MW00452805

MINDSTIR MEDIA

Black, White, and Gray All Over

Copyright © 2021 by Frederick Douglass Reynolds. All rights reserved.

No part of this book may be used or reproduced in any manner whatsoever without written permission, except in the case of brief quotations embodied in critical articles and reviews. For more information, e-mail all inquiries to info@mindstirmedia.com.

Published by Mindstir Media, LLC

45 Lafayette Rd | Suite 181| North Hampton, NH 03862 | USA

1.800.767.0531 | www.mindstirmedia.com

Printed in the United States of America

ISBN-13: 978-1-63848-521-6

BLACK WHITE AND GRAY ALL OVER

A BLACK MAN'S ODYSSEY IN LIFE
AND LAW ENFORCEMENT

FREDERICK DOUGLASS REYNOLDS

ACKNOWLEDGEMENTS

THERE ARE MANY PEOPLE who have contributed to the way my life has turned out. So many, in fact, that I cannot possibly list them all. But there are some whose contributions cannot be ignored. First and foremost, I am grateful to God, whom I had been all but ambivalent to until the events of 2020 opened my eyes and forced me to see that faith in something greater than ourselves is sorely needed in these troubled times;

To former CIA Officer Gary Berntsen and author Ralph Pezzullo, who both gave me the inspiration to even believe that I could write a book;

To my Aunts Arlene and Shirley, who recognized in me a thirst for the written word and taught me how to read, write, and put thought to paper;

To my brothers David and Derrick, who I love more than anything and who I have always tried to make proud;

To my children and grandchildren, who I love dearly and hope that I have left a legacy and something for them to be proud of;

To my mother-in-law Lynne Baker, who was just as much a mother to me as my own was;

To my brother-in-law JD Baker and my sister-in-law Terry Tasby, who accepted me into their family as if they had known me all my life;

To my friends Onuka Henry, Mark and Kim MacGuire, Bryan and Nicole Bavis, and Kathy Cummings, who have always been there for me and my family; To my mother and father, who were architects of a vessel with far too many doors and far too few lights; And lastly, to my lovely wife and the love of my life, Carolyn, who was that one guiding light that I needed to navigate the troubled waters of life.

For my father

CONTENTS

PART TWO

FOREWORD

BY RALPH PEZZULLO

"I have reached the conclusion that those who have physical courage also have moral courage. Physical courage is a great test."

— Oriana Fallaci

SINCE THE TRAGIC DEATH of George Floyd in Minneapolis on May 25, 2020, major cities across our country have been buffeted by massive demonstrations, widescale looting, and violence. On TV, internet, and radio we've heard constant heated talk about Black Lives Matter, police shootings, racism, and political division and hatred. The large majority of this commentary issues from the mouths of political pundits and experts—many of whom have been quick to assign blame to the police.

The knee-jerk solution of some city councils has been to cut police budgets. But increasingly, the public has expressed their desire for a more balanced, thoughtful response. Maybe it's time to consider the perspective of a group of people that has largely been silenced—police officers themselves—those men and women who actually serve our communities, have had to subdue criminals, been shot at in the line of duty, watched a colleague gunned down in cold blood, tried to help a family deal with the grief of losing a young man or woman to gang violence, and seen closeup how the social, psychological, and economic scars of racism and slavery continue to affect our inner cities.

Someone like Black policeman/detective Frederick Reynolds. Someone who has seen how the issues relating to policing and violence play out on the streets in tears and blood. Someone who has been forced to deal with the extenuating circumstances and complications. Someone who has felt the anger, grief, and frustration.

Fred Reynolds, as you'll learn in his book, is the son of poor sharecroppers from rural Virginia. He associated with the Errol Flynn gang in Detroit, was himself a criminal, a victim of racism, a Marine Corps infantryman, and then, when he ran through his savings…homeless. Not homeless, doing drugs, and begging on the streets. But homeless, working two jobs, and sleeping in cars and all-night movie theaters, unable to earn enough to house, clothe, and feed his growing family.

For thirty-two years he served as a cop and detective in Compton, CA—a.k.a. "Hub City," because of its central location with boundaries defined by the 105, 110, 710, and 405 freeways. It's the 10.1 square miles of southern LA County that have become synonymous with gangs, drive-by shootings, and gangsta rap. In 1988, NWA rapped, "Straight outta Compton, crazy motherfucker, from the gang called Niggaz with Attitudes. When I'm called off, I got a sawed-off!"

And they meant it. It was Fred's job as a policeman to keep the peace, or, at least, the violence to a minimum. And when the shooting broke out, it was Fred's job to identify the victims, investigate the crimes, and arrest the perpetrators. As members of the 121-strong Compton PD, Fred and his fellow officers were woefully under-staffed and under-resourced—in part due to corrupt public officials who siphoned off money into their pockets.

Then in July 2000, in a major slap in the face to all of them, the Compton City Council voted to disband their own police department and hired the Los Angeles County Sheriff's Department. Imagine that. They claimed the Compton PD was "powerless to stop the out-of-control violence." Fred reveals that disbanding Compton PD had a whole lot more to do with city corruption and politics. Again, he knows what he's talking about because he was the detective who ran the investigation into police and municipal corruption that caused the Compton City Council to vote to disband the police department. So what happened next? Most of the officers, including Fred, traded their blue Compton PD uniforms for Los Angeles County Sheriff's Department tan and green, and the violence continued.

In 1991, Compton hit a terrible peak of 87 murders. That's a murder rate of roughly 90 per 100,000 people. The rate for the entire county that year was considered high at 9.8 per 100,000. And the Compton total didn't include those labeled suicides because the city's four-man homicide unit was too overburdened to investigate them. Nor did it recognize the dozens of others who were maimed for life or the scores of brothers, sisters, fathers, mothers, and other family members who suffered deep emotional scars.

As Fred points out, the majority of the violence committed in Compton was (and continues to be) gang related—and not just Crips versus Bloods. There are also the CVT-Flats, the CV-70s, Alondra 13, Barrio Los Padrinos, and numerous other dangerous Hispanic gangs, too. Some of the shootings made national headlines, like the vicious shootings of world-famous West Coast rapper Tupac Shakur in Las Vegas in 1996 and East Coast rapper Notorious BIG one year later in LA. The killers of Tupac lived in Compton and most of them would later die there. The murder of BIG is much murkier, although his death possibly leads back to Compton as well.

Fred's story will remind you a lot of the TV series The Wire, but real and more tragic because the blood that flowed wasn't ketchup or prop blood. It was real and even today stains the concrete sidewalks as only real blood can do.

He portrays some heroes and good cops, and some bad ones, too; and lots and lots who landed in the gray. He includes himself in the latter category. One, because he's honest. And two, because even though he was twice named California Policeman of the Year and can boast a ten-page-list of commendations and awards, he admits that he struggled at times. You will understand why when you read his story. One thing that comes across loud and clear is that it's damn hard being a police officer in today's United States. If you're a person with compassion, it's impossible to remain unaffected by the violence, the daily pressures, and the demonization of cops that started as a reaction to the abuses committed during the war on drugs.

If you want the real and unvarnished perspective of a police officer, you've come to the right place. You'll learn what it's like to be a Black cop in this era of political correctness and Black Lives Matter. You'll come away with a better understanding of the pressures on families trying to raise their kids in commu nities like Compton. And you might come to the realization that the only way we'll ever make progress, individually and as citizens of this country, and heal the divisions, the violence, and the rift between the police and the public, is to understand and embrace the truth regardless of political affiliation, race, or ethnic background, so help us God.

I BEGAN writing this book many years ago. So long ago that, at first, I used an ink pen and lined loose-leaf paper. The only thing I was certain of when I began the journey was the title. From what I understand, authors will usually begin writing and often won't come up with a title until well into the work. Sometimes, a title won't be chosen until the end of it. I didn't know why I chose this title. All I knew was that no matter what I ultimately ended up writing, this would be it. Little did I know just how applicable the title would be to my life, both personally and professionally.

I started writing this book because of the emotional and physical trauma I had experienced as a child. But, life got in the way, and I put it away, in that place where grown-ups put away childish things. However, if I thought that emotional trauma was restricted to childhood, I could not have been more wrong. I continued through life, collecting it like bees collect pollen. I went through the normal travails of life: jobs, marriage, and kids, collecting additional trauma at each stage. Inevitably, I arrived at the stage we all strive to reach. After thirty-two years as a police officer and deputy sheriff in some of the worst areas in Los Angeles County, I was able to retire. This time I picked up that modern-day pen and quill, the laptop, and started where I had left off those many years before.

Still, the ink pen and lined loose-leaf paper would continue to play a part, as the majority of this story was written while I was sitting in the driveway of Mr. Clarence Avant's house. Mr. Avant is widely known as the "Black Godfather" and is one of the most beloved and influential Black Americans alive. I had picked up a post-retirement job as his part-time driver and bodyguard, and he provided me with choice nuggets of wisdom and life advice that I will cherish forever as I ferried him around Beverly Hills to lunch and dinner and meetings with other Black heavyweights.

Initially, writing this story was therapeutic, as I dredged up all those painful memories that I had buried deep inside of me for so many years. And the more I wrote, the more I realized just how emotionally broken I was. It was like laying on a psychiatrist's couch day after day. But instead of sharing my pain with another person, I shared it with my keyboard as if it were Freud himself. Because of my chosen profession, the more I wrote, the more I realized just how appropriate the title I had chosen long ago was.

When I had written a little over half of the book, I had a heart attack on April 5, 2020, one of the worst years in modern history. I was rushed to the hospital, where emergency surgery was performed. One of the things I thought about was how my story might now not ever be written. As it was during the Covid-19 pandemic, I was unable to have visitors. After a successful surgery, I lay in my hospital bed, alone, and contemplated the fickleness of life as I thanked God for giving me another chance at it. When I was released from the hospital, I began writing again, this time with a sense of urgency.

On May 26, 2020, I was watching the news when a horrible story out of Minneapolis, Minnesota, came on. A White police officer was videotaped while he kneeled on the neck of a handcuffed Black man named George Floyd as Floyd begged for his life and screamed for his mother. He later died at a local hospital. It was painful to watch, and I grew angry because no police officer I had ever worked with would have done something like that, especially not in my presence. But what hurt just as much was that my eight-year-old son saw it, too. He sees things in strictly black and white; there is no gray area for him. There is only right and wrong. He asked, "Papa, why is the bad man hurting the good one?" That was a watershed moment for me. My children idolized me and had always been proud of what I did for a living. In nine minutes and twenty-nine seconds, some asshole by the name of Derek Chauvin had destroyed the entire perspective of the most special one.

Although I do not believe that law enforcement is riddled with racism, I know for a fact that every law enforcement agency in America has at least one, if not dozens, of Derek Chauvins in its ranks, and that goes for the Federal agencies as well. If you are a cop reading this, you will know that I am telling the truth. If you deny it, then you are part of the problem and an underlying reason why the George Floyd incident happened and why the subsequent fall-out was a societal nuclear explosion. Even if you do not approve of your peers acting in this manner, by not policing them yourselves, you are equivalent to being accomplices. And if you are a supervisor, and a Black cop came to you with concerns about the racist tendencies of a fellow officer and you did nothing about it, then you are even worse.

While I hadn't wanted to write exclusively about racism in America, I knew I had to touch on it as I had experienced it throughout my life like most Blacks in America. Sometimes the racism was subtle; sometimes, it was suffocating. But it was always there, even if it were bubbling just underneath the surface of that star-spangled banner. This book will be painful for some people, most likely White readers, and they may not want to continue past the first two chapters. If those two chapters offend you, perhaps some introspection is required on your part. Simply put, in order to get to where I ended up in life, you must walk in my shoes. And if this nation is to be saved, then we all must have some serious conversations with each other—and not one-sided conversations, either, because there is enough blame to go around. We have all fallen short of who we are supposed to be.

Although I touch on racism throughout my story because it is a necessary part of it, the overall story is about so much more. It is mainly about the fall of a storied police department after 112 years, shoot-outs, political corruption, murdered police officers, and sensational murders. But it is also about a young man's coming of age, the ever-present taboos and secrets inherent in all families, the triumphs and failings of that young man, and ultimately, his redemption.

PROLOGUE

THE DAY started off like any other one.

I worked the PM shift, which started at 4:00 p.m. and ended at 1:30 a.m. Slightly hungover, coming off a weekend drink-fest with friends, I took two Excedrin before eating a bachelor's Spartan breakfast of coffee, toast, a slice of cheese, and two boiled eggs. My coffee table doubled as an aquarium. I watched the exotic fish of all colors swim around as I ate, the gentle bubbling sounds helping to hasten the medicine's effect.

I lived in an upstairs, two-bedroom apartment with a balcony about a mile from downtown Long Beach and six blocks from the Pacific Ocean. Long Beach is just south of Compton, where I worked as a cop. Although the area I lived in was geographically close to Compton, it could not have been more different aesthetically or demographically. At the time, Compton, California, was a predominantly Black city that, although just 10.1 square miles with a population of 90,000, was also an abattoir averaging over 1,000 gunshot victims and seventy-five murders a year.

After my headache subsided, I went on my usual three-mile morning run on the beach, knifing through the bikini-clad women who were rollerblading under the beautiful California sun. Life was good.

At 3:35 p.m., I got in my burgundy 1991 Acura Legend and sped north on the 710 freeway. I hoped that traffic would not be heavier than usual, but if I was late to work, so what?

I was one of the senior officers on my shift and a field training officer (FTO) as well. The other officers looked up to me, and the supervisors respected me. As a result, I got more than my share of leeway for minor infractions like tardiness. At worst, I would just have to write a "102" memo to the watch commander

(W/C) explaining the reason for being late. The memos went into your personnel file for a year, but nobody gave a shit about that. Cops just hate to write in
general unless it is an arrest report or filling out an overtime slip.

While Janet Jackson sang, "That's the Way Love Goes" on the car's cassette
player, my mind drifted to my two kids, Dominic and Haley, who were nine and
ten years old, respectively. At thirty-two, I had been divorced for almost four
years now, and between the rigors of the job, twice a month weekend visits, and
the crap I had to take from their mom, I wasn't spending much time with them.
It is difficult being a cop when you do not live with your kids. When you do,
even though you work long and odd hours and sleep a lot, at least you are there.
Still, I had to find a way to do a better job as a father.

As I weaved in and out of traffic doing 85 to 90 mph, the twelve-story
Compton court building came into view. We called it Fort Compton because
we believed it to be the only safe place in the city. In stark contrast to its sur-
roundings, it was an alabaster structure without much architectural imagination
standing amidst colorful, single-story homes and overpopulated apartments. A
monument dedicated to Martin Luther King Jr. kept silent vigil in its shadow, a
beacon of hope and justice in an otherwise lawless land filled with despair. The
police station, a two-story building with a basement, indoor shooting range, and
a jail with a kitchen for cooking inmate meals, sat next to the Fort. The back lot
was behind the station and used for patrol cars and employee parking. Three
gas pumps, with a huge marquee atop them with the words, 'COMPTON
POLICE' in blue letters, separated the booking stalls immediately behind the
station and where the patrol and detective cars parked. The dispatch center, a
large room without proper ventilation, was next to the entrance to the kitchen
for the jail and had a small window on each of two doors. A three-foot retaining wall was the only thing that separated the back lot from passersby walking
down the sidewalk.

The back lot was a sacred place for everyone who worked at the station. It
was used for everything from private conversations to intimate encounters in
vehicles. And "meet me on the back lot" said in anger was also the precursor for
a fist fight between two cops who didn't necessarily see eye-to-eye on things.

The Heritage House stood behind the back lot and was built in 1869 as a tribute to the city's founder, Griffith Dickenson Compton. It is the oldest house in Compton and a state landmark. We sometimes went there to drink beer after work. It was a common way for cops to unwind and is known in cop talk as choir practice.

I arrived at work with ten minutes to spare. I walked into the locker room to change, looking for lockers with coat hangers so that I could laugh at the latest fuck-up. Whenever a cop did something stupid or disrespectful, such as a rookie being in the locker room when the senior officers arrived, the other officers on the shift would wrap metal coat hangers around the lock on his locker until the hangers looked like a metal ball. The bigger the ball, the more unwritten rules the officer had broken. If the officer did something particularly egregious, like snitching on a fellow cop or missing a weapon during a search, or he was just an unliked asshole in general, the other officers would also splash liquid whiteout on his locker. There were at least five such lockers in the locker room, harsh reminders of the number of snitches, assholes, and incompetent cops I worked with daily.

A boom-box—confiscated from a street corner when gang members ran off and left it as cops drove up—played in the corner of the locker room. It was blasting "I Will Always Love You," which was Officer Kevin Burrell's favorite song at the time. At six foot seven and more than three hundred pounds, he was struggling to put on his bulletproof vest at his locker while trying his best to sing a duet with Whitney. With a personality and charm as large as he was, all the cops loved to ride with him. He had recovered quite nicely from a gunshot wound caused by a fellow officer playing with his gun in the report writing room about a year before. The gun accidentally went off, and the bullet entered Kevin's left upper thigh as he was writing a report.

Kevin was a star basketball player at Compton High School and a three-year starter at Cal State University Dominguez Hills. Basketball skills ran in his family. One of his older brothers, Clark "Biff" Burrell, led Compton High School to two CIF championships and a sixty-six-game winning streak before the Phoenix Suns drafted him in 1975.

Kevin grew up less than three blocks from the station in the Palmer Blocc Crip gang neighborhood. His mother and father, Edna and Clark, had extended a standing invitation to patrol officers to stop by their house whenever they were hungry. There were sometimes two or three radio cars there at a time, the officers eating barbeque and playing dominoes or spades in the backyard while listening to their radios for calls. After they left, Edna always listened to the police scanner Kevin had bought for her, thrilled whenever she heard his voice.

Kevin had wanted to be a Compton police officer since he was a kid. He certainly earned the position. He paid his dues as an explorer scout at fourteen years old before working as a community service officer and jailer. When the city sent him to the police academy, he caught chicken pox and was unable to complete the training. Undeterred, he self-enrolled in the next academy class. As a testament to how well liked he was, every officer on the department chipped in to help him pay for the training the second time around. When he graduated, the city hired him as a police officer.

Only the senior cops were still changing when I arrived at work. The rookies were already in the briefing room, which was in the basement next to the men's locker room. The women's locker room was small, not much bigger than a walk-in closet, and was on the opposite side of the briefing room. There were never more than four or five female patrol officers on the department at a time, so there was no need for a large locker room for them. As was often the case, no female officers were working that night.

The rookies had to arrive at work at least thirty minutes before their shift began and sit silently in the front row. Speaking out of turn was grounds for a ball of wire on their lockers. They had to stand up on their first day and answer embarrassing sexual questions from the senior officers about their significant others, such as whether she wore underwear, how well she performed fellatio, and whether she would be open to threesomes. Profanity-laden hazing was the norm, even in front of supervisors. After the rookies sat down, they were bombarded with erasers, wads of paper, and even notebooks thrown by the officers sitting behind them. Seating placement was based on seniority, with the most senior officers sitting in the last row. Most of them smoked cigarettes and some held empty soda bottles or cans, which they used to spit their chewing tobacco.

The dispatchers sat behind the last row in front of the lunchroom. We called it the Code-7 room because that was the radio code for lunch. The shift briefing started when the supervisors took their seats in front and told one of the dispatchers to close an accordion blind that separated the two rooms.

Lieutenant Danny Sneed was the W/C, and Eric Perrodin was the field sergeant that night. Danny was a middle-aged cop with a short afro and a perpetual scowl occasionally interrupted by a shit-eating grin. Known as the "Plug" because of his short stature and tenacious personality, he was a demanding but compassionate supervisor. Street smart and book smart, Danny grew up in Compton, as did Eric, whose father was a beloved city employee for more than thirty years. Eric's brother Percy was a captain on the department. He and Eric grew up on Central Avenue in one of the most gang-infested neighborhoods in the city. Percy had long since moved out, and their father had passed on, but Eric and his mother still lived in the same house.

Danny assigned me to lead a team of several Zebra units to address the numerous gang shootings that had plagued the city in recent days. The units were called Zebra in honor of the majestic African animals because they are fearless and fleet of foot and because our patrol cars were black and white at the time. I was training a rookie named Ivan Swanson, a suave, fast-talking lady's man. Our radio call sign was Zebra-1. Ivan grew up in Carson, a town south of Compton, and his father was John Swanson, a well-respected homicide detective on the department. Lendell Johnson, a muscular cop from Chicago by way of Louisiana, and his trainee were Zebra-2. Lendell was one of my best friends on the department and was a relatively new FTO. I didn't know much about his trainee, but that wasn't unusual. Senior officers didn't pay much attention to trainees. No one gave a shit about them until they got off probation, which was akin to a rite of passage. They weren't accepted until they had completed their journey. Then, they had to throw an off-probation party and foot the entire bill. The party wasn't for them. It was for the senior officers who now accepted them into the exclusive club of that thin blue line of law enforcement.

Kevin and James MacDonald were Zebra-3. MacDonald, or Jimmy, as we called him, was a reserve police officer. Reserves were part-time officers who worked for just one dollar a year so they wouldn't be viewed as doing the job for free. Most people became reserves to try and get their foot in the door to become full-time cops. Others did it just so they could carry a concealed firearm. Jimmy was a young, mild-mannered White guy from Santa Rosa who smiled a lot. His family still lived there where his father, Jim, owned a successful dental implant business, and his mother, Toni, was a homemaker. Jimmy went to Piner High School and played football, baseball, and basketball. He was the quarterback on the football team and was MVP his senior year. Jimmy attended Sacramento State for two years after graduating before transferring to Cal State Long Beach, where he played rugby as he obtained his degree in criminal justice.

Jimmy requested to ride with Kevin that night because it was his second to last shift in Compton before starting his new job as a regular police officer with the San Jose Police Department. He was going closer to home to be near his family. Mark Metcalf and Gary Davis rounded out the team and were Zebra-4. Metcalf, a level-headed White guy in his mid-twenties who grew up in Orange County, was also a reserve. He and Jimmy were best friends, but reserves could only ride with a regular officer or an FTO, so they never rode together. Like Burrell, Sneed, Eric, and Percy Perrodin, Gary Davis was homegrown, and his parents didn't live far from the Perrodin family. Along with Kevin, Gary was one of the tallest cops on the department. He and Kevin had known each other since they were kids and were teammates on Compton High's basketball team before Gary went on to star at Cal State Fullerton.

That was the uniqueness of the Compton Police Department. Many of the officers were born and raised in the city or still had family there. These kinds of connections are rare in inner cities, as most of them are policed by cops who have no links to them and view the people who live there with negativity and sometimes outright hostility. Some departments have a residency requirement that applicants live in the city or within a certain distance. The thought process behind this is that cops who have a connection to the community will have more compassion for their citizens. The way Compton cops addressed each other was unique as well. We never called each other by rank. Most of us referred to each other by either surname, first name, nickname, or "dumbass," "motherfucking," or "goddamn" before the surname. I was "that goddamn Reynolds" on more occasions than I could count.

The team grabbed a quick bite to eat at Super Marathon Burgers at Compton Boulevard and Santa Fe. The owner was an old Greek guy by the name of Alex. We called him Alex the Greek. He drove an old beige colored Mercedes Benz which he parked by the walk-up order window. Alex the Greek wasn't scared of shit. About ten years before, a gangster from the Imperial Courts housing project in Watts tried to rob him at gunpoint. Alex the Greek pulled out a gun instead of money and shot him dead. As the would-be-robber lay on the ground bleeding, Alex the Greek continued to serve customers as they stepped over the dead body to order.

While listening to my fellow officers' tales of carnal conquests and corny jokes, my mind drifted to thoughts about the woman I was currently dating. Despite my best efforts not to, I had fallen in love and looked forward to seeing her when I got off. In the interim I joined the rest of the team in eating greasy hamburgers and over-seasoned fries on the hoods of our patrol cars. It never crossed any of our minds that we would pay for meals like this years later, which, when combined with the ebb and flow of adrenaline and stress, would lead to high blood pressure, higher cholesterol, and obesity. But for now, we tried to mask the ever-present tension of policing one of the most dangerous cities in America with bullshit stories and humor. We were all afraid but would never admit it to each other. Still, when you work with someone long enough, you learn to pinpoint the telltale signs of their fear. Some of my peers had a tombstone sense of humor, some an overinflated sense of self, some a braggadocious fearlessness and nervous laughter, and some carried a boot knife, two back-up guns, and the biggest duty weapon allowed. A few were guilty of all the telltales.

The radio blared calls of shots fired and gunshot victims all over the city. Our patrol car sirens screamed in perfect harmony with the ubiquitous sound of the Compton police helicopter, better known as a "ghetto bird." The regular patrol units received all the report calls, with the Zebra teams responding to help if gangs were involved. At about 8:00 p.m., we were driving on Rosecrans Avenue toward Willowbrook when I heard gunshots in an area called PCP Alley because of the ease it could be bought. A potent hallucinogenic, PCP was known as sherm because users dipped Sherman cigarettes into the PCP before smoking them. It was also called angel dust because in its unrefined state it is a white, crystalline powder and the high has been compared to walking among the clouds. Users often became catatonic or violent and had insane levels of strength when confronted or agitated. We called them dusters or sherm heads. PCP alley was in the area claimed as turf by the Tree-Top Piru Bloods, one of the city's most violent gangs.

The rest of the Zebra team followed Ivan and me to the sound of the gunshots, where we saw a gang member wearing a red Philadelphia Phillies hat, a white t-shirt, and brown khaki trousers standing next to the driver's door of a gold Cadillac. He was shooting toward the alley with a shiny semi-automatic pistol. I pulled behind his car, and as Ivan and I got out, guns in hand, Ivan yelled, "Compton Police, muthafucka! Drop the fucking gun!" These are the career-defining moments in the life of a police officer, both emotionally and psychologically. We could have shot him, but we could not see what he was shooting at, and he posed no direct threat to us. If he had turned toward us, we would have put him down. But *he* didn't, so *we* didn't.

The shooter dropped the gun and screamed at us not to shoot him as he laid on the ground. Then, in a perfunctory manner showing just how many times we had done this very thing, Ivan handcuffed him, searched him, and matter-of-factly put him in our patrol car while I secured the gun and collected the shell casings. I told Kevin and Jimmy to check the alleyway for victims, but all they found were multiple bullet holes in a wooden fence. The shooter had missed his target, and we would never know the target's identity. This was often the case in Compton. No one called the police if there was a shooting with no victims. The only reason we knew about this one was because we witnessed it.

There were many more shootings than those reported. Every New Year's Eve, at the command of the W/C, all the patrol units had to return to the safety of the station until the gun-loving revelers had satiated themselves. We huddled near the back door under the concrete overhead, listening to the shots and the sound of falling bullets striking the back lot and sometimes, parked patrol cars. The dozens of shots fired calls we normally got throughout the remainder of the year were usually the result of lousy aim, and it was considered snitching to contact the cops if someone shot at you and missed. We found out about the victims who were hit because of mandatory reporting to law enforcement by medical personnel or because the victims were still at the scene when we arrived. If they were still alive, the level of cooperation from these victims was usually along the lines of, "Nobody shot me," "Fuck you," or "I ain't telling you shit."

Lendell asked if he and his trainee could handle the arrest because his trainee needed the practice. I gave the trainee the shooter's gun and shell casings, and he and Lendell took the shooter back to the station to book him and write the report. Afterward, the city grew quiet. There was hardly any radio traffic or calls for service. Not entirely unusual for a weeknight, but typically, it did not get this dead until well after midnight. Metcalf, Kevin, Gary, and Jimmy decided to take code-7 at a Sizzler's restaurant in Long Beach, but I chose to take advantage of the lull in violence to leave work early and see my girlfriend.

At around 11:00 p.m., I was on the back lot bullshitting with Lendell while Ivan was getting our gear out of the patrol car. I went to the locker room to change when it started to drizzle. I had just unlocked my locker when I heard the dispatcher over the station intercom. "Compton officers, we are getting reports of an officer down at Rosecrans and Wilmington. Unit to respond code-3, identify?" I froze. I had been a police officer for seven years and had never heard an officer down call. I slammed my locker shut and ran up the stairs. Ivan and I sped out of the back lot, our overhead emergency lights activated and siren screaming. In my rear-view mirror, I noticed that Lendell and his trainee were behind us just as the dispatcher updated the call, her voice now frantic. "Compton officers, we're now getting reports of two officers down! Two officers down, Rosecrans and Wilmington!" Filled with dread, somehow, I knew the officers were Kevin and Jimmy. What I didn't know was what I would see when I got there, or that it would become a cross I would unjustly bear for years to come.

PART ONE

"We need the books that affect us like a disaster, that grieve us deeply, like the death of someone we loved more than ourselves, like being banished into forests far from everyone, like a suicide. A book must be the axe for the frozen sea inside us.

— Franz Kafka —

CHAPTER ONE

MY PARENTS, Charles Delton, and Theresa E. (Kirby) Reynolds were born near rural Rocky Mount, Virginia, about 300 miles from Annapolis, Maryland. *The Lord of Ligonier,* an eighteenth-century British slave ship, sailed from the Ivory Coast of Africa across the Atlantic Ocean and through the Chesapeake Bay, where it unloaded slaves in Annapolis in 1767. It is the only recorded voyage in the Trans-Atlantic Slave Trade database for this vessel. Only 98 of the 140 slaves who made the trip survived. One of them was Kunta Kinte, an ancestor of Alex Haley, the famed author of the novel *Roots.* According to historical records, William Waller bought Kinte at the auction. Waller and John Reynolds, who also bought slaves from the ship, were Virginia plantation owners from Spotsylvania County, which is about 180 miles from Rocky Mount. Considering I share the same surname as John Reynolds, it is not a stretch to believe that one of my ancestors may have been on the ship, too. Slaves often took the surnames of their masters, a demeaning practice put eloquently into verse by one of the greatest Americans of all:

"The whisper that my master was my father, may or may not be true; and, true or false, it is of but little consequence to my purpose whilst remains, in all its glaring odiousness, that slaveholders have ordained, and by law established, that the children of slave women shall in all cases follow the condition of their mothers; and this is done too obviously to administer to their own lusts, and make a gratification of their wicked desires profitable as well as pleasurable; for by this cunning arrangement, the slaveholder, in cases not a few, sustains to his slaves the double relation of master and father."

— Frederick Douglass

My father was an alcoholic. Born in 1938, he was handsome; a tall, slim, light-complexioned man with beautiful, black, curly hair. His family were sharecroppers, and he dropped out of school in the sixth grade to help farm the land. He was the fourth son of ten children. They grew up in a white two-story structure that looked like a plantation house. It had giant circular pillars on either end of an expansive raised porch that evoked images of ancient Rome. The pillars supported the upstairs balcony where my grandparents would sit and watch the sun go down on the sprawling land that wasn't theirs—land owned by Doctor F.B. Wolfe, a wealthy White obstetrician from one of Virginia's most prominent families. I don't doubt slave owners, possibly the Wolfe's ancestors, once lived in the house. Many sharecroppers were former slaves. Once freed, they had no place to live or any means of making money, so they farmed the land in exchange for housing and a share of the crops produced. Thus sharecropping, much like welfare over a hundred years later, became generational. Ironically, while the descendants of my father's family, the Reynoldses, toiled in hay and cornfields, my mother's family farmed the product with which RJ Reynolds has become synonymous: tobacco.

My mother, a dark-complexioned, buxom woman, was born in 1940, the second oldest child of five brothers and one sister. Her family owned their house and land. The original house was an old, wooden two-story structure on at least forty acres with a stable of hogs, roaming chickens, grazing cows, and at least one mule. Two large wooden sheds, where the picked tobacco leaves were hung to dry, stood within fifty yards of the house. The family cemetery was about one hundred yards in the other direction. Filled with ancestors going back as far as the early 1800s, some of the grave markers only had a name and date of death etched in them; a few only had a first name and year of death.

My mother's father, Rufus Kirby, was an intensely dark-skinned man. Originally from West Virginia, he married into the land passed down to his wife, Helen Tyree, a direct descendant of the property's original owners and a woman so light-skinned she could have passed for White. For reasons still shrouded in obfuscation, the family sent my mother to live with her paternal aunt and uncle in Detroit, Michigan, as a young teenager. She got pregnant at fifteen years old while attending Northwestern High School, and her aunt sent her back to Rocky Mount. The stigma of an unwed pregnancy was unacceptable during that time. The family hid my mother's condition, and in August of 1957, she gave birth in an upstairs bedroom to a baby girl named Linda Faye. No one in Rocky Mount knew the shame of Linda being born out of wedlock. To the good folk of this quaint little town, she was my mother's baby sister, the last of eight children.

Less than a year later, my mother got pregnant again, this time by my father. I never knew how my parents met, just as I never learned why my mother's family sent her to Detroit. Somehow, despite my ignorance, I feel that it is probably the worst-kept secret in a town so small that everyone knows everything about everybody.

My parents were married at 5:00 p.m. on December 24, 1958 in an obvious shotgun wedding, as Doctor Wolfe delivered my brother David just two weeks later. My parents moved into a one-room wooden shack about five hundred feet behind the big white house where my father's family lived. A wood burning stove, which also doubled as a heat source in the winter, was in the center of the room. As there was no way that anyone related to the original occupants of the big house would have lived in a structure such as this, it was, at one time, most assuredly quarters for slaves or newly freed ones with nowhere else to go. And here, on the site of generations of racial inequality, is where I was conceived.

I was born Fredrick Douglas Reynolds at Franklin County Hospital on November 5, 1961. My birth certificate shows my father's occupation as a farmer, and my mother as a housewife. Our races are all listed as "N." Doctor Wolfe also delivered me. I was a breech baby. Breech deliveries are high-risk, and the baby often dies. Sometimes the mother dies as well. The older women in Rocky Mount believed that breech babies were old souls who came into the world ready to run. This belief is apparent in my given name. Most babies born during this era were named after biblical figures. I was named after an escaped slave turned abolitionist and statesman. My genealogy shows that I am Nigerian and Cameroonian with mixtures of Benin, Togo, and Mali. It is no surprise that I have British (Welsh), Irish, and Scottish blood as well. There are no true descendants of Africans forced into slavery in the Americas who do not have any Caucasian blood in them.

The wooden shack where I was born was built on stilts, and I can vaguely remember seeing a black snake crawling out from under it once. The odor of the nearby outhouse where my parents relieved themselves is more vivid, however. Other than one other outhouse near the white house, there were only three buildings on the land: our shack, the white house, and a barn not far from a bullpen. To take baths, my father had to get water from the well, heat it on the stove, and pour it into a metal tub. An old, ornery rooster sounded the alarm every morning just before sunrise, signaling it was time for my father to get up and begin his work for the day while my mother stayed home, cooking, cleaning, and washing clothes by hand on a washboard. She had gotten a taste of the big city lights while living with her aunt and uncle. I am sure it was quite a culture shock for her going from Detroit to living in a small wooden shack and performing tasks such as these.

My father was a simple man, however. He was content living there and helping his family sharecrop the land they lived on, even though many other Southern Blacks had been moving north in search of better opportunities. In a trenchant contrast to the forced diaspora of their ancestors' roles in the Trans-Atlantic slave trade, Southern Blacks migrated to Detroit for a less oppressive culture after the Civil War. Thousands more would move there over the next fifty years, mostly living in a sixty-block area east of Woodward Avenue known as Paradise Valley and the "Black Bottom."

Detroit's population was more than two million by the early 1940s. Ford Motor Company was the leading employer of Blacks at twelve percent of its entire workforce. Detroit became a symbol of cultural rebirth and was known as the "Paris of the Midwest." The phrase, "When I die, bury me in Detroit" was the rallying cry among Blacks far and wide due to the city's growth and employment opportunities. There is no doubt that my mother, having had a taste of that prosperity and urban sprawl, longed to return there. Either because of her wistfulness or insistence, my father joined the ongoing migration. My mother would have been ecstatic and my father apprehensive as they packed David and me and our meager belongings in the car. And after saying our goodbyes to my father's extensive family as they gathered on the porch of the white house, he drove us there in 1963 with the *Green Book: The Black Traveler's Guide to Jim*

Crow America nestled securely in the glovebox. Ford Motor Company hired him the following year.

We lived in at least five different apartments during the early years, all in horrible areas and rooted in squalor. Cockroaches ruled the roost even after the lights came on. Several had rats as big as small cats. A particularly temerarious one bit my mother on the nose while she was sleeping in bed one night. When I was just shy of five years old, I put the stopper in the tub and turned the water on to take a bath. I walked out, and seconds later, I heard horrible screeching and scratching sounds. A kitten-sized black rat was in the tub, struggling to climb out. It had come through the faucet. Instead of calling for my mother or father, I grabbed the box for my favorite toy, a View-Master stereoscope, placed it on top of the rat as the tub filled with water, and held it down with both hands until the thrashing tail was still. To this day, I still have nightmares of screaming rats.

The apartments were all close to my mother's aunt and uncle's house, which we frequently visited. I hated going there. My mother's uncle was a cruel man and taunted David and me incessantly, most often when we mispronounced words. Instead of correcting us, he ridiculed us. He was a small bronze-skinned man with shifty eyes and dark freckles high on his cheekbones. He had short, curly hair and a pencil-thin mustache, blowing smoke from Benson and Hedges cigarettes at us through an insidious smile.

His wife was a plump, brown-skinned woman with short hair who chewed double-mint gum non-stop and wore flower-print dresses and one-inch-heeled shoes. She was extremely cordial to my father, her husband painfully indifferent to him. She never smiled at her husband and sometimes snapped at him while we were there, although I suspect she paid for it later when they were alone. Even at such a young age, I could tell that she was afraid of him. Family rumors persisted that after my mother left their home pregnant, they slept in separate bedrooms and she locked her door at night, especially when he had been drinking.

My youngest brother, Derrick, was born in November of 1965. We lived on the second floor of a two-family flat at the time. It was next to a liquor store and about two blocks behind the Olympia Stadium on Grand River, where the

Detroit Red Wings played hockey. Derrick was much darker than David and me. I would frequently ask my mother why, which angered her to no end, sometimes prompting replies of "shut up, boy," other times, slaps to my head. The demon that is alcohol would grow to haunt my father around this time. During his youth, he often helped his Uncle James "Bus" Nimmo transport bootleg liquor, known as running shine. Uncle Bus had earned his nickname because of his strength, especially when he had been drinking, once breaking his handcuffs after getting arrested. Perhaps my father's demon grew out of a seed planted by Uncle Bus that strength can come from the bottle; some traumatic, uneven circle-of-life event providing it with fertile soil.

My father was either sad or drunk most of the time. I liked him best when he had been drinking because he was the happiest then. He rarely lost his temper and left all corporal punishment to my mother. He hid liquor bottles all over the house, even under my mattress. My mother poured them into the toilet whenever she found them as he watched, pleading with her not to. He never argued with her or hit her. Instead, sometimes when he got paid, he wouldn't come home for two or three days. When he returned, smelling like cheap whiskey and even cheaper perfume, my mother would curse him out for being a "whore-chasing drunk" and make him sleep on the couch.

My father often blew his whole paycheck on wine, women, and song within two days. A few times, he came home walking or in a cab after crashing one of our family cars. On at least three occasions, he was arrested for drunk driving. In retrospect, I understand why he sometimes wouldn't come home. But I also know why he always came back. He loved his boys. All of us. Although my mother clearly showed favoritism toward Derrick, my father treated us all the same. Sometimes he took the whole family to Windsor, Canada just to get ice cream, telling us it was so good they had to make it in another country. And I believed him, too, the taste of the ice cream sweetened by the fact that he and my mother hardly argued the entire time during the trips.

It was around the time my father started drinking a lot that I began having a recurring nightmare. I can see it even now, as plain as day. I hear beating on the side door of our apartment. I look out the window and see a big, inky-black man trying to get inside. He must be a burglar, and he frightens me. I run as fast as I can and hide in a closet filled with dank, musty clothing. There is no one home. *Why am I alone at four-years old?* I'm terrified, scared that the slate-skinned intruder is going to find me. I'm quiet, as still as the field mice that live under the raised front porch of the shack where I was conceived. I grasp my knees and pull them close to my chest, too afraid to even breathe. *Please don't let him find me,* I plead to God. I hear the heavy thud of boots walk past the door, thankful that God appears to have listened. And then I just wait. I wait for my father to save me. *Where is he, anyway?* No matter how many times I have this dream, he never comes back in time to catch the intruder as he plunders the sanctity of our home.

After an eternity, I hear footsteps outside the door, slow and deliberate. The door jerks open, and the dark closet floods with light. It blinds me as I yell, "Please don't hurt me, mister!" I feel a hand grab my arm, and an irritated voice says, "Shut up, boy. Ain't nobody gonna hurt you!" The voice is familiar, and I open my eyes. It belongs to my mother. She has saved me from the intruder. *But where has she been?* My thoughts are interrupted by the crying of my new little brother from another room. *Were they here the entire time?* I don't mention the intruder to my mother; somehow, I think she knows him. I wake up then. I convince myself that it was just a dream, but why is it that, to this day, I don't like small dark places? I never mention the dream to anyone, especially my father. I hated to see my mother yell at him, and something deep inside told me that saying something to him would do more harm than good.

CHAPTER TWO

THE SUMMER of 1967 was sweltering. Martha Reeves and the Vandellas's seminal hit "Jimmy Mack" dominated the airwaves, played almost non-stop by radio personality Martha Jean the Queen. My father was a huge Detroit Tigers fan and often took David and me to games at Old Tiger Stadium, located at the corner of Michigan Avenue and Trumbull since 1911. Nancy Whiskey Pub was just a few blocks away on Harrison Street and had stood there since the turn of the Nineteenth Century when it was known as Digby's saloon. Legendary ballplayers like Cobb, Speaker, and Ruth drank there during prohibition, flirting with adoring women after games while members of the infamous Purple Gang held court. Local 299, home of powerful Teamster's boss Jimmy Hoffa, was just down the street on Trumbull Avenue within a mile of the Detroit River, where many Purple Gang victims found their final resting places. Cobblestone streets with the remnants of old cable tracks bursting through the asphalt added to the area's traditional feel. One could almost still see the trolley cars rolling down the street filled with nattily dressed men wearing fedoras, smoking cigarettes, and reading the *Free Press*.

On Sunday, July 23, the Tigers played the New York Yankees in a doubleheader. My father took David and me to the first game. I saw smoke rising in the far-off distance as we drove to the stadium but didn't think anything more of it. Braving the wooden splinters from the one-dollar bleacher seats in right field, we watched Yankee Centerfielder Joe Pepitone hit a two-run homer off Mickey Lolich and power his team to a 4-2 win. The Tigers would get even in the second game, though, as Willie Horton, a young Black outfielder and one of the team's most popular players, hit a home run to lead his team to victory. Instead of going home after the game, Horton, still in uniform, drove to 12th Street and Clairmont where he had a newspaper route as a boy. The smoke I had seen resulted from rioting, which started at 3:30 a.m. at a Blind Pig at that same corner. Horton was a hometown hero and dearly loved in the Black community. He stood on the hood of his car and pleaded with rioters to stop destroying their neighborhood. Two days later, Lolich would be protecting the city with the Michigan National Guard while Horton and the rest of his teammates were on the way to Maryland to play the Baltimore Orioles.

The racial turmoil in Detroit was palpable throughout the sixties. The city was 40 percent Black, while the police force was 95 percent White. I rarely saw an officer who looked like me. The police were deployed disproportionately in areas where Blacks lived and treated them brutally. The Civil Rights movement was in full effect by 1967; Martin was calling for equality through peaceful means, and Malcolm was demanding it by any means necessary. The blind pig incident was a perfect storm. Two Black servicemen who had just returned from Vietnam were there celebrating. When cops tried to arrest several patrons, the tinder box, coupled with the heat and years of pent-up frustration at mistreatment at the hands of the police, exploded.

My father owned a red Ford Galaxy 500 at the time. To avoid paying for parking, he always parked several blocks away from the ballpark, which meant that we had to walk through Corktown to get there. The people in that neighborhood were tough. After fleeing the Great Irish Potato Famine in County Cork, Ireland, their forefathers had settled there in the 1840s, making it the oldest neighborhood in the city. Corktown was serene as we walked to our car after the game, but I could feel the tension in the air. I got in the back seat, the vinyl burning my legs as I rolled my window down before sliding across the seat to roll down the other one. Hot, humid air clung to my face and the smell of smoke from burning cars and buildings assailed my nostrils as we drove down Grand River. Dozens of looters were running in the street, carrying televisions and stereos, their rallying cry of "Fuck the Police" reverberating in the air. Instead of spinning the hottest Motown tunes on wax, Martha Jean was praying for peace and pleading with the brothers and sisters of Detroit to stop destroying the city.

More looters were emptying the corner store when we got home, my mother watching the news on our little black and white TV with the rabbit ears. Later, I looked out of our living room window toward the Olympia Stadium, watching the glow of fires and flashing lights of emergency vehicles while listening to the blare of sirens for hours. The next day, President Lyndon B. Johnson ordered the deployment of National Guardsmen and the US Army. Tanks, flanked by uniformed troops carrying rifles with fixed bayonets, were soon rolling down the streets. When one turned down ours that night, I was curious and wanted to see it. The tank stopped when I pulled the curtain back, and soldiers yelled and pointed at me as the gun turret slowly turned toward the window. My father pulled me to the floor and laid on top of me with a forefinger to his lips. After what seemed like an eternity, the tank and troop formation continued patrolling. The following night, the infamous Algiers Motel Incident occurred about one mile from the flashpoint of the riot. Detroit cops killed three Black male teenagers. The cops had gone to the motel because of reports of a sniper. They went inside after seeing people in a window, and the incident spiraled out of control when the cops discovered White women hanging out with the three teenagers and four other Black men.

The shedding of my innocence started in earnest that sweltering August day. It was a precursor to an upbringing that would be a dichotomy of emotions, a roller coaster of physical and emotional abuse with a sprinkling of joy in between. Dickens could very well have been writing about my childhood and hometown, as Detroit was indeed a *"Tale of Two Cities."* There were the areas where Blacks toiled and struggled, lived in sub-par housing, and got policed incessantly. And then there were the affluent areas where the residents lived blissfully, ignorant of the cesspool just a stone's throw from their manicured lawns and automatic sprinkler systems.

By 1972, my mother was working at the Michigan Consolidated Gas Company. Her income, combined with my father's after she had taken the drastic step of driving to Ford every payday to pick up his check before he blew it, allowed them to buy a two-story brick house with a basement on Whitcomb Street. Located on the city's northwest side, the house was once owned by Major League pitcher Milt Pappas, a graduate of nearby Cooley High School. Joining the group of Detroiters oblivious to the nearby cesspool, my family had made it. And in the spirit of Blacks who shielded their nice furniture with plastic, my mother finally got a chance to join in on that tradition. Spurred on by "White Flight," within three years, the only White people left on the block would be an elderly couple who lived next door.

Our new house had a large, grey metal gravity furnace, commonly called an "octopus." It had long ducts coming from the central unit that fed into different rooms and a small door that looked like a mouth. The furnace made a loud "whoosh" like the roar of a monster whenever it came on. It was in one of two rooms in the basement. The other room was at the base of the stairs and contained a couch, love seat, TV, eight-track cassette player, and an amplifier for my father's guitar. The rigors of putting rear-view mirrors on Mustangs at the River Rouge plant in Dearborn didn't affect my father's ability to play the guitar at all. Drunk most of the time and trapped in a menagerie of misery, he would sit on the couch playing it while listening to Bobby Blue Bland lament about "Stormy Monday Blues" no matter what day of the week. My father was also a great singer and once part of a legendary group in the Rocky Mount area called the Starlight Gospel Singers. They were like rock stars with no shortage of big-legged groupies following them from church to church. Undoubtedly, my father had his share of them. I am sure that as he sat on the couch playing his guitar and singing, he reminisced about days gone by and things that might have been.

My family went to Rocky Mount to visit my grandparents every summer. We always stopped at my maternal grandparent's house first. My Grandma Helen was very mean, particularly to my mother, Linda, and Derrick. She once held Linda's thumbs to a hot stove to try and discourage her from sucking them. She treated Derrick as an outsider and always addressed my mother dismissively whenever my mother tried to have a conversation with her. After a few obligatory hours, we would leave Derrick at the house, where he had to work in the tobacco fields, topping and priming in family purgatory along with Linda Faye under the watchful eye of my Grandpa Rufus. When I once asked my mother why Derrick had to stay there, she told me not to worry about it as my father remained curiously silent.

Small, modest homes with cows grazing behind barbed wire fences periodically came into view as we drove away. The area's rustic atmosphere was refreshing, a convivial contrast to the concrete jungle I called home. Sometimes we stopped at a local store to get soda and potato chips. The store's owner was the leader of the local KKK chapter. Beforehand, no doubt, with the fate of Emmitt Till weighing heavily on his mind, my father would instruct us not to look at any White women and to address the White men as "sir." With most of my father's life overshadowed by the wings of Jim Crow, he most assuredly knew that the trees in Rocky Mount had borne strange fruit on more than one occasion for far lesser transgressions.

I always looked forward to visiting my paternal grandparents. Their house was in the mountains at the end of a long, winding dirt road a half-mile from Route 220, a major highway. There was a metal gate half-way to the house to keep the livestock from wandering away. After David or I opened it and my father drove through, we would get back in the car after closing it and reach out of the windows, picking blackberries from the bushes that bordered the roadway as we continued to the house. No less than a dozen family members stood on the porch heralding our arrival. Others sat on the multi-person swings near the Romanesque columns. Fallen apples were plentiful, never far from the trees that bore them. Hens roamed freely, often running from the irascible rooster. The odor of freshly cut grass and patties deposited by Buck, the old black bull stalking the confines of the bullpen, was always heavy in the air and intoxicating. Some days more than others, you could smell the pungent odor coming from the nearby outhouse. Whenever it rained, the petrichor created an aggregate of aromas that built lasting and pleasant sensory memories.

My paternal grandfather, Walter Lee Reynolds, was just one generation removed from slavery. He was a short, dark-skinned man who wore bib overalls every day. He would dress them up with a white button-down shirt and necktie and a pork pie hat on Sundays for the family's mandatory church attendance. Grandpa Walter never went to school but had the sagacity of a man who had seen the worst of humanity and knew the strength of family. And although he didn't talk much, everyone immediately shut up and listened whenever he did, patiently waiting for whatever wisdom flowed from his mouth. One of the most memorable things that he said occurred while David and I were helping him in the fields behind the big white house. He said, "Y'all boys stay out of that tall grass. That's where the snakes hide," the absolute best advice two city boys could ever be given.

My paternal grandmother's name was Mary. Loquacious and complimentary toward everyone, she laughed often and heartily, exclaiming, "I declare!" whether in joy, agreement, or disgust. Affectionately known as Mom Mary, she was a truly singular woman. At slightly over six feet tall, she was brown skinned with straight black hair that touched the hem of her ubiquitous knee-length flower-print cotton dress. The stoop in her back was the only clue that she had given natural childbirth to ten children, the last one just before the onset of menopause. She always wore an apron, wiping her calloused hands on it more out of habit than cleanliness, and her long, tapered fingers were the creators of the most sought-after patchwork quilts in Franklin County.

My father had three sisters named Arlene, Shirley, and the baby of the family, Emma, who was born with Down syndrome. After my grandparents died, Shirley, in unbelievable selflessness, would dedicate her life to providing for Emma, never marrying or having children of her own. Emma's face always lit up whenever she saw me, and she said the same thing every time: "That's my nephew Fred. Fred like biscuits and gravy." And I did, too, sopping up my Mom Mary's brown gravy with her homemade biscuits until the plate shone like the gleaming ring in Buck's nose. There was never any arguing while we visited my paternal grandparent's house, and it wasn't an act. They were just genuine people. They spoke to each other warmly and with respect. But as good as the family atmosphere was there, the atmosphere at my maternal grandparent's house was just as bad. Something just wasn't right. I always felt like I would get smothered by skeletons if I opened the wrong closet door. Just maybe, the long-denied denouement as to why my mother got sent to Detroit in the first place would be among them.

I was devastated every time we left Virginia. Starting around the time Derrick was born, rarely do I recall peace or tranquility in our house. It was difficult being there; I struggled to find solace or sanctuary from the turmoil but did the best I could, sometimes hiding under the bed and reading by flashlight. I was smart and a voracious reader who, according to my mother and thanks to Arlene and Shirley, had learned to read by the time I was three years old. Cursed with the disease of inquisitiveness, I was always good at seeing the simple hidden by complexity. I questioned everything, sometimes to the embarrassment of those close to me. I wanted to know everything. I wanted to read even more.

When I was eight, I read the *Narrative of the Life of Frederick Douglass*. Realizing that my name was spelled differently, I began spelling my name like his. I also discovered that I had an innate talent for drawing, often rendering artwork worthy of framing before I was ten years old. I whizzed through elementary and middle school, got promoted from the sixth grade to the eighth, and started high school at twelve-years-old. It was difficult, as I struggled to fit in and was teased and bullied because of my age. I went from turmoil at home to daily ridicule at school. I made friends with two neighborhood kids, Butcher and Keith, who collected Marvel comics and liked to draw. I started reading comics to escape reality, finding a corner in the basement away from the gray monster when my place under the bed was occupied. I should have continued to hang out with Butcher and Keith, but my life was destined to take a darker path.

CHAPTER THREE

MICHIGAN IS known as the "Great Lakes State" because it is bordered by five of the most massive freshwater bodies on Earth. It comprises two landmasses, the Upper Peninsula (U.P.) and the Lower Peninsula (L.P.). The L.P. looks like a mitten, and the U.P. like a rabbit leaping over it. Detroit is the most populous city in the state and is located at the southernmost end of the mitten on the thumb side. Although one of the wealthiest cities in America for decades, it eventually became engulfed in so much violent crime that the mitten is now known colloquially as the "Dirty Glove."

On a cold winter night in 1975, a neighborhood kid named Roney asked me to go to the east side of the city with him to meet one of his cousins. Roney was my exact opposite. He got into fights all the time and rarely attended school. Although just sixteen years old, Roney was well over six feet tall, weighed close to two hundred pounds, and had huge fists and feet. He had a terrible stuttering problem and learned how to fight exceptionally well because he got tired of the other kids teasing him. That, coupled with his size and a nasty disposition, made everyone in the neighborhood afraid of him.

I was sitting on my porch reading *Fantastic Four Issue #52* when I first met him. He walked up to me and took it, laughing as he walked away. I ran after him, but he just pushed me to the ground. My mother came out of the house, cursed him out, and took my comic book back. She then handed the now crumpled and worthless future classic back to me. As tears streamed down my face, she ordered me into the house where she whipped me for not standing up for myself, not far from where my father was passed out drunk on the plastic-covered sofa.

The next time I saw Roney, I was on the porch reading "The Tell-Tale Heart" by Edgar Allen Poe. Roney apologized for getting me in trouble and asked what I was reading. I handed him the book, and he started thumbing through the pages and moving his lips. It was evident he couldn't read, so I offered to read it to him. We sat on the porch, me reading a story about a genderless narrator consumed with guilt after a seemingly motiveless murder, him listening with rapt attention. He took a liking to me. We started hanging out, him teaching me to fight, me teaching him to read. I had a strong suspicion that the dysfunctional family dynamics present at my home were also present in his.

I snuck out after my parents went to sleep. Detroiters called the buses "Damn Slow Rides" because the bus system was officially under the Department of Street Railways, commonly known as the DSR. We called freezing wind the "Hawk," and it was flying high that night. Roney and I stamped our feet at the bus stop and blew evidence of the unrelenting predator into our fists as nearby sewer caps spewed steam clouds. I was nervous about going to the eastside, where the worst gangs in the city ruled unchallenged. They had rather generic names such as the Chain Gang, the Bishops, the Mack Hoods, and the Eastside Coney Oneys, who took their name from a mispronunciation of the family name from the movie epic *The Godfather*.

A new gang, calling themselves the Erroll Flynn's, in homage to the dashing, womanizing movie star of the 1920s and 30s, had recently emerged on the scene. They were flamboyant, well-dressed, and even had a dance and the first gang hand sign, done while dancing with one hand in the form of a karate chop held high above their head and yelling, "Erroll Flynn!" Their arch enemies were the Black Killers, or BK's, another eastside gang that had emerged around the same time. The Flynn's neighborhood, or hood, was Mack Street to the Detroit River and Mt. Elliott to St. Jean. The BK's controlled Mack to the Ford Freeway and Van Dyke to Alter, which meant they often ran into each other. The questions "What up, dough?" or "What it be like?" were challenges when encountering rivals, almost always leading to fistfights, stabbings, or shootings.

Roney took me to a small house not far from the old Paradise Valley part of the city. It was uncomfortably warm but extremely well kept. An older woman sat on the far end of a couch watching Florida Evans, perennially parted from

Good Times, yell at James for losing another job on a small color TV sitting on top of a much larger one. Noiseless except for the screech of plastic whenever she moved, she seemed oblivious to us. Roney introduced me to his cousin, "Cisco." A black belt in Tae Kwon Do, he was about nineteen, short, muscular, and black as oil with a shiny processed hairstyle called a finger wave. He was wearing a pair of black glass-heeled shoes, the equivalent of today's most expensive Air Jordan sneakers. After putting on a black leather jacket, Cisco put a .45 caliber pistol in his waistband before topping his outfit off with a black felt Borsalino hat, commonly referred to as a Boss or Boss-a-leenie. He looked at me and scowled before turning to Roney and asking, "What you doin' brangin' this westside lame muthafucka over here?"

Roney smiled as he answered, "Be c-c-cool, Cisco. T-t-this is my p-p-partna! He a s-s-s-smart m-m-muthafucka."

Cisco sucked his teeth and smirked. "We goin' to a party at my dawg's house. Let's go."

The house was a two-story red brick structure on a corner about six blocks away. The porch had two large columns on either side of the stairs supporting a balcony. Cisco knocked on the front door but never looked at it, his eyes instead scanning for potential enemies. A streetlight burned brightly on the opposite corner, illuminating the words "Earl Flinn" spray-painted on a nearby wall.

A guy named Red opened the door. He and Cisco were about the same age. Red was light skinned with red hair and freckles. Like Cisco, he had a finger-wave hairstyle. He had a black revolver in the waistband of his Swedish knit pants. He quickly locked the door and slapped hands with Cisco. A stick of marijuana in Red's mouth bounced up and down when he spoke. I wasn't paying attention to their conversation, though. Many other people were in the house, most of them smoking weed, drinking wine, and listening to "Love Rollercoaster" by the Ohio Players. I saw a guy in the living room wearing a white boss, a multi-colored Nik-Nik shirt, blue Swedish knit pants, and blue glass-heel shoes. He was surrounded by girls wearing skin-tight window-pane jeans and halter tops who were watching him doing the Erroll Flynn dance. Roney told me he was known as Dancing Dan.

"H-h-h-here. H-hit this." Roney handed me a joint, and I smoked weed for the first time. The unease I felt subsided. My senses suddenly heightened as I became captivated by the women. One of them looked like a black light poster my brother David had in his room, the one of the bandolier-wearing Black woman with a huge, perfectly round afro and ass and titties to match. My new-found euphoria and flights of fantasy were suddenly interrupted by Red peeking out of the living room window. He yelled, "It's two muthafuckas creeping cross the street! I think they BK's!" Red and Cisco pulled their guns and ran outside, followed by Roney and me. I should have been terrified, but the marijuana had had a strangely calming effect on me.

Whoever Red saw seemed to have disappeared. We stood on the porch, looking and waiting for whatever came next. I saw them first, two shadowy figures across the street. One of them was holding a shotgun or a rifle. I pointed and whispered, "There they are. In the bushes."

Suddenly yelling, "Erroll Flynn M&M, muthafuckas!", Cisco and Red fired into the bushes.

The BK's shot back as I ducked behind one of the columns, bullets creating sparks in it and causing small chunks of pinkish-colored brick to fly past my head.

The BK's began running away, and one of them fell. Roney tapped me on the arm and ran. I followed him, my heart tap-dancing in construction boots as we jumped fences and cut through yards with the screams of sirens all around us.

Finally, reaching a bus bench, we collapsed on it. I was so scared I could only think of one thing to say. "What the fuck does M&M mean?"

Roney laughed, lit a cigarette, and passed it to me after taking a drag. "Y-y-you re-re-really is a lame. It me-me-means m-m-m-money m-m-m-maker, d-dumbass." In a night filled with firsts, I took a long, hard pull of the cigarette, watching as the orange glow at the end increased in brightness. I stood up unsteadily when our Damn Slow Ride arrived, dizzy from the combination of nicotine and marijuana, oblivious to the Hawk. Neither of us said anything on the way home. Roney broke the silence after we got off the bus. "C-c-cisco gonna be c-cool with you f-from now on. You did g-good." We gave each other five, and he went into his house through the front door while I crawled through an upstairs bedroom window into mine.

I was constantly with Roney in the days and weeks that followed. I lost interest in school. I had been turned out by the danger and allure of the streets. I preferred the chaos there to the chaos at my house. I started ditching classes and staying out late every night. My grades plummeted to D's and F's. My mother would order me to the basement and give me a beating with one of my father's leather belts or an extension cord every time I brought home a bad report card or got caught coming home late. The beatings became so frequent that I eventually stopped crying and just stood silently as the grey beast roared in concert.

Most of the families that began moving into the neighborhood were from rougher areas of town. The manicured lawns began disappearing; the sprinklers replaced by kids opening fire hydrants for relief during the dog days of summer. The Parks and Recreation Department tried to alleviate this by sending water-filled semi-trailers called swim mobiles to impoverished neighborhoods. They would park our swim mobile on Kendall, the closest cross street to my house. It dead-ended at an alley behind the local supermarket. Many older White women who couldn't afford a ticket on the White flight walked this street to the market. Along with two new guys who had moved on the block, Roney and I began snatching their purses during the first part of 1976. We didn't just snatch purses, however. We stole everything not nailed down. We broke into student lockers at Cooley and stole leather coats. We burglarized houses and department stores, smashing the display windows and taking the mannequins for the clothing. One of the new guys almost lost his head when a shard of glass fell as he was stealing one decked out in a three-piece suit.

We broke into an electronic store on the corner of Whitcomb and Grand River so many times the owner finally replaced the display window with a concrete wall. The remainder of the stores on Grand River soon followed suit but installed collapsible metal gates instead.

The Flynn's and BK's were now always in the news, and not for anything good. Cisco had begun hanging out on our side of town as a result. One day, I was ditching class and broke a dice game near the newer Cooley High building next to Fenkell Avenue. I had learned how to cheat at dice from a neighborhood guy named "Black Ike". He taught me how to spin dice in the dirt and pad-roll on blankets and carpeted floors. Originally from the east side, Black Ike was tall, dark-skinned, and kept a roll of one-hundred-dollar bills in his pockets. The ultimate player, he had dozens of girlfriends and every color of glass heel shoes imaginable, which he often let me wear to school.

Two of the guys at the game were members of the Chene gang, named after a street on the eastside. One of them hit me on the head with a gun and robbed me before they both ran away laughing. I told Roney and Cisco when I got back to the hood. They were pissed. The next day, five or six Flynn's that Cisco called from the eastside caught the bus to Cooley. I led them through the school until we found the guys who robbed me. In an incident that caused Cooley to be the first school in the nation to install metal detectors, the Flynn's beat them bloody and took their gun. They were yelling "Erroll Flynn" and dancing through the hallways the entire time as everyone ran in terror. Afterward, the Flynn's got on the Fenkell bus, slapping and robbing passengers as they continued to let everyone know who they were. But this was nothing compared to the event that would forever etch their name in Dirty Glove infamy.

On August 15, 1976, Kool and the Gang and the Average White Band were in concert at Cobo Hall, where numerous Flynn's were in attendance. At about 8:15 p.m., one of the shortest members, wearing white-rimmed glasses with no lenses and a black boss, yelled, "Erroll Flynn" while waving a closed umbrella. Dozens of fellow Flynn's dressed similarly and waving umbrellas as well or canes responded with, "M&M's!" They then began robbing concert goers and storming the stage. They also raped two White women, one in the Pontchartrain Hotel parking lot and one just outside the arena's entrance doors. While most of the police force responded to Cobo Hall, dozens of other Flynn's simultaneously burglarized stores downtown and cleaned out Kosin's shoe store and Henry the Hatter.

Cisco had a brother nicknamed "Black." Like Cisco, he was very dark-skinned and wore his hair in a finger-wave. He grinned a lot, like he knew something no one else did. Black wasn't a Flynn member, though. He was a street hustler who wore glass heels, a diamond Longines wristwatch, and had every style of the expensive Nik-Nik and Roland shirts imaginable. He made his money cheating at dice until the wrong gambler caught him. The police found him the next morning in the trunk of his car in an alley, shot seven times. On the other hand, Cisco made his money by putting people at the business end of his .45. His favorite targets were dope houses. He was eventually killed when the employees at a house he had already stuck up twice ambushed him. Guys like Black and Cisco were what all inner-city youth admired and aspired to be. These were our role models. We didn't see any Black doctors or lawyers, any Black firefighters or cops. Before athletes and rappers who made hundreds of millions of dollars, the only successful Blacks we saw were well-dressed hustlers and pimps with beautiful women on their arms and the gang members, who were feared and earned street cred through violence and measured coolness. Black men like my father, who worked on an assembly line, were known as squares or suckers.

On June 17, 1977, I got arrested for robbing the local paperboy. I had just finished walking our family dog, a mangy old black Labrador retriever that we named "Ruff" because he never barked. All he did was lay down, yawn, and pass gas. His favorite spot was on the front porch next to my mother when she drank her morning coffee. I was still holding the dog chain and leash when the paperboy rode up on his bicycle, a nice Schwinn with a banana seat and monkey bars. I asked him if I could take a quick spin, and when he refused, I pushed him off and rode away. He was gone when I got back just ten minutes later. I put the bike in the backyard with Ruff and went to my room. My mother called me downstairs a little while afterward. She was standing at the front door with two cops and the paperboy who said, "That's him, officer! He threatened me with a chain and took my bike!" My mother stood in the doorway with her arms crossed as I was handcuffed and driven away in the light blue patrol car of Detroit's finest.

I got into a fight on the first day in juvenile hall because I wanted to watch *The Scene*, a popular dance show that featured students from local high schools, and the other kid wanted to watch something else. I got confined to my room, where there was a single, narrow window that I could look out of and see 1300 Beaubien Street, the headquarters of the Detroit police department. It was next to the old Wayne County jail. I spent hours looking at my potential future before laying sleepless on my cot, subconsciously rubbing the horseshoe-shaped scar on my left arm, its origin known by only me, my mother, and the grey monster.

I went to court on August 5, my Mom Mary's birthday. The judge gave me probation for six months. Just two days after getting off probation, I caught the bus with Roney and four other guys to Redford High school to break into student lockers. The school was on Grand River, about four miles from our neighborhood and about thirty minutes from Oakland County, where a cabal of obscenely wealthy pedophiles was dumping the bodies of sexually abused White kids not much younger than us. Redford was a predominately White school, and when a teacher saw us, he knew we weren't students. Roney knocked him out when he tried to stop us. Had we done our research we would have known that the sixteenth police precinct was just blocks away. Multiple cop cars converged on the school as we ran away. Slowed by four feet of freshly fallen snow, I watched it change to scarlet as I got beat with nightsticks. Roney was in big trouble, however. The teacher was in a coma. Roney ended up going to the Michigan Reformatory in Ionia for several years.

I didn't get released until close to midnight. The officer who opened my cell told me, "Your mama said she ain't coming." I was hoping that my father would have picked up the phone when they called. Now I knew that I was going to get another beating when I got home, this time by an extension cord or leather belt instead of a nightstick. I flipped up the collar of my bloodstained coat to try and stave off the unrelenting hawk as I waited for the damn slow ride.

By now David was attending the University of Arkansas at Pine Bluff. He paid for the first semester with money he had saved while working after-school jobs his junior and senior years in high school. About a year before he left for college, I got kicked out of school for smoking weed. After that, I went to Henry Ford High School but got kicked out within two weeks for selling it. Next, I went to Central High school, where I tried to stay straight and narrow and went to all my classes. My art teacher hung one of my drawings on the classroom wall and wanted me to apply for a prestigious art program in the city. That same day, my English teacher wanted to enter a science fiction short story I wrote into a state-wide contest for high school students. It was the best day I had had in a very long time, and I felt a tremendous sense of worth. I was excited to tell my parents, but my father had crashed another family car. The car was less than a week old, which made my good news irrelevant. That was the maddest I ever saw my mother get. The yelling and cursing got so loud, I left the house and didn't come back for three days. My dreams of being an artist or writer ended the following week after I got caught smoking opium in the school lunchroom. I was sent to Cass Tech night school but dropped out after two weeks, never having gotten past the 10th grade.

During the last part of November 1979, I decided to shoot dice at a new after-hours gambling spot. David had been back home for about a year now after one semester of college. He was working at Ford and making good money. He had a new gold-colored Pontiac Trans-Am with T-tops and a nice wardrobe. I took an expensive black leather suit jacket out of his closet and put it on before walking to the bus stop, smoking a stick of Acapulco gold along the way. Grand River is one of the city's longest streets. Starting downtown near the Detroit River, it runs through some of the roughest neighborhoods in the city to the suburbs of adjacent townships. In Detroit proper, it is home to many abandoned buildings, one of which provided clever concealment for the gambling spot. A Las Vegas-style crap table was in the center of a room illuminated by two overhanging light bulbs.

An old wino was sitting next to a wall, drinking from a bottle of Wild Irish Rose and nodding in tune to the latest hit from Heatwave. I sidestepped him and continued to the table. The man who controlled the bets, known as the stickman, was short, balding, and had bug eyes and a half-smoked cigar wedged between huge, grayish-colored lips. He said, "Roll the dice, Youngblood. Let's see what you got." Gray ashes from the cigar exploded into a bright orange glow as he inhaled and then blew a thick plume of smoke in my face. I coughed lightly, bringing laughter from the other players and giggles from the female spectators.

The establishment, or the house, made its money by cutting craps. Cheaters faced not only the wrath of the other players but also the wrath of the house. If I won tonight it was going to be with the assistance of Lady Luck. I dropped $100 on the table. A pimp standing at the other end matched my bet. He said, "Shoot, little nigga." The pimp had on makeup foundation and wore his jet-black hair in a Jheri curl set off by a barely perceptible widow's peak. His manicured nails

51

perfectly complimented the sparkling full-carat diamond rings on both pinkies and his diamond Longines watch. The widow's peak and the paleness of his face caused him to look not unlike Blackula. The women on his arms only enhanced this ghastly effect. They were also pale, their oversized lips painted blood-red.

I grabbed the dice, blew on them, and threw them across the table where they stopped on eleven. I rolled another eleven, two sevens, and bucked eight, Little Joe, and Big Ben. The last time I had won like this had been by cheating, and my head still bears a scar to this day as a reminder. I decided to let the money ride. The stickman, no doubt praying for a two, three, or twelve, shot me a gold-and-diamond-toothed grin as the pimp covered the bet.

I blew on the dice and hurled them directly at him just as a loud gunshot rang out. I instinctively looked in the direction of the sound. A huge man wearing a long black coat was standing near the door, holding a gun above his head. Smoke curled out of the barrel as small pieces of the ceiling fell gently onto the crap table. He said, "What it be like, muthafuckas? This is a stick-up!" I glanced around the room and saw two other men also holding handguns above their heads.

The wino tried to sneak out the door, and one of the stick-up men hit him with his gun. Blood and teeth flew out of his mouth as he fell against the wall and slid to the floor unconscious. The stick-up man who fired the shot yelled, "Everybody put their goddamn heads down! Look at the table!" I did as he ordered and saw the snake eyes of my last roll staring back in silence. One of the gunmen scooped the money into a bag. I was terrified. *Would these men execute all of us before leaving?* Although I had been robbed before, the fear of losing your life over material things is something you can never grow accustomed to. No doubt, the women whose purses we snatched experienced that same fear. Although growing up in the ghetto was a minefield of potential danger, it was also a veritable kaleidoscope of karma, as yesterday's perpetrator often turned into today's victim.

The leader of the stick-up crew ordered everyone to strip. The other two gathered our clothing and left before the leader smashed the lightbulbs with his gun barrel. The sudden slamming of the door threw us into darkness. The stick-man lit a match, revealing that the gunmen had overlooked his teeth. I followed several of the gamblers outside and saw taillights disappearing at the end of the alley. Clothing was strewn on either side of a pair of tire tracks in the snow. David's jacket was missing. It was going to be a long, cold walk home. Hugging myself to fight off the hawk, a canary yellow Cadillac Seville pulled up to the curb. The window rolled slowly down, and a voice asked, "Hey, you need a ride somewhere, you lucky little muthafucka?" It was my dice-shooting adversary displaying a classic pimp lean behind a mink-covered steering wheel, his rings and watch glaringly absent. His two undead companions were still with him, one in the front seat and one in the back. The heat from the interior of the car helped me make a hasty decision.

The woman in the back seat with me was wearing a red Afro wig, a waist-length faux fur jacket, a pink suede miniskirt, and matching platform heel shoes. She kicked them off and put her feet in my lap, spreading her legs just enough to reveal that the stick-up men had maybe decided to keep more clothing than just David's jacket. As I asked the pimp to drop me off near Grand River and Whitcomb, she pulled a cellophane bag containing small balloons of heroin out of her vagina. The pimp did not approve and snarled, "Bitch! What if da fucking po-leece stop us right now? Stash that shit!"

She said, "Please, Daddy. I need some. I'm getting sick, and what just happened fucked me up bad."

The pimp relented and pulled into a nearby alleyway. The hooker removed one of the balloons and returned the bag to its hiding place. She then reached into a crevice in the seat and grabbed a small purse containing a burnt spoon, a small piece of cotton, a Bic lighter, small yellow rubber tubing, and a syringe. Collectively, these items are known as a dope fiend's "works." After preparing the dope for injection, she ran her fingers over the inside of one of her thighs. She inserted the needle, and the liquid entered her leg as she slowly depressed the plunger before pulling it back up. She did this several times, causing the blood to flow into the syringe and mix with the heroin each time. She smiled slightly and looked at me, her speech slow and deliberate as she said, "You're cute, lil nigga."

She laughed softly just before her amply lashed eyes rolled upward, and her head dropped down onto her chest. She released the syringe, and it hung like a dart as she drooled. I panicked and yelled, "Hey! Something is wrong with her!"

The pimp looked over the back seat before calling her a stupid bitch as he opened the door and slapped her. Her wig slid off just before he removed the heroin from her vagina and threw it to her stablemate. He then looked at me and said, "Get the fuck out of here. The ride and show are over, muthafucka." I walked off into the frigid night air as he dragged her to a nearby dumpster.

My mother caught me sneaking in the house that night, but she had given up on corporal punishment by now. Belts, extension cords, broomsticks—none of that shit worked, so she ramped up the psychological and emotional warfare, often repeating the same warning: "You ain't gonna be shit! You're going to end up dead or in jail! If you're lucky, you'll just be a drunk like your daddy!" What she said hurt, but she was right. I was on a path for prison or, worse, the graveyard. But threats like she made never work when coming from a parent. They don't deter a child from wrongdoing. Instead, they become self-fulfilling prophecies. I began hating myself and engaging in increasingly self-destructive behavior, preferring to always see glasses as half empty. The hatred and adverse reactions never really go away, either. You carry them with you through life until they become too heavy to bear, and you either succumb to the dire predictions, or you don a suit of armor burnished in arrogance.

A week later I was on Grand River looking for shit to steal, when I found myself in front of an Armed Forces recruiting office. A poster with "First to Fight" and depicting a Marine holding a rifle and hiding behind a tree was in the window. I thought about recent events in my life and my potential future and at that moment, I knew I had to leave Detroit. I walked into the building and told the recruiter, "I want to do what the guy on the poster is doing."

He looked at me incredulously and asked, "You want to sign up for the Infantry? To be a *grunt?*" He tried to convince me to look at other Military Occupational Specialties, but it went in one ear and out the other. People rarely sign up for the Infantry. Usually, they are placed there based on test scores. But I had no self-worth at the time, so I literally signed up to be cannon fodder. My boot camp start date was in January of 1980 at the Marine Corps Recruit Depot in San Diego, California. I was excited at the prospect of seeing a real beach and an ocean for the first time in my life, instead of concrete and the odorous Detroit River, the final resting place for a different type of cannon fodder. Maybe I could have gotten a job at Ford like my father and David, but I needed a fresh start; I needed to leave the trauma and turmoil as far behind as possible.

The whole family rode with me to the airport. I hugged my father last before getting on the plane. I smiled as I held back tears. Every fond memory of my childhood involves him, like when he would drive drunk with David and me to Dot and Etta's late at night to get shrimp baskets and frog legs. I would watch wide-eyed as the prostitutes flirted with him while he waited for his order, their peacock-attired pimps keeping a close watch. Flashbacks of my father taking us to the Thanksgiving parade on Woodward Avenue created a mental montage. I was sitting atop his shoulders to see over the crowd as Santa came out of his castle on the second-story façade of the J.L. Hudson building. The following week, we would visit Santa on the twelfth floor and ask for shit we never got.

My father even let me drive the current family car on a date. I was sixteen and had never driven before. She was twenty-five and built to drive men wild. I took her to a Parliament-Funkadelic concert at Cobo Hall. On the way home, I sideswiped a parked car. My father told my mother that he did it, taking the full blame for the damage to yet another family car while I got a mercy fuck after my date found out my actual age. I thought she was my girlfriend until a few days later when I went to visit a friend and saw his three brothers and another neighborhood guy running a train on her on their dirty basement floor.

The only time my father ever punished me was when I spray-painted my name on the side of the White couple's house nearest to our driveway. When my father came home, he punched me in the chest and knocked me down the stairs. He made me scrub the paint for hours to no avail, as a faint outline of my name stubbornly refused to disappear. I know now that I wrote my name where my parents would see it because I was crying out for attention. In 1952, Ralph Ellison equated being Black in America to being invisible. Sometimes the feeling of that invisibility never ventures past family, and one needs to be seen, even in a negative light. Perhaps my mother had experienced that invisibility once as well.

As I boarded the plane, I prayed that she and my father would someday learn to get along. I prayed that he would overcome his struggles with the demon in that bottle of Canadian Club and that she would somehow learn to help him and respect him. Most of all, I prayed that they would come to some type of reconciliation with whatever had happened between them when Derrick was born.

Derrick started Cooley High in the fall of 1980. Frequently teased because of his complexion, he would fight anyone at the drop of a dime, so he joined the football team, which became a perfect outlet for his anger. Even still, Derrick beat up everyone on the block at least once, sometimes twice. When one of the neighbors stole David's T-tops off his Firebird, Derrick beat the neighbor's ass in the middle of the street as my mother sat on the porch drinking coffee. The neighbor's family had a bulldog named Brutus, who barked at everyone and terrorized the neighborhood. When Brutus ran toward Derrick, Ruff, in an atypical display of barking, left my mother's side and attacked him. Brutus and the neighbor both ended up limping home, tails between their legs.

Derrick led the team to the 1981 City Championship. He was strong as an ox and ran like the wind, but he was only about five foot six at best. During his senior year, he was visited by University of Michigan football representatives, but they decided to pass on him because they didn't think he was tall enough. Instead of playing for a D-II school, Derrick joined the Marine Corps. I was torn by his decision, proud that he had chosen to follow my path, disappointed that he didn't go to college. I wanted him to be better and to do better than me. I owed him that much at the least. All my life, I had chosen to ask my mother the tough questions about him: why he looked so much different than David and me and why he was so much darker. Because of his complexion, neighborhood kids always teased him and questioned his familial connections to David and me. Not once had I given a thought that although he had never vocalized any questions he himself might have had, he had to feel the same way. Not once had I considered how he felt, how sometimes neighborhood ostracism and the cruelness so inherent in kids affected him.

I never thought that although I had gone through my share of emotional and physical trauma, he had gone through trauma of an existential nature due to those unanswered questions.

CHAPTER FOUR

OKINAWA, JAPAN, was my first duty station after boot camp. One of the most desirable ports of liberty in the Pacific was the Philippine Islands, commonly referred to as the "P.I." or the Pleasure Islands. The P.I. was known for its exotic women willing to do anything for little money. In truth, most of them just wanted to get to the United States. I never got a chance to go there because the previous year, my new unit was banned for drinking, fighting, and an accusation of rape against several Marines.

I was stationed at Camp Pendleton after leaving Okinawa. The other Marines in my platoon and I would catch the Greyhound bus from Oceanside to Los Angeles or San Diego during weekend liberty. While in Oceanside one weekend, I found a paycheck made out to someone named Antonio Smith. A crook I knew made me a fake ID so I could cash it. After that, my friends jokingly referred to me as "Tony." One of them bought a used car a few weeks later, and he and I drove to the Carolina West, a popular nightclub near LAX airport just outside Inglewood. We needed the getaway, as the entire base had a recent scare when we almost went to war with Iran. On day 443 of hostages being held at the American Embassy in Tehran, we were mustered to board planes for Iran. Twenty-four hours later, Iran released the hostages when Ronald Reagan was sworn in as president.

The tables around the dance floor at the Carolina West had telephones on them. I called one with two young women sitting at it. When one of them picked up, I said, "Hi. I'm Tony." She told me her name was Gilda. She was with her sister, and they were from a city called Compton. I had never heard of it. My friend and I took them to Denny's for breakfast when the club closed. Gilda told me about Compton, which she described as a lovely suburb. We ate and got to know each other before parting ways at about 3:00 a.m.

Within five minutes, an Inglewood police car stopped my friend and me. A tall White officer with a buzz haircut walked up to the driver's door. He said to my friend, "Get out the car, nigger."

His partner was a short, bald White officer with a mouthful of Redman. The short one rapped on my window with his flashlight. "You too, nigger." He said it as casually as if he was asking someone how their day was going. He made us sit on the curb and he went through our wallets while the tall one searched the car.

My friend asked the tall one what we had done wrong, and he replied, "Shut the fuck up before I bash your head in. What you niggers doing in my town, anyway? Where's the dope and guns? Whose car is this?"

The short cop changed his tone when he saw my military ID. "You a Marine?" he asked.

I replied, "Yes, sir, both of us. We just left a nightclub nearby."

He smiled, exposing tobacco-stained teeth, and said, "Well, Semper Fi! Why didn't y'all say so? I was a Marine, too. Y'all gone and get out of here, most ricky tick." He spat a mouthful of brown shit on the ground as he and his partner got in their car, driving off slowly, no doubt to the nearby Randy's, which had the biggest donut in the world displayed on top of the building.

Semper Fi, short for Semper Fidelis, is the Marine Corps motto. It is Latin for "always faithful." My friend and I had recently been ready to lay down our lives for this country. And now, this was how we got treated by cops while on liberty in that same country? And by at least one who had once worn the same uniform as we wore? Not much had changed from 1967 to 1981. At that very moment, I never hated the police more.

The next time I had liberty, I took a Greyhound to LA and then a city bus to Compton. There was gang graffiti on several buildings and tennis shoes hanging from phone lines, but Gilda lived in a lovely house with a well-kept yard. Her mother was polite and cooked dinner for me. I had initially introduced myself as Tony to make my friend laugh, but now I decided to stick with the name. Looking back, I think I did it because I just didn't like who I was at the time.

At midnight, Gilda's mother told me I had to leave. The bus had stopped running by the time I got to the bus stop. A carload of gang members slowed when they saw me before driving off. I was a stranger in their hood. They could have even been rivals to the neighborhood gang. At that point, my survival instincts kicked in. I walked to a nearby payphone and made a call. A woman with a raspy voice that betrayed far too many years of smoking picked up. I could picture her mashing a filter-less cigarette into an overfilled ashtray as she spoke. "911, Compton Police Department. What's your emergency?"

I told her two guys robbed me at gunpoint, and I needed help. She put me on hold for about five minutes.

When she got back, she asked a bunch of questions. I made up more lies. She said, "OK. Stay where you are. A unit will be there shortly." I hung up and looked at my watch before fading back into some bushes near the payphone.

Thirty-five minutes later, a police car slowly drove up and stopped. The car was white with a horizontal blue stripe down the side with the words Compton Police stenciled in white. I had never seen two Black police officers riding together before then. Neither one got out of the car.

The passenger held a cup of steaming hot coffee. He wore glasses and was medium skinned, slightly overweight, and had a large Afro and a salt and pepper Fu Manchu mustache. A cigarette dangled from his bottom lip, a long, lingering ash threatening to join the others on the front of his uniform shirt. The cigarette bounced rhythmically as he asked, "Yo' name Tony?"

The portly driver, dark-skinned with a receding hairline and pork chop sideburns, yawned loudly and farted but otherwise said nothing as he took a bite out of a cheeseburger. I was at a loss for words. The passenger spoke again, impatiently this time as he snarled, "Yo' muthafucka! Is yo' name Tony?"

I replied, "Yes, sir. Two guys with guns robbed me."

With the driver preoccupied with his meal, the passenger asked, "Can you recognize them if you see them again?" He seemed relieved when I said no and said, "Well, it wouldn't do any good to file a report then. You live around here?" He snickered when I told him that I was stationed at Camp Pendleton and in Compton to visit a girl. He said, "Well, Semper Fi, muthafucka! I hope you at least got some pussy. How the fuck you getting back to base? The buses don't start running for another few hours." I asked him if they could give me a ride to the police station to wait.

The driver grunted, farted again, and finally spoke. "Yeah, the last thang we need is a dead Marine on our hands. Get in the backseat, muthafucka." He threw his cheeseburger wrapper out of his window, and his partner flicked his cigarette out of his before cautiously taking a sip of coffee. Then, Compton's finest slowly drove off with me securely seated next to a blood-stained back seat.

The next time I saw Gilda was when she caught the Greyhound down to Oceanside where we spent the weekend at a motel not far from the beach. From that point on, she came to see me. Married military personnel got a marked increase in pay for housing. I was looking for that bump in pay, and she was looking for the stability of medical and dental insurance. With both of us looking for things other than love, we got married in February of 1982 in an impromptu ceremony in Las Vegas. We moved to a small one-bedroom apartment in San Clemente right outside of Camp Pendleton. Gilda was pregnant by January of 1983. I had been demoted three times, twice for insubordination, and once for missing a movement after getting drunk and passing out at a woman's house in San Diego the year before we were married. After we got married, I got my shit together and was promoted to squad leader. I also got my GED and put in my re-enlistment papers.

A month later, the battalion Sergeant Major summoned me to his office. He said, "At ease, Marine. I'm denying your re-enlistment because of your disciplinary record. I don't think the corps is for you." I pleaded with him to allow me to re-enlist, explaining that I was now married with a baby on the way. He said his hands were tied. The Marine Corps, with an eye toward a new reputation, was now denying re-enlistment to Marines with multiple rank reductions. Although I wasn't allowed to re-enlist, I was given an honorable discharge in April of 1983 and therefore had to remain a reserve until completing my full six-year commitment.

I decided to leave Gilda in Compton while I went back to Detroit to look for a job. I felt that I was now mature enough to deal with any peer pressure to fall back into my old ways. By now, it was hard to get a job in the automotive industry. The foreign automakers had cornered the market by selling cars that lasted anywhere from 200,000 to 500,000 miles. Add this to the Ayatollah Khomeni cutting Iran's production of crude oil and shipments to the US in 1979, and sales of more fuel-efficient foreign cars exploded. Ford's car sales alone dropped by 47 percent, eventually resulting in a loss of 100,000 jobs. I went back to Compton after only one month.

Crack cocaine had become a plague in Black communities. What mainstream America has never understood is why. Most everyone that lived in these areas smoked marijuana. They also drank beer and wine, which is why there is a liquor store every two blocks. Impoverished people need to escape from their bleak realities. The ones who don't use drugs or alcohol use prayer, so there are just as many churches. Before crack, people saw cocaine as a status symbol. When smokable cocaine flooded the inner cities, almost everyone who smoked marijuana wanted to try it.

But no one knew the devastating effects crack would have on America. People got hooked by the thousands. Others tried it, got scared of it, and never smoked it again. And then some saw the money-making potential. The neighbor who stole David's T-tops was one of them. He and another neighborhood guy were in business together and made a lot of money. A gunman rumored to have been hired by his best friend who was jealous of his success, eventually killed him on Kendall, where I snatched purses years before. Thirty-five years later, the concrete where he died still bears a bloodstain underneath a pair of shoes hanging from a telephone line. His best friend is still alive, although in a wheelchair, because of an attempt on his life at his money-laundering carwash on Seven-Mile Road.

Roney also fell victim to the allure of smoking crack. During hiatuses from Jackson State prison or Ionia, my parents would feed him after his own parents disowned him for stealing from them. He repaid my parents by breaking into their house and stealing my father's guitar among other things. Karma eventually caught up with Roney when he died several years later of a heart attack while smoking crack. When I heard about his death, I had no remorse. I had realized long before that our childhood friendship had been nothing more than an obscene port in an emotional storm.

People went to any lengths to get crack, including exchanging sexual favors just for a hit. The woman I took to the concert became a crack prostitute, her beauty fading with every suck of a pipe or penis. The owner of the dirty basement floor where she played train caboose also dabbled in the cocaine business until he woke up one morning and found two rival dealers sitting in his kitchen.

The scourge of crack hit even closer than just friends and lovers. Soon people in Rocky Mount were smoking and selling it. One of my maternal first cousins, seeking to expand his empire, got shot to death in a MacDonald's parking lot in southeast Washington, DC. He still had $10,000 in his pockets when the police arrived. His mother, who the family called "Baby Sis," was devastated. Her nickname was ironic, considering the pains taken to make everyone believe that Linda was the baby sister. Baby Sis was inconsolable over her son's death, but not as much as she was when the cops told her she couldn't have the money.

My daughter Haley was born on October 4, 1983. She was the most beautiful thing I had ever seen. But I was scared. Gilda and I were so broke by now that we used cloth diapers because Pampers were too expensive. Forced to go on welfare, we stood in line once for powdered milk and government cheese. I refused to let the government take care of my family and me. The next day, I went to Compton City Hall and filled out applications for every job position in the city, from janitor to firefighter to security officer. I drew the line at police officer, however.

On November 2, Greyhound bus workers went on strike. I was reluctant to cross a picket line, but I was desperate. I got hired as a janitor a week after applying. The striking employees settled for a substantial reduction in pay and came back to work on December 20. The ostracism was visceral. Only one of them talked to me, a young, slim guy everyone called Playboy because he wore his hair in a Jheri curl and came to work in Fila sweat suits and Cazal sunglasses. He started selling crack to make up for his loss in wages. A month later, I overheard some of the other employees talking about him. His mother had died in a fire after she set their house ablaze while smoking some of his crack.

The money from Greyhound wasn't enough, so I got a second job as a security guard at the Meteor Security Company. I no longer had to catch city buses because I had recently bought Gilda's sister's old gray Camaro. It was in horrible shape, which is how I was able to afford it. I always felt the pangs of jealousy whenever I pulled next to a gleaming El Camino or a convertible 5.0 Mustang flossing expensive Dayton wire rims. The rims were extremely expensive and called "Dana Danes" in tribute to the New York rapper, and "flossing" was a term widely used at the time to describe someone who was showing off.

The security company sent out guards to various businesses on an as-needed basis. I worked at a supermarket in Ladera Heights most of the time, where I slept all night near the dumpsters in back on the company golf cart. The work at Greyhound was hard, so I had to get rest whenever I could. Besides cleaning the toilets inside the massive terminal, I had to clean human feces and urine from the outside doorways surrounding it where the homeless called home. I also had to mop the floors inside, careful not to hit the alligator shoes of pimps waiting to pounce on young girls who had come to LA seeking stardom.

A guy from Alabama also worked for the security company. He was assigned to a location not far from the supermarket. One night he woke me and asked me to ride with him to get something to eat. Five minutes later, he stopped near some gang members selling crack. When one of them walked up to the car, Alabama pulled out his job-issued .38 revolver and demanded his stash. Alabama then sped off as the rest of the gang members began shooting at us. I cursed him out for getting me involved in his shit, but he just laughed as he dropped me off at my golf cart and drove off with at least two bullet holes in his back window. I never saw Alabama again.

It is just that simple to get caught up in situations that could land you in prison or the graveyard. They are both filled with Black men who were unwilling accomplices to crimes. It is so ingrained in our psyches not to snitch, probably because of the stigma generationally attached to enslaved Blacks telling slaveo-wners and overseers on other slaves, that we would rather go to prison than tell on someone. And if we would have gotten caught that night, I probably would have kept my mouth shut, too. I mean, what cop would have believed that bull-shit anyway? A week later, I was sleeping behind the dumpsters when a Ghetto Bird woke me up. I drove around to the front, where I saw several LAPD cars.

One of the cops was talking to my supervisor, a nerdy White guy who had been rejected by every police department in LA County. My supervisor asked me why I hadn't stopped the store from getting robbed. When I yawned and stretched instead of answering, he demanded my badge and gun. He was beside himself. He felt that I should have confronted two guys armed with 12-gauge shotguns with my revolver whereas I believed I was lucky as hell to have been sleeping when the robbery occurred. It suddenly made sense why no police department would hire him. He was an idiot. There was only one Black cop at the scene, so I decided to only talk to him. For all I knew, my supervisor had told the White cops that I may have been in on the robbery.

I told the Black cop the truth. He chuckled as he replied, "They knew when to hit. Guys like that will only kill if they have to. You were lucky you were asleep. Fuck your boss. He's an idiot." It felt strange to agree with a cop on something. For the first time, I realized you could be a cop without being an asshole. I got in my car and left one job lighter without mentioning that one of the robbers was probably on his way to Alabama.

After working at Greyhound for two months, I caught a guy trying to steal a suitcase from a Mexican woman with three small kids. She cried and hugged me as if it contained everything they had in the world. At another time in my life, I would have been the one trying to steal her luggage. Now, I suddenly felt right about my reversal of roles. If helping people made me feel that good, then maybe being a police officer wasn't such a bad job after all; perhaps I had been on the wrong side all along. It was an epiphany like no other. I decided to apply to be an LAPD cop. Two White men and one Black woman were on the oral interview board. The men asked several questions, nodding as I answered. The woman asked the next question. "Mr. Reynolds, you stop a woman for speeding and running a stop sign. When you walk up to the car, she spits at you, curses you out, and then refuses to show you her driver's license before rolling up her window and locking her doors. What do you do next?"

Without hesitation, I said, "Well, I would break her window with my nightstick and arrest her."

The woman was speechless. One of the men stood up, extended his hand, and said, "Thank you, Mr. Reynolds. Don't call us. We'll call you."

All my life, I had believed it was normal for a police officer to handle defiance in this manner. I gave the answer I thought they wanted to hear. It was apparent they had no clue what some of their officers were doing in the real world.

I got laid off from Greyhound not long after making an ass of myself at Parker Center. Worse, Gilda was pregnant again. I was almost out of money. Her mother told me I had to leave if I couldn't pay rent, but Gilda and Haley could stay. I didn't want to leave them, so we all caught the bus to Detroit. One of Greyhound's perks was that employees and their families could ride for free. There was plenty of space at my parent's house now. David, good-looking like my father, had always been a womanizer and was currently living with a *Jet* magazine centerfold model in the suburb of Southfield, and Derrick was in Okinawa. I looked for a job every day. I had filled out an application to be a Compton cop before I left California, but I did not try to be a cop in Detroit. I'm sure the neighbors would have had some exciting things to tell any background investigators about me.

Gilda and my mother hated each other from the moment they met. Gilda stayed upstairs with Haley all day and rarely interacted with my mother. I found out that while I was looking for jobs, Gilda was spending time with Baby Sis, who had moved to Detroit shortly after my parents. For reasons never revealed to me, Baby Sis and my mother had never got along. Within two weeks of living with my parents, I was coming from a job search when I saw Gilda and Haley in a cab parked out front. I asked what was going on, and Gilda said, "Ask your mother." I watched the exaggerated exhaust belch from the cab's tailpipes before taking her advice.

Instead of letting me in, my mother yelled, "You take your ass right along with your wife and baby!" She then slammed the door in my face. I stood there, speechless. When I finally turned to walk down the driveway, the remnants and meaning of my spray-painted name on the house next door were suddenly crystal clear. After all these years, I was still invisible.

David drove up just as I was walking away from the house. I stayed with him and his girlfriend for the night. I asked him why he chose a college so far away from home and why he came back so quickly. He said, "Man, I hated all the arguing and yelling at our house, so I went to the farthest school away that accepted me. I ran out of money and I wasn't getting any financial help from Mama and Daddy, so I had to come back home when I couldn't find a job out there." The next morning, he took me to the Greyhound station, where I got on the bus back to LA with only the clothes on my back.

Gilda gave me a letter from Greyhound requesting that I return to work when I got to her mother's house. She refused to tell me what happened between her and my mother. I didn't have anywhere to live so I parked my car near the Greyhound station and slept in it until it got impounded. After that, I would sneak into an all-night movie theater on Broadway through the exit door. I must have seen *Scarface* at least twenty times. I didn't have much money for food, but moviegoers leave a lot of popcorn in boxes, and you can always find milk duds on the floor. On a good day, you might even find a half-eaten hotdog.

I stayed at the Hotel Cecil on Main Street after I got paid. It was a dump, but it was cheap, and you could pay by the day or week. My room had a broken window concealed by heavy, soiled curtains. The hotel, built in 1927, was reportedly haunted. Many strange deaths and occurrences had taken place there over the years. The wind howling into my room at night did nothing to assuage any doubt I had that this was true. Several serial killers had even used the hotel as their base of operation on occasion. Richard "the Night Stalker" Ramirez was a tenant during the time I rented a room there. I don't remember ever seeing him, though. I guess we were working the same hours.

Work at the LA station became scarce. To keep getting a paycheck, I caught a Greyhound to the San Diego station every day for a vacation relief spot as a ticket clerk. The next vacation relief spot was in El Paso, Texas. I roomed with an alcoholic in a local YMCA near the station. Before crying himself to sleep every night, he drove me nuts complaining about how his "bitch wife" had taken everything from him, including his kids. Two months later, I went back to LA when a janitor position became available and rented a studio apartment in Long Beach near Artesia Boulevard across from an Eddie's Market.

My son Dominic was born in November of 1984. Greyhound laid me off a week later. To get away from Gilda's nagging, I would go across the street to the market to play arcade games. The store owner would let me sweep the floors and take out the trash for a few dollars a day. I was at my wit's end. I had to get a real job, even if it was at Burger King. And just when the rent was two months past due, the city of Compton offered me a career as an armed security officer. The news caught me by surprise. Then it hit me. Security officers were part of the police department. There was a chance the city might offer me a job as a police officer next. As I dropped the notification letter to the floor, I whispered, "Son of a bitch," causing Haley to look up at me and giggle.

CHAPTER FIVE

I STARTED working for the city of Compton on January 14, 1985, one more officer added to a security force of six Barney Fifes, some of whom occasionally forgot to load their guns. Other than me, only two of them had any aspirations to become cops. The rest were content with opening doors and making sure visitors signed in before meeting with city officials. One of them was a former hairstylist named Larry Fisher, a short, brown-skinned middle-aged man who wore an impeccably neat Afro. He had decided to become a security officer for the benefits after his hairstyle clients became scarce when the biggest one, Maurice White of Earth, Wind, and Fire, stopped touring with the group.

The first floor of the police station consisted of the front counter, located just south of the lobby and entrance. Unlike most police stations, there was no bulletproof partition separating the records clerks working the front counter from the public. Two locked doors prevented access from the lobby to the remainder of the first floor. One door led to the report writing room and the stairs to the second floor and basement where the narcotics vault was located. The other door led to the records bureau, W/C's office, watch sergeant's office, armory, jail, training bureau, and additional stairs that led to the south portion of the second floor and to the basement. The detective bureau and a large conference room took up most of the second floor, with the chief's office, known as the corner pocket, located in the southeast corner of the building.

Security officers checked out their guns daily from the armory, which was next to the W/C's office and no bigger than a large broom closet. The door was often left standing open, the key attached to a six-inch piece of wood marked "armory" hanging from a nail in the W/C's office. There was a sign-in sheet next to the door to the armory. No one monitored which guns were supposed to be there. One security officer misplaced her weapon for several days before finding it at home. Had she never said anything, I doubt if anyone would've known it had ever been missing.

When I got off work, the cops would be in the locker room changing into their uniforms. The official name for a police officer's gun belt is Sam Brown, but the Black officers called theirs "Jim Brown" after the Cleveland Browns Hall of Fame running back. Female cops called theirs Sally Browns. It was always raucous in the locker room, filled with good-natured teasing, light-hearted insults, and boasts of recent sexual conquests as the boom-box blasted music at full volume. The cops were particularly fond of Whodini's "Freaks Come Out at Night."

I had to catch two buses to get to work, finishing the journey walking north from Greenleaf Blvd along the railroad on Willowbrook. The tracks separated the east and west sides of the street. There was no vehicle access to either side from Greenleaf to Alondra Blvd. The drug dealers, who were all armed with guns, sold dope on both sides. Whatever side the cops drove down, the dealers would just run to the other side. There were also packs of dogs all over the city. Most of them were harmless, but some would chase you and attack for no reason. The cops called them crack packs because they roamed the streets just like the crackheads. I walked past bullet-riddled dead dogs all the time.

My duty assignment was at city hall. I would often be at the reception desk late into the night when City Manager Laverta Montgomery and Councilmen Bob Adams and Floyd James got off the elevator, the odor of alcohol trailing behind them. Mayor Walter Tucker Jr., Councilwoman Jane Robbins, and Councilman Maxcy Filer were with them occasionally. Montgomery always smiled and said goodnight. Adams just glared at me as he took a long drag from his cigarette. James always grinned like a Cheshire cat and waved like a grand marshal in a parade. He and Adams looked like used-car salesmen who gave free samples of snake-oil. Tucker was more menacing, however. He looked like the tall man from the movie *Phantasm* and carried himself with an air of superiority like a casket on his shoulder. He wouldn't even acknowledge me.

Robbins, a direct descendant of the founder of the city, was an old White lady who wore rhinestone library-style eyeglasses with her white hair in a beehive. Filer was a tall man who wore black-rimmed glasses and had an unkempt medium length horseshoe Afro. He wore suit jackets over white short-sleeve, button-down collar shirts with ties loosely worn around his neck. Although a slovenly man who frequently went without socks, Filer had a huge heart and an even bigger smile. Without fail, he would wave and hiccup just before saying, "Good night, officer. Thank you," as he staggered out the door to his house just blocks away.

I also provided security during council meetings. The city was involved in multiple business ventures, and accusations of malfeasance were rampant. Most of the allegations came from Eddie Randolph, a soft-spoken middle-aged former Marine who wore a camouflage bush hat and jacket. It was probably part of the same outfit he wore during his two tours of Vietnam. After serving his country, he was now homeless and slept on a bus bench at Compton Blvd and Willowbrook, spitting distance from where he had engaged city politicians in verbal combat four times a month starting in 1979.

Eddie spoke at every council meeting, patiently awaiting his turn as he sat in the same seat in the front row. The city officials hated to see him approach the podium and frequently ordered security to remove him. He was always a gentleman, politely complying with my requests to leave as his trenchant questions remained unanswered.

A true patriot to the end, Eddie died of natural causes on July 4, 1990. He was found in the plaza just outside of city hall with a copy of the city budget and a recent council agenda inside his two small duffle bags. In life, Eddie was like a Marine on guard duty, standing on the steps of city hall every night until he retired to his bus bench. Everyone knew him, most laughing him off as crazy and dismissing his claims as those of a demented Vietnam veteran who had fallen on hard times. Not me, however. I thought his questions were spot on, mostly because of how nervous and angry city officials got whenever he spoke. I had learned long ago that whoever screams the loudest has the most to hide.

I started as a police recruit on Haley's birthday. I was sent to the LA County Sheriff's Academy for training. I had asked David for a suit jacket because recruits must wear business attire the first week. Being a smart ass, he sent one exactly like the one stolen at the gambling spot. I stood out like a sore thumb even without the leather jacket. Out of over one hundred recruits, there were only seven Blacks, including me and two other Compton PD recruits. The academy is like Marine Corps boot camp. The instructors are called TAC officers. One of them was a short Mexican deputy with a bushy mustache. I knew that I was in for it when he got to me. He pointed his finger in my face and yelled, "Is that a fucking *leather jacket?* Are you some kind of gangster? Where are you from? You can't be a sheriff's deputy recruit! What the fuck are you doing on my parade grounds?"

I calmly replied, "I'm from Detroit, sir. I work for Compton PD."

He threw his hands up in exasperation. He screamed, "Well, that fucking explains it! You're from Detroit *and* Compton PD. You *are* a fucking gangster! I promise you won't last here, so don't get comfortable!"

To assess our writing skills, the class was assigned to write a brief statement detailing our likes, favorite movies, and books. My books were the autobiographies of Frederick Douglass and Malcolm X. My films were *Soldier Story* with Denzel Washington and *Scarface,* of course. This revelation, and the fact that I was Black, from Compton PD by way of Detroit, and wearing a leather jacket, did little to endear me to the other TAC officers, either. One of the other Compton recruits got kicked out because he wrote at roughly a fifth-grade level. The other one got kicked out about two months later because she couldn't pass the physical fitness test. The TAC officers rode me hard, desperately wanting to get rid of all three Compton recruits.

I graduated in the upper half of class #229 on February 14, 1986, affectionately known as the "Love Class." I was one of only five Blacks out of eighty-five graduates. I walked across the stage wearing the Compton PD navy-blue dress uniform, adorned with gold-colored "P" buttons on the shirt pockets and epaulets. A gold-colored keychain connected to the left epaulet was attached to a gold-colored whistle in my left breast pocket. My shoulder patches had "Compton Police. We're making it better" displayed atop an image of the MLK memorial in front of Fort Compton. I struck quite a gaudy figure as I accepted my diploma and shook hands with LA County Sheriff Sherman Block and Chief Ivory J. Webb, the only Black police administrator at the ceremony. The day before, I had received my Honorable Discharge certificate from the Marine

71

Corps, confirming I had fulfilled my reserve obligation. It bears the Latin phrase of "*Fideli Certa Merces*," which means "To the faithful, there is just reward."

We had moved to a one-bedroom apartment about two months before I started the academy. It was on the first floor of a gated, two-story building in one of the worst areas of Long Beach. A sailor stationed at the Long Beach Naval shipyard lived above us with his Filipina wife. They lived next to an older Black guy named "Brother," who just stayed home all day, played gospel music, and tried to bring the love of God into the women in the apartment complex.

The sailor, a blond White guy who smoked too many Marlboro Reds, played Led Zeppelin all night and drank far too many beers, had fallen in love while on liberty in the Philippines. His wife was flirtatious and wore far too much make-up and far too little clothing. When he was home, they drank beer together and fought all the time. When he was at work, she laughed and drank beer with other men who climbed *her* Stairway to Heaven. One morning, he came home to an empty apartment. He was still crying and listening to "Heartbreaker" when I got off work that evening. I had a beer with him and tried to console him, thankful that my Marine unit never got an opportunity to go to the Islands of Pleasure.

On my first day on the job, the training sergeant, Willard Williams, who lived in the middle of the MOB Piru neighborhood, gave me a call-box key. When the dispatchers had messages that they couldn't give over the radio, we had to use one of several call boxes located throughout the city to call the station. I found a bottle of liquor next to the phone every time. The pretty gold whistle I wore for graduation also had a function. We were supposed to blow it when chasing someone. None of us ever did, though. Instead, we blew our other whistle, the one that spat out bullets and smelled like gunpowder.

Lieutenant Jim Fette was my first W/C. The tenured officers called lieutenants "El Tee." and sergeants "Sarge." Rookies referred to both ranks as either "sir" or "ma'am." Fette was legendary among old-school Compton cops. A tall, lean White man with a mustache and horseshoe hairline, he looked like the Bad of the Good and the Ugly. Fette was more like Wyatt Earp than a city policeman. I could picture him chasing a bad guy down Compton Blvd while blowing his real whistle. Most W/Cs didn't wear their gun belts while in the station, but Fette never took his off. A leather strip with extra bullets was affixed to his belt, like cowboys in the Old West wore theirs, and a Hoyt break-front holster securing a four-inch Smith & Wesson .44 Magnum revolver rode high on his right hip. The TAC officers called these holsters "widow-makers" because the gun could be pulled from the holster by someone standing in front of you if you weren't paying attention.

Fette didn't talk much and never to rookies or trainees. The routine for officers getting reports approved was to knock on the W/C's door and wait for an invitation into the office. With his head buried in a newspaper, Fette would sit at his desk and wave you in without looking up. He wouldn't let you sit down while he read your report. If there were problems with it, Fette would get on the sergeant's ass. If the officer was a trainee, he would get on the FTO's ass.

Fette was involved in one of the most famous shootouts in Compton PD history. On August 3, 1966, he responded to a local supermarket to help a woman whose husband, William Herron, had tried to kidnap her earlier. Herron returned just as Fette was talking to her. Herron had a .38 caliber revolver and approached them from behind. He fired five shots, hitting his wife once. Fette returned fire, striking Herron five out of six times. After Herron fell to the ground, Fette noticed that he was still moving. Fette put his foot on Herron's gun and struck him in the head with the barrel of his .44 magnum. Fette then took the weapon out of Herron's hand, dumped the empty .44 caliber casings from his own gun on the ground and slowly removed rounds from his ammo strip, reloading it as he watched Herron lay there dying.

I rode with several officers the first week because my FTO, Jeff Nussman, was on vacation. I learned how to do the daily log, a written report documenting a patrol unit's actions and observations during their shift. I also learned the three most essential radio calls, code-7, code-9: the code for officer needs help immediately, and code-100: the code to take a shit. The dispatcher needs to know when an officer is on a code-100 because it takes time to undo a gun belt and put it back on. These precious seconds could mean life or death to a unit requesting a code-9. And the only safe place for a cop to take a shit was at the station because you did not want to get caught with your pants and Sam, Sally, or Jim Brown around your ankles in a public facility.

On my first night, I rode with Al Skiles, a short, rotund Pacific Islander with a pleasant demeanor who called everyone he encountered "sir" or "ma'am." We handled a gang-related shooting and a fatal traffic collision, both calls that he volunteered us for. He hated lazy cops who "kissed off radio calls" or, in other words, shirked their duties to citizens who called in for help.

The next night, I got into a vehicle pursuit of three burglary suspects with Paul Wing, an overweight White cop with a bushy mustache who wore glasses and chain-smoked Marlboro Reds. He didn't say one word to me the entire night. At the time, I thought he was the biggest asshole ever. At least Skiles had engaged me in conversation and was cordial. One year before, Wing was in a Wells Fargo bank in Garden Grove when Steven Smallwood, a small-time loser who had already been convicted of robbing the same bank twice before, tried it again. Armed with a .38 caliber revolver, he announced, "This is a robbery! Nobody move!" Wing pulled his 9mm pistol while identifying himself as a cop. Smallwood fired first but missed. Wing returned fire and hit Smallwood in the shoulder area, but then Wing's weapon jammed. Wing slipped and fell, and Smallwood continued shooting as Wing scrambled around while grabbing at Smallwood's arm. Smallwood staggered out of the bank when his gun was empty, mortally wounded. Incredibly, he had missed Wing all six times.

Months later, I would learn that Wing had spoken glowingly about me to the senior officers on the shift because of my performance during our vehicle pursuit. The car we were chasing had crashed at Wilmington and Alondra. When the three suspects got out to run, I grabbed the shotgun, chambered a round, and ordered them to get on the ground. Although Wing never said anything to me about my actions that night, he told the other cops, "That motherfucking Reynolds is gonna be alright."

On the third night, I rode with Tom Eskridge. We made three different arrests of gang members who were selling crack, in a stolen car, and in possession of a stolen gun. Eskridge was a cerebral White cop who wore glasses and had thick black hair and a matching mustache. Like Wing, he smoked Marlboro Reds all night, flicking them out the window whenever we were about to get out of the car. Eskridge got me started in earnest with my career, showing me what I needed to carry in my patrol bag, which we called "war bags" because patrolling

Compton was like being in combat. Eskridge told me that I needed extra ammo, blank report forms, a *Thomas Guide,* and maxi pads. At first, I thought this was some hazing bullshit until he explained the pads could be used to stop the bleeding if one of us got shot. It had all been a game until I put those sanitary napkins in my war bag. As I zipped it up before going out into the streets, I realized that I could die out there.

On my fourth night, I rode with Jasper Jeremiah Jackson, aka "J.J." He had a beautifully deep, baritone voice. After briefing was over every day, he would lead the charge onto the back lot, swinging his nightstick over his head while yelling, "Let's go, maggots! There's crime in those streets!" J.J. was a former Army Ranger and Vietnam vet who had 20-inch biceps, which he showed off by wearing a uniform shirt a size too small.

According to J.J., the most important lesson he had for me was to know where all the stores were that gave free shit to cops. These locations were known as "pop spots" and were where he got packs of Kool cigarettes all shift long. Most of the PM shift cops would pull up to Bunny's liquor store on Alondra Blvd and Willowbrook in their patrol cars before the end of their night, loading up cases of beer into the trunks for the impending choir practice. One of J.J.'s favorite pop spots was KFC on Central and Compton Blvd. Every night before his shift was over, he would stop there and get a bucket of chicken to take home. I got the feeling that he wasn't just greedy. His three ex-wives were seriously leaving him almost penniless each month.

J.J. was fearless and a complete psycho. We pulled up on at least ten gang members congregating on a corner. He jumped out of the car with our shotgun, racking it multiple times while chasing them and growling. The gang members were so scared they never even noticed the gun wasn't loaded and just fled in terror, screaming, "Wolf! Wolf! Don't shoot, Wolf!" They had given him this nickname because of his ferocity, unpredictability, and, yes, his tendency to growl. Gang members frequently gave nicknames to certain police officers and to cops in general, such as "Rollers", "Five-O", and "One-Time."

Nussman came back to work the following night after a tour in narcotics working for Sergeant Ramon R.E. Allen. Nussman had gone from looking like a bearded Timothy Leary on LSD to a thin White cop with gold wire-rim glasses, a dirty light brown military haircut, and a scraggly mustache overnight. He also smoked Marlboro Reds, by far the favorite brand for the White and Mexican cops. For the Black cops, it was either Kools, Newports, or Benson and Hedges. Nussman chain-smoked in the car, and as we patrolled the city, I noticed that his eyes sometimes lingered just a little too long on girls wearing scanty clothing. He seemed to prefer the ones who looked like they were seventeen years old the day before.

Nussman was a former Marine and Vietnam vet. He still wore his combat jungle boots and carried a blue-steel Smith & Wesson .44 magnum with a six-inch barrel. Compton PD had a very liberal firearms policy. We could use any caliber bigger than a .38 on-duty if we purchased it ourselves. There were no restrictions on make or model or whether it had pearl handle pistol grips or was chrome, black, blue, or stainless steel. Barrel length was allowed anywhere from four inches to eight.

The first thing Nussman asked was who I had ridden with my first week. Laughing, he stopped me when I got to J.J.'s name. "How much did Wolf get you for?" he asked. I looked at him quizzically, and he said, "J.J., dumbass."

I replied, "Fifty dollars, sir. But how did you…" Now he was laughing so hard I thought he was going to choke. He said, "Don't worry, kid. J.J. gets every rookie. You can kiss that Grant goodbye, though. Lesson number one: Trust is earned in policework. Lesson number two: Don't rat out your partner. Oh yeah, make sure you buy a fucking *Thomas Guide* most ricky-tick, so you don't get fucking lost."

CHAPTER SIX

I WAS thrown right into the fire with Nussman. We were assigned to PM's, the most active of the three patrol shifts. Days and graveyard, or the "yard," were the other two. The yard always had the fewest personnel. Most of the time, only eight officers patrolled the entire city, so there were only four districts during that shift, whereas there were six districts on the other two shifts. The reputations of the officers were obtained based on when they worked. Except for the rookies, day shift officers were considered dinosaurs who just wanted to spin their wheels until retirement. PM shift officers were considered cowboys, cops who thrived on making felony arrests and getting involved in vehicle and foot pursuits. Sometimes upward to fifteen patrol officers, not including the gang and narcotics units, worked PM's.

Graveyard cops were considered lazy. That title was well earned, however. Usually, after 2:30 a.m., there were not many radio calls, particularly in the winter months. Sportsman Drive was on the city's extreme southeast side, tucked away in a little enclave west of Atlantic Avenue. The Compton-Woodley airport, set on seventy-seven acres with two landing strips, was on Alondra Blvd north of the Grandee apartments. Graveyard cops retired to either the airport hangers or Sportsman Drive every night when it quieted down. It was not uncommon to see some of them walking to their patrol cars after briefing, carrying their war bags in one hand with a pillow under their arms.

Call signs for two-person patrol units were 1-Adam, 2-Adam, 3-Adam, and so forth. One-person patrol units were 1-Lincoln, 2-Lincoln, 3-Lincoln, and so on. PM and graveyard shifts were Adam units, and day shift was Lincoln units. Sergeants were 21, 31, and 41, days, PMs, and the yard, respectively. Most agencies use "Sam" to identify their sergeants, such as 21-Sam, 31-Sam, and

41-Sam. Compton PD used this system until the early 70s when a Black supervisor acknowledged a radio call using 21-Sam, and one of the White officers responded with, "Copy that, 21-Sambo," followed by laughter. This ridicule and disrespect ended when future Black supervisors formally protested, leading to the elimination of "Sam" to identify sergeants at Compton PD.

I got my introduction to Compton street gangs through Nussman. He taught me how to recognize them and what areas they claimed as hoods. I learned that Crips wore blue and that Bloods favored red. The gangs chose their clothing based on sports team colors and carried colored bandanas, most of the time hanging them from their back pockets. Crips carried their bandanas in their left pockets, Bloods in their right ones. "Where you from?" was the universal challenge when encountering suspected or known rivals, similar to when Detroit gangs confronted enemies with "What it be like?" or "What up, dough?" Crips called each other "Cuz" and hated words that started with the letters, "B" or "P".

All Blood gangs in Compton were Pirus. Bloods referred to each other as "Blood" or "Damu," which is Swahili for "blood." They hated words that started with the letter "C." To a Crip, bleeding was "slobbing." Bloods substituted any word that began with a "C" with a "B," like *bigarette* instead of cigarette. Crips replaced words that ended in CK with CC because, to them, CK meant Crip Killer. CC also stood for Compton Crip or Coast Crip. Crips called Bloods "slobs" or "blobs," and Bloods called Crips "crabs" or "e-rickets." Pirus often used "roo" at the end of their respective nicknames, such as "Smiley-roo." White members were known as "White Boy," and Hispanics were called "Geronimo." Most gang members got their nicknames according to physical appearance or trait, such as "Frog," "Turtle," or "Potato Head." I knew one gang member whose forearms extended directly from his armpits. His nickname was "Baby Short Arms," and he loved to challenge people to box.

There were multiple Hispanic gangs but only two major factions. One was in Northern California, and the other was in Southern California. The dividing line was Fresno. Southern California Hispanic gangs used the number 13 and preferred blue. They were known as "Surenos." Northern Hispanic gangs preferred red and used the number 14. They were called "Nortenos." Hispanic gangsters used monikers like "Weasel," "Ghost," or "Sniper." In Compton, Hispanics prefaced their gang's name with the initial's "CV" for Compton Varrio.

Some Hispanic gangs had Black members and White ones, too. The Black members were always "Negro" or "Blackie," and the White members were "Huero."

There were also female gang members, but very few. Most of them were just considered "hood rats" and were shared sexually among the male members. There were some exceptions, however, like Chata, a member of the CV70 gang, and Sylvia Nunn, a member of the Lueders Park Piru gang and sister of notorious member Marcus "China Dog" Nunn. I dealt with both Chata and Sylvia on many occasions. They were both fearless and only slept with who they wanted to. Chata confronted a Black Compton cop once during a gang round-up. She was defiant, and the cop slapped her. She smiled, wiped the blood from her mouth with her hand, and licked it off before asking him, "Is that all you got? Nigga, you hit like a bitch."

Sylvia was even more ruthless than Chata. Her brother Marcus killed his wife on July 20, 1990. Officer Reggie Wright Sr. arrested him after an informant told him where Marcus was hiding. Sylvia, believing that a neighborhood smoker by the name of "Big-titty" Jackie was the informant, enticed her to Angeles Abbey cemetery with the promise of crack. When they got there Sylvia shot her in the head and left her for dead next to Big-titty Jackie's mother's headstone.

Crack was the bread and butter of the gangs. They all fought for prime territory and the best crack, known as caviar. Women who sold their bodies for crack were known as "strawberries" because it was just as easy to pick one up as it was to pluck a real one from the vine. We called the smokers who roamed the streets all night "base heads," "crackheads," or "cluck heads". The term cluck head came about because when they were out of crack, they would pick up anything that resembled it, like chickens pecking the ground. We had a specific name for female smokers who roamed Willowbrook. We called them "brooks". This term eventually evolved to refer to all unattractive or poor women.

Nussman loved to write traffic tickets. Pulling over cars is probably one of the most dangerous things a cop can do. They can contain people who have just committed murder, robbery, are armed with guns, transporting drugs, or have dead or kidnapped people in the trunks. Or, as in about 95 percent of the cases, just people who are piss-poor drivers. But that 5 percent will fuck you up every time if you have your head up your ass, better known as getting caught slipping.

The first week we rode together, Nussman pulled up on four Front Hood Crips hanging out at a liquor store on Wilmington Avenue. One was on a bicycle. Two walked into the store, and the other one walked away, discreetly tossing a small bag of crack to the ground. Nussman reached under the seat of the bike and pulled out a larger bag of crack. The guy on the bike ran east across Wilmington, dodging the heavy traffic. I chased him and did something they never showed me in the academy. I threw my PR-24 baton at his feet, and he tripped and fell on the sidewalk. I picked up the baton and was about to handcuff him when he kicked at my groin area. He missed but got up and swung at my head. I ducked, and, using a movement with the baton called the "pool-cue jab", struck him in his solar plexus. He screamed and fell to the ground. I handcuffed him and walked him back to where Nussman was leaning against our patrol car, smoking a Marlboro. He flicked the cigarette away and said, "Good job, rookie. Put him in the back seat with the other scumbag and throw the bike in the trunk."

Nussman couldn't wait to tell the senior officers that not only was Wing right about me, I also wasn't afraid to "whip a scumbag's ass." That was my introduction to the culture of policing in Compton. I was the right type of cop, a warrior who wasn't afraid to get his hands dirty. I was deemed worthy of working the streets. To me, I just used common sense and improvised on what I had been trained to do. I used that force necessary to arrest someone who was trying to avoid arrest. When he stopped fighting, so did I.

Nussman and I got a radio call to assist units in the 900 block of North Long Beach Blvd during our second week. Two Pirus robbed two men flossing their jewelry. One of the Pirus had a handgun with a red bandana tied around the barrel. When we got to the area, they ran right in front of us. They split up, and we chased the guy with the gun. I caught him in the rear yard of 816 North Sloan Street when he fell while jumping a retaining wall. He dropped his weapon, and it landed close to him. He looked at it like he wanted it back. It was my first potentially deadly confrontation. If he reached for the gun, I would have to kill him.

Time seemed to stand still as I put the front sight of my Smith & Wesson .38 caliber revolver on his forehead and moved my finger to the trigger. There would be no accidental discharge; the double-action trigger pull was twelve pounds. I was calm like I was the night Cisco and Red defended their hood from the encroachment of the two BK's. My mind was crystal clear, and at that moment, I chose to forgo all my police training and reverted to the lingo of the Dirty Glove and calmly asked the Piru, "What up, dough?"

He forgot all about the gun and yelled, "Don't shoot, sir!"

Seconds later, the Cavalry arrived, guns drawn and yelling in terms the Piru was more familiar with, "Don't move, dickhead! Freeze!"

Cops call suspects a lot of derogatory names. Nigger, of course, for Blacks is the worst by far. The White and Mexican cops wouldn't dare use this word in front of a Black officer, but scumbag, piece of shit, crook, asshole, and dickhead were used indiscriminately for all races. When called for, I preferred mutha-fucka. I only used dickhead for the worst of the worst. The Piru's real name was Alondro Bennett. He went to prison, but just three years later, he took part in another armed robbery with two other Pirus at Chico's Market, a fami-ly-owned business on Wilmington. Bennett's two accomplices got killed during a shootout with the owner. The owner's fourteen-year-old son was killed in the crossfire. Bennett got shot in the ass. One of the dead robbers was a recently paroled lieutenant in the Black Guerilla Family prison gang. The BGF had a contract on his life because he owed them $10,000, so he got his brother and Bennett to help him rob the market to pay off his debt. Bennett got convicted of three counts of murder, and he went away forever.

Nussman cleared me from the first phase of training after three months. I got a new FTO, a graveyard cop named Jack McConnell who only worked district four. He had been on the department since the early 1970s and had the kind of obeisance that allowed him to say whatever the hell he wanted to on the radio without repercussion. Good-naturedly known as Fat Jack, he was highly respected. He wore the large-framed eyeglasses popular in the 1970s discotheques and had receding red hair and a mustache. A plump White guy with a fatherly persona, he smoked Marlboro Reds like the rest of the White cops. Unlike them, however, he never smoked in the patrol car. He would light up near the trunk while I stayed in the car doing the log sheet. Fat Jack was a gentleman in other regards, too. Some cops farted in the car, rolled the windows up, and turned the heat on, laughing the entire time. Fat Jack never farted in the car. He would stop and get out to do it, lifting one of his legs and shaking it as if to get the smell out before getting back in the car.

While Nussman taught me the basics of policework, Fat Jack taught me more humanistic lessons. He taught me how to temper the tremendous responsibility and authority we had with kindness and respect. Fat Jack called criminals wolves and referred to us as sheepdogs, responsible for Compton's citizens, who were our flock. He was just as likely to park his patrol car in front of a citizen's house and play dominoes with them as he was to arrest someone from that same family.

Fat Jack also used tragic events to ensure that I learned from the mistakes of others, such as the death of Officer Dess K. Phipps, killed on October 12, 1962 during a vehicle pursuit while chasing two teenagers wanted for burglary. Fat Jack always told me that no one's life is worth driving too fast; that crashing on the way to help another officer or while chasing a wolf does far more harm than good and puts our flock in jeopardy. He taught me how to survive professionally as well, continually citing the things that got more cops fired than anything else: booze, broads, and bills, which he called the three B's. Whenever it was boring, and we had nothing to talk about, Fat Jack always sang something that went like this: "Chicken, gonna get me some of that fried chicken." It was nonsensical, totally made up by him, and without melody but it seemed to soothe him whenever it got quiet in the car.

Our first night together, we were going east on Alondra Boulevard at about 2:30 a.m. when we heard screaming. Quickly pinpointing the source, I grabbed the radio mic and said, "Unit 4-Adam."

The dispatcher replied, "Unit 4-Adam, go ahead."

I told her that we heard screams coming from a vacant house at the corner of Poinsettia and Alondra and requested another unit to assist us.

She said, "Unit 4-Adam, there are no clear units at this time, and unit 41 is not answering. Please advise." There were only four two-person units and a field sergeant on duty that night. And while someone was in a vacant house screaming, one of the units was at the hospital with an injured prisoner, one was on the way to county jail with another prisoner, and one was on a code-100.

Just then, a breathless voice came over the radio. "Unit 41 en route. ETA twenty minutes."

I thought, *Twenty fucking minutes? At 2:30 a.m., you could get anywhere in the city well under four.* We didn't have time to wait, and Fat Jack let dispatch know as he snatched the mic and gruffly stated, "Unit 4-Adam, that's too fucking long. We're going in, goddammit!" We parked and went through the back door and saw a man holding onto a naked woman while another man was burning her with a hot fireplace poker. Broken cocaine pipes littered the floor, and the odor of burning flesh permeated the room. Fat Jack pointed his gun at the man with the poker and ordered him to drop it. He immediately complied as he and his accomplice begged us not to shoot.

The three of them had been smoking crack and engaging in group sex, or what smokers called a "freak party," when the men decided to torture the woman. She had burns on her vagina, anus, and the area colloquially referred to as the taint, and the two men were clearly aroused by their depravity. I requested an ambulance after handcuffing the two tumescent dickheads. A few minutes later, the ambulance pulled up just as my radio crackled. "Unit 41, show me out with 4-Adam." Fat Jack sighed heavily and then walked over to brief our leader, who smelled of perfume, alcohol, and just the slightest scent of sex, about what he had missed.

CHAPTER SEVEN

COMPTON WAS incorporated on May 11, 1888. It is known as the Hub City because it is almost in the exact geographical center of Los Angeles County and is bordered by several freeways. The Alameda Corridor, a passageway for twenty-five percent of all US waterborne international trade, leads directly from the Port of Long Beach and runs through the middle of the city.

Just south of the 91 freeway, Compton has a considerable presence in businesses ranging from food products and processing to heavy equipment distribution. It is known as the Industrial area. Numerous murders and body dumps have occurred in this area, as it is deathly quiet and deserted during the early morning hours. The most notorious murder occurred on September 13, 1975. A nude female between the ages of fourteen and seventeen was found dead next to the curb line in front of the Datsun Corporation located at 745 West Artesia. She had been shot in the head. To this day, she has never been identified and remains officially known as Jane Doe #51.

Despite the city's seedy reputation, for the most part, many residences, particularly those on the east side, were well kept. Still, a lot of the houses bear visible remnants of drive-by shootings. One was on the north side of Elm Street, just east of Alameda. The Staves family, or perhaps more accurately known as the "First family" of the Santana Blocc Crips, lived there. The house got hit so often that they stopped repairing the bullet holes and left windows boarded up for weeks. The family gave as good as they got; the homes south of theirs had multiple bullet holes in them as well, caused by family members returning fire at fleeing cars.

Compton was also home to numerous apartment complexes. The largest was the Wilmington Arms, located just east of the Compton Airport. The complex was home to over a thousand people. It was owned by Jewish businessmen and Holocaust survivors Jona Goldrich and Sol Kest, founders of the Goldrich & Kest management company, which had an annual gross of almost $300 million a year. A black, twelve-foot-tall wrought iron fence surrounded the property. Armed security guards inside a shack guarded the only entrance, which led directly to a large roadway that separated the east and west sides of the complex. The residents called it the "boulevard." Drug dealers sold crack on all sides of the complex as the smokers gave them money through the fence in exchange for their dope. The crackheads who lived in the complex sped around as if their pants were on fire, begging for money, stealing when they could, and providing sexual favors in return for as little as a five-dollar piece of crack. Small, zip-lock baggies, torn open by the yellowing teeth of the crackheads to get to the little beige colored rock inside, littered the boulevard.

The Park Village Crips were responsible for most of the crime. The gang was a mixture of young Blacks and Pacific Islanders. The Black members lived in the Wilmington Arms, and the Pacific Islanders lived in the Park Village Housing complex at 600 West Corregidor, located just south of the Wilmington Arms and east of the Compton Airport. The military had used the airport as a truck depot during WWII. The multiple single-family dwellings in the housing complex were the former homes of military dependents. Accordingly, a famous WWII battle inspired the name of the street. The intersection of Wilmington and Alondra also had a local attraction. A young man rippling with muscles would run from corner to corner for hours, stopping at each one to do fifty pushups. No one knew why he did it, but he didn't bother anyone. He just ran. Accordingly, we just called him "running man." Years later, he got shot to death for no apparent reason during a drive-by.

The Richland Farms, where Mayor Walter Tucker Jr. resided, was east of Wilmington Street and south of Alondra. Chickens and roosters roamed the front yards of numerous houses, many of which had wooden posts in front where saddle-bearing horses stood tethered. Some of the homes hosted the lucrative cock-fighting matches that drew gamblers from far and wide. Like everywhere else in the city, several murders occurred in the area. On one occasion, the victim was riding a horse when he was shot dead and fell out of his saddle. The horse then dragged him down the street because his boot got caught in the stirrup. On another occasion, a suspect galloped down the road on horseback with two guns blazing, killing one man and wounding several others.

Angeles Abbey Memorial Park is on Compton Blvd east of Long Beach Blvd. The structure was designed in 1922 by two architects who went to India for inspiration and crafted it with a heavy Middle Eastern aesthetic. Only Whites were buried on the grounds or interred in the crypts until the late 1960s when a Black-owned mortuary assumed control. By 1985, graffiti-covered the walls, there were numerous broken stained-glass windows, and the grounds were filled with detritus. Even this place wasn't exempt from violence. On August 2, 1976, Martha Eddington, a seventy-six-year-old White woman who caught the bus weekly from South San Gabriel to place flowers on a family member's crypt, was raped, beaten, and strangled on the floor beneath it. The case was never solved. The only lead was that groups of Piru gang members frequently hung out at the gravesite of Larry "Tam" Watts, one of the founding members of the Compton Piru gang, drinking and smoking weed.

The family of former long-time City Treasurer Wesley Sanders Sr. purchased Angeles Abbey in 1992. His wife, Jean Sanders, is now the owner. Their son is Wesley Sanders Jr., who was voted into his father's seat after his death. Angeles Abbey is a graphic reminder of the nebulous relationship between crime in the city and the local government. Councilman Bob Adams owned the Adams Funeral Home located at 501 East Palmer Street, less than two miles away, and the bodies often went directly to Angeles Abbey. The funeral home has been a staple of Compton since 1974. Adams made hundreds of thousands of dollars during the 1980s and 1990s, primarily profiting from the gang-related murders in the city. There were so many murders he installed a drive-through viewing area. Survivors and friends of the recently departed could view them as they laid in a casket next to a bullet-proof window. Initially, it was preventive in nature.

Rival gang members had shot up several gang funerals on prior occasions, including an incident where they interrupted a funeral service at a nearby church and turned over the casket, spilling the body onto the floor and shooting it as family and friends screamed in horror.

My first burglary alarm call with Fat Jack was at Angeles Abbey. This place might have been an architectural treasure during daylight hours, but at 3:03 a.m., it looked like something out of a horror movie. As we pulled up with our lights out, other than an occasional owl hoot and the sound of male crickets trying to attract lovers, it was deathly quiet. Fat Jack put the car in park and said, "I'll check over here. You check the mausoleum." I didn't say a word or move until Fat Jack said, "Well, did you hear me? Check the other side." Apparently, after all the years he had worked around Black people, he still hadn't learned that we don't do horror movies. I slowly walked into the mausoleum, gun in one hand and flashlight in the other. I shone the light over the crypts and heard a noise above me. Startled, I pointed my flashlight upward and fired a shot. Dozens of bats flew into view screeching as they left the mausoleum. Fat Jack yelled, "Reynolds! Reynolds, you okay?"

I had never seen him run before. He stopped next to me, hands on his knees, his chest and back heaving as he struggled to catch his breath. I said, "Yes, sir. I'm fine."

Fat Jack looked down at a dead bat on the floor and started laughing between his labored breaths. He said, "Son, this alarm is never good. It goes off about six times a week. I think its old Martha trying to remind us that the son of a bitch who murdered her is still running around. I just thought I would have a little fun with you. Jesus fucking Christ! We're not gonna report this. You would never live it down. And don't worry about the bat. One of those crack packs will handle it for us. Let's go get something to eat."

Fat Jack let me drive after a week. I loaded our war bags and shotgun into the car, checked the lights and sirens to ensure they worked, and drove off the back lot. I had gone north on Willowbrook when the vehicle stopped about six blocks from the station. Fat Jack just sat there. I looked at the fuel gauge and said, "Sir, we're out of gas."

He laughed and replied, "No shit. What now?"

"I'm gonna call for a tow truck, sir."

Still laughing, he said, "Oh, hell no, you're not. Get out and push. I'll steer."

I pushed the car back to the station and refueled it while making sure not to make eye contact with Fat Jack or any of the other veteran cops laughing and pointing at me. One laugh was unmistakable. It was like the person kept getting caught in the middle and had to keep starting over. I later learned that the laugh belonged to Henry "Bud" Johnson, a tall, slim White PM-shift cop with the unmistakable signs of early balding that he tried to balance out with a scraggly mustache. He was one of the most likeable cops on the department, and his laugh was thoroughly infectious. Once he started, he couldn't stop, which led to even more laughter from everyone around him.

Afterward, while Fat Jack and I were patrolling our area with the sound of Bud's laugh reverberating in my head, for some reason, I thought about Officer Phipps. I asked Fat Jack about the lack of a memorial for him in the city. He sighed and took a deep breath before answering. "Listen, son. These fucking politicians don't give a shit about us. What you and I do, we do for the citizens. Goddammit, they may never tell you, but they are goddamned glad we're out here!" I had obviously hit a nerve. He told me to pull over, and he got out, farted, and lit a cigarette.

About two hours later, I was driving down the street slowly, looking for crime. Smack in the middle of his chicken song, Fat Jack suddenly told me to stop in the middle of a block. He said, "I've been shot. Where are we?"

I didn't know. Even though it was just another one of his roleplaying scenarios that he frequently sprung on me as part of training, I froze.

He yelled, "Well? I'm dying! Where the fuck are we, so you can let dispatch know?" I started driving to the nearest intersection. He blew out an exasperated raspberry and said, "Stop. Now get the fuck out and go find out where we are. Take the shotgun with you. Run like you're on a fucking battlefield and hurry up. I'm fucking bleeding to death." I wanted to tell him to just get a fucking Maxi-pad out of my war bag, but I ran to the closest street sign instead while thinking how much more useful one would be than a fucking *Thomas Guide* right now.

CHAPTER EIGHT

ON THE morning of June 23, 1986, dispatch requested a unit to respond to a dead body call. It was 7:30 a.m. Our shift was almost over. Still mad because we ran out of gas earlier in the week, Fat Jack nodded toward the radio mic. The call was in district one, so I knew he was punishing me. I grabbed the mic and said, "4-Adam en route."

The dispatcher quickly acknowledged and replied, "10-4, Unit 4-Adam en route to Poplar and Kemp. Any unit to back?"

The radio crackled. It was Mike Doyle, one of Fat Jack's least favorite people. Doyle said, "1-Lincoln, 10-7. EOW." 10-7 is the radio code for out of service. EOW is an acronym for "End of Watch." In other words, I was SOL because Doyle, who was responsible for district one, was going home. I reached down to put my seatbelt on, ready for a code-3 response. Cops didn't wear seatbelts then unless they went in pursuit or rolled code-3 to a hot call. They thought they would lose precious time if they had to undo a seatbelt before jumping out of the car.

Fat Jack looked at me, blew a raspberry, and said, "Relax, son. That body ain't going nowhere." I released the seatbelt just as he turned north, driving the speed limit, humming his chicken song and obeying all traffic laws. When I pointed out that he had driven past our turn, he just grunted and pulled up to a drive-through donut shop at Compton Blvd and Central. He ordered two large cups of black coffee and two bear claw donuts, handing me one of each. He said, "You're gonna need these." When we finally got to the scene, we parked about twenty feet from a blue tarp, partially wrapped around a man lying in an empty field just west of the canal. He was as dead as Jimmy Hoffa. Ants were crawling in and out of his eyes, ears, and nose, and flies were buzzing around his body. I took a closer look and saw multiple punctures in his exposed upper chest area. An autopsy would later reveal that he had been stabbed eighty-one times.

After securing the scene and checking for evidence, Fat Jack and I sat in the car while I wrote the report and waited for detectives and the coroner to arrive. I noticed a guy walking toward us. He had his palms held out in front of him and said, "Scuse me, offisas. Can I talk to y'all?" His name was Kevin Dykes. The dead guy was his neighbor Otis Perry. They both lived nearby, or rather, one of them did now. Dykes was very fidgety; his eyes were wide open, darting back and forth, and he kept licking his lips. It was apparent he was fucked up off crack. An uninvolved person in his state would have stayed as far away as possible. To come to the scene to talk to the police meant he was probably involved and feeling guilty. I told Fat Jack what I thought and that we should hold onto him until detectives arrived. I bullshitted with Dykes, asking him mundane and generic questions. He didn't mind. His full attention was now on that partially eaten bear claw and half a cup of cold-ass coffee I had given him.

Detectives Marvin "Scomb" Branscomb and Al "Pepper" Preston got there about thirty minutes later. Although both in their late thirties, they worked out in the station gym every day and were two of the fittest cops on the department. Scomb was sinewy while Pepper was more muscular. They looked like old school cops who would slap you on the side of the head with a telephone book in an interview room. Fat Jack worked homicide with them before becoming an FTO, so they trusted his word. After he relayed my suspicions to them, they braced Dykes like he was a suspect and not merely a concerned citizen. Dykes broke down quickly and told the whole story. He was a local crack dealer who frequently got high on his own supply and used John "Hondo" Henderson and Eric "Slim" Smith as his bodyguards. A week earlier, Dykes got into a fight with a guy named Ephraim Martin over an unpaid drug debt. Slim and Hondo stabbed Martin and his mother, leaving them both for dead. Before Perry was murdered, he had confronted Dykes about stabbing Martin's mother. Slim, Hondo, and Dykes had been smoking crack for four days and were out of their minds. Enraged, Dykes stabbed Perry at least forty-five times before Slim and Hondo joined in. The three of them then wrapped Perry's body in the tarp and dumped it near the canal. Dykes felt guilty later and went to check on the body.

He decided to talk to us when he saw our patrol car. Scomb and Pepper got warrants for Hondo and Slim when we were unable to locate them that day.

Fat Jack finally let me drive again a few days later. It was quiet until around 5:30 a.m. when the dispatcher interrupted Fat Jack singing his chicken song. "Any unit to respond to Alondra and Wilmington, we have reports of two suspects wanted for murder in the area. Unit to respond, identify?"

I bought the call and told Fat Jack, "Put your seatbelt on, sir."

When we arrived, Officers Douglas Slaughter, William Farrar, and Reggie Wright Sr. were already there. They were talking to Ephraim Martin. About ten minutes earlier, he had seen Hondo and Slim at 152nd and Dwight Avenue in a blue Chevy Nova. Fat Jack and I, along with Slaughter and Farrar, found the car parked in front of 408 South Maie. Hondo and Slim were getting out just as I skidded to a stop while simultaneously taking off my seatbelt and jumping out of the patrol car. Hondo surrendered, but Slim ran, shedding his clothing and discarding a knife. Slaughter and Farrar detained Hondo while I chased Slim as Fat Jack screamed into the radio, requesting additional units.

Slim jumped a fence and disappeared into the darkness. But he was fucked now. We had his bloodstained clothes and what would turn out to be one of the murder weapons. In short order, every patrol car in the city was within a six-block area. Officer James Lewis saw Slim suddenly run from the rear yard of a house. He wasn't hard to identify; he was the only Black man running through yards wearing nothing but a pair of shit-stained Fruit of the Looms. Lewis, probably one of the fastest cops on the department, lost him too, but we kept the area locked down until the arrival of a sheriff's K-9 unit. A Belgian Malinois named "Nitro" tracked Slim's scent to a large hole underneath a garage at 1020 West Myrrh Street. We knew Slim was there when we heard screams and Nitro snarling.

Officer Mike Doyle was a blond, muscular White cop who laughed a lot and looked like he would be more comfortable hanging ten in Malibu than chasing a murderous crackhead in the middle of the ghetto. He was also an immature knucklehead at the time, always prone to doing stupid shit. Fat Jack hated him. Sometimes the graveyard shift would have lunch together at Alexander's restaurant on Long Beach Blvd. We always sat in a large booth in the back.

Bruce Frailich, a handsome, clean-shaven Jewish guy who wore his hair in a pompadour, would talk about his Franklin Templeton investments while Doyle smashed water bugs and cockroaches crawling up the wall with his 187-bea-vertail sap. Fat Jack would curse him out and call him a stupid motherfucker every time. A sap is a blackjack. Its size is named for the severity of a crime in the California penal code. The code for murder is 187, so the 187 sap is the largest one. Most cops carry a 245, the second largest, and the penal code for assault with a deadly weapon. The smallest one is a 415, the code for disturbing the peace. Doyle smashing bugs with his sap was the equivalent of shooting a cannon at a sparrow.

Doyle leaped into the hole as the K-9 handler screamed at him to stop. Nitro had a good bite on Slim's leg and pulled him out of the hole as Doyle hit Slim in the arms and the other leg with his beavertail. No one else had gone into the hole with Doyle. We just stood around the edge, watching him make an ass of himself. When he climbed out, leaving Slim handcuffed and bleeding from the dog bites and bruised from the beavertail, he looked at me with a huge grin, laughed, and said, "All in a day's work, rook. I'll get my cuffs later."

As Doyle started to walk away, Fat Jack grabbed him by the arm and hissed, "Where the fuck do you think you're going, numb nuts? This is your fucking arrest now." Fat Jack looked at me, so mad that his face matched his hair, and said, "Come on, son. Let's go book the clothes and knife into evidence." Doyle ended up sitting with Slim all day at the county hospital. Had Fat Jack not been my FTO, Doyle would have stuck me with the arrest and babysitting.

In addition to protecting their trainees from clowns like Doyle, FTOs were responsible for teaching them how to dodge the peer-created landmines they would encounter throughout their careers. FTOs protected trainees, but the Compton Police Officers Association was supposed to protect us all. During the 1970s, the White officers ran the CPOA. In 1975, City Councilmen Hillard Hamm and Russell "Buddy" Woolfork got indicted after receiving money in exchange for their votes on a land deal. Before the indictments, Thomas Cochee, the first Black police chief in California, got fired for insubordination. He had accused Hamm and Woolfork of corruption and asked state government officials to investigate. Cochee believed he got fired in retaliation.

Cochee was not well liked by the White officers. His most radical move was introducing the "salt and pepper" policy. He believed in integrating every patrol car, but the White cops didn't like being told who they had to ride with, especially if it was with a Black cop. In January of 1976, a division emerged between Black and White officers over charges of discrimination. The CPOA held a meeting to vote on supporting Cochee. The vote divided along racial lines. John Soisson, a White detective and president of the CPOA at the time, publicly stated, "This is a political issue, and we should stay out of it." It ultimately didn't matter one way or another, as Cochee would win his appeal anyway and get his position back.

The Black cops formed a counterpart union known as the Guardians. One year they sponsored a banquet for Black police officer associations statewide at a hotel in El Segundo. Stoney Jackson and R.E. Allen, both detectives at the time, were on an elevator with Wanda McGreggor when two Oakland police officers got on. From Pittsburgh, Pennsylvania, Stoney was a tall, slim, dark-skinned US Army Vietnam vet who had joined the Marine Corps reserves after his term with the Army ended. He was a member of both the Army and Marine Corps boxing teams and won several police Olympic medals while on the Compton PD boxing team. Wanda, who would later marry R.E. and become secretary to several police chiefs for many years, was a gorgeous woman with an hourglass figure. When the Oakland officers began flirting with her, Stoney got pissed because even though she was dating R.E. and not him, the Oakland officers didn't know that. He felt like they were disrespecting them both. Stoney was charming but had a legendary temper if provoked. The Oakland cops continued flirting with Wanda, and R.E. said nothing.

Stoney had a slight speech impediment, and the more upset he got, the more pronounced it became. He snarled, "H-h-h-hey mu-mu-muthafucka! C-c-can't you see s-s-she's with us?"

One of the Oakland cops then made a horrible decision, snarling back, "Fuck you, muthafucka! I don't g—" He probably didn't even see Stoney's punch just before he fell against the elevator wall, sliding down and coming to rest on his ass. His partner tried to grab Stoney, and Stoney ended the fight with a left uppercut, landing him unconscious on the floor next to his amorous friend.

93

Stoney's watch had come off his wrist, and his Walther PPK pistol had fallen out of his waistband during the fight.

R.E., thinking the Oakland officers lost them, told Stoney, "I got me a gun and a watch now."

Stoney, perturbed because R.E. hadn't lifted a finger to help him, snatched the items and said, "Man, g-g-give m-m-me my shit!" as he stepped over the unconscious cops and walked out of the elevator when the door opened.

The CPOA sponsored a Fourth of July firework stand every year at various locations throughout the city. In 1986, it was at Rosecrans and Central, across the street from Tam's Burgers. Fat Jack drove to the stand one night to check on the off-duty cops working it. Almost the entire PM shift was there, standing in a circle and drinking beer. They were all drunk, some of them waving guns in the air. Fat Jack didn't want any part of their shenanigans. While walking back to our car, we heard a gunshot. One of them had accidentally dropped a 1911 Colt .45 in the middle of the inebriated circle jerk. We ran over to make sure everyone was okay, but they just laughed and continued to drink. Somehow, someway, that .45 caliber slug had managed to miss everyone.

Commander Dallas Elvis summoned Fat Jack and me to his office later that morning. Elvis was an old White guy who wore glasses, a toupee, and had a salt and pepper barbershop quartet mustache. He had been on the department since 1958. After Fat Jack and I left the firework stand, apparently the drunken cops had decided to use the Tam's Burgers marquee for target practice. There were more than fifty bullet holes in it when the owner arrived to open for the day. Knowing that a cop-operated firework stand was across the street, it didn't take much to figure out who was responsible. Elvis told Fat Jack to wait in the hallway. Seeing me as a possible weak link because I was still on probation, Elvis threatened to fire me if I didn't tell him who was at the firework stand. I told him I was doing the daily log sheet and never got out of the car. He didn't believe me, and before telling me to get the fuck out of his office, he said that he would fire me if he ever found out I knew what had happened.

Elvis eventually found out who was there when one of the involved officers told on everyone else. The rat and six other cops got suspended. They are now known in Compton PD lore as the Central Seven. The rat ended up transferring to another police agency, but before he did, he cut coat hangers off his lock and scraped white-out off his locker every day. The most ironic thing about the entire incident is that one of the officers shooting at the sign was using a .44 caliber Magnum that he bought from Elvis just six weeks before.

Even though they differed in training style, Fat Jack and Nussman were both great FTOs. I took the best parts of each of them and created my own style of policing. They were different in more ways than just etiquette and philosophies regarding policework. Nussman knew I was a former Marine, but he didn't want to know anything about my personal life beyond that. Maybe it was some Vietnam thing, where he didn't want to become vested in that part of me in case I was killed on the job or didn't make it off probation. Or perhaps he just didn't give a fuck. On the other hand, Fat Jack was extremely interested in my life. We talked a lot, mostly about how vital it was for me not to get caught up in stupid shit when I was off duty. I learned a great deal from Fat Jack. One of the more memorable things that he taught me was, "If they fight, we fight back. But when they stop, so do we. Let them decide how they choose to go to jail. Kicking and screaming or with dignity, they are still going."

And Fat Jack certainly practiced what he preached. We were driving a guy to jail once when he spat a big gob of saliva through the cage at Fat Jack. Livid, Fat Jack yelled, "Goddammit!" and pulled over to the curb. I thought Fat Jack was about to beat the shit out of him. Instead, he went to the trunk, got a towel, and wiped the guy's face. Fat Jack then hung the towel over the cage so that it was between the front and back seats. He looked at me and said, "Son, I want to beat this guy's ass so bad I can taste it. But he's handcuffed. We don't hit handcuffed people." Fat Jack didn't believe in using force unless it was necessary. He was also compassionate toward the citizens and didn't see race when enforcing the law.

Years later, Lendell Johnson told me about an incident that happened while he and Fat Jack worked background investigations for police applicants. Sue Nelson, a blonde-haired, blue-eyed White woman, was a former Torrance PD officer who had recently applied to be a cop with Compton. Lendell reviewed her file first and saw that she didn't complete probation at Torrance. He looked a little further into her personal life and found out she had a Black boyfriend and immediately suspected why she didn't pass probation. Lendell, being a

Black man, knew that Torrance PD personnel wouldn't give him the truth. He decided to let Fat Jack speak to them about her, but he didn't say anything to him about her boyfriend. Just before Fat Jack left, he told Lendell, "Okay. Let's go through the motions, but she probably ain't fit to be a cop."

A few hours later, Fat Jack came back in a rage. He slammed Nelson's file on his desk and yelled, "Those racist motherfuckers! They didn't let her pass probation because she's fucking a Black guy! Well, goddammit, we're sure as shit gonna hire her now!"

Fat Jack loved the city and its citizens, but he hated the city officials. As we drove past city hall every day after leaving the back lot, without fail, he would say, "One day they're gonna pull a jail bus up to that fucking place and march all those thieving sons of bitches out in handcuffs." Fat Jack believed that the city politicians would eventually fuck up the budget by stealing so much that either the sheriff's department would be forced to take over or the city would open the door and invite them in. He thought it might happen before his career was over. He was positive that it would happen before mine was.

CHAPTER NINE

I GOT released from training in July of 1986. Now I had to ride alone for six months on the day shift to get off probation. It is the most critical time in a cop's career, as a probationary cop can get fired for things that a tenured officer wouldn't, such as being habitually late or making a mistake on a radio call.

My supervisors were Brent Neilsen, Cornelious Atkins and Ron Malachi. Neilsen was a White man who would have been right at home hanging out in front of the KKK store in Rocky Mount. He smiled and patted all the White cops on the back for a "job well-done" no matter how simplistic but appeared not to notice good work by the Black cops. He also took an inordinate amount of time approving reports written by Black officers in compared to the White ones.

Atkins was a tall, slim, very dark-skinned older cop with a bald head who wore glasses and lived in the heart of the Southside Crips hood. He was a house mouse who struck a dashing figure in his uniform; he still wore his shiny gold whistle with his ever-present long sleeve shirt and tie and spit-polished shoes. He and Malachi were at opposite ends of the spectrum. Malachi was a huge man with a huge Afro who couldn't give two shits about his uniform appearance. He had served in the army and was a Vietnam vet who took his nightstick wherever he went, even on code-100 in the station.

Just two years before Malachi got hired as a cop, he had been awarded the Distinguished Service Cross for extraordinary heroism. Over two days, he attacked Vietnamese bunker and mortar positions with machine guns, killing multiple Viet Cong and saving the lives of countless Americans. Malachi lost one of his legs in a motorcycle accident several years after becoming a cop. Even with a wooden leg, he was still on the streets more than Atkins. Malachi loved to write tickets and because of his disability, we always had to back him up, which drove the dispatchers crazy. He was married to Evelyn Malachi, a coquettish woman who frequently smiled and batted her eyes at the younger officers. They were both sergeants at one time. Malachi was an intensely jealous and competitive man, prone to bouts of PTSD from time to time, especially when it came to Evelyn, who he sometimes treated as an extension of his battle with the Viet Cong. When she got promoted to lieutenant before he did, he congratulated her by gifting her with two black eyes.

Crack had kicked the crime rate in Compton into overdrive. When we cleared for service, there were so many calls from the previous shifts that the dispatchers would tell us to prepare to copy ten, sometimes fifteen of them. It was not uncommon for an oncoming shift to be down fifty radio calls that the previous one didn't handle. Patrol officers hated handling pending radio calls. Instead, we would immediately arrest someone for possession of crack or a gun. One of the most common pending calls was always "Vag-Loits," a combination of vagrant and loiterer, who were just crackheads and winos.

Most of the officers on the day shift disliked all the cowboy shit on the PM shift and didn't want to stay up all night on the yard. Some of them were peacocks with freshly pressed uniforms, shiny badges, whistles, and polished shoes, but most of them were dirtbags who wore the same uniforms for days and never met a can of shoe polish that they liked. Except for James Lewis, Serette Mitchell, Brett Garland, Clarence Holzendorf, and one other guy I'll just call J.W., they were all older men. All they did was kiss-off radio calls all shift long before going to John's Bar on Compton Blvd to drink until closing. On several occasions, a PM or graveyard unit had driven behind the bar only to discover one of the dinosaurs in the middle of a down-stroke on a waitress or some drunk badge bunny.

The dinosaurs had names like Junkyard, Pete, BB, Code-9 Calvin, and Russ and had been on the department for twenty or more years. One of them had responded to my bogus robbery call years earlier. He didn't recognize me, and I never reminded him. There were also other dinosaurs on day shift, cops like former Marine Bob Page, a tall, striking peacock whose interest in policework had long since passed, and two Mexican officers. One was an arrogant, morbidly obese cop, exceptionally skilled at kissing off calls. The other one I will just call

S.A. He was a surly middle-aged man with graying hair who had killed two dusters trying to take his gun.

Perhaps the emotional trauma from these incidents played a part in the bone-headed crime he committed. After briefing one payday, S.A. drove to Capital Bank on Compton Blvd to cash his check.

The teller was very polite, accustomed to seeing uniformed cops at the bank on payday, their presence making her feel safe in a city filled with thieves. She accidentally gave S.A. his check back with the cash. The following day, S.A. tried to cash it again with the same teller. The next paycheck he got was from the unemployment office.

One day not long after that, one of the dinosaurs asked for code-7 and told the dispatcher that he would be, "by the radio." This means that if the dispatcher needs you for a call, you are still available to respond. Sixty minutes later, the dispatcher tried to raise the officer on the radio, but he didn't respond after repeated attempts. The dispatcher got worried and rightfully so. The cop could have been hurt, dead, or even taken hostage by someone. The dispatcher notified the W/C who launched a citywide search for the officer. We were driving everywhere looking for him. We found the dinosaur's patrol car parked at the rear of Centennial High school near the gymnasium. The entire shift, detectives included, converged on the location and entered the gym, guns drawn. The missing officer was inside, dressed in full basketball referee attire, refereeing a basketball game for a league which paid him. When he saw the contingent of armed officers, he just weakly blew his whistle.

John "Wilk" Wilkinson was the only White officer on the day shift and had been on the department since the 1970s. A rail-thin, middle-aged cop with a calm demeanor and soft voice, Wilk ate, drank, and shit Compton PD. His mother worked in the chief's office in the 1960s and 70s, and he grew up in Compton when the city was just beginning to change demographically. Wilk was atypical for day shift; although technically a dinosaur, he was still a hard worker.

James Lewis was my best friend on day shift. He graduated from the academy one class ahead of me. Lewis wasn't a big guy but was a phenomenal athlete and a great baseball player. He had a soft, melodious voice, and his conversations always consisted of who his new lady was and where they were going on his off days.

Like a lot of Compton cops, he graduated from Compton High. Brett Garland was a slim cop who looked Puerto Rican. About the same height as Lewis, he had beautiful wavy hair and a large bushy mustache. Garland was, in fact, a handsome motherfucker who had chicks waiting in line for him. We called him Prince because he resembled the Purple One. He was a prankster, too, the kind of guy who would put a gopher in a closed evidence bag, put it on the table in the Code-7 room, and hope that a dispatcher or records clerk looked inside.

Lewis and Garland were womanizers, but Clarence Holzendorf took it to a whole new level. He had a finger wave hairstyle and sometimes wore eye shadow and make-up foundation. His shift consisted of pulling over every brook he saw or stopping at phone booths throughout the city to return pages on his beeper to phone numbers ending with code "69." When it rained, he would approach cars holding an umbrella in his gun hand and his ticket book in the other hand. A dinosaur trapped in a newly hired officer's body, he primped and preened the entire shift, and rarely if ever, made any arrests.

Serette Mitchell was the only woman on the shift, but there was certainly nothing feminine about her. Although everyone called her "Candy," she was tough as nails. She had a deep voice and wore her hair in a military buzz cut, and sparred with male boxers in her spare time. She was very friendly, though, and greeted everyone with a smile. When I first got to day shift, I backed her up on a call. She was standing in front of a gangster with arms like J.J. when I got there. He was yelling at her as she just stood there calmly listening. When he made the mistake of pointing his finger in her face, she knocked him out with one punch. I handcuffed him as he lay at her feet. When I looked up, she was smiling. Years later, having been diagnosed with brain cancer, she took her life with her duty weapon while sitting in her garden.

J.W., a small, reserved guy who wore black rimmed glasses, was a Jehovah's Witness. Every day after briefing, he would volunteer to handle all pending report calls to get out of dangerous shit. Since cops hate writing reports or "scratching paper," he never got any opposition from the rest of us. Some cops considered it a victory to get through an entire shift without scratching any paper. Arrest reports were different, though. But J.W. hardly ever arrested anyone, so he rarely had to scratch one. With J.W. volunteering to take all the report calls and Holzendorf always on the hunt for one of the "B's" Fat Jack preached about, me, Wilk, Lewis, and Garland held it down on the shift, making the most arrests and handling the most calls. If we had a loudmouth on a scene, we just called Candy.

J.W. resigned after only a few years, citing family issues. In truth, he was a conscientious objector and feared having to kill someone. It turns out he had nothing to worry about. He had carried an unloaded gun his entire career. Perhaps he really resigned because he knew that he would eventually run into that person who didn't share his reverence for life. I'm glad there was still an opening for him at his old job. Policework ain't for everybody.

For the first six months, my home life consisted of me going to work and Gilda complaining about the hours. Police officers on probation are required to be at work extra early and they frequently stay late. I was coming home completely wiped out every day. Policework was proving to be more demanding than I thought it would be. The mental stress of continually seeing death and the reality that every day could be my last one alive was more draining than getting into a fight. It didn't help that Gilda and I didn't have much extra money, so we stayed home a lot. And the fact that we had gotten married for selfish reasons instead of love was starting to loom large. I could feel us drifting apart.

On Halloween in 1986, I got a radio call of an assault victim on Pearl Street. I heard screaming coming from the open front door of the house when I got there. A woman was lying motionless on the living room floor, covered in blood. Her head was as big as a pumpkin, the features of her face unrecognizable. A blood bubble appeared in the area where her nostrils were with every rise and fall of her chest. An older woman was kneeling next to her. As I requested an ambulance, she yelled hysterically, "He killed my baby! I knew he was gonna kill her sooner or later!" She screamed his name and told me he left for his mother's house. After she gave me the address and the type of car he was driving, I advised the other units over the radio.

One of the dinosaurs showed up at the scene. I asked him if he could stay with the victim while I looked for the suspect, and he replied unenthusiastically, "I'll stay, but the paper is yours." Good old day shift. The dinosaurs never failed to disappoint, but sometimes they would surprise. By the time I got to the woman's house who gave birth to dickhead, two of them were in the backyard fighting with him. Younger and more robust, he was beginning to get the best of them. I kicked him in the stomach, and he vomited before falling face-first into it. I'll admit it. I was furious at him for what he did to that woman and causing her mother so much pain, so I kicked him a lot harder than I should have. But man, did it feel good seeing him lying on the ground blowing snot and vomit bubbles.

The dinosaurs invited me to drink with them at John's bar when the shift was over. Senior officers never socialized with rookies at all, much less invited them for an after-work drink. I had to go. I called Gilda, excitedly telling her about my day and the rare opportunity. I told her to take the kids trick or treating because I was going to be late. I hung up when she started yelling and cursing. I sat with the dinosaurs, matching them drink for drink. When I staggered home at close to 11:00 p.m., Gilda yelled so loudly that Sleeping Beauty and Casper woke up crying.

I didn't even try to make Gilda understand why I had to go drinking. I knew she wouldn't care how much it meant to be accepted by the people I worked with daily, people who might be called on to lay down their lives for me. Was I at fault for not coming home to take the kids trick or treating? Or was she, for not taking them in my stead and just talking to me later rather than engaging in a yell-fest in front of them? I didn't yell back. I just grabbed my pillow and slept on the couch, trying to drown out the yelling and crying. Before drifting off, I realized something in my drunken stupor. I was becoming my father and Gilda was becoming my mother.

A few weeks after the Pearl Street incident, the victim's mother sent a handwritten note thanking me and the other officers. It was the first commendation of my career and is my most cherished, misspelled words and all. She listed every involved officer except the one who had been worried about scratching paper. When he found out about the letter, he wrote his name on it before it got copied for our personnel files. Several months later, I saw the victim in court. I didn't even recognize her. She was gorgeous. The guy who had beaten her to a pulp was sitting next to his lawyer. It took everything I had not to make him blow bubbles again as he looked at the victim and me and smirked and sucked his teeth.

I had been a most unlikely candidate to be a cop. But now that I was one, I vowed not to be one of those crooked or dirty cops who stole money, planted dope, and lied on reports. I remembered how little we thought of police who did shit like that while I was growing up and how much we respected the ones who did shit the right way, even if they beat our asses. We always figured on getting an ass whipping if we got caught; it was just part of the game. Cops stealing, planting evidence, and lying? That was cheating, coloring outside of the lines. The standard I would set for myself would be to treat people how I would expect to be treated by a cop. Cops shouldn't just treat people like shit because they can. Someone that they give a chickenshit ticket to today could be a juror on one of their cases tomorrow.

I certainly knew the difference between criminals and law-abiding citizens. I had been straddling that fence for years. If I had to beat someone's ass, I would do it, but I would also always be respectful until I was forced not to be. It is a crucial distinction. Criminals can sense weakness and will show no mercy when they find it, especially in a cop. The hardest struggle for most cops is knowing when to turn it on and when to turn it off. They can go from appearing at a grade school to do a presentation on just saying no to drugs to a fight for their life with a duster when they get a block away. I can recall at least five occasions where I was justified to shoot someone in the eyes of the law. But those aren't the eyes that look back at you from a mirror. All police are afraid at times; however, if they can't conquer that fear and act accordingly, they should find another job. Still, there has got to be accountability on both sides. If you fight with a cop over a gun, you will probably get shot. If you reach for a weapon, you will probably get shot. And this might happen *no matter what fucking color you are.*

Being a cop is a challenging, thankless job. No one likes to be told what to do. Unfortunately, some people don't know how to act without guidance or rules and regulations. It would be wonderful if society could be utopic without a need for cops. But we live in the real world, where there are monsters and evil walks among us. Sometimes monsters and evil individuals wear badges. It is just the law of averages. It was even more challenging being a Black cop. Although I faced potential death daily, I still had to balance the peril with respect for my people. I had to deal with racism and discrimination within my profession and scorn from without.

It was also difficult being a Black cop because Blacks often respected or feared the White cop more so than they did the Black one, in a perverted way seeing the White cop in the role of master and the Black one as a house nigger. But just for a second, imagine if there were no Black cops. Black people would be up in arms, screaming racism to MLK's mountaintops. Despite the difficulties Black cops faced, we still had to do the job. Otherwise, Blacks would be policed only by Whites. Still, we can't have it both ways. Skin color is not a shield to be used to commit crimes. It is wrong when Whites commit them, just like it is wrong when Blacks do. At a time in our country when everything is considered racist, crying racism has become a get out of jail free card. Evil is evil, regardless of skin color. There has got to be law and order across the board. Just because racism still exists, it does not mean that every time a Black person gets shot or arrested, it is because of racism. If everything is racist, then nothing is.

The slope becomes quite slippery, indeed, when we get to the point where color grants immunity. We fought for years to make that go away when it applied to Whites because it was inhumane. To reverse the ideology makes it no less so. I was frequently at the bottom of the monthly stats when it came to tickets written and vehicles towed, and I lost track of how many times I caught someone with crack, stepped on it, and told them to go home. Most of these people were sick, not criminals. The justice system filled our prisons with them, overcrowding the prisons to the extent that violent criminals often got out early because of it. Every situation does not have to end with someone going to jail. The primary role of a cop is to keep the peace, which is why cops are called peace officers.

I always considered it a win to do that without taking someone's freedom. Some cops have no compassion or common sense, either. I stopped to check on a fellow day-shift cop on a traffic stop one day. A young woman and her three kids were sitting on the curb near their car. I asked the cop what was going on, and he told me he was towing her car because her tags were expired. When I asked him how she and her kids were getting home, he told me, "That's their fucking problem." It wasn't a racial thing, either. The cop was Black, and the woman was too. The difference was, he was an asshole who needed his locker wired. I took the woman and her kids home and waived the towing and storage fees so she could put the money to better use, like for food and clothing for her kids. Several years later, she witnessed a murder and would only talk to me.

On another occasion, a young Mexican couple with a baby got detained for shoplifting in the Thrifty's store in the town center across from city hall. They were trying to steal diapers and Enfamil. The store security guard was adamant about them going to jail. He said, "They committed a 459, officer, and I want them to go to jail." He was trying to impress me with his command of the California penal code, as 459 is the code for burglary. But he was wrong. The individual in question must enter the store with the intent to steal for the elements of burglary to be met. I knew this more than anyone, considering how many times I committed the crime during my youth. I asked the security guard if the couple told him they came into the store to steal. With a stupid look on his face, he answered, "Well, uh, no."

Unable to conceal my sarcasm, I replied, "Well, it ain't burglary then, Sherlock."

Clearly embarrassed, he shrieked, "Well, I'm sick of these people stealing while I'm on-duty. I want them arrested!"

In the first week of the academy, recruits learn that cops cannot refuse a citizen's arrest, which is used for misdemeanors not committed in a peace officer's presence. To me, policework, like life, is not just black and white. They both abound in grey, fading in and out, morphing, ebbing, and flowing depending on the situation. I have met those deemed criminals and discovered their morals and ethics were far superior to those considered honest and law-abiding. In my eyes, life comes down to one caveat: Sometimes, doing the wrong thing for the right reason is the right thing to do. In other words, fuck what the security guard wanted. I tried to be diplomatic first and appeal to him, telling him that I didn't think it was a big deal and an arrest was unnecessary.

The security guard refused to relent, so I paid for the diapers and Enfamil and told him, "I ain't taking them to jail. Fuck you." Afterward, I drove the couple and their baby to a nearby rundown apartment where they lived. The woman was in tears, and her baby daddy, who years later became a cop for one of the larger agencies in LA County, couldn't thank me enough. This simple arrest could have adversely affected the rest of this man's life. Maybe he would have gone on to become a hardened criminal instead.

The security guard called the station later to make a complaint. He got the wrong W/C. John Garrett had answered the phone. Garrett called me to his office the next day after briefing. After I told him what happened, he said, "I agree. Fuck that guy. Don't worry. I'll handle it." I never heard anything about it again.

I thought Garrett was a great supervisor. He had been on the department since the mid-1960s and was a tall, dark-skinned cop with skinny legs and a beer gut who dyed his Jheri curl jet black. He had a deep voice and mumbled bafflegab when speaking, frequently stopping mid-sentence and wiping the white drool from the corners of his mouth with one of his gorilla-like hands. His favorite punishment for officers who had run afoul of him was the dreaded "102." He demanded them for everything from being tardy to briefing to having unpolished shoes. Garrett was stubborn, too. If he thought you misspelled a word on a report, he would even tell you Webster's dictionary was wrong if you showed it to him. Like the Sarge character from *Soldier Story*, Garrett believed that Blacks had to get rid of the "shuck and jive" routine and that using slang diminished us and made us look like fools or "Geechee" niggas. As a result, he had the utmost respect for the young Black officers on the department who were articulate in speech and the written word.

Garrett owned an ice cream parlor near Compton Blvd and Wilmington called the "Sweet Shoppe." A chain smoker for most of his life, a cigarette was always in his mouth as he prepared ice cream cones for customers. Sometimes, ashes would fall from his cigarette, providing an unhealthy topping as the neighborhood kids gleefully waited.

I was working the yard once when a burglary-in-progress call on Long Beach Blvd came out. I heard two loud gunshots as I turned the corner. Garrett was standing next to the driver's door of his patrol vehicle holding his .38 over his head, smoke from the barrel dancing with smoke from a cigarette dangling from his lips. I found the burglar underneath a nearby car and arrested him. Garrett was reloading his gun when we got back to him. He pointed at a smashed storefront window before driving off, no doubt to get the Sweet Shoppe ready for business.

I got off probation in February of 1987. I was sent to the yard, where I primarily worked district four. Most of the time, I rode with Robert "Blue" Williams, Roberto Valentin, Lendell Johnson, and Bruce Frailich. Frailich was an academy classmate of Kevin Burrell's. He grew up in the San Fernando Valley and came from money. He ended up in Compton because his father had a business that picked up grease from restaurants, one of which was in Compton. Frailich drove the grease trucks before Compton PD hired him. He was a good cop who had a positive outlook about everything, which, I guess, is easy when you never have to worry about money.

One morning after getting off work, I was trying to get some sleep when I heard yelling at my front door. I got out of bed and saw Gilda arguing with two women. The women pointed at me and yelled, "Yeah, motherfucker! We got somebody for you, too!" before running toward the front gate. Two evenly spaced metal cylindrical poles supported the upstairs balcony of the apartment building. One of them was about five feet from my front door. The staircase's supporting wall jutted out, so the gate wasn't visible from the door, but I heard it open after the women disappeared. I went to get my off-duty weapon, a Smith & Wesson 9mm semi-automatic pistol.

A guy dressed like a Crip appeared from behind the staircase just as I got back to the door. Partially blocked by the closest metal pole to my door, I could see him holding a stainless-steel revolver. He pointed it at me and asked, "What's up, cuz?" I noticed Dominic walking toward me, and I pushed him away just as the Crip fired. I shot back multiple times. The Crip ducked and covered his head while running out of view behind the staircase. I didn't get a good shot at him because I was concerned for Dominic, but I had definitely put the fear of God in Cuz's ass.

I yelled at Gilda to call 911 as I ran after him. I stopped next to the supporting wall and peeked around it in case he was waiting to ambush me, but he was gone, along with the two women. There was a bank of mailboxes on the wall near the entrance gate. At least six tenants were going to have bullet-riddled welfare checks. While waiting for Long Beach PD to respond, I looked frantically at my apartment for the bullet hole but couldn't find it. Two White officers arrived first. They were unimpressed when I showed them my badge and ID. One of them was skeptical when I told him what happened and asked, "Well, if he did shoot at you, where is the bullet hole? I mean, we see the mailbox you killed, but where did *his* bullet go?"

I was about to lose my temper until his partner said, "Found it. Here it is." The bullet had struck directly in the center of the metal pole near my front door about five feet from the ground.

Gilda feigned ignorance as to who the women were or what they wanted. I had seen this movie before. The last time her co-star was my mother. I knew Gilda was lying. The women were acting like she was messing around with one of their boyfriends or husbands, and because they knew that I was a police officer, they brought an armed accomplice. We had to move now. I told Gilda to pack a bag and take the kids to her mother's house while I stayed at a nearby motel. About two days after the shooting, James Lewis and I went back to the apartment to get some of my things. I heard Brother and a woman laughing when we walked through the front gate. I looked through his screen door. He was with one of the women, the lust in his eyes belying his standing with God. I grabbed the woman by the throat and threw her on the floor. I put my gun in her mouth while Lewis pointed his weapon at Brother and made him call out to Jesus.

I called LBPD, and they took the woman into custody. A few days later, I was on the second floor of Compton Station when I heard a familiar laugh coming from Lieutenant Al Smith's office. The woman was sitting with him. She was wearing a halter top and a short skirt with her legs crossed, exposing an expansive portion of her thigh as a high-heeled shoe dangled from her foot. She was there to file a complaint against me, and Smith was hanging on her every word.

I didn't have a problem with him taking a complaint from her. I had a problem with the way he flirted with her.

Hired in the early 60s, Alfred Smith was one of the first Black officers on the department. He was from New Orleans, had a weakness for younger women, and tried to stay hip by dying his collar-length Jheri curl jet black like Garrett's. Quite happy with his lot in life, all he did was laugh all day, a loud, cackling shriek heard long before you saw him. When Smith was the day shift W/C, he would bring roadkill to the station and clean and cook it in the jail kitchen. As part of a potluck during a Christmas luncheon in the detective bureau one year, he brought a festively dressed possum as his contribution.

David W. Smith, who we called D-dub, was a short, overweight detective who fancied himself a stand-up comic. With an ever-present toothpick in his mouth, he sometimes wore a small apple hat in his best attempt to appear urban instead of the rustic individual that he really was. He had the entire bureau laughing when he said the possum looked like James Lewis with an apple in his mouth.

Although the woman I arrested had given the LBPD detective a nickname for the guy who tried to kill me, the detective never found out his true name. Unable to prove she knew the shooter's intent the DA's office rejected the case. The detective scoffed when I told him I thought the woman was lying. From that point on, he gave me the runaround whenever I called, maintaining that they were unable to find out the shooter's real name. Either he was the most incompetent cop ever, or he just didn't care.

Although the pole had most certainly saved my life, the incident signaled the death knell for my marriage. If not for the kids, I would have left Gilda that day. It was just a matter of time now. Leaving the kids was the last thing I wanted to do, but I knew that I couldn't stay. I didn't want them subjected to the same toxicity I had to endure while growing up. I was also fanatical about proving my mother wrong about me ending up a drunk like my father. I had to be successful, and I couldn't do it if I had to drink every day to escape the reality of a toxic marriage. But I knew the demon of alcohol lurked in my genes as well and I would have to keep it caged as best as I could, even if I was in a profession where the rate of alcoholism as a coping mechanism was sky-high. To be successful,

I had to work hard, and alcoholism would certainly be an impediment to that goal. I had to show everyone that I could be the best at whatever profession I chose. I wouldn't find out until much later in life that an alcoholic and a workaholic are synonymous in many ways, and neither is conducive to being the type of father that a child needs in their life. In that regard, my father and I were already the same.

CHAPTER TEN

THERE WERE seventy-six documented street gangs in Compton. A very conservative estimate of thirty members in each one put the total number at 1,320. The number of cops was never more than 125 in the 1980s. Despite this sobering fact, we had an outstanding gang unit led by Sergeant Hourie Taylor and comprised of Reggie Wright Sr., John Pena, Eric Perrodin, Mark Anderson, and K-9 Officer Tom Zampiello and his Belgian Malinois, Saroni.

Eric, tall and lean with a hearty, guttural laugh, was a graduate of Cal State Dominguez Hills and considered to be one of the more intelligent officers on the department. Pena was a stout, muscular Mexican cop with a Pancho Villa handlebar mustache. Zamp was a good-natured White cop built like a barrel who always had a smile on his face and wore black leather gloves no matter the temperature. Mark Anderson was White and wore his hair like he was the fifth Beatle, but we called him Big Bird after the Sesame Street puppet. He was a huge man. Kevin Burrell, Gary Davis, and Bobbington "Big Bob" Brandt, who stood close to six foot six and weighed well over three hundred pounds, were the department's biggest Black cops, but Anderson was even larger than them.

Reggie was clearly the star of the gang unit. He was a short, light-skinned man in his late thirties who could out-talk a Baptist preacher consoling a widow. Reggie wore large-rimmed eyeglasses, had a mustache, and suffered from male pattern baldness like Bozo the Clown. He exaggeratedly swung one of his arms back and forth in rhythm with his steps when he walked. Reggie was small but had more heart than anyone I ever met. He grew up in the Imperial Courts Housing complex in Watts, where he was an icon. Before becoming a cop, he coached inner-city basketball teams, so he knew all the gang members in the area. He coached several kids who would make it to the NBA, most notably Reggie Theus, David Greenwood, and Roy Hamilton.

In September of 1969, Reggie got hired as a meter reader for Southern California Edison, located at 700 North Bullis Road just south of Lueders Park. After the Watts riots, Black families began moving into Compton en masse. Reggie endeared himself to many of them by not turning off their electricity despite being armed with shut-off notices. He was hired as a reserve Compton police officer in 1976 by his cousin, Joseph Rouzan, who was the police chief and later the city manager. Reggie and his brother Giles were hired as full-time police officers three years later. By this time, their mother lived in Compton in the MOB Piru neighborhood.

Reggie was respected and loved by the citizens in Compton and Watts. He often received calls from informants identifying the perpetrators of shootings and murders. And Reggie would not only know the killers, but their parents as well. He and Fat Jack worked together as partners in homicide for a brief time. Fat Jack once told me that a murder suspect had fled the city and was hiding in Texas. Reggie got the suspect's mother to have him call, and then he talked the suspect into not only turning himself in but also convinced him to pay for his own airline ticket.

I learned a lot from Reggie. He loved the department and carried water for it no matter who was in charge. When officers complained about the lack of personnel and the workload, Reggie would just smile and promise that help was on the way. The first time I met him, I was on probation and working day shift. I had responded to a radio call of a nude man causing a disturbance in a furniture store at the corner of Compton Blvd and Long Beach. I knew he was a duster, so I turned off my siren and overhead lights when I got close because noise and lights are triggers for them. The man was as big as Mark Anderson and growling at a terrified woman trapped in a corner of the store. I held my gun along the seam of my trousers, praying that I didn't have to use it as I said, "Hey, brother. Look over here." He looked at me with murderous intent, but at least I had diverted his attention. He sauntered toward me, growling and swinging his fists back and forth like wrecking balls. As I raised my gun, Reggie came out of

FREDERICK DOUGLASS REYNOLDS

nowhere and jumped on his back and choked him out. Help had finally arrived, at least for me.

We always took dusters to Augustus F. Hawkins mental institute and put a seventy-two-hour hold on them according to the 5150 Welfare and Institution Code. This is where the term 5150 used to describe people acting crazy comes from. I handcuffed the duster and put a hobble on his ankles, affixing it to the handcuffs in preparation for the trip. Known as hog-tying, at the height of the PCP epidemic, this mode of restraint was frequently used on dusters until they started dying of positional asphyxia in the backseats of patrol cars. Reggie was strutting George Jefferson-like out the front door when I looked up. I called out to him in appreciation and without looking back, he replied, "All in a day's work, rook" as he vanished into the hustle and bustle of Compton at rush hour.

Despite Compton's demographics when I got hired, it was once one of Southern California's most racist cities. In the 1930s, the Compton chapter of the KKK would ride out in full regalia on horseback and line up on the south side of Imperial Hwy. It was their way of intimidating Blacks in Watts, telling them that Imperial was as far south as they could come. When Maxcy Filer moved to Compton in 1952, the city was 95 percent White. He went to a city council meeting every week and wasn't allowed to speak until a Black man ran for a council seat in 1958.

The first Black police officer, Arthur Taylor, was hired on the first day of the year. During a subsequent council meeting, the all-White city council and mayor discussed having the sheriff's department, which was almost exclusively White at the time, come into Compton to keep any more Blacks from policing the city. By 1965, Compton was half Black with a handful of Mexicans in the unincorporated areas. The other half was White, making Compton the only integrated city in LA County. Alameda Street was the dividing line, with Blacks on the west side and Whites on the east side. When additional Black officers got hired, they could only police the west side of the city. Whites called Alameda the Asphalt Curtain, and Blacks called it the Alameda Wall. On August 11, rioters from Watts and Willowbrook stormed Compton, sending a significant number of the remaining Whites to other parts of LA County and beyond.

Although now the majority, Black citizens were still ignored, and they had no political voice. As late as 1966, there was an establishment in Compton called the Plantation Bar. Riots devastated Black communities nationwide, particularly after Martin Luther King Jr. got assassinated. Malcolm X, once known as "Detroit Red", was assassinated in 1965 and the rise of Black revolutionary groups started a year later. The most famous or infamous, depending on political affectations, were the Black Panthers, founded in Oakland by Huey P. Newton and Bobby Seale. They allegedly formed to address racial inequality and provide protection against profiling and brutality by the police. They were really pro-communist Marxists and advocates for overthrowing the country. As a child growing up in Detroit in the 60s, I remember the Panthers trying to win our hearts and minds by handing out box lunches and cartons of milk as we walked to school.

At the time, racial profiling by the police was so pervasive that it even led to the bungling of capturing one of the most elusive serial killers in history. On October 11, 1969, Paul Stine, a White cab driver in San Francisco, picked up a frumpy, average-looking White guy who wore glasses. He then shot Stine in the back of the head and tore off a piece of Stine's bloody shirt. Several kids in a nearby house heard a commotion outside and saw the White guy leaving. They called the police and reported what they had seen. Responding police units immediately thought that robbery was the motive. One of them stopped the killer walking not far from the scene of the crime. The officers asked him if he had seen a Black guy even though the kids never gave a racial description. The killer pointed in the opposite direction and told them he saw a Black guy holding a gun run that way. The feckless cops then went on a wild goose chase, looking for an armed Black man who did not exist. Simultaneously, the White guy, who just happened to be the Zodiac Killer, walked off into history after mailing the piece of clothing to the *San Francisco Chronicle*.

Embarrassed police officials later said there had been a "miscommunication" regarding the murderer's race. Most likely, absent a verifiable race description, responding officers associated a murdered cab driver during a robbery with someone Black as the culprit. FBI profilers described the Zodiac Killer as a narcissist who deemed himself intellectually superior to the police. He must have felt that his interaction with cops while in possession of the murder weapon and a piece of Stine's bloody shirt was his magnum opus. The two patrol cops likely never got over the humiliation of letting America's equivalent of Jack the Ripper slip right through their fingers.

Less than six months later, on July 1, 1970, Compton almost became ground zero for an all-out assault on law enforcement by the Panthers. Tommy Lige Harper III was about to enter the police station, carrying a suitcase filled with explosives, when he accidentally blew himself up. A search of his apartment uncovered more explosives, stacks of Black Panther literature, and a collection of the writings of Mao Tse-tung. Officers Julio Hernandez and John Cato were on the 300 Block of West Fig Street just four months later when a sniper shot out their overhead emergency light bar. Multiple officers responded to assist, including Hourie Taylor, Stoney Jackson, Ron Malachi, and the badass version of Bob Page before he stopped giving a fuck.

Neighbors told the officers that the shooter and another man ran into the back door of 361 West Fig Street. One of them was Tommy Harper's brother. He was arrested, but the other man got away through a homemade tunnel underneath the kitchen sink. Gas masks, explosives, guns, walkie-talkies, ammunition, and Black Panther Party and Chinese Communist literature were in the house. Harper's brother told the cops he was a Black Panther awaiting orders to begin the revolution. The Panthers would start fading away by the early 70s, clearing the path for complete domination of inner cities by street gangs.

Although Nussman had given me an introductory lesson on gangs, Reggie Wright Sr. gave me the advanced course, teaching me the history of LA and Compton gangs in the aftermath of the Panthers. A young street tough named Raymond "Truck" Washington, a former member of a gang called the "Avenues" which was ran by brothers Jimmy and Bobby Lavender, is credited with starting the Crips in the early 70s in South (Central) LA. He befriended another street tough named Stanley "Big Tookie" Williams and they decided to unite the many different gangs in the area. Truck came up with the name "Cribs" because he wanted to "gang bang from the baby crib to the grave." The members began mispronouncing the name when they were drunk, slurring it as Crip. The word gained traction because they used walking canes, which doubled as weapons.

When LAPD officers interviewed a witness to one of their crimes, the witness described them as "those crippled niggas," and the name stuck. The gang soon split into the Eastside and Westside Crips. Tookie would lead the east, and Truck would head the west. They grew exponentially as Tookie and Truck challenged leaders of smaller gangs, asking, "Is it gonna be Crip, or what?" If they accepted, they became Crips. If they declined, they got beat down and became Crips anyway. In the Nickerson Gardens, the Bounty Hunters, one of the toughest gangs around, stood their ground.

The Crips terrorized the community, beating people up and taking their leather jackets. One of their victims, Robert Ballou, died after such a beating, making him the first official murder committed by members of the Crip gang. The Crips would use the annual Watts festival to showcase their numbers and strength. Tookie and members with nicknames of "Barefoot Pookie", "Cowboy", and "Godfather" walked around shirtless exposing their massive physiques.

Mac Thomas formed the Compton Crips. He despised another gang in Compton called the Piru Crips, founded in 1972 by James "Jimmy Earl" Tyiska, AC "King Bobalouie" Moses, Larry "Tam" Watts, Lorenzo "Lo" Benton, Sylvester "Piru Puddin" Scott, and Darrow King. The Piru Crips conducted their meetings at Centennial High school. Truck was once a student at the school and wanted to become allies with them. Thomas refused, telling Truck that the Piru Crips, particularly Piru Puddin, were his mortal enemies. Although historically attributed to a clash of personalities, the real reason for their beef was animosity over an extremely attractive neighborhood girl.

At a subsequent party on Piru Street, Tookie and Truck talked with Tam, Pudding, and Thomas to squash the beef, but Thomas still refused to become allies with them. The party almost ended in gunplay when one of the Compton Crips took a hat from a Piru. The Piru Crips aligned with the Bounty Hunter Bloods to shore up their ranks and became Piru Bloods. The Pirus and Bloods now considered all Crips their enemies. The Compton Pirus split and formed two separate gangs: the Westside and Eastside Pirus. The Westside Piru gang members were the original Compton Piru Crips and remain the largest Piru gang with two major cliques: deuce-line, which references 142 Street in Compton's Rosewood neighborhood, and four-line, which references 134 Street in Compton. The Eastside Pirus would eventually become the Lueders Park Pirus and spawn numerous smaller Piru cliques just as the Westside Pirus and the Crip gangs had.

Crips referring to each other as "cuz" stems from Truck Washington. He believed all members to be family and, as such, called them cousins. It caught on, and he and Tookie shortened it to "cuz." Also, in the Black culture, unless a family member was involved, only one-on-one fighting was allowed. Crips got around this by referring to fellow gang members as their cousins. The term "Blood" has a long history in Black culture, beginning during slavery when Blacks were sold and lost track of family members. They started calling each other blood because they could be related and not even know it, so the term refers to kinship. The Bounty Hunters adopted this term of endearment among their members, and as a result, they became one of the original Blood gangs along with a gang called the "Bishops."

There are many theories about why Crips chose blue, and Bloods chose red. The real reason is simple, as are most answers to complicated questions. An original Westside Crip by the name of Curtis "Buddha" Morrow always wore a blue shirt, blue pants, and blue suspenders. He either wrapped a blue bandana around his head or hung it from his left rear pocket to coordinate his outfits. When he got shot to death in 1973, his fellow Crips wore blue bandanas in memoriam. The Bloods chose red for a much more apparent reason and decided to display their bandanas in their right rear pockets.

Although gang violence had been on the rise since 1972, the 1975 Compton High homecoming football game against Dominguez seems to be the flashpoint for the coming wars between Crip and Piru gangs in Compton. Blood was already boiling as a Piru had been recently shot by a Crip at the traveling Carnival set up near the old Sears building, now the site of the Compton Swap meet, on Long Beach Boulevard. At the football game the Crips sat on the Compton side of the field, and the Pirus and Bloods sat on the Dominguez side. Several fights broke out in the stands. Legendary gang members with colorful street names like Bartender and New Yorker, Skull and Part-Time, Sugar Bear and Lil Tim, Top Cat and Knuckles, Buntry and Country, Spud and Porky, Love and Willie 'T', Troubleman and Bo-Peep, and Salty Dog and China Dog were involved in the fighting.

After the game, Puddin, Bo-Peep, and Buntry were shot at by Crips during a party on Butler Street. Just hours later, Tam, one of the most popular Pirus, was shot to death on West Arbutus Street by a Westside Crip. The funeral was held on October 18, 1975. The following day, two Pirus shot Tookie as he sat on his front porch at 537 West Palm Street. Although originally from LA, Tookie was instrumental in forming the Boot Hill Crips, which became the Grandee Crips and later the Nutty Blocc Crips, one of Compton's most ruthless gangs. Tookie was later executed for the 1979 shotgun murders of four people. Truck Washington was murdered by members of the Hoover Groovers, the only Black non-Crip or Blood gang in LA County, that same year.

Despite the proliferation of gangs in Compton and surrounding areas, only Bob Page and Tom Barclay comprised the Compton gang unit initially. But they weren't called "gang" units then. So as not to glamorize the gangs, they were called other more innocuous terms such as, "graffiti teams" or "Banish". Stoney Jackson replaced Page and Barclay after they were given other assignments. Stoney would frequently team up with Black members of the newly formed LA Sheriff's "gang" unit known as O.S.S. (Operation Safe Streets). Stoney rode with Curtis "Red Neck Slim" Jackson, who the Black sheriff character in the movie *Colors* is based on. Along with Kenny Bell, Herb Jerome, and Richard Valdemar, they were formidable gang investigators during the early days of the Crip and Blood gangs.

The 1990s brought the racial gang wars between the Black and Mexican gangs. The Mexican Mafia, or "La EME," and the Nuestra Familia are prison gangs. Their power is so great it extends to the streets, where the street gangs are beholden to them, as the gang members know they will eventually end up in the prison system. The Crips and Bloods, usual enemies on the streets, must band together in prison to protect themselves from the Mexican Mafia and Aryan Brotherhood, comprised of neo-Nazi skinheads and other White supremacist groups.

During the Black v Brown wars in the 90s, the Mexican Mafia issued a death edict against Mexican gang members who committed drive-by shootings after a child was murdered. The gang members could then only commit walk-up murders. This directive would later be rescinded several years later, however. Racial violence in the prisons had also erupted on the streets as the Mexican Mafia issued orders to kill Blacks. Racial epithets spray-painted on houses and other structures became commonplace throughout the city as dozens of Black on Brown murders began to overwhelm Compton and the entire county of Los Angeles. The crimes were commonplace because the gang members lived in the same neighborhoods, often on the same blocks.

There were many killers in Compton, but some of them were outright sociopaths. It doesn't take much to drive past a yard full of people and fire indiscriminately into a crowd, but to execute people in cold blood takes a sociopath of the first order. Known as "Riders", they build the rep of the entire gang. They didn't always kill strictly for the benefit of their gang either. Sometimes they killed for selfish reasons, but the reputation of the gang benefited anyway. Twenty-one-year-old Anthony Lloyd Crumpton, aka "Tony C," was one such individual. Although he killed rival gang members and even members of his own gang, his specialty was robbing and killing drug dealers. Crumpton is suspected of murdering twenty-one people, most of them during dope rip-offs, between 1987 and 1990. He even handcuffed some of his victims to shower rods and tortured them with chainsaws reminiscent of *Scarface's* bathroom scene.

Crumpton first came to the attention of Compton PD in March of 1990 when he and Front Hood Crip Lafayette Jones, along with two other men and a woman, murdered Dennis "Beaver" Farmer during a drug rip-off at 926 North Pearl. Crumpton also robbed a Compton drug house operated by Grape Street Crip Wayne "Honcho" Day, who had a stranglehold on PCP sales and crack in Watts in the 80s and 90s. Crumpton's half-brother was Flentard "Flint" Coleman, a hitman for Thomas "Tootie" Reese, one of the biggest drug dealers on the west coast for over twenty years. The family's murderous reputation extended back to the early 1970s, when their brother, "Fat Bennie" Coleman, shot and killed "Son" McDaniels at an illegal gambling spot in Compton on West 131st Street.

On June 11, 1990, Mark Anderson received a tip that Crumpton was in the area of Broadway and West 64th Street in Los Angeles. He told Stoney, the

119

investigator on the Dennis Farmer case, and Stoney called legendary LAPD Robbery-Homicide Detective John "Jigsaw" St. John. St. John had been a cop since 1942 and was involved in the infamous Black Dhalia murder case. He had the LAPD Special Investigations Squad, better known as "S.I.S." or the Death Squad, stake out Crumpton's vehicle. This unit was only assigned the cases involving the most violent offenders, and the people they went after rarely survived the encounter. When Crumpton got in his car, one of the S.I.S members blocked his path with an unmarked police vehicle, and the rest of the Death Squad filled him full of lead.

The Death Squad knew no boundaries and didn't care about jurisdiction, either. On October 8, 1989, they killed Farm Dog Crip Demetrious "Bird" Russell on Caldwell Street. The only way Compton PD even knew what happened was because of 911 calls from neighbors about shots fired on the street. When I got there, Bird was lying dead in a driveway with a .12-gauge shotgun on the ground near him.

Anthony "Tony Bogart" Parker was a close associate of Crumpton's and a shot-caller in the Imperial Courts housing complex. He told St. John that whenever Crumpton murdered someone, Crumpton attended the memorial services and obtained an obituary as a souvenir. When S.I.S. killed Crumpton, he had an obituary in his car for Front Hood Crip Deltony "Warlock" Warnock, murdered in Compton on April 29, 1990. Warnock's murder remains open, as does Beaver's. Although Crumpton is dead and Jones was arrested and convicted for killing Beaver, the two other men and the woman who assisted remain unidentified.

I ran across Crumpton several times while working patrol. He was always respectful and reserved, but whenever any of the gangsters with him got loud, he shut it down with just a glance. Crumpton never had a gun or drugs when I searched him, but he always had a pocketful of money, and most of the time, I found a gun and a bag of crack hidden nearby. I knew they were his, but I believe he had a grudging respect for me because I never lied and put anything on him or his associates. Probably one of the more obvious gray areas of policework, this is a perfect example of how coloring outside of the lines can sometimes be beneficial. Had I lied on Crumpton and arrested him, how many lives would I have saved?

Eighteen-year-old Oscar "Ghost" Figueroa was just as evil as Crumpton. A member of the CVT-Flats gang, Ghost had an insane hatred of Black people and killed at least four within one month in 1994. On June 17, a husband and wife had just finished cleaning the parking lot of an apartment building where T-Flats members sold crack. When they asked for payment in the form of crack cocaine, Ghost shot the husband in the head. He then shot the wife multiple times before finishing her off with a bullet to the head as she crawled away. Three weeks later, he killed a guy thought to be a neighborhood snitch after knocking on his window and shooting him in the face when he looked out. The following day, he stabbed a strawberry in the head and took the four dollars back from her he had given her for a blowjob.

On February 13, 2000, Ghost shot three people near a concession stand during a concert at the LA Convention Center billed as a "Valentine's Super Love Jam." An LAPD officer shot and killed him, bringing Ghost's racist reign of terror to an end.

Popular gang members were known as shot callers. When they got killed, gangs sometimes banded together in search of revenge, like when beloved Palmer Blocc Crip Herbert "Hub" Rowe got killed by a Tree-Top Piru on January 27, 1987. Within days, Honcho organized a meeting of Compton and Watts-based Crips on the Compton High football field, collectively referring to them as CC Riders, to talk about the need to only fight Bloods. Honcho also discussed tactics, such as calling 911 and reporting a fake crime on one side of the city while committing a crime on the opposite side. After the gang summit was over and while every patrol unit was on the west side of town looking for the non-existent victim of a shooting, at least fifty Crips yelling "CC Riders" ran into the Indoor Swap Meet on the east side. In a carefully planned operation reminiscent of the Cobo Hall incident in Detroit, the gang members stole more than $500,000 in merchandise.

The Swap Meet was in neutral territory. The MOB Piru hood was to the east, and the Santana Blocc Crip gang was to the west. Gang members from all over LA County shopped at the Swap Meet, which the gang members called the

"Indo." It was a popular spot to get their t-shirts custom made and purchase the sports attire that represented their respective gangs. A stereo installation shop was at the back of the Indo. At least ten vehicles waited on any given day to get the latest top-of-the-line stereo systems and phones installed, paid for with crack proceeds, while homegrown Rappers NWA and DJ Quik sometimes sold their original mixtapes in the parking lot out of their car trunks.

More than two-hundred shootings and twenty murders occurred in Compton alone in the months following Honcho's speech at Compton High. None of the violence was Crip on Crip, but Honcho would forego his vision of a Crip kumbaya when his younger brother Kenneth "Lil Honcho" Day got car-jacked and murdered in Southside Crip hood on November 27, 1987. The car had the highly sought-after gold Dana Danes on it. Most of the time, carjackers wouldn't even ask drivers to get out of vehicles that had these rims on them. They just shot the drivers in the head, dragged them out, and drove off in their cars. There were so many killings utilizing this method that the rims became known as Killer Dayton's.

Seeking revenge, Honcho allegedly sent four carloads of Grape Street Crips to Southside. They killed one man and wounded ten others during seven separate drive-by shootings. Lil Honcho had been killed by three gang members from Long Beach, who just happened to be passing through Compton when they saw his car. They didn't know who he was, and the Southside Crips paid the price. No one was ever arrested or charged for the SSCC shootings. No direct evidence ever linked Honcho to the crimes, even though we all knew who gave the order.

There were 387 gang-related murders in LA County in 1987. I responded to dozens of the more than eighty-six of them that occurred in Compton. One of the most gut-wrenching ones occurred in front of Bunny's liquor store. A gang member named Willie "Bull" Deal was shot to death with an AK-47. When I got there, Deal was lying at the curb line near the gutter. Half of his head was gone. A young woman was kneeling on the ground, rubbing his blood and brain matter on her face and clothing as she screamed, "They kilt my baby daddy!" over and over.

Yet no one outside of the inner cities wanted to acknowledge that there was a gang problem. As of 1988, it was LA County's secret—thousands of bullet-riddled skeletons in its 4,751-square-mile closet. But when Karen Toshima, a graphic artist for a Studio City advertising agency, was killed during a gang shooting in affluent Westwood on January 30, the fallout was immediate. LAPD Chief Daryl Gates ordered a series of massive sweeps through the city's worst neighborhoods, interrogating or arresting young Black males who looked like gang members, which, of course, to most White police officers meant *ALL* young Black males. Twenty-four thousand got arrested in the first nine months of the sweeps, but barely half were gang members. And this is how thousands of kids who weren't gang members got put into the gang database, originally called the "G.R.E.A.T" system, an acronym for Gang-Related Enforcement and Tracking. It is now known as Cal Gangs. Police units put together to combat gangs were now appropriately called "Gang Units." The cat was officially out of the bag.

The number of gunshot victims in Compton, a large part of South (Central) LA, Lynwood, and Watts put a tremendous strain on the only local trauma center, Martin Luther King Jr. Hospital. So many were treated there the US military began sending their trauma teams to the hospital for combat surgery training. It became derisively known as "Killer King" because of the number of gunshot victims who died there. It was an undeserved nickname, as most of the victims were shot with high-powered rifles or multiple times with handguns, and no amount of medical care could have saved them.

While we were still armed with six-shot revolvers and .45 caliber pistols from the WWII and Vietnam era, the gang members were now armed with high-capacity semi-automatic pistols and rifles courtesy of the wealth generated by crack. The death rate increased exponentially as a result. We would soon be responding to shootings with as many as ten victims laying on the ground. No one was safe. Children and the elderly were often unintended victims, killed while playing in their front yards or sitting in rocking chairs, knitting, or watching the evening news. And in the middle of a gang-infested city that routinely led the nation in murders per capita every year, Compton had a gun store complete with a shooting range.

CHAPTER ELEVEN

MIKE VIRGILIO was a red-haired, middle-aged White man who walked with crutches because of a gunshot wound sustained during a burglary at his home. He lived in beautiful, serene Manhattan Beach located about fifteen miles from Compton, but he owned Boulevard Auto located just a block from Lueders Park. The business's name had nothing to do with what he sold. Some residents in Compton called it the house of the devil and referred to Virgilio as Satan. During Jesse Jackson's presidential campaign speeches in 1988, Jackson vilified the store as a place where "assault" rifles were easily accessible.

Boulevard Auto was painted camouflage green with a bullseye containing a semi-automatic pistol and a magazine clip in the center just south of the entrance. There were no windows. The store's perimeter was lined with evenly spaced four-foot-tall concrete cylinders to prevent vehicles from ramming into it. The interior was like a vault, the walls lined with blackened sheets of reinforced steel to prevent break-ins. Handguns of all calibers were on shelves inside of bulletproof cases. Dozens of magazine clips, including one-hundred-round drums, and various types of semi-automatic rifles and shotguns were affixed to the walls behind the counter area. There was a tiny section in the back of the store reserved for auto parts to justify the business's name.

For almost twenty years, Virgilio sold ten to fifteen semi-automatic rifles and handguns a week. The weapon of choice for Compton gang members was a Chinese version of the AK-47 with an attached bayonet. The destructive capability of these weapons was unbelievable. On October 24, 1987, seventy-year-old Mable Elam was sitting at her desk at a daycare center when a bullet fired from one tore an egg-sized hole in the concrete and wood wall. It slammed into her back and broke a rib before destroying one of her kidneys and part of her liver.

She died instantly. Two years later, the city council adopted an unconstitutional ordinance that banned the sale and possession of semi-automatic rifles. Sixty people had been murdered between 1986 and 1989 by these types of firearms in Compton alone.

Two days after the city council adopted the ordinance, two-year-old Phillip Fisher was playing in his front yard located across the street from where Eric and Percy Perrodin grew up. A vehicle occupied by three gang members drove past, and one of them opened fire with an AK-47, killing the child and one of the neighbors. The gang members were arrested and prosecuted, but this provided little solace for the toddler's father, who lamented, "There's a war going on out here. All we're missing are the tanks and the warplanes, but you should hear the gunshots at night. I bet Vietnam wasn't this bad."

During the first week of 1994, Boulevard Auto opened a $500,000 gun range. Even though it should have been clear that the optics of having a gun range in a city besieged by gun violence was terrible, the city council approved the project despite objections from the chief of police. City Clerk Charles Davis was a hugely influential city official who held his position for thirty years. He believed that the city would be safer if gun owners had a place to practice away from residential neighborhoods. "Maybe some innocent people won't get hit," he said. The following year, there were eighty-two murders in Compton, the most in five years.

The reality that Boulevard Auto was selling guns to gang members came to light after Officer Joseph "Joey" Reynolds was involved in a shooting on December 3, 1987. He and his partner, Raymond Banuelos, saw a drug transaction between two men at 204 North Sloan. The men ran, and Joey, armed with a Smith & Wesson .44 magnum revolver with a six-inch barrel, chased them down the driveway. He was confronted by Kevin "Orek" Johnson, who was holding an AK-47 with a fifty round banana clip. Joey shot him in the stomach when Johnson turned toward him. The AK-47 was the second one Johnson had purchased from Boulevard Auto. The police confiscated the first one after Johnson got arrested for threatening someone with it. When he told Virgilio about the confiscation, Virgilio sold him the second one at a discount.

Additionally, Johnson got arrested two months before that for possession of a loaded 12-gauge shotgun, also purchased at Boulevard Auto.

Virgilio would continue to sell guns to gang members until March of 2007, when federal agents working with members of the Los Angeles County Sheriff's Department raided his stores in Compton and Ventura County. The raids were a result of months of operations where undercover officers purchased firearms. Almost four thousand firearms and more than 1.6 million rounds of ammunition were seized. From 1996 to 2007, 1,328 weapons used in crimes were traced to the Compton store, including twenty-eight directly tied to homicide investigations and the attempted murder of a cop. We will never know the exact number of firearms sold the previous ten years that were used in crimes. Virgilio might not have been Satan, but he was without a doubt a merchant of death.

Joey Reynolds was a lean, clean-shaven White officer who wore size fourteen boots. He had a long, sleek nose that perfectly complimented his full head of dark hair with just a splash of white in front. Joey called everyone "Bro" and always told terrible jokes, laughing before delivering the punchline in his thick New York accent. I met him for the first time while we were sitting outside of the training office. Joey was new. The department had hired him after he paid to attend the Rio Hondo Academy like Kevin Burrell did. I was waiting to meet with my background investigator, Dennis Auner, a White guy with a pock-marked face who smoked unfiltered Camel cigarettes and wore glasses, three-piece suits, and wingtip brogue shoes. Joey was in uniform and continually bounced one of his legs while rubbing his knee. Every time he spoke, he emphasized the word "bro" by hitting me on the arm with his unoccupied hand. He said, "Hey, bro, I can't wait to get out in the streets, bro. I hear there's a lot of action in Compton, bro. Where you from, bro? I'm from New York, bro."

I wanted to fall on my knees in prayer when Auner finally called me into the office. Instead, I stood up, tapped Joey on the arm, and said, "Stay safe out there, bro."

Joey would certainly get his wish for the action he craved, as serious incidents followed him throughout his career. He was what cops call a "shit magnet," meaning that he was always involved in shootings, fights, and vehicle pursuits. On May 11, 1995, he was riding with Officer Eric Strong. Strong was just about as perfect a police officer as there could be. Tall, good looking, and smart as a whip, he was the honor cadet in his academy class. Years earlier, Strong was selected the honor recruit in his Marine Corps boot camp platoon. He bow-hunted wild boar, scuba-dived, skied, and jumped out of airplanes for enjoyment. Strong and Joey were driving east on Alondra Blvd toward Willowbrook when they saw a stolen Mack truck driving in front of them. The driver, Jerry "Black Ice" Guess, was dusted. He failed to yield and continued driving at speeds less than ten miles an hour. Officer Christopher Paredes arrived to assist. He drew his Glock .45 caliber pistol with an extended twenty-round clip, walked in front of the truck, and fired six shots into the windshield, bringing the pursuit to an abrupt end.

In addition to shooting Oren Johnson, Joey shot two other armed gang members within the next two years. All these critical incidents began to take a toll on him, but one more than any other had a particularly devastating effect. Several months after the incident involving Black Ice, Joey and Strong were radio car partners again. Joey was driving westbound on Greenleaf Blvd when they got in pursuit of a stolen car. The driver ran a red light, struck another vehicle at 100 mph, and was ejected and killed. He was only fourteen-years old.

Not long afterward, Joey was about to go into the field when he was summoned to R.E. Allen's office to discuss a disagreement he had with Lieutenant Al Smith over a court subpoena. Smith never liked Joey, and the feeling was mutual. Joey had just checked out a shotgun from the armory, so he brought it with him. I saw him leaning against the wall in the hallway as I walked to the bathroom. He cracked a joke, fucking up the punch line as usual. A few minutes later, Joey was in the office, arguing with Smith, when he suddenly screamed, "Leave me the fuck alone! I'm sick of this shit!" He threw the shotgun to the floor and repeatedly kicked the wall. He then picked up the gun and stormed down the stairs. Joey had scared the shit out of everyone on the second floor, but no one more than Smith. This incident, coupled with all that excitement he had been clamoring for, eventually caused Joey to go out on a stress-related retirement. The experience shook Smith, too, as we didn't hear his cackling nearly as much after that.

Chris Paredes was Filipino and small but built like Bruce Lee. He wore his hair in a Mohawk and dyed it various colors. One day it was blue, the next day, it was green, the day after that, it was blond. Paredes loved guns and had an apparent *Terminator* fetish. He would come to work wearing an ankle-length trench coat with a double shoulder holster containing twin Glock .45 caliber pistols. He wore fingerless black leather racing gloves, sunglasses like the pair worn by Arnold in the movie, untied combat boots, parachute pants, and tank tops.

In addition to shooting Black Ice, Paredes shot four other men, killing three of them. One of the shootings happened at a Denny's restaurant on February 22, 1992, in nearby Torrance, an affluent city with many citizens who were descendants of the White flight from Compton in the 1960s. The Torrance police department was known as one of the most racist in LA County. With well over two-hundred cops, they never had more than one Black one at a time. A Black man could not drive through Torrance without getting stopped by the cops, at which point he would either get his ass beat, arrested, or cited. None of this deterred two members of the Hoover Groover gang, however, as they decided to rob the restaurant that night. Paredes, whose choice of color for his Mohawk was blond that day, and Officer George Betor had gone to the restaurant when they got off work. As soon as they sat in a booth near the front door, the Hoovers walked in. Amazingly, they didn't recognize Betor and Paredes as off-duty cops.

Betor was a balding White man with a beer gut who wore "God Bless America" t-shirts and a fanny pack, for crying out loud, and Paredes, well, he was just Paredes. Despite the tell-tale signs that Betor and Paredes were cops, the two Hoovers went full steam ahead. One of them turned toward Betor and Paredes with a gun, and Paredes fired six shots from one of his Glocks, hitting him five times. Betor cornered the other Hoover in the rear of the restaurant and took him into custody. The guns used by the Hoovers had been taken during a residential burglary in Compton just days before. The burglars entered the house through a rear window and stole seven handguns, three hunting rifles, and two semi-automatic rifles. They hung the victim's dog in the backyard, most likely to keep it from barking.

Paredes bought a Desert Eagle .50 caliber pistol to carry on duty after that. Instead of rewriting the firearms policy, the chief reassigned Paredes to the helicopter unit as an observer when he found out. It did little to temper Paredes's enthusiasm for the smell of gunpowder. Within three months, he leaned out of the helicopter and shot out the engine block of a stolen car during a pursuit. Paredes would retire from the department in 2000. After the Towers went down on 9/11, the rumor was that he went to the Middle East, where he worked for Blackwater.

I believe that every cop who worked at Compton PD suffers from various degrees of PTSD. In addition to all the violent crime incidents I responded to, I also responded to horrific fatal traffic accidents, including hit-and-runs involving pedestrians, some of whom were children. Unexplained phenomena frequently occur at horrific events. For some reason, pedestrians killed by motor vehicles always get knocked out of their shoes, whether they are slip-on or lace-up. I have seen someone die from a .22 caliber gunshot wound to the ass and someone live Phineas Gage-like with a 9mm gunshot wound to the head. I was the first officer on the scene of a fatal traffic accident involving a bandit cab and a train at Willowbrook Avenue and Greenleaf. When I got there, the taxi had been torn in half. The driver was still in his seat, embedded as one with the wreckage. His five passengers' mangled bodies were neatly laid out and staggered on either side of the track as if purposefully placed by some divine hand.

No one ever considers police dispatchers when talking about PTSD. Just because they don't face the actual danger of confronting an armed individual or witness horrific atrocities, they are victims in another sense. They must listen to the screams and agony of callers, to the cries of a mother who just saw her child brutally murdered, to the pleas of a victim just before taking his or her last breath. If cops are the sheepdogs protecting sheep from wolves, then dispatchers are the shepherds. Injured cops have survived wounds, comforted by a dispatcher's soothing voice while waiting for medical help. Dispatchers feel the adrenaline of officers involved in high-speed chases and they feel the fear of an officer getting shot at just as they feel the trauma of an officer who dies on their watch. And not only are they lifelines for cops; they are also lifelines for the very communities they serve.

Even our records clerks, jailers, and parking control officers would be candidates for PTSD. They were subject to verbal and even physical assault almost daily. There was no partition protecting the records clerks from the citizens, and when a crazed lunatic leaped over the front counter one morning, one of the clerks hit him in the head with a heavy-duty stapler. During a jail check, the W/C came across one of our jailers getting sodomized in a cell. The jailer swore he was being raped, but the W/C swore that wasn't what it looked like to him. A parking control officer took to carrying a .357 magnum in her vehicle after one of her peers was assaulted while writing a parking ticket. Another one, a kindly old man close to seventy years old, once chose to chase a stolen car in his little parking control vehicle while calling out the pursuit on his radio.

One of the more popular officers on the PM shift was a neurotic White cop who shied away from all radio calls. Instead, he preferred to go from pop spot to pop spot, getting Marlboro cigarettes and coffee all shift. After one violence-filled night, he drove home and parked in his driveway. His wife found him still sitting in his car an hour later, sobbing uncontrollably. He refused to get out until she called the W/C to come and talk him down. The officer went out on stress after this incident.

Another cop was becoming increasingly frustrated with Lieutenant Steve Roller, an intelligent, silver-haired White cop who wore designer eyeglasses. He was a stickler for grammatically correct paperwork and continually had the officer make corrections to a simple vandalism report. After the fourth time, the officer smiled and said, "I'll be right back."

He got an AK-47 from his locker and was on his way to the W/C's office when Reggie Wright Sr. stopped him and asked, "Hey, where you going with that fucking thing?"

The officer replied, "Reggie, I'm gonna kill Roller! I'm sick of that asshole!" Reggie calmed him down and took the rifle, but that was the officer's last day on the job.

During one extremely busy night filled with gunshot victims and several murders, a female officer and her partner responded to a call of a stab victim. When they got there, the victim was lying on the floor, a pair of scissors in his throat, wobbling back and forth in rhythm with his death rattle. Tired of the gratuitous violence, when she got home, she barricaded herself inside and threatened to commit suicide. After hours of negotiations, she surrendered to the local law enforcement agency but never returned to work. Violent death was a constant in Compton. Some of us could handle it better than others, but a few of us couldn't handle it at all. And the murders always seemed to come at the most inopportune times.

On April 25, 1987, at around 2:15 a.m., I was riding with Officer Oscar Van Wie when we got a radio call of a "hit-n-run" victim at Willowbrook Avenue and Spruce. I had hoped that the night wouldn't be like the previous one when we were on Compton Boulevard at three in the morning and heard gunshots. Van Wie was driving. He looked left. I looked right and saw someone in a car shoot a woman before speeding off northbound. But that was just Van Wie, always looking the wrong way at the right time. I yelled, "There! Somebody in that car just shot a woman," as I grabbed the radio mic. "4-Adam, we're in pursuit northbound on Poinsettia from Compton. Roll paramedics to Poinsettia just north of Compton Blvd for a gunshot victim." It was a short pursuit. The shooter turned down an alley a few blocks away and jumped out of the car. He tumbled a few times before hopping to his feet and running away with a gun in his hand.

Van Wie was the shortest cop on the department. Mixed with Mexican and Filipino, he looked like a fatter version of *The Hangover's* Mr. Chow and was clumsy as fuck and blind as a bat without his glasses. As I closed on the shooter, I aimed at the sky and blew my whistle. The shooter stopped and tried to throw his gun on the roof of a nearby building, but it hit the second story façade and fell to the ground about twenty feet in front of him. As I was handcuffing him, I heard another gunshot behind me. I looked and saw smoke coming from the barrel of Van Wie's gun while he was on his knees looking for his glasses.

The gunshot victim was a strawberry from Long Beach Boulevard who had given the shooter a $10.00 blowjob. He shot her after she grabbed his wallet when she was getting out of the car. I told him that if he didn't say anything about us blowing our whistles, I wouldn't say anything to his wife and kids about why he blew his.

One of the favorite eating spots on the yard was Puritan's restaurant on Rosecrans Avenue and Willowbrook. After grabbing a bite to eat, most of the shift did a "bar check" at the Golden Garter strip club on Long Beach Blvd near Lueders Park. The dancers were all strung-out White dope heads with faded tattoos, sagging titties, and stretch marks, but they had no shame and danced like nobody was watching. One cop transferred to another police agency and had his going away party at the club. A stripper impressed him so much during a nude lap dance he ended up marrying her.

Before the hit-and-run call, it had been quiet after our nightly post-briefing meal with the other graveyard units at Puritans. Van Wie had had his usual cheeseburger, plain with extra mayo, and a large cup of black coffee. "Barstow" Bob Davis, a short, extremely overweight cop who looked like the Stay-Puft Marshmallow Man, was one of the most senior officers on the yard. Every night he had a double patty melt with extra, extra bacon, and an extra-large diet Pepsi, and that night was no different. While Barstow Bob and his partner headed off to the airport with their pillows and warbags, Van Wie and I drove to the call where we saw a Mexican man with dog-eared pants pockets lying dead in the street near the railroad tracks. He reeked of beer and was bleeding from a stab wound to the chest.

A small group of people in sleepwear had gathered on the corner near PCP alley. Not unusual, despite the late hour. There was always yellow crime scene tape somewhere in Compton, and people always stopped to look. Usually, they would lose interest and leave. Not this group of people, however. They were still on the corner when the detectives arrived an hour later. These people were keenly attentive as if they had a vested interest. But they were Black, and the victim was a drunk border brother. *Why hadn't they gone back to sleep by now?*

John Swanson, Stoney Jackson, and Edward "Red" Mason were the responding detectives. When I told Swanson about my suspicions, he thought it was unusual as well. As we made our way over to talk with the spectators, one of them suddenly hung his head and walked toward the duplexes. We stopped him and noticed that he was extremely nervous. Swanson smiled and said to me, "Hook him up, officer. This young man did it."

I took out my handcuffs, and the young man held his palms out in an upright position near his chest and screeched, "Whoa! I didn't do it! My brother did it!

He told us he jacked a Mexican and stabbed him, so we just came out of our apartment to see!"

Swanson had me and Van Wie cover the rear of their apartment just as the suspect jumped out of the back window and ran. Van Wie cuffed him after I tackled him. Swanson found a blood-stained steak knife in the apartment. It turned out that the suspect periodically preyed on the Mexicans frequenting the bar because they would not contact the police for fear of being deported.

Swanson, Stoney, and Red were legends on the department, a link to glory days long gone. And they looked the part of detectives from a by-gone era as well. Swanson was a huge man with hands and feet supporting the axiom that everything from Texas is bigger. He wore ill-fitting suits and had a small, neatly cut Afro. Despite his relatively young age at the time, he had to wear reading glasses because of his love for reading and writing. Swanson was a wizard at solving cold cases and once solved a triple murder that was twenty years old, tracking down the culprit who had taken on a new identity and moved over a thousand miles away. Stoney was always well dressed in tailored suits. He smoked Baraccini Capriccioso pipes and always wore a fedora rakishly to one side, which masked the evidence of his rapidly thinning hair. Red was a thin, light-skinned cop with a smattering of freckles high on his cheekbones. Like Swanson, he also wore a small, neatly cut Afro and had to use reading glasses. His handwriting was barely legible, but he could sell oil to an Arab and call out someone telling him a lie in a heartbeat. He had high-blood pressure, was always on edge, and frequently took gulps from an ever-present bottle of Maalox he carried in his back pocket.

These three men were part of a Compton PD homicide unit once considered one of the finest in the nation, clearing an astounding ninety percent of murders when the number was manageable. They were now part of a unit with less than six detectives responsible for investigating an average of eighty murders a year, clearing slightly over fifty percent of them annually. The three of them were all smart, savvy detectives gifted with talents uniquely suited for their chosen profession: Swanson, the gifted writer with bulldog investigator qualities; Stoney, the well-dressed, pipe-smoking, fearless fighter; and Red, the loquacious charmer with a hearty laugh and a penchant for sniffing out bullshit.

CHAPTER TWELVE

ON MAY 3, 1987, I was riding with Officer Gary Eaves. We called him "Jaws" because he was a big White guy with a granite jawline and huge teeth. Jaws carried a .44 magnum with a six-inch barrel, which he pulled out quite often. Several times when we were on a scene, I would notice him holding it behind his back, even when the situation didn't call for it. I had always considered the White cops to be racist until they proved they weren't. It was wrong and stupid, but it was my defense mechanism against White people, specifically White cops. Jaws never did anything to prove to me unequivocally that he was racist. He just didn't "fit" Compton, in my opinion. He was always overbearing and aggressive when confronting Black men, which I knew was his tell.

At 6:00 p.m., Jaws and I assisted Officers Rene Fontenot and Reggie Wright Sr. with a call of a dead body at the One Stop Body Works, an abandoned building on Compton Blvd that was known as a hangout for crackheads and strawberries. We found a dead White woman named Mary Corman lying face down in an oil pit. A handcuff key and two books titled *Malcolm X on Afro-American History* and *Under the Hood: A Report on the KKK in Greater Los Angeles* were on the ground near the oil pit.

The reporting party was a strawberry who told us that the victim and several other smokers had engaged in a freak party a few days before the murder. A guy nicknamed "Moja" got upset with the victim when she wouldn't let him sodomize her, so he handcuffed her to a pole, strangled her, and stabbed her in the chest before throwing her in the oil pit. The homicide detectives were Pepper Preston and Davey Arellanes, a middle-aged Mexican cop with silver hair and a silver tombstone cowboy mustache. He frequently pulled his stainless steel .357 magnum for no reason and licked the six-inch barrel while laughing maniacally.

Everyone knew he was certifiably 5150 but just laughed it off by saying, "Oh, that's just dumbass Arellanes."

Pepper and Davey didn't have to try very hard to find out the killer's real name or his location. It was Jeffrey Collins, and he was currently a guest at the Men's Central Jail. Jaws and I had arrested him just a week earlier. He was walking in the middle of Long Beach Blvd not far from the Body Shop, and when I hit the siren to alert him, he flipped us off. I did a stop and frisk and found a bag of crack as Jaws stood nearby, holding his big-ass gun behind his back. Given the state of the victim's decomposition, Collins most likely murdered her the night we arrested him. The books found at the scene belonged to him, so it was clear what his thoughts on race relations were. Perhaps in his cocaine-fueled aggressiveness and paranoia, the refusal of anal sex was just an excuse to exact racial revenge on her.

On June 27, my mother's uncle in Detroit died of black lung disease contracted while working in coal mines in McDowell, West Virginia, during his youth. He died as he had lived, a wretched man whose own wife wouldn't talk to him and hadn't willingly slept with him for over thirty years. Three days later, his wife died of breast cancer. I believe that she died in misery; regretful that she had given her life to such an awful man and never had children of her own, remorseful that she had taken my mother into her home those many years ago. My mother's uncle left Linda Faye a good portion of their belongings in their will, forever ending any speculation surrounding her biological father's identity.

I was still somewhat estranged from my family. I hardly ever spoke to my mother, and when I spoke to my father, it was never about anything emotional or of any substance. It was always about sports or the Clint Eastwood and Bruce Lee festivals at the Fox Theatre in Downtown Detroit he took us to as kids. Derrick was made for the Marine Corps, both in physique and killer mentality and was rapidly advancing in rank. David lived in Minnesota, forced to transfer to a Ford assembly plant there, or be laid off from the River Rouge plant. My father, still balancing the installations of rear-view mirrors on Mustangs with the allure of a drink of Canadian Club with a half-inch of sugar at the bottom of the glass, didn't have to make this choice because of his seniority.

Gilda and I were barely on speaking terms. I could not get over the shooting at our apartment and the fact that she never told me why it happened or what happened in Detroit. I hated going home now. All she did was start arguments. We were living in a three-bedroom apartment in a complex in Bellflower. Other than Mrs. Jones, an old White lady I nicknamed Mrs. Kravitz because she was always looking out of her window, the complex was a decent place to live. I knew Gilda was seeing someone else, but I couldn't have cared less. On several occasions, while I lay in bed, I heard her in another room whispering on the telephone after midnight. I wasn't going to stay in an unhappy marriage and planned to leave when the time was right. But as Frailich used to tell me, "*Mann Tracht, Un Gott Lacht,*" Yiddish for "Man plans, and God laughs."

While at Thrifty's drug store in Compton the day after hearing Gilda display her cupidity during a midnight conversation in the bathroom, I met a cute, chocolate-skinned cashier with one of the most beautiful smiles I had ever seen. I was smitten. I said, "Hi. I'm Fred." The name Tony never even came to mind. I had finally realized there was no need to be ashamed of who I was or how I was raised. I had seen far worse family situations than mine in the course of my job.

For the sake of confidentiality, I'm just going to call the cashier "Darlene." She was about five years younger than me and didn't have any kids. I told her I was married with two kids, but she didn't care. We dated in secret for the next two weeks. After taking her to a movie, I stopped by my place to get my work boots. I knew it was risky taking Darlene with me, but Gilda was at work, and the kids were at their grandma's house in Compton. I parked about a block away in case Mrs. Jones was in her window. I didn't count on her walking her dog, however. She saw Darlene sitting in the passenger seat as I was getting back in the car. Not wanting to appear suspicious, I spoke to Mrs. Jones. While her little rat dog pissed on a nearby bush, she turned her nose up and said, "Hmmph. Who's in the car with you? It's definitely not your wife."

I replied, "No, ma'am. It's a co-worker."

She looked at Darlene and then back at me before saying, "I see. Come on, CC. Let's go home, girl."

I drove off as Darlene looked at me worriedly, asking, "You think she believed you?"

Without taking my eyes off the road, I answered, "Not a chance in hell."

Meanwhile, at work, six murders and at least seventy-five shootings had happened over three days. Three of the killings came within hours of each other on the same day I got caught with Darlene. That night, my partner was William Jackson, a smart, young Black cop who I got along well with. We went to all three murders. The first one occurred at midnight. A crackhead named Johnny Lee got killed at 1317 East Glencoe Street by Southside Crip John "New Boy" Sandifer. New Boy and Lee had been smoking with several other crackheads. New Boy blew Lee's head off with a sawed-off shotgun because Lee was hogging the pipe. The second murder occurred just minutes later. Southside Crip Jimmy "Buggs" Mapp was shot in the face with a shotgun outside of the Del Mar motel about a block away near Greenleaf Boulevard. Jackson and I heard the shot and a vehicle speeding away while we were still looking at Lee's brain matter and bone fragments scattered amongst broken crack pipes.

Less than two hours later, while still at the Del Mar, we heard gunshots at an apartment complex just two blocks away. Jackson, Officer Roberto Valentin and I stopped Neighborhood Crips Charles "Buster" Goshen and Kevin "Slip Rock" Rice running away from the complex. While Jackson and Valentin detained them at gunpoint, I followed the smell of gun smoke to a downstairs apartment. Donald "Don Juan" Stallworth was sitting on a couch, dead from a bullet hole in his heart. Another man was on the floor with a bullet in his ass. Buster had killed Stallworth for talking shit about his brother, Jody "Popcorn" Goshen, recently murdered behind the Coronet Motel. Buster shot the other man for laughing.

When I got home the next morning, my clothes were piled up on the drive-way, and my academy and Marine Corps pictures were ripped in half. Gilda refused to let me in as she yelled and cursed at me through the door, all while Mrs. Kravitz and CC sat in their living room window. I gathered my things from the driveway and rented a room at the Willowtree Inn in Compton just north of the 91 freeway. I had no idea that it would be my home for the next six months. My divorce was quick since neither of us owned anything, but my credit went to shit because of my new child support payments. I survived by frequently picking up a bucket of chicken from KFC before getting off work. I worked as much as I could to keep my head above water, so I didn't see my kids that often.

I asked Darlene to marry me before the ink on my divorce papers was dry. I was still living at the Willowtree. She lived in Compton with her parents and was from an excellent family. Not only that, Darlene was smart, and a hustler who was good with her money and could possibly help me get on my feet, or at the very least out of that Goddamned hotel where there had been three unsuccessful attempts to steal my car as I slept. Her mother was a sweetheart, and her father was an honest, hard-working, and decent man, but he didn't seem to like me for some reason. He never disrespected me or said anything untoward, but my instincts about people were seldom wrong. A week before the wedding, I stopped by Darlene's house to take a nap. I was lying on the living room couch when I heard her father talking to her mother in the kitchen. He said, "I still don't know about her marrying this guy. I don't think it is fair she should marry into a ready-made family and have to take care of kids that ain't hers." With the riddle of why her father didn't like me solved, I called off the wedding. Darlene slapped me and ran away in tears, but she would get her revenge years later by sleeping with another Compton cop who smiled in my face every day because he thought I didn't know.

Not long after the break-up, I was at an illegal after-hours gambling spot in LA near Crenshaw Blvd. I was having a good night on the crap table and went to the bathroom to take a piss after I finally crapped out. I heard the front door to the building crash in just as I finished and then voices yelling, "Police! Police! Don't move!" I may have considered gambling a harmless vice, but my chief would have fired me had I been caught. I stepped on the toilet seat and climbed out the window, dropping onto the alleyway and running away with about $1,200 more than I had when the day started. The cops didn't have the back covered, and I made them pay for their mistake. The next day, I bought my kids a brand-new Dell computer.

CHAPTER THIRTEEN

IN 1989, President George H.W. Bush called drugs the most significant domestic threat facing our nation and vowed to escalate funding for the war on drugs. He approved the 1033 program, which equipped local and state police with military-grade equipment. Crack houses, fortified with bars on the windows and doors, had been around for several years. Buyers handed their money through the mail slots of barred doors in exchange for crack. Impenetrable to would-be robbers and law-enforcement alike, these crack houses made millions of dollars a year. Daryl Gates was the first police chief to take advantage of the program, using tanks equipped with rams to crash through the fortified doors. This entry method would become so common that Compton-bred rapper Toddy-Tee wrote a popular song about it titled, "The Batter Ram."

During the heyday of crack houses, our narcotics unit, led by Sergeant R.E. Allen, served multiple Search warrants a day. A uniformed officer went with them to the front door, and another one went to the back door. Patrol officers were never allowed in the houses. We were there strictly to transport prisoners and stop people from running away. The first time I helped on a warrant, R.E. had me go to the front door. He told the other cop, a heavily muscled, medium-complexioned guy without much common sense named Robert "Chilly" Childs, to stand by the back door. When R.E. and his team broke the front door down, a dealer ran out the back past Chilly and got away. R.E. was furious. He asked Chilly why he didn't stop the dealer, and Chilly replied, "You told me to stand by the door. So that's what I did."

Laws for people caught with crack cocaine had become far stricter than for people caught with powder cocaine. Crack was prevalent in the inner city, powder commonplace in the suburbs. As a result, the prison system soon became overcrowded with Black and Brown people. Most were guilty of nothing more than being addicted to a substance that was ostensibly introduced to them by the same government that was now imprisoning them for their addiction. At one time, cocaine was rare in the inner-city, and suddenly, courtesy of CIA-backed Central American drug lords, it was everywhere. Even law-enforcement officers got caught with their hands in crack cookie jars, as two Compton cops got fired for incidents involving the drug. One was fired after beating up his wife, also a Compton cop, during a cocaine-induced furor. Another one stole cocaine during a sting operation after persistent rumors that he was robbing dealers. R.E.'s narcotics team arrested him on the backlot as he was about to go home, still in possession of the crack stolen during a fake radio call he was sent to.

Every cocaine arrest led to a subpoena for the officers who witnessed the crime and booked the dope as evidence. They would then get overtime for a minimum of 2.5 hours with every appearance in court. Some officers cleared briefing and kissed off calls and chased crackheads all shift to ensure they received a subpoena every day. The war on drugs was a farce; it became equivalent to bounty hunting. Sometimes there would be ten to twelve officers in the second-floor lunchroom of Fort Compton getting paid overtime for cases they would never even testify on. Duane Bookman was one of the most prolific bounty hunters on the department. He was a muscular, dark-skinned cop from Texas who had a slight paunch and a small Afro with a pencil-thin mustache. He hated crack dealers and smokers. His first wife got addicted to crack. After that he saw red whenever he came across a dealer or smoker. Many of them felt his prowess with his 187 Beavertail sap firsthand. Bookman made so many dope arrests the defense attorneys began comparing notes. His reports became known as "Bookman drops" because they all read the same: "While driving my patrol car on [insert street], I saw the subject look at me with a startled look on his/her face before tossing a small clear baggie to the debris-free ground. Upon exiting my car, I saw that the baggie contained a beige, rock-like item resembling cocaine. I then placed the subject under arrest."

The defense attorneys launched an all-out effort to get Bookman barred from testifying if not indicted. Several prosecutors agreed, refusing to file his cases, and the chief put him on desk duty for several months. The prosecutors left him alone after several of them went on ride-a-longs and saw first-hand as smokers and dealers dropped crack on the ground at the sight of approaching police cars. It might seem stupid to a layperson that someone would take a chance and drop drugs in front of the police, but people discarded drugs because cops routinely violated their Fourth Amendment rights. They knew that they were subject to being stopped and searched for no reason. They figured why not take a chance and discard the dope and hope the cops didn't see it, rather than have the cops find it on them and lie about how they found it? By disregarding citizen's fundamental constitutional rights, cops had perverted the system by having citizens take a chance on incriminating themselves out of fear of having those rights violated.

One of the most popular locations to buy crack in Compton was the 600 block of South Santa Fe Avenue, known as the Santa Fe Gardens. The gang controlling the crack business was the Santa Fe Mafia Crips, headed by Vincent "Dog" Watkins and his brother Glenn. There was a large alleyway on the west side of the street behind the complex.

Cars lined up in the alley like they were at a fast-food restaurant. It was difficult catching the dealers, as they all had walkie-talkies and were in communication with lookouts. High-powered rifles and high-capacity handguns were either on their persons or stashed nearby in bushes, hallways of the apartments, or the wheel wells or trunks of parked cars. During one PM shift, Evelyn Malachi was the field sergeant. She had a friend who owned a limo company. She borrowed a stretch limo and loaded it up with cops. When the limo pulled into the alley, the cops jumped out and arrested the dealers.

The Santa Fe drug dealing got shut down for a few hours, but all it meant was that other drug dealers in the city made more money as the customers went to them instead. Ironically, the commander-in-chief of the current war on drugs lived in the Santa Fe Gardens in 1949 and 1950. He worked for Dresser Industries selling oil-drilling equipment while his wife Barbara took care of their son George W. Their daughter Robin was born in Compton. Twenty years later, four teenagers were playing in a garage behind 625 South Santa Fe when one accidentally fell over a naked dead woman. She had been kidnapped, raped, and stabbed multiple times at a house in Los Angeles before being dumped across the street from the former residence of two future presidents of the United States.

Robert "Blue" Williams grew up around the corner from West Park on Alondra Boulevard, yet another location rife with crack dealers. His parents still lived in the same house, and we stopped there for code-7 many times. Blue was a dark-skinned cop with a shaved head who weighed 245 pounds, ran a four-four 40, and bench pressed over 400 pounds. He was an All-South Bay running back for the State champion Compton High School football team in the early 1980s and is now a member of the school's hall of fame. He went to Washington State University on a full-ride scholarship and then returned to his hometown and became a cop after obtaining his degree.

Other than James Lewis and Marvin Pollard, a former Banning High School football star named one of the five best defensive backs in the nation in 1986, Blue was the fastest cop on the department. He was also one of the quirkiest. He loved the song "Vapors" by Rapper Biz Markie, and in an intensely deep voice which was a mixture of James Earl Jones and Isaac Hayes, he frequently quoted the hook while cocking his head to the side whenever he thought someone was full of shit. Blue was very familiar with most of the Nutty Blocc and Tragniew Park Crips because he had gone to school with a lot of them. On one occasion we stopped a Nutty Blocc Crip, who Blue knew was selling crack because Blue saw him doing it when he was on his way to work.

We made him put his hands on the hood of our patrol car with his feet spread apart so Blue could search him. He was wearing a Yankees Starter jacket and a Yankees ball cap. NBCC gang members chose New York Yankees gear because of the prominent "NY," which to them stood for "Nutty." Their base of operations was the Grandee apartment complex located across from the Compton airport. The complex was in a "U" configuration, so they called it Yankee Stadium. Blue found a bag of crack in the Yankee fan's socks and held it up. Blue said, "Now, what do we have here?" The Yankee fan suddenly sprinted off. Blue tossed the crack to me and said, "Hold this, Fred," before running after him.

I leaned up against the hood of our patrol car and lit a Newport. After taking a few puffs, I flicked it away and drove to where Blue was handcuffing him.

Blue wasn't even breathing hard. Although a recipient of a degree from a highly regarded university courtesy of his athletic prowess, his reports were notorious for improper syntax, grammar, and spelling and were the bane of John Garrett's existence. Blue was my friend. Plus, I didn't want to be in the station all night while he and Garrett jousted over the arrest report, so I looked at him, smiled, and said, "Since he caught the vapors, I'll scratch the paper." Blue just cocked his head to the side and put the exhausted gangster in the back seat.

Compton PD was one of the lowest-paid police departments in the state. Most of us had to work security jobs to make ends meet because of either child support, alimony commitments, or mistress and brook support. Several detectives had contracts with businesses that employed off-duty cops as security. Detective Phillip Bailey had taken advantage of the havoc wreaked at the Swap Meet by the CC Riders and now had off-duty officers working there from opening to closing seven days a week. A few other detectives had security contracts, but Blue was the only patrol cop who had one.

In the mid-80s, the city contracted to have a hotel built on Artesia. After experiencing a series of setbacks and financial difficulties, the city took over the hotel's day-to-day operations and hired Satra Zurita as the hotel manager. Her first cousin was Omar Bradley, a city council member who had considerable influence over the hotel's operations and the daily bingo games. The games generated a great deal of cash, so there was a need for security. Blue and Hourie Taylor, then the chief of police, butted heads big time over this issue. Early on, Satra had offered Blue the opportunity to obtain the lucrative security contract.

Retired Police Commander Thomas Armstrong had thrown his hat in the ring to get the contract, and Hourie was pulling for him to get it. Hourie was in over his head, though. Omar was the de facto head of the hotel and bingo games. When he said he wanted Blue and Satra to have the security contract, it was a done deal. Satra and Blue partnered to provide security for the hotel, with Blue as the muscle and face, and Satra as the brains behind the scenes.

They named the company RSK Security, an acronym for Robert, Satra, and the initial of the attorney's last name who drafted the business's paperwork to obtain licenses. I was one of the first cops they hired.

Satra was born and raised in Compton. She was on the cheerleading team the year Blue's team won the State Championship. She was smart, pretty, and had a sparkling personality and a firm grasp on the city's pulse. While I was working at the hotel one night, a gangster was giving the front desk clerk a hard time. He was wearing black khaki trousers and a red Pendleton shirt. He looked at me like I was a bug on the bottom of his red Chuck Taylor's when I walked over. He yelled, "What the fuck you want, Blood? You better get the fuck out my face!" I told him to calm down and he looked at me menacingly and asked, "What, muthafucka? You know who I am?"

Satra walked up before I had a chance to answer. He calmed down when he saw her. She spoke to him in a soothing voice, saying, "Sylvester? What are you doing here? Come on, baby." She then took hold of his arm like they were on a date, and they walked away. About ten minutes later, she saw me walking in the lobby.

"Boy, you got some balls on you. You know who that was?"

I smiled and answered, "Naw. Is he supposed to be important?"

She laughed and replied, "Fool! That was Piru Puddin.'"

The hotel was one big playground for us. We did whatever we wanted. There was a nightclub near the front entrance called the Indigo Jazz Blue Room. Satra's first cousin was the bar manager, so we drank top-shelf liquor and bullshitted around until well after closing every weekend. When my brother David visited me one year, Satra threw a surprise birthday party for him in one of the larger suites, complete with food and champagne. On another occasion, she let Santa Fe Mafia Crip Glenn Watkins rent out a ballroom for Ice Cube's Lench Mob to perform. Blue and I worked security that night with several other cops. I woke up in a strange bed the next day, between a woman whose name I couldn't even remember and a crying baby in a playpen.

Lieutenant Mardrue Bunton was among the first Black cops hired at Compton PD. We had his retirement party at the hotel and gave him a rocking chair. When Bunton and the older cops and their wives went home, the younger cops had an after-party. I was friends with several strippers—and not Golden Garter trailer-trash, but ones with tiny waists and big booties with just the right amount of stretch marks. I had a few of them come to the hotel to dance in one of the ballrooms. Kevin Burrell was a legendary gourmand but couldn't hold his liquor to save his life. After only two beers, he stripped down to his white Fruit of the Loom jockey underwear and joined them. We played along and made it rain, and Kevin ended up with more money than the strippers. We had to use a wheelchair to get him to his room after he passed out. Before leaving, we ensured that two of the strippers stayed with him to welcome him back when he woke up.

The bingo games were the hotel's moneymaker and were run by Rueben Kandilian and Michael Aloyan. They were subservient to Omar, doing anything he said to keep their dream of a full-fledged casino in the future alive. Aloyan was a short, chubby, jovial man who smoked Ararat cigarettes. He wore cheap black suits with white dirt-stained collared shirts and smudged shoes. He had immigrated to America from Armenia in 1987, landed a job at Murcole Inc.; a trash firm with a contract in Compton, and by 1991 was the general manager. In 1992, he joined Kandilian in a bid to open a casino at the hotel. Neither man had ever held a gaming license in California.

Kandilian was a monster of a man. He had a thick grey and white beard, stood well over six feet, and weighed over three hundred pounds. He dressed far more casually than Aloyan, always wearing short sleeve polo shirts and khaki trousers. Kandilian was aloof with everyone except Aloyan, Satra, Blue, and Omar, who visited the cash room often with his brother-in-law Lonnie Howard. The cash room was across the hall from the bingo games. On more than one occasion, I saw Omar and Howard, always in possession of a briefcase, go into the room with Kandilian. I don't know what happened in that cash room. But I do know what I saw. And except for the employees who worked in the cash room, I never saw anyone other than Kandilian, Aloyan, Omar, and Howard go back there.

A lot of suspicious shit took place at the hotel over the years. But to get it to the point where it became our playground and the city to where it became financially unstable, you have to go all the way back to the early 1970s.

CHAPTER FOURTEEN

NAFTALI "TULI" Deutsch was a Holocaust Survivor and an orphan of parents murdered by Nazis. After WWII, he made his way to Israel and then to the United States, where he became a self-made multimillionaire in real estate and construction. By 1973, he was the principal owner of the Westbrook Development Company. Under his leadership, the company developed a $3 million commercial center featuring a thirty-two-lane bowling alley in the city of Garden Grove, one of many great accomplishments.

In 1975, Maxcy Filer and Jane Robbins replaced disgraced council members Hillard Hamm and Russell Woolfork. Three years later, Compton developed a city-owned property tract by selling $21 million worth of Walnut Industrial Park Project bonds. The same year, UDAG, a new U.S. Housing and Urban Development program, gave Compton a $2.1 million grant to start its first home construction in twenty years. The city loaned the money to Hub City Urban Developers, a non-profit firm organized by a group of community leaders who used a renovated Foster Freeze ice cream factory on Alondra Blvd as its headquarters. Soon after that, the city had to loan them another $3 million to complete the construction project.

In August of 1982, ground was broken on a 1,600-room, $200 million Hilton Hotel in Anaheim. The C-D Investment Co.—a firm jointly owned by Deutsch and Alexander Coler—served as the construction management company. Earlier in the year, Deutsch and Coler became limited partners in sixteen properties, including the LA Airport Hilton and adjoining Century Center complex.

In 1984, the city council hired Paul Richards, a close friend and former business associate of Bob Adams's son, Laurence, to fill the newly created post of city council chief of staff. Councilpersons Filer and Robbins opposed the hiring because they considered the position unnecessary. Still, their two votes were not enough to overcome the votes of Councilmen Bob Adams, Floyd James, and Mayor Walter Tucker Jr.

In December of 1984, the city issued another $10 million in revenue bonds to finance the Walnut Park Project and construct a three-hundred-room hotel. The proposed tax increases on Compton citizens projected to $1.6 million annually for thirty years. The city hired the Tucon Construction Company as the general contractor for the hotel and a future convention center complex, which were to be owned by D&B Development and Lazben Financial. Tuli Deutsch and his sons, Laurence and Benjamin, owned all three firms. Despite Alexander Coler and Tuli's recent partnership in constructing the Anaheim Hilton, they chose not to partner for the Compton project. It is unclear why, given their recent success together, but shortly after the city hired Deutsch to build the hotel, Tucker Jr. held a fund-raising campaign dinner at the LA Airport Hilton.

Among the most significant contributors were AFCOM and the LA investment banking firm of Bancroft, O'Conner, Chilton, and Lavell. The firm underwrote the bonds for the construction of the Compton Hotel. AFCOM also developed 291 units in the Compton Sunny Cove housing project in 1984, with $22 million in city-sponsored mortgage revenue bonds. When a car dealership in the city-sponsored Alameda Auto Plaza had gone bankrupt a few years earlier, the city bought the property for $2.4 million. Less than three months later, the city gave Brett Mitchell, a young Black entrepreneur, a sweetheart deal to open a Chevrolet dealership there. Mitchell had previously bought two parcels of land in downtown Compton from the city for $35,000. Within one year, he sold them back to the city for $725,000. He used the money to move into the Alameda auto plaza and open Brett Mitchell Chevrolet. The city gave him a five-year subsidized lease on the property, and for the first year, he was charged only $200 a month. During his first two years in business, he gave thousands of dollars in campaign contributions to Tucker Jr., Bob Adams and James in addition to donating money at the campaign dinner. Adams and James received $22,000 of the money raised that night. The three of them consistently formed the decision-making majority on the city council, and between 1985 and 1987 received about $262,000 from campaign contributors.

On January 29, 1985, Governor George Deukmejian appointed City Manager Laverta Montgomery as one of the first commissioners of the newly created State Lottery Commission. With her new duties, she was hardly ever in Compton. Council members, most notably Bob Adams, complained about her not doing her job, and she was fired. Jim Goins was hired as the new city manager over Howard Caldwell, Montgomery's assistant city manager. Goins created another new post called the "special assistant to the city manager's office," and appointed Laurence Adams despite Maxcy Filer's accusations of nepotism. Laurence was Bob Adams's middle child and the most ambitious. A corpulent man who smiled a lot, he always reminded me of someone who would shake your hand and make you think to check for your wallet as he walked away.

Within a year, Goins promoted Adams to redevelopment director and promoted Paul Richards to another newly created position, the "assistant city manager for community development and public policy." Richards would subsequently be elected Mayor of Lynwood with the help of $13,000 raised by Laurence Adams and passed through Bob Adams's re-election committee the following year.

In April, Tucker Jr., wearing a hard hat and wielding a gold-plated shovel, broke ground on the Compton Hotel. Three months later, the San Pedro City Council approved the construction of a 232-room hotel in San Pedro by Beacon Street Associates and the Lazben Hotel Investment Company at a projected cost of $20 million. Beacon Street Associates was an arm of Goldrich & Kest Industries, the same corporation that owned and operated the Wilmington Arms Complex.

By October, the city officials were worried about the $5.1 million loaned to Hub City. Laverta Montgomery had previously written a memo to city officials about Hub City being unable to repay the loan, having missed $68,500 in interest payments on a million-dollar construction loan from Family Savings and Loan. Compton had allowed an unusual escape clause in its 1979 contract with Hub City that forgave the repayment of a $1.19 million interest-free loan, enabling them to buy the Foster Freeze factory. Regional HUD officials said they had never seen such a provision in any of the over forty-five UDAG programs they had issued to date. Unlike most HUD grants that underwrite a single project, UDAG money should be recycled from one community development to another as it is loaned, repaid, and loaned again, which means that any debt forgiveness defeats its primary purpose. HUD officials came to regard the Hub City endeavor as one of their biggest failures.

In 1986 the city council approved a $40 million redevelopment bond sale that would funnel $11 million back to the city's general fund. The other $29 million was to help finance various redevelopment projects, including the hotel, an entertainment complex, and a shopping mall. The city would pay off the bonds over thirty-six years at an interest rate not to exceed 9.6 percent. Filer questioned the legality of it but was disregarded by his peers. He also did not believe the city could handle the additional debt, especially when added to the Walnut Industrial Park bonds, loans, and other recent revenue loss. Work at the hotel halted while city officials scrambled to arrange a $5.5 million loan request by Deutsch to complete construction. Besides the loan, a council majority voted to allow him the rights for ten years to purchase the five acres where the hotel, convention center, and parking garage would be built.

The city also voted to allow him the rights for two years after completing the hotel to develop the five-acre parcel of land next to the hotel. Filer was the only one to vote no. Two years after being awarded the contract to build the hotel, Tuli Deutsch spent $30,000 of Compton taxpayer money to find a name for the new hotel. According to him, after consulting several public relations firms and running hundreds of possible names past prospective clients, he found the perfect one—Lazben, which was a combination of his son's first names: Laurence, Andrew, Zachary, and Benjamin.

In May of 1987, Brett Mitchell told the city council that he needed a loan of $175,000 to expand his business. Tucker, Bob Adams, and James voted to give him the loan with Adams going so far as to compare Mitchell's struggles to those of Lee Iacocca, who is credited with saving Chrysler from bankruptcy. The city loaned Mitchell the money at 7 percent interest, far below what banks were charging their best commercial customers that year.

The following year, Mitchell was awarded the Young Entrepreneur Award by the U.S. Small Business Administration and showcased in an issue of *Jet* magazine featuring Latoya Jackson. At the time, Mitchell's reported annual sales were $12.6 million. Most of his sales were to local drug dealers and gang members. Every time I stopped a Chevrolet IROC Z-28, a drug dealer was driving it, and it was bearing Brett Mitchell Chevrolet paper plates or license plate frames. Less than a year after the Jet magazine article was published, the DMV suspended Mitchell's operating license, and the State Board of Equalization issued a lien for $110,721 against his dealership. Despite his reported gaudy annual sales numbers, he still owed the city $115,887 on his loan and $12,000 in back rent. He subsequently went out of business, bouncing a check to the city for $9,000 on his way out the door.

On November 20, 1988, Tuli Deutsch sent a letter to council members claiming the city was responsible for paying back wages to hotel construction workers after state labor officials ruled the workers had been underpaid. The state Department of Industrial Relations disagreed. Since the hotel was a public works project built with city redevelopment funds and city-backed loans, Tucon was responsible for paying the wages, not the city. Tucon subsequently laid off two hundred workers right before Thanksgiving. They now owed $3.3 million in penalties and back payments to the workers. The state also levied a $186,000 fine against Tucon because Tucon failed to provide workers with itemized payroll deduction statements. In December, State labor officials froze payments from the city to Tucon.

Deutsch told city officials that he could not continue working on the hotel because he was $3 million short. He agreed to raise $1.5 million if the city loaned him the rest. The city council voted 4-1 to lend him the money. Filer was the lone dissenting vote. This latest loan brought Deutsch's debt to the city to $6.75 million, which he was supposed to pay in its entirety plus interest by May of 1990. Other than Filer, no one cared that the city was essentially giving him almost half of what the state had ordered him to pay in penalties and back wages.

By the beginning of 1989, the federal government pressed Compton to demand repayment of the UDAG loan steered to Hub City. Hub City also never repaid Compton $3 million in other loans. On March 30, Dalton Construction, the contractor on Compton's multipurpose transit center, was in default for failing to complete the project. The city had already paid the firm $2.5 million of the $4.1 million allocated for the project. Not surprisingly, the firm's owner had periodically given sizeable campaign donations to Tucker Jr., Bob Adams, and James.

In April, Jim Goins told the city council that the city must come up with $11 million to balance the 1990 budget or lay off multiple city employees. He also proposed raising taxes on phone, gas, and electricity bills, joining a cooperative liability insurance pool with other cities, even selling South Park. Goins suggested just about everything except collecting the debts owed by Deutsch, Brett Mitchell, HUB, and Dalton Construction, which would have made the city whole again *without* laying off employees. In July, Tucker Jr. directed Goins to demote four police lieutenants and four sergeants to save money in the interim. He also called for the dismantling of the department and contracting with the sheriff's department due to the police department's "inability to deal with the city's high crime rate." Meanwhile, his wife Martha had pleaded guilty to three grand theft counts just one year previously for swindling $300,000 from ten people during real-estate transactions.

Laurence Adams wore many hats, including that of president of the local chapter on Camp Fire, Inc. In August, Jim Goins fired him after Adams requested that each developer doing business with the city contribute $6,000 to his Camp Fire chapter. James Chilton was a Century City investment banker and developer. He had helped the city float several million dollars in redevelopment bonds in the recent past. He alleged that Adams asked him to contribute around the time that the Community Redevelopment Agency (CRA) and Chilton's firm were wrapping up the deal for the Walnut Industrial Park project.

Shortly after Goins fired Adams, the city council fired Goins and promoted Howard Caldwell. Within a month, Caldwell placed City Controller Timothy Brown on administrative leave for "revealing the city's bleak financial situation" during a council meeting. According to Brown, the city had almost $6 million in outstanding bills, contracts, and purchase orders from the previous fiscal year. City Treasurer Wesley Sanders Sr. confirmed the deficit. The city had only $3.2 million on-hand compared to $7 million through the same period. The city's bi-monthly payroll was $1 million, and weekly expenses were between $200,000 and $300,000. The deficit caused Compton to delay payments to vendors to ensure that employees received their paychecks. Within two years, Caldwell hired Laurence Adams as his special assistant. Despite the city always being in financial distress, the same people were being hired, fired, and rehired.

Chief Ivory Webb retired on February 28, 1990, under an early retirement incentive designed to ease the city's budget problems. Commander Terry Ebert, a White, somewhat reserved twenty-three-year veteran, was named chief. By April, the other three commanders—Tommy Armstrong, Tony Ruiz, and Dallas Elvis—retired after the city replaced their positions with three lower-paid captain positions. As many as twenty other city employees also retired instead of being laid off or fired, saving the city $450,000 through June 30. Additionally, the city canceled future promotions and cut our overtime, even though there had been an average of seventy murders a year since 1985.

Webb was a great chief and visionary during his brief tenure, having been able to get the city to purchase two helicopters, two K-9 units, and four traffic unit motorcycles in 1986. His brightest moment as chief came on September 9, 1988, when he pinned helicopter wings on Angelia Myles, making her the first female police helicopter pilot on the West coast. But no matter how many innovations Webb introduced, he couldn't change the demographics of the department. As such, his accomplishments did little to garner respect from surrounding law-enforcement agencies. Some of them still employed officers from the turbulent 1960s and, in some cases, the 1950s. To these agencies, Compton PD was a department run by "niggers, gangsters with badges and guns." Sheriff's deputies had little respect for Compton PD personnel and even ridiculed our helicopter, painted yellow and blue to reflect our uniforms, by calling it a flying banana.

Deputies also often maligned us during contacts with Compton citizens and criminals, calling us "F-Troop," "Dum-Dums," and much worse. Deputies came into Compton frequently to make arrests, a practice known as "poaching" because they were out of their areas. They would then lie to their supervisors to justify their reasons for being in Compton.

During one incident, deputies poaching in Compton resulted in a confrontation that could have led to a tragedy of epic proportions. On August 29, 1991, Douglas Slaughter, a Black Compton officer, was working undercover on a bicycle at the Metro Rail transit center due to a rash of auto burglaries. He left to get a cup of coffee at Louis Burgers just a few blocks from the police station.

Slaughter was suddenly surrounded by four LA County Sheriff's deputies, three White and one Latino, who had arrived in two cars. Slaughter held up his badge and identified himself, but the deputies still ordered him to lay on the ground at gunpoint. They handcuffed him even after seeing his police radio and his repeatedly telling them to get his photo identification from his back pocket. Sergeant Garrett arrived in full uniform and a marked patrol vehicle, and the deputies still refused to remove the handcuffs until their supervisor arrived twenty minutes later. Sheriff's Department Chief Duane Preimsberger later wrote a letter of apology to Slaughter and attended all three Compton shift briefings to apologize.

The slow descent of the department began in earnest with Webb's departure. The future of the department was in jeopardy. Five officers transferred to the Redondo Beach Police Department, three went to the Rialto Police Department, one to Downey PD, one to UCLA PD, one to Glendale PD, one to Bell PD, one to LAPD, and two to the sheriff's department. Most of them were tenured officers with a wealth of knowledge and experience. Their departures severely impacted the department, as the void it created represented close to fifteen percent of the total number of Compton cops. The city officials didn't care. There were always plenty of reserves willing to work. The city was now paying them ten dollars an hour, even though all the other agencies still paid theirs one dollar a year. The city was saving a tremendous amount of money by not filling the vacancies. I can recall any given night on the PM shift that there would be at least six reserve officers working. Some of them wanted to be regular officers, but the city put a freeze on hiring to continue saving money.

The city had a budget for the police department, which included salaries and benefits for 135 officers. The department never reached this number, so it was salary savings for the city. Most years, the department never had more than 121 officers. If the budget was $24 million, this accounted for officers not yet hired as well. Every year the department wasn't at full strength, the money remained in the general fund. It was obviously being used for something else, but certainly not to balance the budget.

In the spring of 1990, the Deutsch family defaulted on $6.8 million in construction loans from the city. Although three years past the original expected completion date, the hotel's top four floors were still not finished. By now, the city had invested $35 million in the hotel. Tuli declared personal bankruptcy and was now merely a consultant. He signed many original agreements with the city, guaranteeing repayment and interest on $14.3 million of the bonds issued. In declaring bankruptcy, he no longer had any financial liability or any economic interest in the companies involved in building the hotel. His sons now owned and controlled all three firms. By September, the Lazben was the Ramada Hotel and Convention Center. Without the knowledge of city officials, the Deutsch family had purchased a franchise from Ramada for $88,200. The contract with the city regarding the hotel had precluded the developers from entering into agreements without city permission, but they did it anyway.

On October 1, 1990, Walter Tucker Jr. died of cancer. His body laid in state at city hall with two police officers from the department he had been so desperate to get rid of posted on either side of his casket. His son, Walter Tucker III, won a special election to replace him. Born to a family that many considered the Kennedy's of Compton, Tucker III graduated from Compton High in 1974 and then attended Princeton before finishing his studies at USC. He obtained a Juris Doctorate from Georgetown Law School in 1981. He returned to Compton afterwards where he served as a Los Angeles County Deputy District Attorney at Fort Compton from 1984 to 1986 until he was fired for falsifying evidence and lying to a judge. Following in his father's footsteps, one of his first acts as mayor was to call for the sheriff's department to replace the police department.

On June 30, 1991, Maxcy D. Filer's tenure with the city came to an end. Tucker Jr. may have hated the police department, but Filer loved it. He passionately defended it every step of the way, no doubt remembering when the all-White city council tried to bring in the sheriff's department to stop additional hiring of Black police officers. Known as Mr. Compton, Filer had been a watchdog for Compton's citizens and fought for their best interest at every turn. As honest as the councilman he replaced was corrupt, he could not have been a better choice. With his departure from Compton's government, there would be no one on the horizon to keep the agents of avarice under control. A fierce advocate for equal rights and social justice, he was a former president of the Compton NAACP. His commitment led to his being the flag bearer for the organization's Southern California delegation's 1963 March on DC, where MLK delivered his "I Have a Dream" speech.

After obtaining his law degree, Filer took the state bar exam forty-eight times between 1967 and 1991 before finally passing it. Some have called him incompetent for having failed it so many times. I look at it in another way. To me, it is a manifestation of the spirit he had displayed during the Civil Rights Movement; an unwavering commitment to an ideal and dogged determination to obtain something at all costs. That fervor for justice ran heavily in his bloodline, as his son, Kelvin Filer, would become a defense attorney and later a judge at Fort Compton. Kelvin's brother, Anthony, and his daughter, Kree, would also become attorneys.

Omar Bradley won Filer's seat. Bob Adams and Floyd James had lost their seats in 1989, so Tucker III, Omar, Patricia Moore, Jane Robbins, and Bernice Woods now formed the city council. Howard Caldwell promoted Laurence Adams to Community Redevelopment Director again in July of 1991. Adams stepped right into dealing directly with the Deutsch family. He said an appraisal showed that the hotel was worth $40 million even though the top floor was still under construction, and 5,800-square feet at the back of the hotel didn't have electricity, plumbing, paint, or carpet. Just two months later, the city council voted to take control of operations of the now nearly deserted hotel and convention center. The city contended that Tuli Deutsch breached the contract. Deutsch countered, saying that he invested millions of dollars of his own money in the hotel and demanded *compensation*.

The city council voted to grant LA Raiders pro football player Greg Townsend a liquor license and open the "Raider Sports Bar and Club" in the unfinished area. Townsend estimated that renovation and opening costs would be about $300,000. Council members voted to loan him half at 8 percent interest from the city's allotment of federal funds. The renovation was completed within three months. The club opened in September of 1991 but closed just six months later. Shortly afterward, the city agreed to sell the hotel to Cal-State Progressive, Inc., for just $24.4 million. When the company failed to live up to the terms of the contract, the city kicked them out, hired Satra Zurita as the hotel director, and allowed Rueben Kandilian and Michael Aloyan to run nightly bingo games.

In October of 1992, the Lynwood City Council voted unanimously to hire Laurence Adams as the new city manager. At the time, Paul Richards was the mayor, so perhaps this was his way of paying Adams back for Richards's created positions in Compton. Richards was also friends with Tucker III and Omar. The four of them now had a stranglehold on the Compton and Lynwood governments.

Before the hotel debacle, the Community Redevelopment Agency had been incredibly sound financially. Real estate in the redevelopment zone, which included the downtown area and the Walnut Park project, jumped from $159 million in 1973 to $479 million by 1984. Annual revenues to the redevelopment agency increased from $1.9 million to $7.8 million during the same time frame, which covered agency payments on the $36 million bond and paid off old bond debts, too.

The blame for the hotel fiasco doesn't all lie with Tuli Deutsch and his sons, however. Most of it lies with the city of Compton. People get taken advantage of in business all the time. And if nothing else, Tuli and his sons were business-men. But the political corruption going on in Compton was beyond belief. The city politicians were thieves who stole the dreams of their constituents. They didn't use guns; they used words and contracts, falsehoods, and fragile ideals. Eloquent politicians who are charming speakers with hidden agendas are much more dangerous than honest, inarticulate buffoons, which was how Filer's peers viewed him and possibly how potential investors and grifters saw him as well. In a city awash in blood, the more innocuous white-collar crimes and political graft went unnoticed by everyone but Filer and Eddie Randolph. The abattoir contained in just 10.1 square miles was the perfect diversion, reminiscent of Washington, DC, where wars and other military actions divert attention from the ever-present red and blue hands in the cookie jars of every home in America.

Patricia Moore and Walter Tucker III, now a US congressman, would be indicted by a federal grand jury on August 31, 1995. Moore, who tooled around the city in a black Rolls Royce, extorted $62,000 from Compton Entertainment Inc. and Compton Energy Systems. The businesses were seeking licenses to operate a card club in the Ramada Hotel and to build a waste-to-energy facility in the city. Tucker III extorted $37,500 from two other waste companies and attempted to extort $250,000 from Compton Energy Systems in 1991 to back the company's project. Michael Aloyan, also indicted, was granted immunity after agreeing to testify against Tucker III and Moore. They were convicted and sentenced to twenty-seven and thirty-three months in federal prison, respectively.

After Moore and Tucker III went away, Omar, his Aunt Delores Zurita, Yvonne Arceneaux, Marcine Shaw, and Fred Cressel were the latest Compton kakistocracy, with Omar as the mayor as he had defeated Moore in a special election after Tucker III became a member of congress. The council voted to lease the hotel to Hollywood Park and San Francisco 49ers owner Edward DeBartolo Jr. for fifty years. Hollywood Park leased the convention center to Ruben Kandillian and Compton Entertainment, who parlayed the bingo games into a high stakes card club. Hollywood Park then put $30 million into the hotel and renamed it the Crystal Park Hotel and Casino.

Within two years, Kandilian ran his part of the business into the ground by gambling with the players, defaulting on a $5 million bank loan, and failing to pay his monthly rent of $350,000. There was doubt that the city would move against him since the casino employed Omar's wife Robin and several other family members. Soon that decision was taken out of their hands. In October 1997, Hourie Taylor, John Swanson, Stoney Jackson, and Sergeant Tom Barclay assisted the Department of Justice in shutting down the casino because Kandilian did not have enough cash to cover his outstanding chips and owed $1 million in back gaming taxes.

As a courtesy, the DOJ had let Hourie know about the investigation and requested the police department's assistance when they served the warrants. Hourie and Howard Caldwell were good friends and confidants. Hourie told Caldwell what was going on but expressly told him not to tell Omar. Omar was furious when he found out. The incident would lead to lasting hatred between Omar and Hourie, as Omar began to doggedly believe that Hourie was assisting federal agencies in investigating city officials. After the DOJ's intervention, the good times came to an end for us, and our playground was shut down for good.

Declaring bankruptcy certainly didn't hurt Tuli Deutsch. As of 2012, he lived in an 18,400-square-foot mansion in Beverly Hills with an even larger property next door where his sons lived. The properties have a combined value of nearly $17.5 million. Tuli and his sons were now neighbors with Tuli's long-time partner, Alexander Coler, who in 1988 had purchased an eleven-bedroom, nineteen-bath, 37,000-square-foot chateau that was valued at $30 million, at the time one of the most expensive homes in the nation.

As of 2017, the hotel was owned by a Chinese investor and the casino was owned by the Keligian family. It is now named the LA Crystal Hotel and Casino. The revenue from the hotel is based on a Transit Occupancy Tax that was initially voted down by the citizens. An unconfirmed rumor has it that it was because the voters believed that it was literally a tax on "transients." The casino generates between $1.5 million and $2 million a month. The city gets a portion of that revenue based on a sliding scale depending on the monthly revenue, so the city gets approximately 10% or $2 million annually from just the casino.

Even still, as of 2020, Compton was facing bankruptcy and faltering on delivering basic services to citizens. It is facing a $113 million deficit, and from 2017 through 2020 it was ranked as the worst city financially in the state. The city has no credit or bond rating, and the citizens pay some of the highest taxes in the state.

RIP and Semper Fi, Eddie Randolph, and God bless you, Maxcy Filer. You both always knew the depths of corruption in Compton and tried to sound the alarm, but no one bothered to listen.

CHAPTER FIFTEEN

I WAS assigned to district four my entire patrol career. The biggest and most active gang in the area was the Southside Compton Crips (SSCC). I knew most of them. Fat Jack had religiously preached about district integrity, meaning you stayed in your assigned area as much as possible, only coming out if the dispatcher gave you a call in another district or if a unit asked for help. Fat Jack had a soft spot in his heart for an SSCC member named Michael "Owl" Dorrough. His mother, Carrie, had once worked for the police department in the property and evidence room and was extremely well-liked. Fat Jack told me it broke his heart when her son went down the wrong path.

The SSCC gang took their name from South Park, located at the southern portion of their hood, just north of Greenleaf Boulevard. There was a canal just west of the park, which the members used as a graffiti canvass to glorify themselves, mourn fallen soldiers, and threaten rivals. The park structures were painted blue and yellow to represent the gang's colors, taken from the Seattle Mariners baseball team. Every gang in the city had what they referred to as "Hood Day", an annual event where the members got together to drink, smoke weed, barbeque, and handle hood business. The SSCC gang's hood day was on May 5, because May is the fifth month of the year and 5/5 resembles SS, for Southside.

The gang's main hangout was a house on the northwest corner of Temple and Glencoe, one of the few rundown areas in the neighborhood. There was a two-story structure behind the house that everyone called the treehouse because it was next to a large tree and had a long single flight of stairs to a door on the second story. Several people were murdered at this corner over the years, including tennis legends Serena and Venus Williams's sister in 2003.

I also knew many homeowners in my area. Most of them were hard-working people tired of the constant shootings and drug dealing. Other than a few houses with remnants of shots gone astray, most homes in the neighborhood were well kept with closely cropped grass, trimmed trees, and rose bushes. If you didn't know anything about the neighborhood and were just passing through, you would think it was a friendly, bedrock community as it was in the 1950s when it was one of the most affluent areas in the city. Now, it was just window dressing, as some of those well-kept residences were home to the most violent gang members in Compton. Unfortunately, the dressing on those windows were black steel bars, just like on the doors. Most of the houses, like most of the others throughout the city, had unleashed dogs patrolling the backyards. The dog of choice was overwhelmingly of the pit-bull variety, most of whom bore the battle scars so prevalent in the winners of the big money dogfights staged by the well-heeled gang members. The losers never made it back to their respective backyards; they were shot to death by their owners or killed outright in the ring.

I was off duty one day visiting a woman who lived in the neighborhood. We were kissing in the living room when Reggie Wright Sr. chased a guy who had just committed a robbery through the house. Reggie caught him in the backyard. Reggie looked at me and shook his head as he walked the guy to his patrol car. The guy he arrested had recently gotten out of prison and was the woman's brother. The next day, Reggie approached me at my locker. He said, "You dumb motherfucker. Stay out of that neighborhood when your off duty. They fucking hate you."

I policed the SSCC gang heavily because they caused the most trouble in my area. Correspondingly, Reggie was right. They hated me, but I couldn't care less. They weren't supposed to like me. Every chance I got, I stopped and searched them for guns. What was I supposed to do to gang members who I knew were carrying guns? Wait until after they shot someone? Drive past them and then come back later to clean up the bodies? Fuck that. Civil rights organizations and others call "Stop and Frisk" a violation of the Fourth Amendment. Yet the same groups support abolishing the Second Amendment to prevent mass shootings. They wanted to do the same thing I was doing. Violate an amendment and take guns to prevent shootings. What I was doing wasn't harassment. It was good policework. I was trying to provide the law-abiding citizens respite by giving the ones causing all the problems hell.

One of the more violent SSCC members was John "J-Bone" Cass. He was diminutive but dangerous, suspected of involvement in multiple murders. One night he did a drive-by shooting near Kevin Burrell's house. One of the victims was Kevin's cousin. Terrance Idlebird and Steve McMorris, a loud-mouthed, light-skinned Cajun from New Orleans who laughed non-stop, hung out at John's bar every night, and called all women "cher," got in pursuit of J-Bone's vehicle. I was the second unit behind them. J-Bone bailed out of his car when he got back to his hood. Idlebird and I tackled him and handcuffed him. When I grabbed his arm to get him to his feet, he began resisting and cursing at me for the benefit of a growing crowd. "Fuck you, Reynolds, you punk ass bitch" quickly turned into "Reynolds, you motherfucker! You broke my arm!" as I yanked him to his feet. I didn't try to break his arm, but he was resisting, and he was light in the ass. Idlebird and McMorris transported him to the hospital for treatment. When he threatened them, Idlebird promised to break his other arm if he didn't shut the fuck up. J-Bone took Idlebird's advice but later threatened the judge, prosecutor, and defense attorney when he was sentenced to thirty years in prison.

Darnell Brim was one of the most respected members of the gang. He had Southside Compton Crip tattoos on both arms and his nickname and PBK, an acronym for "Palmer Blocc Killer," on his right arm. His brother Wesley Earl was shot to death at Cincotta Park by Palmer Blocc Crips in 1982, which led to the PBCC vs. SSCC feud and Brim getting the PBK tattoo.

On August 26, 1991, I was driving with a trainee in heavy traffic in the MOB and Cross Atlantic Piru hood. I saw Brim driving a green Chevy IROC Camaro just ahead of us. Three other SSCCs were in the car with him, all wearing blue and yellow Seattle Mariner baseball caps. I immediately knew what was up. They were trying to inspire slow singing and flower-bringing in the very near future.

Brim saw me in his rearview mirror and sped off south on Atlantic Avenue, coming up fast on numerous cars stopped at the red light at Rosecrans. I thought he was going to rear-end one of them, but at the last minute, he swerved to the right. He drove southbound on the west sidewalk of Atlantic, causing multiple people to dive out of the way. Brim drove back onto Atlantic and sped out of sight as drivers swerved and slammed on their brakes. I pulled into the 7-11 at the northwest corner. The trainee was confused and asked, "Aren't we going after him, sir?" I ignored him, grabbed the radio, and put out a crime broadcast. Some cops probably would have gone in pursuit, further endangering the lives of innocent people. Not me. I knew who was driving.

We may have lost whatever guns they had in the car, but we had saved lives either from a shooting or from vehicular manslaughter. I wrote a felony evading report, thoroughly describing the danger that Brim put innocent citizens in as he recklessly drove through the city with his Brett Mitchell Chevrolet license plate frames proudly on display. Reggie Wright Jr. arrested Brim near the tree-house the following day as Brim stood next to his IROC. Brim didn't get any prison time for the incident, but he did get his first felony strike.

Gang members thrived off violence and fear in the community, preying on the weak and taking advantage of them. They terrorized the law-abiding citizens helplessly trapped in their own homes. The citizens were just as versed in what to do when a drive-by shooting occurred as they were when an earthquake did; children knew to get in the bathtub when they heard shooting, under the tables when they felt the ground shaking. While necessary, their survival instincts were just as tragic when considering that no child should have to worry about getting shot in their own home. No matter what you may think of a cop, they run toward the sound of gunfire while everyone else is running away or hiding. Most of the time, in Compton, gang members were the source of those shots.

I got promoted to FTO in January of 1991. During the first week of March, the department sent me to a two-week FTO training course. When I got to class on Thursday, March 7, the other students were gathered around the TV watching Rodney King get the shit beat out of him. Little did I know at the time that George Holliday, a White guy who videotaped the beating from his condominium in Lakeview Terrace, would one day become the father of police reform by turning on the kitchen light and exposing blue-hued cockroaches.

Although the incident had initially occurred after a vehicle pursuit on March 3, the news didn't show the video until several days later. I was the only Black cop in the class. The rest of the class didn't seem to think the beating was a big deal. They were wrong. Now there was irrefutable evidence supporting long-standing allegations of police brutality against Blacks. I knew there were going to be consequences if the involved cops were not held accountable. All White cops are not racist, just as all cops are not corrupt. To categorize all members of any race or profession in such general terms is moronic. But the reaction of the cops in that class was troubling. These were supposedly the cream of the crop from their respective agencies, tasked with training new police officers.

Their reactions to a Black man being beaten by White cops suggested a strong undercurrent of institutionalized racism in law enforcement at that time. There is no profession where one individual can bring disgrace on their peers more so than law enforcement. If someone deals with one bad or racist cop, they form the opinion that all cops must be like that. If one cop treats you like shit on a traffic stop, you think they are all assholes. And cops can't blame it on a bad day. They have to be better than that, which means that they must police each other. A sheepdog guarding its flock will attack another sheepdog if it endangers their flock. Cops must be the same. They have to protect the citizens and criminals, even from other cops, at all costs. Some cops got so hung up on catching bad guys they forgot we also needed to nurture relationships with citizens. Without trust from the community, bad blood will simmer until it eventually boils over.

Less than two weeks after King was beaten, Latasha Harlins, a fifteen-year-old Black girl, was shot and killed by a female Korean store owner over a bottle of orange juice that Harlins had tried to steal. Even though this incident was captured on video as well, the store owner only got probation. Something had to give. The legal system and the Black community were not working well together at all. The atmosphere in Los Angeles in 1991 was like the atmosphere in Detroit in 1967.

While the legal wrangling over the Rodney King incident unfolded and the furor over the murder of Harlins simmered, I continued training new police officers. One of them was from Detroit. I didn't know him, but I liked him, so it hurt when I recommended that he not be hired. I didn't think he had the common sense needed to be a cop. The other Black cops weren't happy about it. Several asked me why I was fucking over a Black officer when the White officers always took care of each other. To me, it was never about taking care of people for culture's sake. It was about making sure that the right people got the job no matter their race, gender, or sexual orientation. I didn't care what other cops did. I couldn't base my decisions as an FTO on theirs. Sure, I felt terrible about washing out another Black man, but I would have felt worse had he gotten killed or killed someone over something stupid.

Another trainee I had was from New York City. While most trainees struggle with money during their first few years on the job, this guy drove onto the back lot in a brand-new Mercedes Benz on his first day. We later found out that he had five families of New York Mafia connections. He ended up retiring on an injury he got in a car crash. Years later, he would be under investigation by sheriff's homicide for the murder of an associate found buried in the San Gabriel Mountains.

My best trainee by far was Eddie Aguirre, an Ecuadoran who grew up in the Eagle Rock area of Los Angeles. He had a soft, almost soothing voice and was extremely smart, well mannered, ethical, and eager to learn. Eddie had the ideal temperament to be a cop, and his evaluations were a joy to write, except for the first one. Since most Compton cops carried their own firearms, I had a habit of running the serial numbers of my trainees' guns when I wrote their evaluations.

I did this because I did not want them to get involved in a shooting with an unregistered firearm. When I ran the serial number of Eddie's gun, it was in the system as stolen. I asked him about it later that day. He opened his eyes in surprise as he told me that the department issued it to him. I reported it to the training staff, and they took the gun and gave Eddie another one. I ran the serial number right away, relieved to see this one was registered to the city of Compton. I never asked about the circumstances surrounding the gun being in the system as stolen. I was sure it was just an oversight, some type of clerical error. But coupled with the security officer who misplaced her gun years before, it demonstrated a systemic lack of administrative control at Compton PD.

Eddie and I made some spectacular arrests, once stopping a carload of gang members cruising in a rival gang area. All four of them had guns. This arrest earned Eddie the first commendation of his career. I would go on to teach him a great deal, passing on the best parts of what I had learned from Fat Jack and Nussman. And I would learn just as much from Eddie as he learned from me. Our first week we got a call of a domestic violence incident. I handled it because Eddie hadn't dealt with a call like that yet. I wanted him to watch, but I had spent the day arguing with Gilda over some stupid shit regarding our kids, so it was not a good time for me to be listening to someone else's marital problems.

In what should have been a training lesson on how to handle a call like this, I was rude and insensitive to the victim. She had simply wanted us to talk some sense into her husband because he always blew his paycheck on two of the three "B's." Instead of showing Eddie how to handle the call appropriately, I looked at her husband, lying drunk on the plastic-less couch, and sneered, "Stop fucking up the money. If we have to come back, we're gonna take your drunk ass to jail." I turned to her next and sarcastically asked, "You happy now?" I was out the door before she finished nodding her head.

Eddie stopped me before we reached our car. He said, "Sir, I know I'm still new, but I don't like the way you handled that call."

I was stunned. Trainees weren't supposed to talk to their FTOs like that, but he had the guts and the conviction to stand up for what he felt was right. I had no choice but to respect that and said, "You're right, Eddie. I was wrong. Let's go do it the right way."

I was having a bad day, but Eddie had policed me. It doesn't matter how much time a cop has on the job. We are supposed to be hiring them because of their moral and ethical standards. We don't need robots or those seeking approval from their peers at any cost.

Afterward, Eddie and I were patrolling our district when the dispatcher called us. Eddie was driving that night, so I grabbed the radio mic.

"4-Adam."

"4-Adam, respond to a 459 silent at 1515 East Compton Blvd. 4-Adam?"

"4-Adam copy, en route." I put the mic back and said, "Step on it, Eddie. That's Angeles Abbey. Those burglar alarms are always good. When we get there, I'll check the outside, and you handle the mausoleum."

CHAPTER SIXTEEN

I HAD BEEN living at the Willowtree Inn for six months. My credit was so bad by that point I couldn't even get an apartment in my name. After telling Officer Bill "Junkyard" Brown of my plight over drinks at John's bar one night, he suggested that he could help me rent an apartment in the building he lived in without filling out a credit application. It was in a terrible area on Cedar Street near Anaheim in Long Beach. Someone got killed in the alleyway the first week I moved in. My kids were playing in the courtyard at the time.

Junkyard was a private guy and he certainly drank and smoked too much but he was the salt of the earth. In the Black race, there is a multitude of different shades of skin color. Most of us are brown skinned, some of us are so light we can pass as White, others are a shade darker, which we call "high-yellow" or mulatto, and a few are so black we call them "blue-black." Junkyard was blue-black, as was my brother Derrick. Junkyard was about fifty years old, and his eyes were always bloodshot. He worked the day shift when the department had a police officer and a security officer assigned to several sub-stations at parks throughout the city. Junkyard and the security officer who once misplaced her firearm were assigned to Kelly Park, but after the events of April 2, 1989, she refused to work there again.

There was a kid's birthday party going on in the park. Dozens of people of all ages, including members of the Kelly Park and Atlantic Drive Crips, were in attendance. The adults were drinking, eating, and listening to music while watching the kids play on the playground. A few hours after Junkyard got off work, SBCC member Paul "Potato-head" Watson drove past the park and opened fire with an AK-47, killing Atlantic Drive Crip Earl "Hulk" Solomon and a pregnant female. While the shooting was occurring, the armed female security officer ran into the sub-station and locked the doors, hiding under a nearby desk as dozens of people beat on them frantically.

Junkyard's specialty was gathering intelligence on the prostitutes working Long Beach Blvd, which he kept in binders in the watch sergeant's office. The hookers loved him. Maybe he reminded them of the men they worked for because he wore his hair in a process like a pimp. He also wore three colossal gold and diamond rings on each hand and carried a pearl-handled, nickel-plated .45 caliber semi-automatic pistol. Junkyard smoked Benson and Hedges and, just like my father, drank Canadian Club with an inch of sugar at the bottom of the glass. I think I liked him so much because of that commonality. I had no idea why he liked me. Perhaps it was because we had things in common as well. There had to be a reason he was living in a shithole like that after twenty-plus years on the job.

I did not hang out with too many cops off-duty. One of my best friends was as far from being a cop as anyone could be. His name was Onuka Henry, but I always called him by his surname or, as he liked to say, his "government name". Originally from Vicksburg, Mississippi, and militant as hell, he was screaming for forty acres and a mule from the moment we met when he was a gunner's mate in the Navy. He was married to Gilda's sister Valerie while I was married to Gilda. He and Valerie had two daughters who were diagnosed with autism at early ages. Henry was devastated, and I shared his devastation because he was my friend. After he broke up with Valerie, we became each other's moral compasses, all but ensuring that our morality had no direction at all. I should have been worried about the alcoholic gene that I had but I didn't even care at that point. We drank and chased loose women every night. I threw selection to the winds. It didn't matter, just so long as I could take one home, get drunk, and have sex. I even woke up next to a dwarf once. She didn't appreciate it when I rushed her out and into a cab before the neighbors saw her. She slapped the shit out of me before I closed the car door.

Henry knew an old, retired Navy guy by the name of Bo-Pete who lived in Long Beach near 21st and Lewis, about eight blocks from where I lived. The local Crip gang heavily influenced this area. A life-sized cutout of a man wearing all blue clothing was prominently displayed like a scarecrow on the corner of

Martin Luther King Blvd and 20th Street not far from the World-Famous VIP record store.

Bo-Pete held blackjack games at his house every night. He collected money from the players to facilitate the games, which made it illegal. Most of the gamblers were current and former sailors and the occasional street hustler and gang member. Henry and I started hanging out at Bo-Pete's house almost every weekend, drinking and gambling. A few nights, I left flat broke, but some nights I left with over $3,000 and even won a diamond ring from a sailor.

One night Henry and I, along with Bobbington "Big Bob" Brandt, went nightclub hopping. Big Bob wasn't a cop yet, but I knew him because he was friends with one of Gilda's cousins. I had a red 8-cylinder Chevy Camaro with glass T-tops at the time. After leaving the last club for the night, we were driving in Inglewood near the border of Los Angeles. We were all drunk, and I was still on probation. Although I wanted desperately to be successful, for some reason I just couldn't control myself from engaging in reckless behavior. Big Bob was nodding off next to me while Henry sat in the back seat, smoking a cigarette, talking shit, and bobbing his head to "Candy" by Cameo. I elbowed Big Bob and said, "Watch this, dog." I gunned the accelerator, unaware that I was coming up on a sharp turn. I lost control, spun out, and careened into the curb before slamming into a concrete light pole. The three of us were dazed but managed to get out of the vehicle just before the light pole smashed through the T-tops. Big Bob panicked. He looked frantically from side to side like a cornered animal before sprinting off into the night without saying a word. I sat on the curb while Henry clumsily tried to stop my head from bleeding.

Within minutes, several Los Angeles and Inglewood police cars arrived. One of the LAPD cops just happened to be the same Black cop who had responded to the market robbery when I was a security guard. Henry got my badge and ID from my pocket and showed them to him. The cop leaned down next to me and said, "Listen, I'm gonna get you out of here before my supervisor arrives. Get in the ambulance and keep quiet. I'll meet you at the hospital later." He then walked over to the Inglewood cops on the scene and told them that he would handle the investigation.

I don't know if he remembered me or not, but this was the second time he had looked out for me. My first contact with him inspired me and was part of the motivation that eventually drove me to become a cop. This time, he had saved my career as a cop. This man, whose name I will never mention, had reached down and pulled me up twice. Was it a coincidence? Or divine intervention? With a past like mine, did I really have a cop for a guardian angel? We all need helping hands at some point. None of us can attain any of our goals or successfully navigate through life without some kind of compass, be it moral or otherwise. But how was it that this Black cop, in a profession filled with White ones, a lot of whom at the time didn't have the best interests of Black people as a priority, just happened to be there for me on two occasions when I needed help the most? As hard as I was trying to derail my life, something was trying just as hard to keep it on track.

CHAPTER SEVENTEEN

ON MARCH 29, 1992, LA County Deputy Sheriff Nelson Yamamoto was shot by an illegal immigrant who had already killed three people and was a fugitive from justice. Transported to MLK Hospital and initially stabilized by hospital staff, Deputy Yamamoto died two days later. I didn't know him, but multiple people have told me that he was one of the best people you could ever meet. On the first anniversary of his death, two deputies who he had worked with went to pay their respects and found his girlfriend sleeping on his grave.

Deputy Yamamoto had been given a better-than-average chance of survival but died after a doctor gave him a lethal combination of heart drugs. A medical board found that the four doctors who treated him and the hospital's vice chairwoman of surgery were grossly negligent and incompetent. Still, there were widespread accusations among deputies that the negligence was intentional. The Rodney King trial was underway at the time. On the day that Deputy Yamamoto died, Officer Laurence Powell had taken the witness stand and lied, testifying that he feared for his life as his reason for beating King.

There had been a long history of animus between hospital staff and law enforcement officers, and with justification on both sides. In recent history, a Compton cop had arrested a surgeon at MLK for refusing to draw blood from an uncooperative drunk driver. The surgeon sat handcuffed in the back seat of a patrol car for several hours. Understandably, the hospital staff was incensed. I knew that if the LAPD officers were not found guilty with this type of mentality between citizens and cops, there would be hell to pay.

A month later, I was working the PM shift. I walked into the Code-7 room, and a group of officers were crowded around the TV watching the news. Jurors in Simi Valley had found Powell, Stacy Koon, Theodore Briseno, and Timothy

Wind not guilty. I knew what was coming. I had seen it before through eyes far less mature and less in tune with the nuances of racism. Now I was able to look at the inequality with clarity that I didn't have then. Ron Malachi was the PM W/C that night. I told him there were going to be problems and that he should hold over day shift and call in the graveyard shift and all the reserve officers. His reply was a frightening example of the hubris of a decorated war hero. He said, "Fred, relax. That shit happened in LA with LAPD. It ain't coming to Compton."

I was riding with a trainee named Russell Townsley, who I nicknamed Barney Rubble. It was low-hanging fruit; my name is Fred, and he was short, White, and wore his blond hair with a cowlick in front. Less than two hours into our shift, we were driving down Long Beach Blvd, watching dozens of angry Black teenagers and kids, some as young as six years old, walking in the middle of the street chanting, "No justice, no peace!"

I used the loudspeaker to keep them from stopping the traffic flow, and one furious young man said, "Get out of the car, *brother!* Why you riding with that White boy, you fucking Uncle Tom!"

I knew that the protagonist in *Uncle Tom's Cabin* was based on a slave named Josiah Henson, a man of conviction who helped dozens of slaves escape to the north. But I didn't have time to reflect on why this young man thought the term was so offensive to Blacks. Neither did I have time to explain that in the story, Tom saved the life of a little White girl named Eve, whose grateful father later bought him. That while on her deathbed years later, she asked her father to set Tom and all his slaves free, but Simon Legree, a brutal slave owner, killed her father before he had a chance to do so, which caused the slaves to run away.

There was too much going on for me to explain to the angry young man now throwing bricks at storefront windows that Legree had whipped Tom to death because Tom refused to tell Legree where the runaway slaves were. I didn't have time to ask the angry young man, now running down the street carrying as much stolen shit as he could hold, why, then, was Uncle Tom such a horrid term among Blacks when he was so obviously a compassionate, honorable, and loyal man? Harriet Beecher Stowe's depiction of Tom was one of praise and admiration, and although the book referenced some unfavorable stereotypes about Blacks, the essence of the tale is that Black people are, in fact, remarkable individuals. I wanted to make time to tell the misguided young man that the book itself is credited with fueling the abolitionist movement to end slavery, but there was just too much going on.

I forgave him as I watched him run away, dropping articles of clothing that didn't even appear to fit him. In this moment of insanity, I realized that it wasn't his fault. I realized that he most likely had no fucking idea who Stowe even was and that he was merely the recipient of information fed to him by people blissfully bereft of knowledge or common sense. Less than five minutes after I was called an Uncle Tom, a unit on the other side of the city asked for help with looters at a supermarket at Wilmington and 133rd Street. The market went up in flames just minutes later.

The State Parole and Probation Office on Compton Blvd was next. The radio went crazy with calls of structure fires, looting, and officers asking for help. Back at the station, Malachi and several records clerks were feverishly making phone calls ordering officers to report for duty. Meanwhile, in the vanguard, I grabbed our shotgun and told Barney Rubble to follow me as I walked into a store on Long Beach Blvd, carefully avoiding looters running out with merchandise. I fired at the ceiling and yelled, "Everybody get the fuck out!" It was a temporary fix, at best. As soon as we left, the looters came back.

A liquor store owned by Blacks was at the corner of Compton Blvd and Central, across the street from where I had called to make the false police report ten years earlier. A few other stores and a Korean-owned Swap Meet took up the remainder of the block. Every building was destroyed except for the liquor store. Korean store owners throughout the city caught on quick, futilely writing "Black Owned" on their businesses to save them. When writing on their stores didn't work, they took to the rooftops armed with rifles and handguns.

We worked nineteen hours the first night. When I got off, I drove home with a pistol on my lap as I maneuvered around rioters to the freeway. By the next day, forty-three buildings had been destroyed or damaged by fire, eighty-seven stores looted or vandalized, and more than 150 people were arrested for looting. The youngest was just eleven; the oldest was seventy. Malachi had obviously been wrong. It was much bigger than just a jurisdictional issue.

FREDERICK DOUGLASS REYNOLDS

Constant stormtrooper tactics by police officers in the inner cities had reached a crescendo. Some cops were taking Ronald Reagan's 1982 declaration of war on drugs literally.

When children see older people in their community harassed and beaten by police, it frightens them. But it also gives them resolve, sowing seeds that all cops are the enemy. Reagan had gotten us into a war with no exit strategy. He saved me from one war and put me on the frontlines of another. Police departments across the country already had a history of mistreating people of color, thus, Reagan's declaration of war on drugs was, in effect, a declaration of war on the inner cities. We created a generation of people who hated and despised us in the communities we were supposed to protect and serve. We went from playing dominoes with community members and getting information on the real criminals to worrying about being sniped. Holliday's video evoked images of Blacks hanging from trees as crowds of White people stood around smiling, the scabs of festering wounds ripped off thanks to the father of police reform and the citizens of Simi Valley.

There was another factor involved. As crack tore through the inner cities in the 80s, women prostituted themselves at an alarming rate. Sex had never been cheaper. In Compton, Long Beach Blvd was a virtual parade route of women offering sexual favors for money and crack. Almost none of them used protection, and numerous babies were born addicted. The children were placed in foster homes most of the time, but many were raised by grandparents too old to parent and properly guide them. And now, some of these children were pre-teens and at the most impressionable stage in their lives. Angry and bitter in most instances because they never knew their parents and unstable because of their addiction to crack before they could even breathe independently, the chickens were now back home to roost.

I saw smoke threatening to completely obscure Fort Compton when I drove to work the next day. I wasn't in the mood for music, so there was nothing to drown out the screams of seagulls as I looked in my rearview mirror and thought about the people rollerblading less than twenty minutes from the absolute hell I was going to. When I got there, it was even worse than I could have imagined. Entire families were looting, running out of stores with their children in tow.

And not just Black families. Mexican families, some of their children barefoot, were carrying stolen goods while screaming, "Free Rodney King" and the now all-too familiar, "No justice, no peace!" in thick, Spanish accents.

Pick-up trucks loaded with stolen furniture were speeding down the streets. The smell of smoke from burning cars in the middle of intersections was overwhelming as it billowed upwards, joining other smoke coming from structure fires as I heard sirens and gunfire all around me. I was fucking scared. When society breaks down, it is frightening to behold, and it happens quickly. Bookman was a Federal Firearms License dealer. I stopped by his house and picked up an AK-47 with a thirty-round clip. I carried it in the trunk of my patrol car for the rest of the riots. I wasn't the only one. Bookman loaned rifles and shotguns to several other Compton cops to even the odds against the gang members, who were better armed and now shooting at us indiscriminately.

Three hours before I got to work, Stoney Jackson shot and killed a looter at the Shoe Warehouse on Rosecrans near Long Beach Blvd. Thirty minutes after that, Thanh Lam, a young Vietnamese man whose family owned a store on Alondra near Willowbrook, was shot to death while driving a pick-up truck filled with beer he was trying to salvage.

A car full of Black gang members had rammed Lam's vehicle, and one of them shot him while the others stole the beer. It was so dangerous in the area we couldn't even establish a crime scene to look for evidence. We could only form a circle to protect his body until the coroner collected it and sped off. While this was going on, other cops had circled the wagons around the Swap Meet and were exchanging gunfire with snipers at the MOB Piru apartment complex on Bullis Road. The highest priority had been given to the Swap Meet and the Towne Center, which featured the newly built Circuit City electronics store as its crown jewel. Hourie Taylor was the acting chief because Chief Terry Ebert was away at a training seminar. Hourie stationed cops with shotguns and riot gear in front of these locations. The brand-new Foot Locker shoe store on Rosecrans received no such protection, however. For months after the riot ended, everyone in the neighborhood was still walking around in brand new Jordans.

Our fire department was overwhelmed, so departments from surrounding cities were sent to help them. In contrast to Compton firefighters, the firefighters from those departments were all White. Four from the nearby town of Downey were fighting a fire at the Taco Bell on Rosecrans and Central when a mob began throwing rocks and bottles. Just when they were about to get overrun, an unmarked police car skidded to a stop near their fire engine. It was Kevin Burrell. He got out and fired a shotgun over the heads of the rioters and told the firefighters, "I ain't leaving you crackers alone in this mess." The firefighters were unable to save the Taco Bell, but Kevin continued to follow them around the city, providing protection as they fought other fires.

By Friday morning, we were using the Ramada Hotel as the Command Post. A captain, formally designated as "Duty Commander," was now in charge of the cops on duty instead of a lieutenant. This happens whenever a major critical incident occurs, as the span of control is more significant due to increased personnel. Many reporters, doctors, nurses, and other professional people were at the Command Post. City officials were also present, most of them looking for news cameras. A psychologist saw Officer Gary Eaves walking around chain-smoking cigarettes with a shotgun slung over his back. He was wearing a flak jacket and helmet with two bandoliers of 12-gauge shotgun rounds across his chest in an "X" configuration. The psychologist pointed at him and told Hourie, "That man needs to be taken out of the field immediately." That was it for Jaws. No more cops and robbers in the ghetto. He retired not long afterward.

Governor Pete Wilson had deployed the National Guard after a request from LA Mayor Tom Bradley. They arrived in LA on the second day of the riot. Still, they didn't come to Compton other than blocking significant intersections and thoroughfares with sandbags, using them as fortification for the men armed with M-60 machine guns behind them. We had to show our badges and identification at the roadblocks to enter or leave the city.

US Marines from Camp Pendleton arrived to help us on May 1 and staged at the Ramada Hotel. Two days later, my trainee and I were called there to pick up some of them to ride with us. We didn't need the Marines now. It was all a show at this point, camouflage window dressing. Almost all the looted buildings had burned down. There was nothing left to steal. The city had started to quiet down. Even the Crips and Bloods had called a ceasefire. The duty commander assigned me to be the team leader of four two-officer Compton PD units with two Marines in each car.

At 11:30 p.m., we got a call of a man shooting a shotgun at 119 East Cypress Street. It was an apartment complex about one block from the Heritage House and consisted of two multi-unit, two-story apartment buildings separated by a large driveway. We parked just east of the driveway, and Michael Markey, Carl Smith, J.J., Van Wie, and I walked to the apartment. The other officers staged along the driveway on the west side. We left the Marines behind to watch our cars.

A woman in a downstairs window gestured toward an apartment above hers. Several steps leading to a small landing separated the first and second floors, where there was a walkway between two apartment doors, one to the right and one to the left. The area in front of each door was just wide enough for two people to stand shoulder to shoulder. The apartment we were interested in was to the left. Markey and Smith walked to the door. I stayed behind them on the steps separating the upper and middle landings. J.J. and Van Wie remained on the landing separating the two floors. We heard arguing coming from inside the apartment. Markey knocked on the door and yelled, "Compton police! Open the do—! Hold up; someone is running!" Markey kicked the door and almost fell. Smith then got in position to kick it just as someone fired a shotgun blast through it, hitting Markey in the left arm and Smith in the right one. Markey fell backward and screamed, "I'm hit! I'm hit!" I thought of my father pulling me to the floor in 1967 as I crawled up the steps and pulled Markey to the landing. J.J. dragged Smith to the landing, too, and the four of us and Van Wie covered our heads as dozens of shots from the cops staged along the driveway obliterated the apartment.

J.J. and I had to get Smith and Markey to the hospital, but we would have to go back underneath the apartment window. When the shooting stopped, J.J. grabbed Smith, and I grabbed Markey. I yelled, "Two officers shot! We're coming out! Cover us!" As soon as the last word came out of my mouth, a barrage of gunfire rained on the apartment. I could see the Marines and Compton cops and two deputy sheriffs shooting over our heads as J.J. and I ran down the driveway carrying Markey and Smith. The deputies had joined in after seeing our police cars parked on the street, and the Marines followed them. Smith and Markey were hospitalized for the treatment of multiple pellet wounds. Had they not been wearing bulletproof vests, they may have been killed.

Carl Smith was a tall, high-yellow cop who worked primarily on the yard and had invested heavily in a goose-down pillow, which he dutifully carried to his patrol car after every briefing. He had a tombstone sense of humor and was well liked among the Black officers. On the other hand, Markey was a slightly over-weight, condescending White cop who spent most of his waking hours being annoying to everyone. Before this incident, what I remembered most about him was when he farted close to Bob Page's face while Page was sitting down in the locker room putting on his boots. Page chased Markey all over the locker room and would have killed him had other officers not stepped in. But none of that went through my mind when Markey was lying on the landing screaming for help. His race didn't matter, nor did his personality or crassness. The only thing that mattered was that a fellow officer needed help.

After a brief stand-off, the shooter surrendered to a Sheriff's Special Enforcement Bureau team. In addition to the shooter and his girlfriend, four toddlers and two teenagers were in the apartment. The cops and Marines fired 185 shots into the apartment. Amazingly, none of the occupants were injured. Had it been a ground-floor apartment, they may have all been killed, but if the Marines had stayed by the cars like I told them, this shit would have never happened.

In military terms, providing cover means to lay down a base of gunfire, con-centrating it on the area of the threat. For cops, it means to keep your firearm trained on the threat and only fire in the event of being fired upon or the aggres-sive display of a weapon. The Marines simply followed orders, but the cops fell victim to the contagious fire malady. In the eyes of the military, the Marines had done their jobs. This was evident when their commanding officer came to the scene. He looked at the bullet-riddled apartment and said, "Good job, Marines," before getting back into his chauffeured jeep to go back to the Ramada. Hourie, on the other hand, looked at the apartment, shook his head, and just walked away. The shooting would live on forever in law-enforcement circles as the "cover me" incident. Years later, cops from all over Southern California still bring it up during war story time, engaging in games of Chinese Whispers. The tale got taller and taller every time I heard it, never saying a word as the number of shots grew to over a thousand, depending on the number of drinks purchased.

The riots ended on that potentially fateful day on Cypress Street, but we dealt with the fallout for several more weeks as we went about the task of trying to recover stolen property. In a highly controversial action, city officials instructed the police department to seize new furniture from any residence and transport it to the station. We determined which houses to go into based on old furniture sitting out for trash pick-up. For weeks, the back lot looked like a furniture store. I don't know what eventually happened to all the furniture, but there was less and less still there every day when I got to work. Not surprisingly, the higher quality furniture began disappearing first.

Sixty-three people lost their lives, and over 12,000 people got arrested during the rioting throughout Los Angeles County. The Board of Supervisors formed the Kolts Commission to report on police brutality. One of the findings determined that sheriff's deputy cliques were found primarily at self-described "ghetto stations" or stations in areas densely populated by minorities. A particularly notorious group was known as the Lynwood Vikings, whose members were deputies assigned to the Lynwood station. The next closest station was Firestone, where that station's clique was known as the Stoney boys. They were feared not only in the Firestone area but also in Compton and other surrounding areas. Compton residents were much more frightened of them than they were of Compton officers. When I first moved in with Gilda's family, her brother and I were walking to a nearby liquor store when he told me, "Man, we gotta watch out for the sheriffs, especially the Stoney boys. They all big ass White boys who love to thump on a nigga's head just for the fuck of it."

I asked him about the Compton cops. He said, "Who? Compton Dum Dums? We ain't gotta worry about F-Troop. Fuck them."

CHAPTER EIGHTEEN

CHIEF TERRY Ebert was attending a training seminar in Pomona when the riots started. While he was gone, someone tipped off Howard Caldwell that he may have been stealing from the narcotics buy fund account. Caldwell requested a surprise audit, which showed that money was indeed missing. Ebert was subsequently placed on administrative leave on May 1, 1992, at the apex of one of the biggest riots in the history of the United States.

The investigation revealed that Ebert would get money out of the account for personal use and then replace it before the next scheduled audit. No one knows who tipped Caldwell off, but Ebert never entered the vault alone. Hourie, who was over the gang and narcotics unit at the time, opened it for him several times. Although cops assigned to the narcotics unit have the combination to the vault, the only person with access to the buy fund locker is the police chief. No one should know if money is missing from the fund until the results of an audit. For someone to tip off Caldwell, that person had to have knowledge of the narcotics vault and buy fund money, and have a suspicion that Ebert was stealing. It would also help if the person had Caldwell's ear.

Ebert would eventually plead guilty to one count of grand theft and resign in August. His attorney said Ebert was stealing the money to help his special needs son, but all everyone at the station talked about was how much Ebert liked to frequent the card clubs in nearby Gardena. With Ebert's downfall, Hourie was on his way to achieving his childhood dream as he was named the interim chief of police. Raised in the city and a graduate of Compton high, he had made his bones as the gang unit supervisor and was a nationally recognized expert on Crips and Bloods.

Hourie's nemesis was R.E. Allen, a huge supporter of Ebert which led to Ebert promoting him to Captain. Had R.E.'s promotion depended on Hourie instead, it most likely would not have happened. R.E. was a climber and made no secret about it. A former LAPD officer, he had been gunning for the chief's position since he pinned on a Compton PD badge. R.E. was a member of an erudite family who lived on the west side of Los Angeles. His mother was a teacher, and his brother and father were doctors. R.E. made his bones as the Compton PD narcotics unit supervisor, widely rumored to have been corrupt. I often listened with envy as I heard them talking about how much fun they had at the Carnival in Rio De Janeiro while I struggled to take my kids to Disneyland. Every officer assigned to R.E.'s unit had slant-nosed Porsches and took cruises and extravagant vacations twice a year. Some of them even wore $2,500 crocodile and alligator boots, Rolex watches, and owned custom-made Harley-Davidson motorcycles. Ever the individual, R.E. chose to drive a white BMW 600 series and wear Omega and Cartier watches in his typical subdued elegance.

Hourie was known as "Bear" because of his love of bear claw pastries and the size of his hands. More than one gang member felt those paws against the side of his head during the 70s and 80s. R.E. was simply known as "Weed," possibly a bastardization of R.E. or maybe for some other reason given his love for working narcotics. Brown-skinned and handsome, R.E. walked with a pimp's gait and was suave, articulate, and ridiculous in his pomposity, the kind of guy who calls the "taint" a perineum. Hourie was an intelligent, overweight, self-effacing man with bad knees and a lousy posture who didn't care about his appearance or how he was perceived. R.E. smoked cigarettes and wore his hair in a slicked-back style comparable to pimps in the 70s. Hourie wore his hair in an Afro and couldn't stand smoke. R.E. had a soft, silky smooth voice reminiscent of an old Detroit D.J. known as the Electrifying Mojo, and Hourie was sometimes crass and vulgar when he spoke. The two men could not have been more different. And in a fierce clash of pettifoggery, they never got along or agreed on anything.

Sometime after the riots ended, Hourie assigned Frailich and me to the gang unit because of an increase in shootings and murders after the short-lived Crip and Blood truce. I was in the best shape of my life at the time. I lived alone, ran every day, drank black coffee, ate raw tuna, and did 100 pushups every morning, hangover or not.

Reggie Wright, Sr. was the supervisor of the gang unit. Tim Brennan, Bob Ladd, J.J., and Raymond Banuelos comprised the rest of the team. To be a capable gang investigator, you must love your craft. Being a gang investigator in Compton was like a fledging art lover rooming with Jackson Pollock; it was sensory overload. The gang members painted obscene, grotesque works of art with sophisticated weaponry, using the streets as their canvases and blood as their medium. At least one gang claimed every neighborhood, and they were always fighting. Every hood had soldiers in wheelchairs, survivors of unsuccessful drive-by shootings. Piru gangs fought Crip gangs, Crip gangs fought other Crip gangs, Piru gangs fought other Piru gangs, and Hispanic gangs fought them all. At least three people were shot on average every day. And someone was murdered on an average of seven times a month.

We were proud of the ruthlessness displayed by our gangsters and often bragged that Compton gangsters were the baddest motherfuckers in America. It was a badge of honor to police the worst of the worst, as if it somehow made us tougher. But in truth, Compton gangsters were no more ruthless than the ones in Long Beach, Watts, or any other gang infested area in America. You could transplant the worst gangster in Detroit, Newark, East St. Louis, or Harlem to Compton and they would thrive and be just as ruthless.

The Compton gang unit's philosophy was to know as much about the gang members as possible and the reasons behind rivalries. We wore "soft" clothing: black or blue windbreakers with "Police" in bold yellow letters emblazoned on the back, and jeans and sneakers to distinguish ourselves from the uniformed cops who the gang members perceived as uncompromising assholes. Reggie was the master at obtaining gang intelligence, relying on his past employment as a kind-hearted meter reader to pay dividends.

Banuelos was tall and stocky with a full head of dark hair. He was smart, didn't take any shit, and his bilingual capability was vital due to the ever-increasing Hispanic population.

Brennan and Ladd were arguably the best gang cops in LA County. Brennan was known as "Blondie," so dubbed by rapper DJ Quik when he clowned

Brennan on an underground rap song in the 80s. The nickname was derived from the protagonist of the Clint Eastwood spaghetti westerns. Brennan was a poor man's version of Brad Pitt high off a souped-up dose of adrenochrome. Good looking and arrogant, Brennan, a skinny White guy from Chicago, was relentless in his pursuit of violent gang members. He had blond hair and a raspy, guttural laugh due to smoking unfiltered Camels and drinking black coffee non-stop. I was surprised when I found out that his beginnings were humble like mine. He was homeless and slept in his truck when he first got to California before being hired by Compton PD.

Ladd had a relaxed, laid-back demeanor. A White guy with a full head of dark hair, he was often quiet and unassuming, but he knew policework like the back of his hand. Ladd and Brennan were perfect partners. They were fire and ice, yin and yang, and sometimes Beavis and Butthead when they were drunk. I called Ladd Batman and Brennan Robin, which pissed Brennan off to no end because he never wanted to be considered anyone's sidekick. They both lived in Orange County but loved working in Compton and solved some of the most notorious gang-related cases in Compton's history.

Within a week of being assigned to the gang unit, Frailich and I were driving on Compton Blvd when we saw some 151 Piru gang members at a vacant house on Nestor Street. We stopped and had them all put their hands on the hood of our patrol car. Frailich patted them down and discovered that one smelled like PCP. We told everyone to leave except the duster, who we were going to 5150 at Augustus Hawkins. Frailich asked him to put his hands behind his back, and the duster snarled, "Fuck you, you blue-eyed devil!"

The duster started growling at the sound of an ambulance siren in the distance and suddenly grabbed at Frailich's Sam Brown. Frailich spun away as the duster grabbed the antenna of his handheld radio and pulled it from the holder. I pulled the duster by the shoulder just as he swung the radio, narrowly missing Frailich's head. The radio flew out of the duster's hand and struck the ground, exploding into multiple pieces. For it to break like that, it had hit with a tremendous amount of force. It may have killed Frailich had it hit him. The duster then turned toward me, still growling but now foaming at the mouth.

I punched him in the face as hard as I could. He fell back onto the hood of our car and immediately bounced up, blood flowing from his mouth and nose. Two of his front teeth were now missing. Pinkish colored foam bubbled through the newly created space, my face now a fresco of expired blood spatter due to his heavy breathing. I muttered, "Oh shit," as Frailich yelled for a code-9 on the car radio. The duster leaped at me, but I managed to evade him and slipped behind him and put him in a chokehold. I couldn't get it right, and we both went down next to the curb. Even though I had him by at least forty pounds, I ended up on my back. I wrapped my legs around him and did my best turtle imitation to protect my face as he thrashed his head back and forth. As I wrestled with this insanely strong motherfucker, all I could think of was that I didn't want to die in a gutter in Compton.

Frailich hit the duster on the head with a flashlight, causing blood to flow into the duster's eyes as he continued to growl and fight. Despite the slipperiness caused by the blood, I hung on to his neck for dear life, comforted by the faint sound of sirens approaching. The louder the sirens got, the more he struggled, and the louder he growled. While pulling at my forearms with one hand, he was frantically searching for my gun with the other. I screamed, "Fuck that flashlight, Frailich! Shoot this muthafucka! He's trying to get my gun!"

The sirens were getting louder, but I was tiring rapidly. I didn't know how much longer I could hold on. And just as Frailich pulled out his gun, tires skidded to a halt directly behind us, and I knew that the Cavalry had arrived. Eric Perrodin was the first cop I saw. He carried an extra-long metal flashlight known as a "Kel Light." They are extremely heavy because the longer they are, the more DD batteries they hold. I think Eric's held eight, and he began putting it to use right away. Cops were now everywhere. Releasing my unsuccessful chokehold, Frailich and I bent over, gasping for breath as they beat the hell out of the duster with batons, flashlights, and beavertails. He got a brutal ass-whipping, but he lived.

A week later, Frailich and I were driving in Inglewood, looking for a witness on one of our cases. We came across two Inglewood cops who had three Blood gang members stopped with their hands on the patrol car's hood. I slowed down, and one of the officers gave the universal cop signal that they were okay, holding up four fingers in a display of the "code-4, no assistance needed" radio code. I continued driving. When I was half a block away from them, I glanced in the rear-view mirror and saw that the same guy who gave the code-4 was now chasing one of the gang members. He stopped when he realized he couldn't catch the fleet-footed gangster and went back to his partner. I turned down the first street in front of the gangster, pointed my gun out the window, and told him to freeze. He stopped next to a curb drain, pulling a gun out of his waistband while simultaneously turning away from me. I didn't shoot because I instinctively knew that he was pulling it to throw it in the drainage hole. Frailich handcuffed him, I retrieved the weapon, and we took them both back to the embarrassed Inglewood cops. At least the new breed had learned to tell the difference between real gangsters and Marines on a pussy hunt.

A few months after the Inglewood incident, Hourie took me out of the gang unit because I was needed to help train several newly hired officers. When he called me to his office to give me the news, he told me that he also needed to replace Banuelos, but he wanted another Spanish-speaker to take his place. He asked me if I had any suggestions. I said, "Eddie Aguirre."

Hourie sat back in his giant leather chair and looked at me over the top of his eyeglasses, which he did more out of habit than necessity. He said, "Are you sure? He barely has two years on the department."

I replied, "I wouldn't give a fuck if he only had two months. He's gonna be a superstar gang detective. Trust me." Hourie listened to me, and Eddie was a detective for the next twenty-five years.

On December 2, 1992, I was riding with Reserve Officer Tom Gibby because my trainee called in sick. Gibby was a White guy with a goofy smile and a Hitler mustache who wore eyeglasses with coke-bottle lenses. He owned a small security business where cops moonlighted to make extra money. He was also the owner of an auto repair shop in Downey, often providing services to cops for little or no money because he was trying to get hired as a full-time Compton cop. We got a radio call of a gunshot victim at Super Marathon Burgers. Smokey, a thirteen-year-old Mexican gang member, was playing *Street Fighter II* on an arcade-style video machine near the entrance when someone shot him in the back of the head. The smell of blood is like metal. If there is enough of it, it gives the false sensation that you can actually taste it. When I walked into the restaurant that night, the smell was so thick and heavy it laid on my tongue like a warm metal spoon. Alex the Greek was pissed when we made him shut his business down. He thought we could just work around his customers.

I knew Smokey well. He was a personable kid who always smiled, even when he was trying to be tough. I always liked him. Maybe it was because I empathized with him; he once told me he would rather hang out in the streets than go home. I still think about this murder from time to time. Most of them I didn't dwell on because they just happened so goddamned frequently. But this one bothered me. Smokey was about the same age as I was when I began going down the wrong path. The kid lying on the floor in a pool of blood and brain matter could have been me. To this day, every time I see or hear *Street Fighter*, I think of Smokey and how my life could have turned out.

It also demonstrated just how little life is regarded in impoverished areas. Yet people don't quite understand the entirety of the dynamics of why this is so. The degree of apathy has nothing to do with race. The murder of a poor White kid in Compton was treated the same as the murder of a poor Black or Brown kid. It didn't matter. Social status, degree of wealth, and location are determining factors. Had Smokey been murdered in Beverly Hills or Malibu, every news station in Los Angeles County would have been at the scene, and the cops would have been given unlimited overtime. Had Bill Cosby's son been murdered in Compton, the story would have been just as huge.

In Compton, Smokey's murder didn't even make the local news. No extra overtime was authorized, and only two overworked and underpaid detectives responded to the scene. I went with them to make the obligatory death notification. Smokey's mother cried as she held an infant in her arms while three toddlers ran around her one-bedroom apartment besieged with roaches. Two hours later, the detectives had finished with the scene investigation, I was at the station writing my report, and Smokey belonged to the ages.

Hourie got appointed as permanent chief on January 1, 1993. Not all was peaches and cream about the decision. Rumors abounded that Omar Bradley didn't think Hourie was a good representative of the department due to his weight and sloppy uniform appearance. This was just fluff, however. Omar truly didn't like Hourie because Hourie and Stoney, along with Percy Perrodin, were the main three cops who raided the bookie joint Omar's family ran on Central Avenue in the 70s and 80s. Hourie and Stoney had also arrested Omar's brother Henry several times in the past, so there was no love lost between the Bradley family and Compton PD personnel. This enmity would loom large in the coming years, especially after the fiasco with the DOJ and the Ramada Hotel and Casino.

Hourie was regarded as an honorable man by the rank and file, for the most part. But some officers believed that he played favorites, and that movement within the department was impossible because officers he appointed to the best positions stayed indefinitely. There was a reverse racial aspect involved, too. Some Black officers felt that Hourie believed that only White officers could do those jobs. Although the accusations of racial obsequiousness may have been born out of jealousy, the department was nevertheless beginning to divide. And then, like a bolt of lightning, none of it mattered as Hourie's baptism of fire as chief would be one none of us would ever forget.

CHAPTER NINETEEN

IT WAS 11:16 p.m. on Monday, February 22, 1993, and I was speeding down Compton Blvd at close to one hundred miles an hour, unconcerned with the steady drizzle of rain. I glanced over at Ivan Swanson and saw that he was holding onto the chicken handle above the passenger door, his face fixed in a grim visage. In my rear-view mirror, I could see Lendell Johnson and his trainee, their car's overhead lights flashing, our sirens ominously in sync. I turned north onto Wilmington and saw the emergency lights of a patrol car in the distance. It was Gary Davis and Mark Metcalf's car angled in a manner that traffic couldn't go westbound on Rosecrans. Gary was standing in the intersection, waving his flashlight as we approached. Normally mild-mannered and self-assured, he was now panic-stricken as he pointed to another patrol car stopped on Rosecrans about two hundred feet away.

The car was in the number two lane facing westbound just east of the "Hercules Burger" restaurant. It was vehicle number twenty, Kevin and Jimmy's assigned car that night. The engine was still on, and the overhead emergency lights were activated. Jimmy was lying on his back near the front of the vehicle on the driver's side. He had a gunshot wound to his face. His eyes were open, staring into nothingness, and his head was in a small puddle of blood. The driver's door of the car was slightly ajar, but the front passenger door was standing wide open. The passenger side spotlight was on and pointed west. A long skid mark in front of the car led in a westerly direction toward Central Avenue, giving the appearance that the patrol vehicle had been on a traffic stop.

As Ivan and I got out of our car, it started raining a little harder. The slight odor of gun smoke lingering in the air combined with the rain created an acrid, unpleasant smell, unlike the petrichor that evoked memories of my father's childhood home. It was just at that moment that I saw Kevin. He was lying face down on the front passenger side of the car, his head in a large pool of brain matter, coagulated blood, and vomit. Kevin and Jimmy's duty weapons were both still holstered with the safety straps securely fastened. Kevin's back-up, a Beretta 92 F, was securely fitted in his left front pocket. Jimmy's flashlight and baton were lying on the street nearby. Kevin's baton was still in the car. He rarely carried it in his baton holder, choosing instead to leave it next to his seat. His flashlight was lying in the gutter. As I stood there assessing the scene, the rain began to wash some of Kevin's blood and brain matter slowly down the drain, with the flashlight serving as an impromptu levee for the rest.

Everyone in Compton knew Kevin. Jonathon Bowers and John Thompson, two of the responding paramedics, often played basketball with him. I saw a tear roll down Bowers's face when they put Kevin on a stretcher and rolled him to an awaiting ambulance. The front page of the LA Times, dated February 23, 1993, would depict them wheeling Kevin away from the scene as Metcalf, Ivan, and I stood in the background.

Kevin and Jimmy were transported to MLK with several patrol cars following and blocking intersections. Lendell and his trainee blocked eastbound traffic on Rosecrans from Central.

Kevin was also well liked by the hospital staff and safety police officers assigned there. It clearly showed through the tear-stained faces of individuals wearing uniforms and medical attire. All the blood spilled out of Jimmy's body when the ER personnel cracked his chest to massage his heart. Their efforts were futile. He had bled so little at the scene because he bled to death internally. Doctor Stafford officially pronounced James MacDonald, age twenty-four, dead at 12:31 a.m. and Kevin Burrell, age twenty-nine, dead at 12:36 a.m. Kevin only had five years on the job. Jimmy had eighteen months.

Monica Chambliss was the initial dispatcher that night. She couldn't regain her composure and the supervisor, Bettye Jones, took over. Bettye loved Kevin, but in a strictly platonic way. When she found out that Kevin was dead, you could hear her screaming and wailing over the open mic in dispatch. Every dispatcher who spoke on the radio that night was sobbing.

Percy Perrodin and Hourie met with Clark and Edna Burrell at the hospital. Dozens of Compton cops began arriving, both on and off-duty. Percy eventually had to order them back to the city. Edna was inconsolable, screaming in the hospital lobby as Clark held her tightly. She would later say she "felt it in her bones" that Kevin was one of the officers killed when she didn't hear him on her police scanner. She only turned it on when he was at work to listen to his voice. Kevin loved to talk on the radio. Sometimes, he would even sing to the amusement of his many admirers in dispatch.

The only thing we knew about the killer was that he was a Black man wearing a military-style jacket, who drove off westbound on Rosecrans in a red Chevy pick-up truck with a black stripe and stock rims. A records clerk on her way home after work was driving westbound on Rosecrans. She saw Kevin standing behind the man searching him as they both faced the driver's door of the red truck. The records clerk didn't think anything of it; it was something she had seen Compton cops do dozens of times before. Less than 30 seconds later, a woman and two passengers were also driving westbound on Rosecrans. They saw the man struggling with Kevin and Jimmy between the truck and the patrol car. The passengers looked out the back window and saw what they described as the man "dancing" between the two officers and shooting at them as they lay on the ground.

Gary and Metcalf were the first cops on the scene. A registered nurse on her way to work stopped when she saw Jimmy and Kevin lying on the street. She helped Metcalf turn Jimmy onto his back to provide medical assistance. Kevin's wounds were just too devastating.

Officer Paul Mason was Red Mason's son. He was Kevin's roommate and probably Kevin's closest friend on the department. Paul drove up to the scene just after the ambulances left. I gave him and his partner the descriptions of the killer and his truck and pointed west. He sped off, followed by several other patrol cars. He and Eric Perrodin found out from an attendant at a gas station on Central Avenue that a red pick-up truck had driven onto the station lot and did several donuts before speeding off northbound toward Watts. Thinking the killer may have been a Blood because of his truck's color and travel direction, Eric and Paul drove to the Nickerson Gardens housing complex, home of the notorious Bounty Hunter Blood gang. Nothing. The ordinarily active complex was eerily quiet; no one was outside, not even crackheads or strawberries.

As things calmed down, the magnitude of what happened dawned on me. Unable to collect my thoughts, I walked away from the horrible scene to a small bridge nearby that goes over the Compton Creek. I put my head on the concrete railing, casting my eyes downward as the rain softly pitter-pattered on me. Every horrible thing I had experienced in my life converged as I looked at the creek, watching a small stream of murky water creep down the center. I'm back in that little dark closet, but this time I have one of my Mom Mary's quilts for comfort. Suddenly, the room is flooded with a blinding light, and I'm standing in the bathroom. The quilt is gone. A legion of screeching rats flows from the faucet, forming a macabre opera with the grey octopus bearing witness to ritualistic maternal abuse. A hand grabs my shoulder just as an extension cord whistles through the air, and I am back on the bridge. I turn and see that the hand belongs to Danny Sneed. He tells me he needs me to handle the scene. I nod silently and leave one nightmare and return to another.

Ivan and I returned to the station afterward with the evidence and Kevin and Jimmy's bloody uniforms. We took everything into the report writing room to catalog, sitting directly across from the seat where Kevin got shot not too long before. Detective Catherine Chavers helped us. As we quietly went about the process, I was interrupted by her slowly rocking back and forth in her chair, sobbing as she hummed old Negro spiritual hymns while looking down at Kevin and Jimmy's bloodstained badges.

Hourie ordered me to go home after discovering I had worked twenty hours straight. Instead, I went to my girlfriend's house, where I had been trying to go to when I abandoned my Zebra team. I had no desire for sex now. I just needed a shoulder to lean on. I knocked on the door of her apartment, resting my head on it. I could hear music playing softly in the background as she asked, "Who is it?"

In a shaky and hoarse voice, I replied, "It's me. I need you." She cracked the door just enough to stick her head out and tell me she wasn't feeling well. Her hair, ordinarily long and silky, was in disarray. Despite her best efforts to conceal her body, a large mirror behind her showed that she was wearing my favorite lingerie. It was painfully obvious what was going on inside. I was devastated, but I didn't have the strength to get upset, let alone fight. I simply walked away, feeling even lower than when my mother put me out in the cold.

I bought a fifth of Remy Martin cognac before going home. I slid a tape of the Five Blind Boys of Alabama into my cassette player when I got there, realizing that other than the differences in technology, I now shared my father's need for music and alcohol to soothe the stinging pain of regret. I put my gun on the coffee table, stared at my bloodstained hands, and for the first time since the last time in the basement of my childhood home, I cried. I drank shot after shot as I listened to the Blind Boys croon about the reality that everybody is going somewhere until I lay down on the couch, looking at my gun, no longer able to resist the beguilement of death's gentle cousin.

I woke up on the floor about twelve hours later, staring at the barrel of my gun and the empty bottle near the coffee table. I had no recollection of how either item got there. My head was throbbing like a jackhammer in downtown New York City. Not even the gentle bubbling sounds and the beautiful fish swimming around inches from my face could soothe it. The sudden ringing of the doorbell made it even worse. I heard my girlfriend yelling from the front of my apartment. I went to the balcony and looked down onto the street. She said, "Frederick! Let me explain! Let me come up!"

I walked over to where my gun and the bottle lay on the floor. For just a second, I couldn't decide which one to pick up. The bottle barely missed her as it crashed at her feet. I had been aiming for her head. I yelled, "Get the fuck out of here, you funky bitch!" When she left, I staggered to the liquor store, replaced the broken bottle with a new one, and started all over.

CHAPTER TWENTY

OVER THE next few days, a task force consisting of Compton PD, LAPD, and sheriff's personnel was created. They used two floors at the Ramada Hotel as their headquarters. Scomb was the lead investigator. The sheriff's department assigned Detectives Mike Bumcrot, a cranky old White guy who could barely contain his contempt for Compton PD personnel, and Bob Snapper, another old White guy with a baldhead who always wore fedoras, to assist him.

The task force put so much heat on the streets that five people turned themselves in for other murders and an attempted murder. In one of the murder cases, the killer confessed but added a disclaimer: "Yeah, I killed that other nigga, but I didn't kill Big Kev and that White boy!" And, in a twisted bit of ironic justice, the attempted murder had been one of the many shooting calls the Zebra units responded to the night Kevin and Jimmy got murdered. After a little over a month of intense investigative work, including a segment on *America's Most Wanted* and the offer of a substantial reward, we found out that the killer was twenty-two-year-old Regis "Reg" Thomas, a member of the Bounty Hunter Bloods. Eric Perrodin and Paul Mason had been correct in their initial decision to go to the Nickerson Gardens to search for the culprit.

The investigation revealed that in the hours preceding the murders, Kevin, Jimmy, Metcalf, and Gary had a late code-7 at a Sizzler's Restaurant in Long Beach, where Kevin took full advantage of the all-you-can-eat steak and shrimp special. Although a lightweight as a drinker, Kevin's insatiable appetite for food had often been the source of good-natured teasing by his peers, and that night was no different. He topped off his meal with a massive slice of carrot cake before they returned to Compton. Not long afterward, dispatch broadcasted a call of shots fired near Wilmington and 131st Street in the Front Hood Crip hood. They drove to the area, and for the first time the entire night, the Zebra units split up to investigate a call. Kevin and Jimmy turned left on 131st Street, and Gary and Metcalf turned right toward Anzac and Nord, where the Anzac Grape Crips, bitter rivals with the Front Hood Crips, hang out.

While Gary and Metcalf were looking for possible perpetrators or victims of a shooting, Kevin and Jimmy saw Thomas's truck and decided for whatever reason to stop it. Kevin approached it on the driver's side, Jimmy on the passenger side. Kevin had Thomas step out and he did a pat-down search of Thomas next to the driver's door, missing a gun Thomas had concealed in his clothing. Kevin was a great cop. He arrested armed gang members three, maybe four times a week. He knew what he was doing in the streets. But it was late in the shift, and he had just eaten a massive meal. This combination may have contributed to his being haphazard and lazy in his search technique. It wouldn't have been the first time a cop missed a gun during a search.

Kevin walked Thomas back to the patrol car to have him put his hands on the hood, as was the common practice of cops at the time. Most likely, Jimmy had his gun drawn the entire time until Kevin walked Thomas toward the patrol car. Kevin was going to search Thomas's truck while Jimmy watched Thomas. Thomas was street wise, always looking for an advantage. Seeking to put them at ease, he was cooperative at first to alleviate any fears Kevin and Jimmy may have initially had. Once Jimmy holstered his weapon, Thomas made his move, pulling his 9mm Sig Sauer semi-automatic pistol. The sight of the gun took Kevin and Jimmy off-guard because they thought he was unarmed. They tried to physically overpower Thomas instead of pulling their own guns, possibly because they were still close to him. During the struggle, the gun went off, and its loud retort in the still night air likely startled Kevin and Jimmy and caused them to briefly stop struggling.

A little less than two years before, Kevin had responded to a radio call of an armed robbery at a liquor store on Long Beach Blvd near Greenleaf. Kevin shot the suspect when the suspect pulled a gun. When I got there, the suspect was lying on the grass being treated by paramedics not far from Kevin's patrol car. Kevin was sitting on the ground next to it. Still holding his gun, he was sobbing, his massive shoulders shaking his entire body. Tears were streaming down his face as he said, "I told him not to grab his gun, Fred. Why didn't he listen? Why did he make me shoot him?" Although Kevin was justified in shooting, the fact that he had to do it shook him to the core. This incident, coupled with the memory of getting shot himself recently, may have been on his mind, causing him to hesitate just long enough for Thomas to gain an advantage.

After the pause in the struggle, Thomas shot Kevin in his right arm, breaking it and rendering him nearly helpless. He then shot Jimmy at close range, striking him in his left arm before shooting Kevin in the face, foot, and the top of his head, most likely as Kevin was falling or ducking. Jimmy turned, and Thomas shot him twice in the back, causing him to fall face-first. Thomas looked at Kevin and knew Kevin was done. He then walked over to Jimmy, who exhibited no sign of visible trauma, and shot him in the back of the head. Thomas's murderous actions now complete, he sped off in his red 1992 Chevrolet 454 pick-up truck to a nearby gas station where he did celebratory donuts, mocking the cops he just murdered.

Despite Thomas believing he had delivered an executioner's shot to the back of Jimmy's head, this was not a fatal wound, as it exited his face and struck the pavement. The two shots to Jimmy's back weren't fatal, either. His bulletproof vest defeated those. The bullet that killed him was the one that hit him in the arm, penetrating it and entering his chest cavity underneath his armpit, an area uncovered by his bulletproof vest. It had taken a horizontal trajectory and severed his aorta.

Kevin and Jimmy were each shot four times. I counted nine 9mm shell casings scattered between their bodies. After the first shot went awry, Thomas probably fired the other eight in under five seconds. Inevitably, Monday morning quarterbacks questioned how one man could get the jump on two trained police officers and kill them both and why Jimmy turned his back. People who are inexperienced with guns and their capabilities will never understand just how fast someone proficient with a semi-automatic pistol can pull the trigger with accuracy and precision. As to why Jimmy turned his back, perhaps he panicked after the first shot penetrated his aorta and tried to seek cover behind the patrol car. For all intents and purposes, he was a dead man walking at that point.

Gary and Metcalf were nearby when Kevin and Jimmy encountered Thomas, so close they heard the gunshots reverberating in the night air. Gunshots were a common occurrence in Compton, so frequent that patrol units wouldn't even immediately respond to radio calls of shots fired unless there were multiple callers. Sometimes people just shot into the air to test new guns or in celebration. But the gunshots Gary and Metcalf heard that night were different; first one, a pause, a staccato, purposeful rhythm to several others, then another delay before the final one. Had Kevin or Jimmy broadcast their intentions to stop a vehicle over the radio, Gary and Metcalf would have been present during the traffic stop or, at the very least, on the way.

There was also a lot of Monday morning quarterbacking as to why Kevin or Jimmy did not radio in the traffic stop. It was not uncommon for Compton cops to not advise dispatch of traffic stops. No one wanted to be known as the cop who always radioed in for help or who let dispatch know everything they were doing. Those cops were ridiculed as being "scary" and given condescending nicknames, which is how Code-9 Calvin got his.

The day after the murders, Thomas was at an associate's house watching the news when the story came on. Thomas immediately jumped off the couch and boasted, "I smoked them muthafuckas! I caught 'em slipping." He later told Calvin Cooksey, a Bounty Hunter associate, to get rid of the murder weapon. Cooksey sold it instead of throwing it in the *ocean* like he *frankly* should have. When Cooksey heard about the reward money, he contacted a sheriff's gang detective named Larry Brandenburg. He told Brandenburg that Thomas had given him the murder weapon to get rid of, but he sold it instead. An undercover sheriff's deputy and Compton police officer William Jackson went with Cooksey to buy back the gun. The task force also found Thomas's red truck at his girlfriend's house in San Pedro. Feeling the heat and with his attorney by his side, Thomas turned himself in at the Carson sheriff's station on April 6, 1993, at 9:35 a.m.

The trial of "The State of California v Regis Thomas" took place on the high-security ninth floor of the Criminal Courts Building in downtown Los Angeles. The prosecutor was Mark Arnold, and Thomas was represented by Jay Jaffe. Cooksey refused to testify and went into hiding. A few days later, he and his attorney had a press conference. Cooksey was wearing a bulletproof vest and a hood and claimed that he was fearful for his life. He had good reason to be afraid of Thomas. He was a sociopath. His persona was clearly on display during the trial. He sat stone-faced no matter what evidence or testimony was being shown or heard. When a female witness identified Thomas as the shooter, she broke down on the witness stand and began crying, saying she was terrified to be in the same room with him.

Jaffe, attempting to paint Cooksey as a greedy liar, said Cooksey would never have come forward without the lure of the reward money. We all knew Cooksey wasn't testifying for altruistic motivations; he didn't give a shit about Kevin or Jimmy. But because he knew how vital the gun was to the investigation only proved that he knew it was the murder weapon. Cooksey was a criminal, not a choir boy. The fact that he had access to the murder weapon shows the extent of his criminality. Like the scorpion catching a ride on the frog's back, he merely did what was in his nature. The prosecution also tried Thomas for the murder of Carlos Adkins on January 31, 1992. Adkins, a student at Cal State Long Beach, was visiting a friend in the Nickerson Gardens. Thomas shot Adkins twice in the chest after asking about his gang affiliation. A jury found Thomas guilty of all three murders.

On Tuesday, August 15, 1995, Judge Edward A. Ferns sentenced Regis Thomas to death. During victim impact statements, Kevin's father said, "I taught Kevin each and every day to respect everybody, from the President of the United States to the wino on the street. If you give respect, you can get respect. How you can go around and take another person's life is hard to say. Mr. Thomas took three. I hope he pays." Jimmy's mother also spoke, saying, "Regis's mother said she knows what we feel, but no one knows what we feel until they too have lost a child. Maybe when Regis is dead, she'll know what we feel." The following day, someone spray-painted "BIP REG" and "Fuck the police" on several walls in the Nickerson Gardens. BIP stands for "Bounty, or Blood in Peace." Bounty Hunter Bloods were paying respect to Thomas by writing him off as dead due to his sentence. They were also exhibiting their feelings toward law-enforcement.

Thomas's real motive for killing Kevin and Jimmy is unknown. He may have been paranoid that the Nickerson Gardens murder had come back to haunt him. He was also a trafficker of PCP, so there was speculation that he was transporting at the time. I believe the real reason Thomas chose to execute two police officers that night was born out of revenge. Four hours into the Rodney King riots, a seventeen-year-old Bounty Hunter named Deandre Harrison was shot and killed by LAPD at Central and 112 Street. Meanwhile, anarchy reigned in the Nickerson Gardens as people were shooting at firefighters and police officers. The officers returned fire, and two other Bounty Hunters, Anthony "Romeo" Taylor and Dennis "Bull" Jackson, were also killed. Conflicting reports indicated that none of the three men were armed. Thomas, one of the most active members of the Bounty Hunters, killed Kevin and Jimmy less than three months before the first anniversary of the riots. Three of his fellow gang members getting killed by cops certainly would have been an issue of contention for him and still fresh in his mind when he was stopped by Kevin and Jimmy.

Kevin was supposed to ride with Gary Davis the night he was killed. They were regular partners, but Jimmy wanted to ride with Kevin because it was his next to last shift ever riding in Compton. Gary and Kevin worked well together and could anticipate each other's moves. Had they ridden together that night, the events of February 22, 1993, may well have gone a different way. But then again, perhaps not. One way or another, the devil always gets his due.

CHAPTER TWENTY-ONE

THE MURDERS of Kevin Burrell and James McDonald deeply affected everyone on the department. Eric Perrodin went to law school and dedicated his degree to their memory. He retired not long after and became a Deputy District Attorney for the County of Los Angeles. Metcalf blamed himself because he had talked Jimmy into working that night. After becoming a regular officer, he had recurring nightmares, and every gunshot victim that he saw for the rest of his career would remind him of that night.

Lendell became more focused at work. He had always approached our profession as just another job. After February 22, he realized this shit was real, that if he didn't pay attention when he drove off that back lot, the name of the person next to him could be linked to his forever. Lendell's trainee that night got fired not long afterward. He just wasn't cut out to be a cop. Ivan Swanson decided to forego a career as a cop, choosing to work as a talent agent in the entertainment industry rather than subject himself to constant misery and death.

Gary suffered a great deal of angst over the years, second guessing himself for not riding with Kevin that night like he usually did. He was also very bitter toward the city and the department. He felt that neither entity cared about the police officers, who were in tears as they worked the day following the murders. The city never provided mandatory psychological services for us. If not for Gary's extensive and supportive family and his pastor, he believed that he would have lost his way.

I, on the other hand, did lose my way. Gary had a support system that I didn't have, as I had neither family nor faith. I dealt with depression and drank too much. Like Edgar Allen Poe wrote in a letter describing his wife's illness in 1842, "I became insane with long intervals of horrible sanity."

Most of the time, I didn't want to be a cop anymore. More importantly, I vowed never again to get serious about a woman, much less fall in love with one. My private life was a complete train wreck now, as I was consistently in violation of all three "B's." I didn't want my kids to see me. I didn't want them to have the same kinds of memories of me as I had about my father. I became even more reckless than ever. I went out to nightclubs almost every night, waking up with different women, sometimes in strange beds in dangerous areas. I was living on the edge, sprinting down a path to self-destruction.

I also dreaded the reality that I might have to be responsible for another young police officer's well-being. I couldn't shake the feeling that the deaths of Kevin and Jimmy were on me. My mind played what-if scenarios over and over. If only I hadn't been trying to get off work early, I would have been there. If only I would have ensured that Kevin and Jimmy were in the station before I tried to leave for the night. If only I had never met that woman. If, if, *if.* The guilt became so overwhelming that I wished I could have given my own life instead. I should have spoken to a psychologist, but I didn't want to appear weak in the eyes of my peers. Portraying a certain machismo in the aftermath of horrific tragedy is not unusual among law enforcement and military personnel. Why the fuck did I need to talk to someone? In my mind, I believed that I could handle this shit. Realistically, I knew that I couldn't, but I couldn't let my peers find out.

Jimmy's family flew his body to their hometown of Santa Rosa for his funeral services. Kevin's funeral was held at Double-Rock Baptist church in Compton. Hundreds of LAPD, LA sheriffs, and cops from all over the country were present. J.J. opened the ceremony, reading a beautifully written ode to police officers by LAPD Officer Al Engles titled, "Walking in the Footsteps of Heroes." The following year, a bronze plaque with the title and images of Kevin and Jimmy would be embedded in the cement where they lost their lives, and in the table where Kevin sat during briefing.

Governor Pete Wilson, Omar Bradley, and Patricia Moore spoke after J.J.'s opening. Governor Wilson offered warm words of encouragement to Kevin's family and fellow officers. Omar spoke glowingly, providing some much-needed comic relief when he talked about the long arm of the law arriving whenever

Kevin rolled up on the scene of a crime. Patricia Moore chose to use the Rodney King incident as a political platform and excoriated LAPD.

Moore and Omar wound up running against each other for Tucker III's recently vacated mayor's seat. Moore's statements backfired, making Omar look like a big supporter of law enforcement and an upcoming star in politics, displaying the type of effulgence he could ride all the way to DC. In the interim, it appeared as if he was poised to become just what Compton needed. Omar and Pat Moore's statements were perhaps the tipping point in the election. Kevin had so many family members and friends in Compton that their votes most likely delivered the election to Omar's doorstep. Kevin would not have been pleased. He had always hated Omar and believed that he was a crook.

As the funeral service concluded, Whitney Houston's version of "I Will Always Love You" played while we filed out of the church. The song had become synonymous with Kevin's life. Even news stations played it on the air as their reporters talked about the case. Kevin most often sang Luther Vandross in the locker room before Whitney Houston's hit was released. He would sing Houston's song or hum it during his entire shift and may very well have been doing so as he approached Regis Thomas's truck. The perfect epitaph, the song was an exclamation point on how we would feel about Kevin and Jimmy forever.

It took ten pallbearers to carry Kevin's flag-draped casket from the church. The funeral procession to the Inglewood Cemetery was five miles long. Kevin's mother screamed in anguish when the Compton PD Honor Guard performed a twenty-one-gun salute. She was still sobbing when Hourie, struggling mightily to take a knee, gave her the flag before the casket went into the ground.

The Burrell/MacDonald murder investigation and ongoing Rodney King trial dominated the news. As a result, other newsworthy events went unnoticed. During the 1992 school year, the Compton Unified School District had received a stipend of $4,400 per student from state and federal sources, slightly more than the state average. But the district squandered enormous amounts of money, prompting the school board to fire the district's business manager and order an audit. It revealed that staff members had run up millions of dollars in deficits, kept sloppy records, and, in some cases, lied to the school board to cover up their errors. As many as six secretaries did the work of one, known as featherbedding. County education investigators charged that political cronyism and nepotism were at the root of the problem.

Inside the classroom, student performance was just as bad. Test scores were the lowest in California. At one high school, fewer than ten percent of the entering freshmen graduated, and of those who did, less than half had a C average or better. Between 1986 and 1991, while the statewide dropout rate was falling, Compton's rate rose thirty-five percent. In the Spring of 1993, the CUSD, almost $20 million in the red, became the first school district in California to be taken over by the state because of economic and academic deficiencies. Within six months, Doctor Stanley Oswalt, the newly state-appointed administrator for the district, was on his way to a board meeting when someone fired multiple shots at him. His bodyguards, hired because of the contentiousness surrounding the state takeover, ushered him into an awaiting vehicle and sped away.

On April Fool's Day, the *Long Beach Press-Telegram* printed an explosive story regarding Lynwood politics. Donald Morris alleged that his wife, City Councilwoman Evelyn Wells, was having an affair with Lynwood City Manager Laurence Adams. The next night, someone shot Morris to death in his front yard. Adams got fired shortly after Morris was murdered, but he once again found employment as a high-ranking Compton city official. And, of course, he later married Wells. A city graffiti-clean-up worker was quickly arrested and convicted of the murder, but his motive and whether someone hired him remains unclear.

On April 6, Darrell Harts, a thirty-year-old Black man on the waiting list to become a Compton cop, was shot to death near Main Street and 93rd by two undercover LAPD Officers. Harts shot a pit bull attacking his dog, and the officers, allegedly in the area on a stakeout, killed him. They said they shot Harts after he fired at them first. No witnesses heard the officers identify themselves before firing. Although the DA's office didn't file charges against the officers, the DDA reviewing the case wrote the following in his legal analysis of the shooting:

"Because this claim of self-defense cannot be effectively or completely refuted, we conclude that it cannot be proven beyond a reasonable doubt that the shooting of

Darrell Harts was criminal under the circumstances. The details of the circumstances of his death may never be known."

A lot of Compton officers knew Harts. He often went on ride-a-longs and he loved cops. It is hard to believe that he shot at police officers after they identified themselves. Harts was also a crucial witness for the plaintiff in an upcoming LAPD police brutality case. The dubiety and skepticism of the reviewing DDA, in my eyes, is well founded. In addition to these questionable incidents, something else was going unnoticed in Compton. Kevin and Jimmy's high-profile trial and the jousting for control of the schools provided perfect cover for at least one Compton cop to seize on the tragic deaths and the department's fugue state to engage in corruption on a massive scale.

PART TWO

"In each of us, two natures are at war—the good and the evil. All our lives
the fight goes on between them, and one of them must conquer. But in our
own hands lies the power to choose—what we want most to be we are..."
— Robert Louis Stevenson —

CHAPTER ONE

FLATFOOT IS a name used to refer to patrol officers because they walked a beat in the earliest known form of community-based policing. Around the turn of the nineteenth century, the term "gumshoe" was used for police detectives because they had to sneak around to catch thieves. And after spending so many of my teenage years as a thief, I was promoted to gumshoe in May of 1993. I was assigned to work robbery cases. I also worked forgery for about a month after the original detective got sent back to patrol when the lieutenant found four boxes of unworked cases and a half-empty bottle of gin underneath his desk.

Historically, there was a friendly rivalry between patrol officers and detectives. When I was in patrol, detectives were "old, fat, lazy motherfuckers who had two-hour lunches every day." Now that I was a detective, patrol officers were "dumb fucking cowboys who couldn't recognize evidence at a crime scene if it bit them in the ass." However, one event brought detectives and patrol officers together as one every year: the Christmas Parade.

It was usually held two weeks before Christmas on a Saturday. The parade started near Lueder's Park and ended at city hall. It was quite a spectacle. Beautiful and talented cheerleaders from every high school in the city participated, performing to the latest hip-hop songs. City officials and the grand marshal were always chauffeured in beautiful antique cars, often followed by the Compton Cowboys riding dolled-up horses. Gleaming low-riders from various car clubs bounced up and down and side to side to the thrill of onlookers. And, of course, the gang members were always there.

Our job was to keep the rival gangs separate, detectives and patrol officers working together, breaking up gang fights and chasing gang members the entire parade. By the time the parade was over, the jail van had always made multiple trips to and from the jail, filled with gang members arrested for crimes as minor as spitting on the sidewalk to the more serious crimes of possession of firearms and assault with a deadly weapon. The following week, detectives were lazy and fat again, and patrol officers were dumb fucking cowboys.

Robberies were the crime I most loved to investigate. Robbery suspects can be violent and are often murder suspects as well. I got assigned three hundred cases in my first three months as a detective. One of them was a carjacking committed by MOB Piru William "Boo" Tagger Jr. After he got out of prison several years later, a thirteen-year-old boy won his money during a dice game. The next day, he strangled the boy and dumped his body in a trash bin.

Now that I was a detective, I worked 8:00 am to 4:30 pm and had weekends off. I was dating a beautiful young lady I met in downtown Long Beach, but I didn't want to get too close to her for all the reasons I have previously mentioned. Plus, my ex-wife Gilda being such a pain in the ass did nothing to mitigate my feelings about this. She called the station for everything; if I was one day late with child support, if I brought the kids home late after a visit, or if I was late picking them up. It was a nightmare. During Christmas one year, I took gifts to my kids and their new little brother. While I was opening presents with them, the guy Gilda was currently dating walked into the house. She talked to him for a few seconds before pulling me aside and stating bluntly, "You gotta go. You can't stay here."

I replied, "But I just got here."

She folded her arms and said, "I don't care. You gotta go." I kissed the kids before I left, including the new one who called me dad because he didn't know his own. My girlfriend was spending Christmas out of town with family, so I went over to Frailich's house because I had nowhere else to go. He and his wife Shirleen, a court reporter at Fort Compton, were always accommodating and gracious, even though they celebrated Hanukah. After that, I would sometimes take gifts to their kids on Christmas day, prompting Frailich to call me a mensch.

At the time, I was living in their condominium. The condo was on the third floor of a four-story building. The living room window and patio overlooked the street below. You couldn't enter the building unless someone buzzed you in through the lobby door. You then had to take an elevator to the upper floors.

The elevator stopped directly in front of my door. Before moving in, I had been evicted from my apartment. I still had lousy credit and was unable to find a place to rent. Several Black Compton cops, some of them detectives that I worked with, owned apartment buildings in Compton. Even though most of the buildings were the sites of drug-dealing and murders over the years, none of the cops would rent to me at a discounted rate until I got on my feet. When Frailich learned of my situation, he offered to rent the condo to me for less than half of what he could get from someone else. It pained me that my own people wouldn't lend me a helping hand when I was in need, but here, this Jewish man, a member of a supposedly greedy "tribe" who lives for profit, had.

Frailich didn't have to do what he did. He was losing money every month by renting to me. But he did it anyway. This is when I first began to realize what Martin Luther King meant. The color of your skin means shit. Nothing matters except for the content of your character. People of good character don't see race. And I'm talking about the so-called "liberals" who call themselves helping Blacks because we can't help ourselves. We don't need your pity, your condescension, or your extra test points because of our skin color. In my eyes, to accept such help is an admittance that Blacks need help because Whites are superior. We just demand the same opportunity. Nothing more, nothing less.

Compton PD, like most law enforcement agencies at the time, was extremely misogynistic. When I got hired, the most desired badges were the ones that had "Policeman" on them instead of "Police Officer." There were never more than ten total female cops on the department, and there were only two in positions of authority: Angelia Myles and Evelyn Malachi. Evelyn had reached the rank of lieutenant before being demoted in the wake of the hotel disaster. Now she and Myles were both sergeants. Catherine Chavers was one of only two female detectives. The other one was Betty Marlow, a blonde, White woman with a pleasant personality and an endearing smile. Chavers was known as "Cat" for short. She was originally from Texas and had cat-like eyes and sultry mannerisms supporting her nickname. Her long nails were always exquisitely manicured and her hair flawless.

Despite averaging seventy murders a year, only four detectives and a sergeant to supervise them were assigned to investigate homicides. There were so many murders that at least one Compton cop took matters into his own hands to keep the numbers down. The city of Long Beach is immediately south of Compton. Everything south of Greenleaf Boulevard and east of Compton College is the jurisdiction of Long Beach PD. The officer in question, upon coming across a dead body on Greenleaf east of Long Beach Boulevard, dragged the body to a vacant field south of Greenleaf. He then advised dispatch to notify Long Beach PD regarding a homicide in their area. Members of both departments stood over a dead body arguing over who was going to handle the case for close to an hour. Eventually, we took the murder, and the overzealous cop was fired. Obviously, this did nothing to mend the already contentious relationship between Long Beach PD and Compton.

Cat was the sex crimes detective. She and the homicide detectives worked in a room on the north side of the detective bureau. The room had several windows that faced city hall, Willowbrook Avenue, and the transit center. John Swanson was the supervisor. The rest of the bureau detectives sat on the south side of homicide in a large room with multiple windows that faced Willowbrook. These detectives were referred to as the floor detectives and worked the robbery, assault, burglary, forgery, and auto theft categories.

Willie Bundage, a quiet, reserved, middle-aged Black cop who dressed like it was Easter Sunday every day, was the court officer. His job was to file misdemeanor cases and to present our felony cases to the filing DDA at Fort Compton. Tom Barclay and Pepper Preston were the sergeants and sat at a large desk on the west side of the room. Ken Baratta, Dwight Dobbin, Marlow, Frailich, and Michael Markey were the only White detectives. Baratta was a quiet guy, middle-aged with a white handlebar mustache and salt and pepper hair. He was way past the point of giving a fuck by the time I was promoted to detective, but he was a black belt in karate and dressed like Elvis on occasion, so nobody fucked with him. Either he or Norman Nelson came in early every day to review and assign cases that came in overnight. Some days we got so many new cases, we never had time to get back to the older ones. And any post-conviction investigation was out of the question.

Norm was a middle-aged cop with a medium-length Afro and a bushy mustache. He was assigned to burglary and had carved out quite a niche for himself by providing off-duty cops as security to businesses for $25 an hour, taking $10 off the top for each hour they worked. We called him Stormin' Norman in jest because he never did anything with a sense of urgency. He had spent the last twenty years of his career preparing for the first year of his retirement.

An annoyingly happy guy who was always smiling no matter how turbulent the department was, Norm was married to Chickee, a beautiful deputy sheriff with light-green eyes. Whenever they were together, they dressed exactly alike, down to the shoes. Whenever they weren't, Norm wore a fanny pack and biker shorts.

One homicide detective and one detective from the floor were on call for homicides from Sunday to Sunday and got compensated at two hours of overtime per day. If no homicides occurred during that stretch, they received fourteen hours of overtime. It was rare not to catch a murder when on call, so they received the fourteen hours plus whatever other overtime was generated by the call-out. Cat was in the homicide rotation as a lead investigator for call-out purposes only.

A captain and a lieutenant commanded the detective bureau. The captain's office was south of the floor detectives, and the lieutenant's office was across the hall. R. E. Allen was the captain when I first got promoted, but Percy Perrodin replaced him about a year later. The lieutenant was Al Smith. His office was across the hallway from the entrance to the detective bureau. The bureau secretary sat in a small room at the bureau's entrance across from the lieutenant's office.

Joe Flores replaced Al Smith after I had been a detective for about two months. He was a middle-aged Mexican cop with dark hair, a thick mustache, and forearms of steel. Flores represented the department in several Police Olympics and won multiple gold medals in arm wrestling. He wasn't well liked, but he was honest and set in his ways, a by-the-book supervisor who didn't play favorites. Flores had good instincts for people and diagnosed me early on, sensing that I had had a troubled childhood and a lot of pent-up anger. He told me that until I could somehow resolve those issues, my adulthood would be troubled to the point it could derail my career, but if I ever got my shit together, the sky was the limit. My reply perfectly summed up who I was at the time. "Fuck you, El Tee. You don't know shit about me."

I was assigned to assist Cat most of the time when she was on call. On one of our callouts, Joey Reynolds had responded to a gunshot victim call on the 300 block of West Magnolia. Cat and I were at our desks when the call came in. We got there quickly, as the location was just three blocks from the station. Joey was standing near his patrol car with vestiges of a chalky substance on his hands and trousers while his rookie partner was knocking on doors, looking for witnesses. The victim, dressed in blue sports attire, was lying nearby on the sidewalk in a pool of blood with chalk outlining his body. Cat and I talked to Joey to get some preliminary information before taking a closer look at the body. Out of the corner of my eye, I saw the victim sit up groggily and swipe the front of his shirt as he looked at his bloodstained hands. He shrieked, "I'm slobbing, cuz! I'm slobbing! Somebody help me, cuz!"

Cat and I looked at Joey as he exclaimed, "Bro, he was dead! I swear to fucking God, bro!"

There are five situations where medical personnel are not needed to pronounce a victim dead. One is decapitation. The others are burned beyond recognition, decomposition, severe evisceration, and livor and rigor mortis. Joey's miscalculation caused patrol officers to call paramedics for *every* traumatic injury after that. A week after the dead guy's resurrection, a day-shift officer responded to a call of a gunshot victim. She called for paramedics, and after they trampled through the crime scene, they were not happy coming upon the victim and seeing a baseball-sized hole in the center of his chest. As they passed the officer on the way back to their vehicles, one of them whispered, "He's dead, officer. Real dead." It ended up being Stoney's case. He was infuriated when he found out what happened. He went to patrol briefing the next day to chastise the officers and give training on when not to call for paramedics. No one learned anything because he just cursed and stuttered the entire time.

LA County courts were among the first courts in the country to install metal detectors at the entrances. The county also hired private security guards to help with security at the entrance doors. While going to Fort Compton on one of my cases, I walked into the front entrance and bypassed the metal detector as I flashed my badge. The security guard working the door just happened to be the security supervisor who fired me years before. His eyes widened in surprise at the sight of my badge, and he was a bit humbler this time around. He said, "Go right ahead, sir. Have a nice day."

I could have rubbed his face in the irony of the turned tables, but instead, I just smiled and kept walking.

Nowhere was completely exempt from crime in Compton, not even the Fort. Even though it was one of the safest places in the city, there were sometimes gang fights in the hallways outside of court proceedings. There had even been a murder in the parking lot where a man shot his ex-wife after being ordered by a judge to pay her almost his entire life savings in back child support and alimony.

The most high-profile incident occurred during the summer of 1993. A well-liked judge and his mistress were at a seaside restaurant in San Pedro having lunch. They argued over the future of their relationship, and the mistress threw a glass of wine in the judge's face. She later alleged that when they returned to the judge's chambers, he grabbed her by the throat and threw her against a bookshelf. Even though I was a brand-new detective, R. E. Allen and Joe Flores assigned the case to me, probably because the more seasoned detectives had all turned it down.

Christopher Darden reviewed the case. He was rude and dismissive of my investigation and looked at me with contempt as I explained it to him. He then told me to go back to the restaurant and interview every employee. I didn't have time for all that shit. People were getting robbed and murdered in Compton. To me, the only thing that mattered was what happened in the chambers. Nobody at that restaurant saw what happened there. Darden ultimately rejected the case after the victim withdrew her complaint. Less than a year later, the judge crashed his Mercedes Benz. His mistress was killed. The judge left the scene and did not turn himself in for four hours. In an ironic twist of fate, his attorneys were Johnnie Cochran and Robin Yanes. The latter also just happened to be Cat's baby daddy, a debonair Jewish lawyer who wore Armani suits and was a deep-sea diver who caught lobsters with his bare hands. Cochran's reputation speaks for itself, but Yanes was also a brilliant attorney in his own right. Smooth as butter, he wasn't confrontational or vitriolic. He didn't beat you up on the witness stand. Instead, he just politely painted you into a corner with the kindest words possible to expose flaws in your case and your incompetency.

Yanes and Cochran said the judge "wandered away from the accident because he was in a state of shock," lawyer-speak for he was drunk, scared, and didn't know what the fuck to do. The judge later pled guilty to vehicular manslaughter. A little over three months later, OJ murdered Nicole Simpson and Ron Goldman. It is hard not to think of how fate may have played out for Darden's career had he only filed that first case against the judge. Perhaps charging a judge could have been career suicide for a DDA. Or maybe it would have elevated Darden's career to the point that he no longer had to try cases. More importantly, charging the judge might have been the impetus for him to end the illicit affair. Realistically, everything would have probably happened just the same.

Many years after the OJ case, I testified at Fort Compton on a gang-related shooting. Darden was the defense attorney. He lost this case too, but I found him more gracious in defeat this time than when he went up against Johnnie and his Dream Team. We talked afterward in the hallway, not about either case, just general conversation. I realized that he was a nice guy who had just gotten caught up in the tidal wave of Black rage sweeping America in the aftermath of Rodney King and Latasha Harlins. Perhaps I had misjudged him during our first encounter. Or maybe he had been humbled in defeat on the biggest courtroom stage in American history.

CHAPTER TWO

IN OCTOBER of 1994, Reserve Officer Tom Gibby asked me if I wanted to work security at a video premiere for rapper Snoop Dogg. I agreed to work for him because it was a golden opportunity to test the waters of being a bodyguard in the entertainment industry. The event was for the "Murder Was the Case" video release and came on the heels of the phenomenally successful *Chronic* album, produced by Dr. Dre on the Death Row Records label. The CEO was Marion "Suge" Knight. I didn't even know who he was at the time. I later found out that he was a former college football player and childhood friend of Reggie Wright Sr.'s son, Reggie Jr., also a Compton cop. Suge was drafted by the LA Rams before becoming a bodyguard for Bobby Brown, which paved his way into the music industry. The first time I ever saw him was that night.

About ten other Compton cops worked the event, including Hourie Taylor's adjutant and Lendell Johnson. Danny Sneed was head of planning and assignments. Gibby had no apparent connection to Suge or Death Row, but Danny used him for the evening because he had a security company. It made sense; Sneed was the reserve coordinator at the time, and his wife's family knew Suge's family. Reggie Jr. also worked that night. His friendship with Suge would pay generous dividends, as he would start the Wright-Way security company and eventually become the head of Death Row security. Hourie approved off-duty work permits allowing us to work security for the event that night and later for Death Row.

My assignment was to bodyguard Dr. Dre. I found him quiet and reserved, atypical of other rap/hip-hop community members yet to come. All he wanted to do was make music and money. I would go on to bodyguard him on several other occasions. He called me "Detroit," most likely because it was easier to remember than my last name. When Dre was with the group NWA, they were arrested in Detroit in 1989 after performing "Fuck Tha Police" at Joe Louis Arena. No doubt, Detroit resonated with him from that point on. Even though I was a cop from Detroit and Detroit cops arrested him, he always treated me with respect.

The only thing of note that ever happened while I was with Dre was during his birthday in New York in February of 1995. We were at a restaurant in Manhattan when a drunk White woman rubbed his head. He unleashed a verbal barrage that embarrassed the shit out of her. Later that evening, Dre had his limo driver stop at a park, and Dre and his future wife Nicole got out and talked. I stood nearby, close enough to protect them if needed but far enough away to give them some privacy.

A guy wearing a fur-hooded bomber jacket, sagging jeans, unlaced Timberland boots, and a knit skull-cap saw them and asked, "Yo, my mans! Is that that nigga Dre? Word?" He then pulled out a straight razor and stood about twenty feet away from me as he folded his arms and displayed the razor. He was quick, but I was quicker. He noticed my pistol held along the seam of my trousers and said, "Yo, I ain't tryn' take it there. It's all love, na' mean? I got y'all's back, son! We got mad love for the nigga Dre on the beast coast." He turned his back to me as I kept my eye on him until Dre and Nicole got back in the limo. I showed appreciation to the impromptu bodyguard, yelling, "We out, son!" as we peeled away from the curb.

That same weekend, the Notorious BIG and his entourage came by the bar and grill where Dre had his celebration. It was all love as Suge looked on, smiling and smoking a cigar. It was evident that he had arranged the meeting to lay the groundwork for a future collaboration. Dre, BIG, and Snoop together would have been something for the ages. Suge, Dre, and Snoop knew that BIG was a genius and destined to be a megastar, but I think Suge was trying to steal BIG from Bad Boy Records. Although gangster and thug are just two of the words generally used to describe Suge, two others are just as applicable: Visionary and hustler. Regardless of where he got the seed money from, he was able to capitalize on it and build one of the biggest labels in history. When he couldn't get BIG, he set his sights on Tupac, in prison and at odds with BIG over getting shot at the Quad studio in NYC. Suge knew that Tupac blamed BIG for the incident and seized on the opportunity to sign him. It was a brilliant chess move. Tupac probably would not have signed with Death Row under any other circumstances. Pairing Tupac with Dre set the stage for Tupac's rise to becoming one of the greatest musical artists of all time, sharing the pantheon of greatness with Gaye, Lennon, BIG, and Hendrix.

Several White officers at my agency often asked why I wanted to bodyguard gangster rappers. My reply was always, "Why not?" In my mind, they were only gangsters to sell records. It was no different from the White officers who guarded rock stars who shot heroin, snorted cocaine, or engaged in orgies with underage groupies. They all used off-duty cops as protection. And Compton officers weren't the only cops that worked for Death Row. Black officers from LBPD, Inglewood, LAPD, and the sheriff's department also provided security for the record label at one time or another.

As Death Row became more and more notorious, I told Reggie Jr. that I was quitting. Suge never liked me anyway and only tolerated me because of his affection for Reggie Jr. But Reggie Jr. wanted me around, for some reason. Perhaps he knew that he was swimming in shark-infested waters and needed someone he could trust near him. A female recording artist for the label named Jewell was up and coming, riding high off the success of her remake of the Betty Wright classic, "Woman to Woman." Reggie Jr. convinced me to stay by paying me to be her exclusive bodyguard. She had recently shot Piru Puddin during a domestic abuse situation, and Reggie Jr. feared that there could be repercussions. Puddin was now in a wheelchair because of his injuries, but he was still a force and well respected among Blood gang members.

I bodyguarded Jewell for a few months, but Lendell and I became increasingly concerned as Death Row Records was continually mired in negative controversy. Neither of us were around when Tupac or BIG got killed. It had been the wrong choice to work for Reggie Jr., but it was during a time when I think we both had questions about remaining cops after Kevin and Jimmy were murdered. Lendell saw what I had seen that night. I'm sure it fucked him up as badly as it did me.

Bookman had been promoted to detective by this point. He worked weekends at the local VFW as security, and he asked me if I wanted to work with him. I told him yes, and Hourie signed the requisite work permit. He and Percy Perrodin were always there anyway, as they drank there after work with other city employees. They were good friends and spent a great deal of time together. Everyone knew that Percy would back Hourie to the bitter end, no matter the circumstances. The other two captains on the department, R. E. Allen and Steve Roller, were not part of this exclusive club and often found themselves on the outside looking in as it related to personnel decisions.

The VFW was in the Santana Blocc Crip neighborhood, and gang members were there every weekend. All Bookman and I had to do was search people before they entered. Other than that, we just flirted with females and drank Remy Martin all night. We rarely had any problems with the SBCC members or any other Compton gang members. The ones from LA and Long Beach were a different story. Five Bloods from LA tried to get inside the club one Friday night without paying. SBCC members Big Jonesy, Kizzy, and Rock stepped up and stood with us against them.

Jonesy was as big as John Coffey from the movie *Green Mile*. During a disturbing-the-peace call at his house, it took seven cops to arrest him, and then only after they split his head open with a metal flashlight. He was beating the shit out of cops that night. At one point, three were on his back, three others were hitting him with flashlights, and one was hanging onto one of his ankles for dear life. Whenever we arrested someone, we had to stand them in front of the W/C's office and tell the W/C if they were injured or had any medical problems.

When Jonesy got to the station after getting medical attention at MLK, battered, bruised, and wearing a turban for his head injury and three sets of handcuffs, W/C Ron Malachi asked him what happened and if he was okay. Jonesy looked down at Malachi like he was a child and replied, "Didn't shit happen. I'm good, but you better see after your cops."

But on that Friday night at the VFW, Jonesy was ready to beat the shit out of some LA Bloods. I don't know if it was because of Jonesy or because the Bloods found out Bookman and I were real cops, but they left without any further incident. The following week, Jonesy and the SBCCs were doing their dirt again, and we were trying to catch them. That was the type of relationship we had with most of the Compton gang members. They knew the rules of the game. It was never personal.

On Tuesday, April 25, 1995, I was at a movie theater in Long Beach with some woman whose name I can't even remember now. We were watching *Bad Boys* with Will Smith and Martin Lawrence. After the movie was over, we went back to my condo. I turned on the TV as she started to make herself comfortable and pour us drinks. I saw on a news flash that a deputy sheriff got shot to death in Lynwood. I took a sip of my drink just as the news showed a picture of the deputy. It was Steve Blair, a fellow member of the Love Class. I swallowed hard before putting my glass on the coffee table and telling my guest, "Go home."

She looked at me in surprise and asked, "What? What do you mean, go home?"

I said, "You heard me. Get the fuck out. I can call you a cab if you want."

She called me a motherfucker and said she would find her own way home.

After she gathered up her belongings, she walked out and waited for the elevator. I watched from the balcony as she made her way down the street, still putting on her shoes and adjusting her bra strap. Frowning, I poured another drink and finished watching the news. Blair and his partner were patrolling a gang area when they saw two Young Crowd gang members. One of them discarded a gun, and the other one kept walking before suddenly turning and shooting Blair with a .44 caliber revolver as Blair was getting out of his car. Like the murders of Kevin and Jimmy, this one hit home as well. I worked with Kevin and Jimmy. I was good friends with Kevin and had played dominoes and spades at his house on multiple occasions when he lived with Paul Mason in Paramount. I went through the academy with Blair. Going through the academy with someone is like going through boot camp with them. The camaraderie never goes away. We always refer to each other as classmates, no matter how many years have passed.

Blair was one of the most popular guys in our class. Everyone loved him, just like everyone loved Kevin and Jimmy. I had been a cop for almost ten years by now and had worked with some real assholes. Why did it seem like only the good cops got killed, the ones who never had their lockers wired or white-out splashed on them? I knew this wasn't true, but the emptier that bottle of Remy Martin got, the more real it felt. And why had I treated my guest that way? She certainly didn't deserve it and may have even provided comfort had I given her a chance. But no one was there for me when Kevin and Jimmy got killed. I didn't need anyone then, and I didn't need anyone now. As I was about to pass out, I remembered thinking one thing: *Fuck everybody.*

CHAPTER THREE

WITHIN SEVEN months of being sworn in as the sixteenth mayor in Compton's history, Omar Bradley started angling to be king instead. He pushed for a fifth council seat, setting the stage for more mayoral power, and pressed for the same card club that Michael Aloyan had bribed Patricia Moore and Walter Tucker III to get. He also proposed making the mayor and council positions full-time with hefty pay increases and giving the mayor authority to set agendas for council meetings and *veto council decisions.*

Omar was an egomaniac. But he was also quite brilliant. I had several conversations with him over the years. Sometimes his brilliance bordered on the eccentric, like when he told me that the *Star Wars* movie series was an indictment of Black men: "Think about it, brother. Darth Vader's helmet looks like the head of a penis. He wears all Black, so he is representative of a Black man's reproductive organ. His stormtroopers? They are all dressed in white, like semen, which is the seed of life. If you think about the concept of the film, Vader tries to take over the universe by impregnating it and breeding the other races out. This is what White America fears from us, my brother. That we will breed them out of existence. Vader is the villain who must be defeated at all costs. He is evil incarnate, representative of everything that White people fear. He is the very epitome of the huge Black phallus that White men have feared since the Good Ship Jesus of Lubeck landed in the Americas in 1562. Who are Vader's enemies? The lovable, romantic White heroes who, despite overwhelming odds, always overcome and restore order."

It sounded preposterous, but the more I thought about it, the more plausible I thought it could be. That is when I knew that Omar Bradley would be a formidable adversary if it ever came down to that. Someone able to watch *Star Wars* and come away with that metaphor was crazy like a fucking fox.

On August 2, 1995, Bookman and Blue stopped a fifteen-year-old girl driving a stolen red Jeep. She told them she got it from a man she had been smoking crack with for the past few days at a nearby motel and was on a food errand while he waited for her. When Bookman and Blue knocked on the door, Southside Crip Shawn "Strawberry" Bowden tried to run through them. He picked the wrong cops. They tossed him up like a shortcake doll and arrested him. When they searched the room, they found a handgun, crack pipes, and several credit cards and IDs belonging to various people. They also found a glow-in-the-dark keychain in the shape of a large "1."

Stormin' Norman assigned the case to me. I released the female to the Department of Children Services after interviewing her. In my mind, she was a victim. Next, I turned my attention to Mr. Bowden. I checked out his criminal history before talking to him. He had been recently released from prison after serving time for robbing an off-duty deputy sheriff and taking her badge and gun. I introduced myself, and he replied, "No need for all that, muthafucka. Everybody in the hood know who the fuck you are. I ain't did shit. Now get out my face, cuz."

Frailich and I then checked recent unsolved robbery cases and contacted the owners of the IDs and credit cards. We found out that after taking the Jeep on July 22, Bowden robbed people in the cities of Lynwood, Compton, and Long Beach at least once, sometimes twice a day. He forced people watering their lawns into their homes at gunpoint, where he stole from them as they watched. He robbed single women at bus stops and elderly couples in their homes. One of these couples were eighty-nine and ninety-two years old, the other couple were in their eighties. His victims were Black, White, Mexican, and Asian. An equal opportunity dickhead, Bowden didn't give a fuck who he robbed. Since he had been smoking crack with an underage girl, I expanded my search to include sexual assault victims where the suspect matched his description. Although the girl never admitted it, I knew that if they were in a motel room together, she was having sex with him. I figured that every time they ran out of cocaine, he would pull another heist to get money for more while she waited in the room. He left the food errands for her. Maybe he did more than just rob people while he was out.

The Lakewood sheriff's station had a recent case where a White woman who worked in Paramount claimed she was kidnapped and raped by a Black guy driving a red sport utility vehicle. The detective on the case seemed skeptical of her story and was more than happy to give me the investigation. After talking to the victim, I knew she was telling the truth. Bowden had kidnapped her as she was getting off work and forced her to withdraw money at gunpoint from a bank ATM as he stood next to her. He then took her to a motel and raped her. I got a copy of the bank video. You couldn't see his face because he was holding his head down, intentionally avoiding the camera, but that keychain in the shape of a large "1" hanging around his neck was unmistakable.

The patrol deputies from Lakewood station had had the good sense to take the victim to the hospital for a sexual assault examination. I got a warrant for a DNA sample from Bowden, who was now at the Pitchess Detention Center near the Magic Mountain amusement park. Frailich went with me to get the sample. Bowden was playing basketball with other inmates when we got there. He saw us and grinned before shooting an airball. When a deputy brought him to an interview room where Frailich and I were waiting, he said, "What up, Reynolds? I still ain't got shit to say to you."

I gestured to a nearby chair and said, "Well, Shawn. I kind of figured that. I just need some of your DNA."

Defiantly, he kept standing and asked, "What if I refuse?"

I showed him the warrant and said, "Well, I will just get two of the biggest fucking deputies in this muthafucka to give us a hand. I would prefer saliva, but blood works just as good."

For just a second, I thought I saw fear in his eyes as he answered, "All that shit ain't necessary. Do what the fuck you gotta do, cuz."

Bowden looked at me after providing the sample and said, "Anything else? I need to get back to the game now, cuz. They need me."

I thought about his airball before I replied. "One more thing before you go. Remember that White woman you raped? It's a good chance you left some of your strawberry seeds in her, cuz." The blood drained from his face, the basketball game losing all importance.

Bowden had good cause to be concerned. The DNA test later confirmed that he had indeed raped the woman anally and vaginally. The DA's office charged Bowden with thirty-six felonies, but he was only convicted of thirty-four because two of the victims were too elderly to appear in court. He was sentenced to 652 years in prison. Within days of the sentencing, SSCC members spray-painted "S.I.P Strawberry" and "Fuck Renolds" on several walls in their neighborhood.

S.I.P stands for "South in Peace." As the Bounty Hunters had done with Regis Thomas, the Southside Crips were writing Bowden off as dead. They were also explicitly showing their disdain and hatred for me, not to mention their spelling deficiencies.

Robin Yanes defended Bowden. Yanes was congenial in a rare defeat and wrote a letter to Chief Hourie Taylor regarding the "Outstanding Investigative Work" I did. It was unheard of for a defense attorney to commend a cop for investigative excellence, and it was probably the only time he did it in his entire career. I got the California Organization of Police and Sheriff's Officer of the Year Award for this case. I had also cleared ninety-five percent of my cases that year and got the city of Compton Employee of the Year award as well.

Several years later, I saw the girl who led us to Bowden walking on Long Beach Boulevard, tricking for crack near the same motel. Now of legal age, she was another failure of the child protective system and yet another casualty of the war on drugs.

CHAPTER FOUR

DESPITE THE high number of murders in LA County during the 1980s and 90s, suspects got charged only forty-seven percent of the time. Only sixteen percent ended with murder convictions, with another fourteen percent resulting in convictions for the lesser charge of manslaughter. Unbelievably, seventy percent of people who committed murder in LA County were getting away with it. Compton made a significant contribution to the overall number of killings every year. There is no street in the city where I can drive down and not remember a murder.

Almost all murders in Compton were gang-related, where the only evidence was shell casings, spent bullets, and sometimes a stolen, burned car found later in a neighboring jurisdiction. Our gang unit was very successful in solving most of these murders by using a network of street informants, who were either paid or trying to work off a case. We cultivated them by looking the other way on gun and drug possession charges, either holding the charges over their heads or booking the evidence as found property after telling the lucky soul, "You owe me one." Other murders, like the ones with only biological or other forensic evidence and no witnesses, were rarely, if ever, solved.

Dwight Dobbin had been on the department since the early 70s. He wore glasses and clip-on ties with short sleeve shirts. He leaned forward when he walked, his eyes glued to the floor between his orthopedic shoes. His collateral duty was crime scene investigator since the city had eliminated the full-time position. Despite Dobbin's appearance as a dogged, aging sleuth and last of a dying breed, I can't recall one instance where he made a case on prints that he lifted, and most of the crime scene photographs he took were of low quality, at best. It wasn't all his fault, though. He was just as overworked as the rest of us, and we were discouraged from calling out the sheriff's department to process our crime scenes because of misplaced pride. However, we *needed* the sheriff's department's crime scene investigation expertise to help us with some of our murders. Now, the horde of unsolved cold-case murders with compromised or no evidence will most likely never be solved.

We had one case where someone massacred an elderly woman with a butcher knife in her kitchen. The case should have been a piece of cake to solve; there was a plethora of biological evidence, including bloody footprints that didn't belong to the victim. The case remains unsolved, primarily because the scene was never properly processed. We had another case where a young mother of three was gutted in her own home while her children were at school. The kids found her when they returned home. There was blood evidence everywhere, but the investigators tried to process the scene themselves and fucked it up. We also had rapes where the Sexual Assault Response Team (SART) kits were never refrigerated, and as a result, the kits became contaminated. A serial killer or rapist would have had the time of his life in Compton; we were too busy concentrating on whether Brazy or Gangsta-roo killed C-Crazy, or if Oso killed Bull.

Most of the murders Cat and I handled were run of the mill, but some of them were ruthless and went beyond the norm. On July 17, 1994, we got called out to 500 East Pine Street. Lonzie Thompson, a forty-seven-year-old homeless man, had been found shot to death in the middle of the road, a bullet hole in each kneecap and his brains blown out with a large caliber pistol. He had been pushing a shopping cart collecting cans for his heroin habit when he was killed. Word on the street was that a twelve-year-old Mexican kid killed him as part of a gang initiation.

Once, we got called out to a scene where a paraplegic man got strangled at a playground. The killer stuffed his body in a port-a-potty, folded his wheelchair, and placed it on top of him.

A six-year-old who went to relieve herself found him when she opened the door. We handled another case where a fourteen-year-old boy stabbed his uncle forty times with a kitchen knife because the boy wanted to leave during nighttime hours, and his mother and the victim wouldn't let him. Even though the mother called the police, she tried to fight us when we arrested her son.

There were roaches all over the house, even on a birthday cake sitting on the kitchen table. On at least two occasions, I saw one crawl on the heads of the fourteen-year old's younger siblings. No one made any attempt to kill them; it seemed like just business as usual. Although I could not fathom why the four-teen-year-old felt he had to kill his uncle, I understood why he had wanted to leave the house so badly.

Another case that we handled happened on Thanksgiving. A woman stabbed her brother because he clucked off the family's Butterball the night before for a $20 piece of crack. He was lying in the kitchen with a carving knife sticking out of his chest when we got there.

One of the more memorable murder investigations I responded to occurred on West School Street in 1994. Three men executed a man in front of his wife and several small children. The wife was able to run out the back door, but the gunmen chased her. The couple's older son, fourteen-year-old Marcos Yanez, was in another room upstairs. He armed himself with an AK-47 and, from an upstairs window, killed two of the gunmen as they ran across the front lawn. The third one got away. There were hundreds of pounds of marijuana and a gold-plated Delta Elite 10mm pistol with intricate etchings of Jesus Malverde, the patron saint of drug dealers, in the house. The victim was an informant for the DEA. The killer who got away remains unidentified to this day. Either he lost his head when he returned to Mexico or is somewhere in the Federal Witness Protection Program. My bet is that his head wound up rolling out of a duffle bag across a disco dance floor in Sinaloa.

Four years later, Compton officers served a search warrant at Frederick "Gangsta" Staves's house after receiving information that Santana Blocc Compton Crips were fencing stolen goods there. Marcos Yanes opened the door. The cops found sixty pounds of marijuana, $36,000, stolen electronics, guns, and bulletproof vests in the house. The SBCC gang was dealing directly with Mexican cartels, and Staves laundered the dirty money through "OG's Paging Network" on Compton Boulevard, run by his wife, Guadalupe *Yanes*-Staves.

On September 7, 2001, sheriff's deputies and federal agents would serve multiple search warrants targeting the SBCC gang for running a sophisticated cocaine distribution network. Gangsta Staves got arrested along with two dozen other members, but Marcos Yanes eluded capture. After his blood-bathed baptism of fire, he had gone through quite a transformation to drug kingpin. And nobody even gave a fuck because the Twin Towers went down four days later, and every federal agent in the country dropped everything and went on the hunt for some motherfucker hiding in a cave halfway across the world named Osama bin Laden.

CHAPTER FIVE

ON AUGUST 14, 1995, I went to the PM shift briefing to sell candy for my son Dominic's school. I noticed the most recently hired dispatcher sitting at the back of the briefing room. She wore glasses and weighed about ninety-five pounds with rocks in her pockets. It wasn't the first time I had seen her. Cat and I were at a homicide scene at the corner of Rosecrans and Central Avenue about two weeks before. Witnesses had called the police after smelling a foul odor coming from the trunk of a car. Responding officers opened it and found a human head. The new dispatcher was on a ride-along with Sergeant Angelia Myles that night, and they came to the scene.

Sergeant Myles was talking to her while pointing at Cat and me as we went about the business of detecting. Some crime scenes were so extensive we frequently ran out of the yellow-colored evidence markers. At shootouts, there could be over one hundred shell casings. We just wrote the next number on a piece of paper whenever that happened. As horrific as this particular scene was, it only required two, though, one on the car's roof and one in the trunk. Just as I was placing number two next to the decomposing head with a bullet hole between the eyes, the dispatcher looked at me and smiled.

Her name was Carolyn Baker. She was unmarried and had three kids. As I remembered the way our eyes met over a corpse-less head, I thrust a box of World's Finest chocolate almond bars in her face and said, "Hey. Buy some candy for my kid's school."

She recoiled with a look of disgust and replied, "Uh, no! What makes you think I would buy anything from you with an approach like that?" I stepped back. I was a big-shot detective. It wasn't supposed to go this way. She should have been handing me a $20 bill with her phone number on it by now.

I was offended and reacted like the arrogant dipshit that I was at the time, telling her "Whatever," before moving on to the next potential customer.

As bad as our first contact had gone, I couldn't stop thinking about her when I got home. But I knew I had to try and get some sleep because Cat and I were on call. As soon as I got undressed for bed, the phone rang. It was the W/C. A Mona Park Crip named Billy "Lil Bill" Washington had been shot to death at Alondra Boulevard and Long Beach. It would end up being just another one of the thousands of unsolved gang murders in LA County.

I met a woman that night by the name of Easter Perkins. She was cute, had a pretty smile, and good conversation. She gave me her phone number and told me to give her a call sometime. I called her the next day and asked her out on a date. It wasn't unusual for cops to meet women on the job. We met them all the time, which is one reason cops have such high divorce rates. I still wasn't in the market for a long-term relationship. I just wanted to take her out for dinner and drinks and have sex later. Does that make me a heel? An asshole? A piece of shit? Yes. I was all those things and more. She spent the night at my condo, and the next morning, I kissed her goodbye and called her a cab like I had done for dozens of other women over the years. I was broken inside at the time. My childhood trauma mixed with my undiagnosed PTSD had created an unemotional Frankenstein. Yet, for some reason, I couldn't get Carolyn Baker off my mind.

A few days later, I was at my desk when the secretary told me I had a visitor in the lobby. I went downstairs, and Easter was there. She had a worried look on her face. I smiled and said hi. "I'm pregnant," she said.

I thought she was kidding until her facial expression didn't change at all. I didn't believe her. I thought to myself, *how could she know so quick? She was probably already pregnant and is now trying to hook me because I have a decent job and benefits.* I got angry. "Bullshit. If you're pregnant, it ain't mine. I got work to do, so…"

She didn't get angry. She just walked away as I closed the door. I didn't give it a second thought.

A week after that, I was sitting at my desk when a woman called and asked for Detective Reynolds. I answered, "This is he. How can I help you?"

After a brief pause, another woman said, "Hello. It's Carolyn."

I said, "Carolyn who?"

Audibly irritated, she replied, "Baker. Carolyn Baker? From dispatch?"

I was glad she couldn't see me smirking when I said, "Oh, okay. I'm kind of busy right now. I'll call you back."

"Wait, you don—" CLICK. I leaned back, smiled, and put my feet on my desk.

Frailich took notice and asked, "What the hell are you smiling for, Freddie?"

Without looking at him, I clasped my hands behind my head. I said, "That was that new dispatcher. I think I like her."

Frailich rolled his eyes as he slammed his palms on his desk and yelled, "Then why did you hang up on her, dumbass? You didn't even get her home number!"

This time I looked at him and said, "Hey, meshuguna! I'm a fucking detective. You think I can't find that out? And watch your mouth, you fucking kike." Frailich laughed as I thought about why it was okay for me to call him a kike but not for him to call me a shvooga. But I *was* a dumbass for not asking Carolyn for her number.

A few days later, Carolyn still hadn't tried to call me back. I called dispatch and told the supervisor that I needed Baker's home number because I had a subpoena for her on one of my cases. I called her later. She told me that she had had a dream about me and was going to call me when she got to work. I smiled. She was as full of shit as I was.

Our first date was on August 24, 1995. We went to Legend's Sports bar in Long Beach on Second Street. I liked Carolyn right away. She was everything I thought a woman should be. She was goal-oriented and wanted to make something of herself for her kids. Sure, she had gotten pregnant at sixteen, had her first son at seventeen, dropped out of high school, and had her second son at eighteen. She had been involved with a guy with whom she had had her third child about two years before we met. She told me how badly she wanted to get a college degree one day but bemoaned how difficult it would be with three kids and a full-time job.

She came to my place for our second date. We watched a sub-titled Mexican movie called, *Like Water for Chocolate*. We just sat in the living room afterward drinking cognac, listening to music, and watching my fish. She tried to match me in drinks but ended up throwing up all over herself and passing out. I showered her before putting my robe on her and carrying her to the bed. I washed her clothes while she slept.

The next morning, I made bacon and eggs and had Excedrin and orange juice sitting on the nightstand for her. Smiling through her obvious embarrassment when she woke up, she sheepishly thanked me. I replied, "For what? Your clothes had vomit all over them. I couldn't let you sleep like that."

Carolyn said, "I know. But you didn't have to do what you did." She then looked at herself in the mirror on my dresser and exclaimed, "Oh, God! My hair!" I smiled, kissed her on the forehead, and we had breakfast together for the first time. I realized this was out of character for me. Typically, I would have ushered a woman out the next morning, but I just couldn't shake the feeling that there was something special about *this* woman.

Thirty-six hours later, four-year-old Joshaney Henderson was shot to death by three Barrio Los Padrinos gang members at 1218 East Golden Street. She was in a car driven by her father. The gang members were lying in wait, pretending to work on a disabled vehicle. When they saw her father, they began shooting at his car, and an errant round struck Joshaney. This is the epitome of a cop's life, the constant transitioning from beautiful dreamlike events to nightmares borne of spilled blood, shattered bones, and misery. Just two weeks before the murder, Joshaney's father had visited a Mexican friend who lived in the area. BLP gang members later spray-painted "Don't bring niggers over here" on the friend's house. Eddie Aguirre and Ray Richardson, a tall Black cop who wore his hair in a high flattop like the lead singer of Cameo, knew most of the BLP members and were able to identify the culprits based on their descriptions.

Carolyn introduced me to her kids about a month after Joshaney was murdered. I liked that she didn't immediately try and thrust them into our relationship. It told me that if she wasn't into me, her kids would never get the opportunity to meet me. Her sons were named Jeremy and Deon, and her daughter was named Courtney. Jeremy and I shared the same birthday. Carolyn and my Mom Mary shared the same birthday as well, which was the same day as my court appearance for armed robbery many years before. It was a beautiful synchronicity that I just couldn't ignore.

Deon was a smart, lovable kid who attached himself to me from the start. Courtney was the baby. She was a beautiful little girl like Joshaney, only two years younger. I fell in love with all of them right away, especially Courtney, who I met first. I was in my doorway when the elevator door opened. Courtney, a little miniature version of her mother, just stood there, hesitant to get off the elevator. She was timid and quiet but had inquisitive eyes, a brightness burning behind them illuminating a latent intelligence.

Carolyn came from a great family. Her father was a retired Navy chief and veteran of two wars, and her mother was a retired purchaser for the Korody-Colyer Corporation and was also a property owner. Carolyn's sister, Terry, graduated valedictorian from Compton High in the same class as James Lewis. Carolyn also had incredibly competitive twin brothers, JD and JC. When one got a job at UPS, the other got a job at Fed Ex. Carolyn's mother worked long hours, and her father was a bedridden double-amputee. As a result, her brothers bore the brunt of raising her. Carolyn's undying love for the LA Dodgers developed from them, as they took her to numerous games when she was a little girl. Although close to them both while growing up, Carolyn was far closer to JD, a dynamic that remains true to this day.

Gilda and my kids had moved in with the guy who had her tell me to leave that one Christmas Day. When the kids were with me, I took them wherever they wanted to go to make up for my absence. We even went to Rocky Mount so they could experience the same joy that I had every summer as a kid. They always seemed so happy, but material things can never take the place of time. In a futile attempt to give my kids a better childhood than I had, I would come to realize that I had fallen woefully short. I didn't even know how to talk or interact with them. My solution was to give them money or buy them whatever they wanted. These were the things missing from my childhood, and I wanted to make sure they had them. But emotional bonding and physical attachment were also missing from my childhood. I couldn't give them these because I had never learned how. When Carolyn met my kids, she treated them just like her own. They were standoffish initially, but eventually, they warmed up to her. I would later find out that she was more of a mother to them part-time than their own mother had ever been to them full-time.

Carolyn and I dated in secret for over two years. Frailich was the only person who knew. I was afraid to make a verbal commitment, the fear suppressing the courage of unconditional love. It was selfish of me. I knew she wanted more by this point. She didn't need a man, but that didn't mean that she didn't *want* one. And even though I still felt like I didn't need *or* want a woman, she made me forget about the hurt and the pain I had endured. Through Carolyn, I reconnected with my family and began talking to them regularly. She made me realize the importance of family and that no man should be an island; she made me want to be a better person, to wash the squalidness of unfulfilled potential from the resume of my life. The heart can't speak, but you have to listen to it anyway. Before long, Carolyn became the only fish in my coffee table.

CHAPTER SIX

EASTER SENT pictures of a beautiful baby boy in June of 1996. His name was Abree Miloni Reynolds. He looked like me. Still, I decided to get a paternity test. The results were positive. He was mine. I should have been happy, but I wasn't. I was devastated. My world had been turned upside down. I was a bachelor working a demanding job with all kinds of odd hours. Easter was originally from Northern California. After I told her that I wouldn't be able to help her with the baby, she moved back there with him. I went on with my life, paying child support and ensuring that he had medical and dental benefits. I was never a deadbeat dad. I was worse. I was a father who wasn't actively involved in his son's life. I should have moved heaven and earth to be close to him, to have an ongoing bond with him. But I didn't, and that is something that I can never take back. There are just no do-overs in life.

On September 7, 1996, Tupac Shakur and Suge Knight got shot in Las Vegas. Tupac died a week later, on Friday the thirteenth. Several hours before the shooting, Suge, Tupac, and other members of the Death Row entourage beat down Southside Compton Crip member Orlando "Baby Lane" Anderson in the lobby of the MGM. Over the next two days, more than two dozen shootings and at least five murders occurred in Compton involving members of the SSCC, MOB, Lueder's Park, and Elm Lane Piru gangs.

One of the shootings involved Darnell Brim and ten-year-old Lakeisha McNeese. Someone shot them as they were walking into a neighborhood store. Brim and Lakeisha didn't know each other; she was just an innocent victim who happened to have a hankering for some candy at that moment. Frailich and I got the case. Lakeisha was in surgery when we got to the hospital, so we talked to Brim. He wasn't happy to see me at all. He said, "Fuck you want, Reynolds?"

I replied, "What's up, Darnell? I'm sorry about what happened, and I know for you it's just part of the game, but a little girl got shot too. I don't even care if you come to court. Just help me make it right." He closed his eyes and, with a barely audible voice, said, "Fuck you, cuz. I didn't see shit, and I ain't got shit to say. Now I'm tired, so get the fuck out my room."

A witness had obtained the first three characters of the suspect vehicle's license plate. An informant told Brennan that Leuders Park and MOB Pirus had bragged about shooting Brim. One of them had a car with a plate that matched the partial plate. Frailich and I saw it parked in the driveway of the registered address. When we showed the witness photographs of the car, he/she said it was a different make, model, and color. The witness was also unable to identify a photo of a Piru associated with the car. I ordered a printout of all vehicles with similar partial plate information in LA County. Before Frailich and I got a chance to go through them or show the witness additional photographs, Hourie took us off the case because of my past employment with Reggie Jr. It was the low point of my career. To this day, I believe I would have solved it.

A few weeks after Brim and Lakeisha got shot, over three hundred cops served search warrants written by Brennan at thirty-seven houses. Twenty-three gang members, including Baby Lane, were arrested. The entire operation, dubbed "Heatwave," netted firearms, bulletproof vests, $17,000, and six pounds of cocaine, marijuana, and meth. My team searched at Brim's house. We found a .45 caliber pistol, crack cocaine, $10,000, and an unmailed letter from Brim addressed to Ronald McMillan, an inmate at Pelican Bay State Prison. The US flag stamp on the letter was upside down. This was common among gang bangers, done to show their antipathy for America and law enforcement, like when professional athletes kneel during the national anthem. The irony is that a nation's flag, displayed upside down, is a distress signal in wartime, which the government of Compton most assuredly was in.

The letter was dated October 1 and read, in part: "Big Ron what's up Homie. Yea I'm just chillen Homie. I just got out the hospital Thursday Dogg. Yea I'm doing cool. I'd be in good condition in about two months. I can't walk that good, but it will get greater homie. Yea I got hit five times, 3 in the back & 2 in the arm, yea Dogg niggas tried to have me & you know they paid for it dearly the homies was putting it down you know."

In other words, after Brim got shot, Southside went on a shooting rampage against those responsible. To my knowledge, no one ever continued to investigate the shooting of Brim and Lakeisha. No one ever talked to Frailich or me about anything we did on the case. I don't even know if Lakeisha was ever interviewed, either. My heart truly goes out to her and her family. As for Brim and the motherfucker who shot her, they can just charge it to the game.

Our entire gang unit at the time, which consisted of Reggie Wright Sr., Bobby Ladd, Tim Brennan, Aguirre, and Richardson, knew Baby Lane killed Tupac and the motive by the second day. Reggie Wright Jr. was responsible for the security team the weekend Tupac was murdered. If you don't think he told his father what happened, you must hang out in PCP Alley. Had Las Vegas PD listened to the gang unit early on, they could have tracked everyone involved in the incident. Starting with Baby Lane's movements, they could have obtained footage from surveillance cameras in hotels, casinos, and parking lots.

The 15 Freeway is the only road leading to Los Angeles from Las Vegas, and it is filled with California Highway Patrol cars. With the knowledge that a white Cadillac had just been used in a murder and was on the way to Compton, the likelihood of it being stopped was high. But early on, LVPD chose not to deal with Compton PD because of Reggie Jr. and his familial connection to Reggie Sr. In an unprecedented exhibition of tunnel vision, LVPD believed that all Compton cops were dirty and divulging information to us would jeopardize their case.

Like the cops who let the Zodiac killer slip through their fingers because of preconceived notions, LVPD let the killer of one of the most transcendent figures in music history slip through theirs. By suppressing their preconceptions and just listening, LVPD could have learned the histories between the two gangs involved; they would have known that the SSCC gang had a significant presence in North Las Vegas. They didn't even have to share their information on the case with Compton PD. All they had to do was listen to our gang unit. But they chose not to and look where they are twenty-five years later—foils of one of history's greatest unsolved murders.

Solving this case wasn't rocket science. It was Cop Work 101. To this day, everyone in Compton can tell you who killed Tupac. SSCC member Dwayne "Keefee D" Davis already has. During a proffer session with law-enforcement officials, he confessed to sitting in the back seat next to Baby Lane when Baby Lane killed Tupac. According to Keefee D, SSCC members Deandre "Freaky Dre" Smith and Terrance "T-Bone" Brown were the other two men in the car. Keefee D went so far as to say that he would have pulled the trigger himself if he had a chance to.

Less than six months after Tupac's murder, the Notorious BIG was killed. The SSCC gang was possibly involved in this incident as well. Brennan wrote a search warrant for several locations, including Keefee D's house. Sergeant Henry Robinson supervised the search team at Keefee D's house, which consisted of me, Frailich, and Dwight Dobbin's son Tim. Keefee D was not home. We found a bill from the Monte Carlo Casino in Las Vegas, possibly where he was staying the night Tupac was killed. LAPD RHD Lieutenant P. Conway and Detectives Russell Poole and Fred Miller helped with the search. They impounded a dark-colored Chevrolet Impala under a tarp in the backyard because it matched the description of the car used in BIG's murder.

Tupac's murder and the motive were pretty cut and dry to me, but I don't know much about BIG's murder. I do believe that the reason is much murkier and more of a *labyrinth*, however. Poole became obsessed with solving the murder of BIG and doggedly believed that LAPD officers were responsible. I have no idea who killed BIG, but I would tend to lean toward one of the oldest motives for murder that there is: profit. If you really want to solve this murder, follow the money. Poole's obsession would eventually end his life. On August 19, 2015, while at sheriff's homicide headquarters talking to the captain about reopening the BIG case after Suge's arrest for an unrelated murder, Poole died of a massive heart attack. The tinfoil hatters were immediately out in force, saying that Reggie Jr. was at the meeting and killed Poole using an undetectable poison. Besides being preposterous on its face, Reggie Jr. wouldn't have been able to get within a mile of the building unless he was wearing handcuffs.

An honest cop is a crooked cop's worst nightmare. The honest one can ride with a crooked one for years without knowing. The corrupt cop may do something to test the honest one initially, like finding money and making a joke about not turning it in to gauge the honest cop's reaction. If it doesn't go over well, the crooked cop will never test the waters again. The corrupt cop will always be on his or her best behavior from that point on. I rode with Reggie Jr. several times in patrol. He never did anything illegal, nor did he test the waters. He had to get his pound of flesh every night, though, to ensure that he had an adequate number of subpoenas for his overtime via the "Bookman Drops" that he always seemed to notice that I never did.

Based on how I grew up, it might be hard to believe that I never stole money or drugs or lied on a police report to put a case on someone. I once arrested a man who was convicted of attempted murder and sent to prison. When new evidence came to light, I signed a declaration supporting my belief that he was innocent. The document was the single biggest reason that he was eventually released from prison. I caught a lot of heat from my peers for doing this. Some cops believe that if someone goes to jail for something they didn't do, it's okay because of all the other shit they probably got away with. I didn't care what my peers thought. I knew it was the right thing to do. If I fucked up a case, I was brave enough to document the mistakes and let the DA's office know. I was able to look in the mirror. I wonder if that DDA who sat on the information for almost twenty years could do the same.

I was far from perfect. Everyone is. We have all done shit that we will take to the grave. Some of us have small change purses to carry it in; some of us have duffle bags. Cops are no different. Like everyone else, they are inherently flawed and prone to moments of clarity and epiphany throughout their entire careers. We all must be able to recognize when change is required or needed. If you can't learn to swim with the tides of history, you will get swept away by the undercurrent of time.

CHAPTER SEVEN

ON MAY 5, 1997, the Redondo Beach Police Department hired Carolyn as a dispatcher. She left Compton PD because Redondo Beach dispatchers made almost twice as much. Shortly before she got her new job, a crew of armed men began robbing stores all over Compton. I knew that if I didn't catch them soon, someone was eventually going to get killed. On May 18, I came to work hungover from a night of drinking. After a night like this, I often sat at my desk wearing sunglasses and rubbing my head as Stormin' Norman took delight in dropping a pile of cases next to my phone. He would smile and laugh before walking away to the next desk, oblivious to me softly cursing. Some days, my displeasure at the volume of cases I was assigned was a lot louder. On those days, the more I swore, the louder Frailich laughed.

I took a couple of Excedrin as I thumbed through the reports. One of them jumped out right away. The day before, four armed men robbed the Riteway Market on Alondra Boulevard and took the owner's Glock 9mm pistol. Riteway was about a mile from what was formerly the Happy Little Cow Market. The owners rebuilt it after rioters burned it to the ground in 1992. Now it was just the Little Cow. Rioters also burned Riteway to the ground, despite the "Black Owned" disclaimer spray-painted on the windows. Unlike the other stores the crew robbed, Riteway had surveillance cameras. I recognized one of the crooks. I didn't know his name, but I had seen him in Nutty Blocc's hood before. Frailich and I spent the next few days driving around there looking for the robbery crew.

During my first week on the job, J. J. taught me that when two cops are riding together, they should never look at each other. Their attention should always be focused outside of their windows and in front of them. He also taught me that cops should never ride with their windows rolled up, no matter how hot or cold it was outside. A cop needs the smell, the sights, and the sounds of the city to properly patrol it. Even still, cops talk about the most mundane shit that has nothing to do with police work. As we were looking out our respective windows while driving down Kemp Street, Frailich asked how it was going with Carolyn. Without looking at him, I answered, "Two souls with but a single thought. Two hearts that beat as one."

He broke the rule and looked at me, asking, "What in the fuck are you talking about, dumbass?"

I said, "That's Keats, meshuguna."

Frailich slapped his forehead and said, "Oh, brother. Let me out of this fucking car already."

I laughed as I parked at a liquor store at Central Avenue and Alondra. We just sat there, hoping one of the assholes would go in to buy a forty-ounce or even try and rob the store. While TV shows and the movies make it seem as if police work is nonstop shootouts, car chases, and fighting, real police work is long bouts of boredom, mundane conversations, and insults interrupted by short bursts of terror and fear. Just boredom, insults, and dumbass talk this time, though, and we went home for the weekend no closer to solving the case.

On June 2, three men committed a home invasion robbery in Long Beach. One of them raped a woman. Long Beach PD officers spotted the getaway car and chased it to the Wilmington Arms, where one of the men got shot during a gunfight. The other two men got away. The wounded guy was the one I had recognized in the video. His name was Devonne O'Dell. The detective handling the case acted like I was bothering him when I called, so I just continued working on the Riteway case. Two weeks later, a Long Beach cop named Mark "Mac" McGuire called me. He was assigned to the gang unit, partnered with another Black officer named Vic Thrash. Mac told me about two robberies in Long Beach that Compton gang members may have committed.

The modus operandi was almost the same as in the Compton robberies. Six days after Long Beach PD shot O'Dell, two gunmen robbed the Cork-N-Bottle convenience store at 1302 East Artesia Boulevard. The other robbery occurred on June 12. Two men, only one armed this time, entered the market where I played video games years before and killed Mr. Moon. They then left in a van occupied by two other men. I was shaken by the news. Here was a compassionate White man, who had gone out of his way to help me, a down-on-his-luck Black man, and these idiots had just snuffed out his light. Mac's call resonated with me because he seemed to care. No other Long Beach cop had ever tried to reach out to me before. His calling someone from Compton PD was no small thing based on the relationship between our agencies.

On June 19, a parole agent and two Compton patrol officers found the gun stolen from Riteway during a compliance search at the house of a local gangster named Calvin Chism. The parole agent didn't know any of his accomplices other than Samuel "Ghost" Taylor, who was not involved in the Riteway robbery. This didn't mean that Ghost wasn't involved in Mr. Moon's murder, though, and it just so happened that his girlfriend owned a van. She was scared shitless when I knocked on her door the next day. She told me Ghost used her van the day of the murder and left with Chism and another guy she knew as Mark. She viewed the videotape of the Riteway robbery and identified Chism, Mark, and one of the others as a guy known as "Fade." She didn't know the fourth guy on the video. I did a computer search and found out that Fade's real name was Michael Pride.

I interviewed Chism at the county jail. He admitted to robbing Riteway and told me his accomplices were O'Dell, Pride, and Marcus "Mark" Johnson. Chism said he didn't know they were going to rob the store, and he only took the gun to protect himself from the store owner. I knew he was lying, but I didn't interrupt. He went on to try and distance himself from the weapon, saying that he gave it to O'Dell after the robbery, but O'Dell's girlfriend brought it back to his house without his knowledge. At that point, I knew that Chism killed Mr. Moon and had more than likely used the stolen Glock. A ballistic check would later confirm that I was right.

The following day, patrol officers arrested Marcus Johnson and two other guys for robbing QT's Market located on West Compton Boulevard. The entire robbery crew was now in custody or at least identified. I started writing search and arrest warrants, which is painstaking work because you must ensure you are going to the right house. Hitting the wrong one can result in a hell of a lawsuit or the death of an innocent person. An operations plan is prepared to ensure the proper steps are taken to hit the right house. The plan is always given a name. I just called this operation "Ops Plan" with the date. My boss at the time, Lieutenant William Wallace, a grizzled old White cop who had worked as a California Highway Patrol Officer before coming to Compton PD, told me to give it a name. I changed it to "Reynolds Ops Plan." He didn't like it and told me to give it an appropriate name. He was beside himself when I submitted it again, calling it "Operation Deez Nutz." He finally named it himself, calling it "Operation Nutty Buster."

We served the warrants on August 12, arrested Pride and Ghost, and recovered evidence connected to several of the robberies. While Pride admitted to robbing Riteway, Ghost didn't say a word. I filed the robbery cases in Long Beach in conjunction with the murder case. Marcus Johnson and Ghost got convicted of five counts of armed robbery and one count of murder. O'Dell got convicted of rape, theft, and shooting at the police. Ghost, O'Dell, and Johnson received life in prison. Chism, the triggerman in Moon's murder, was sentenced to death. Shawn Randolph, a beautiful woman with blonde hair and green eyes, was outstanding in her prosecution of the case. She was one of the best DDAs I ever had the pleasure of working with. Extremely grateful for the work I put in on this case, she wrote me a formal commendation. I never received any type of thank you from Long Beach PD, but the family of Mr. Moon, a man who had let me earn a little money and lent an ear when I was at my lowest point, was grateful, and that's all that mattered. That, and the fact that I had met Mac, who would become a lifelong friend.

Mac was a unique individual who lent credence to the old saying about the size of the fight in the dog. Standing at about five foot four, give or take an inch, he was a year older than me but had chosen to become a cop several years after I had. He was a professional drummer who toured worldwide with the incomparable Barry White before entering a profession with medical and dental benefits. His values and mores as they related to police work and life, in general, were the same. His motto—*Investigate the Crime, not the Culture*— would have a profound impact on me for the remainder of my career.

Not long before the Riteway Market case, two young women in a car got arrested for armed robbery. I interviewed the driver, who was armed with the gun. I knew right away that she was guilty. The other woman told me the driver had just asked her to take a ride with her. I could certainly empathize with her unexpected dilemma, so I did something most cops would never have done. I let her go. Years later, she would become an LA County probation officer and marry a great guy. They are now raising two children, one they had together and one she had before. Police work isn't always about locking people up; it's about helping them, too. I realized that I had been practicing Mac's motto for my entire career.

Compton cops went through a period when the crooks decided to use us for target practice instead of the paper targets at Boulevard Auto. Officer Terry Smith was a well-liked, light-skinned cop who laughed heartily, chain-smoked Newport cigarettes, and enjoyed an afternoon drink so much that sometimes he wouldn't even wait until he got off work. On June 10, 1997, he responded to a call of a man armed with a gun. Palmer Blocc Crip David "Day-Day" Greer opened fire on Smith's vehicle with an AK-47, hitting the passenger side seventeen times. Miraculously, Smith was not injured, but his partner surely would have been killed had he not called in sick that night. Greer was later found not guilty. The incident and subsequent verdict had a profound effect on Smith, and he began to descend into the depths of abject alcoholism.

Two weeks after Greer tried to kill Smith, Officers Mark Metcalf and Gonzalo Cetina were driving on Caldwell Street when they saw a muscular man, atypical of the cluck heads milling around, standing in the driveway of a crack house near Wilmington. The man fired six shots at Metcalf and Cetina with a long-barreled revolver just before scaling a wall.

Metcalf shot back but missed as the shooter vanished in the darkness. He got arrested the next day after an informant told cops where he was hiding. Van Wie and Scomb had been called out to investigate the shooting. I heard them talking about the case when I got to work. They couldn't figure out why someone would shoot at cops over a simple gun possession charge. I thought about something else that happened at the same house about five years earlier. Lendell Johnson and Chris Paredes had responded to a call of a drive-by shooting near the Wilmington Arms. I started driving to the area to back them up and heard

Paredes on the radio. He said, "Unit 3-Adam, we are in pursuit of the suspect vehicle southbound on Wilmington from Laurel Street. Roll backup, please."

I saw the vehicle speed south on Alondra with Lendell and Paredes behind it. It turned left onto Caldwell and screeched to a stop in the driveway of the house. I stopped next to Lendell and Paredes as they pulled behind the car, occupied by three gangsters. The driver and front-seat passenger got out with their hands up. Lendell ordered them to lay on the ground at gunpoint as the third guy slowly got out and told Lendell, "If you didn't have that badge and gun, I would whup yo' ass, nigga!" Lendell looked at me. I shrugged my shoulders, and he holstered his gun, took off his badge and Jim Brown, and handed them to me before squaring off with his challenger. He swung at Lendell and missed, almost falling to the ground. Lendell punched him in the back of his head, helping him complete his journey.

After Paredes handcuffed him, I noticed he was missing a tooth. I found it on the grass near the driveway. He told me to stick it up my ass when I asked him if he wanted it. Instead, I hurled it as far as I could across Wilmington. Lendell found a recently fired gun under the backseat of the gangster's car. And although Lendell's challenger took an ass-whipping, I'm sure he much preferred that to what would've happened had he reached for the gun in the presence of Paredes.

While listening to Branscomb and Van Wie, I remembered three recent armed robberies at businesses on Long Beach Boulevard. The suspect was a bald Black guy missing a tooth. In one of the robberies, he shot a cashier in the head with a long-barreled revolver. I hadn't thought about the incident with Lendell in association with the robberies until I heard Branscomb and Van Wie talking about their case. I asked Branscomb if their suspect was missing a tooth, and he replied, "Yeah, one of his front teeth. Why? What's up, money?"

I said, "His name wouldn't happen to be Gerald Miller, would it? I think they call him Lucky." Van Wie and Branscomb looked at each other wide-eyed before looking back at me.

Van Wie asked, "How the fuck you know that?"

I quickly brought them up to speed on the robberies. I told them I believed the motive behind their case was likely because Miller thought he was going to get arrested for mine. Multiple witnesses and victims on my cases later identified him from a photo lineup, and he was convicted and sentenced to forty-five years in prison. His nickname might have held true had I not come to work the day after he got arrested, or if he had taken advantage of the generosity of the California State Penal system's free dental care the first time around.

CHAPTER EIGHT

I GOT assigned to Homicide in June of 1997. On my first day, Swanson dropped forty-six cases on my desk. In detective work, the cases where someone is in custody have priority. The ones with named or identified suspects come next. Then cases with a significant amount of evidence. High-profile or "red-ball" cases trump both of those, however. These cases are those with prominent people involved, missing children, officer-involved shootings, multiple murders, or child murders. If you get one of these, you drop everything else.

On October 6, 1997, at 2:45 p.m., I was in the detective bureau with Scomb, Swanson, Van Wie, D-dub, Cat, and Gil Cross, a brown-skinned man of medium height. Like Steve McMorris, Cross was from New Orleans, had a pre-dilection for calling females "cher," and loved eating alligator poppers and shrimp etouffee. But whereas McMorris struggled with money and lived paycheck to paycheck, Cross wore alligator boots and Rolex watches. We were just shooting the shit, watching Cat play with giant red lobsters caught by her baby daddy as they crawled around on the floor while Cross talked about the crawdads in his hometown.

I was wearing a cobalt-blue double-breasted suit. D-dub had everyone dying in laughter when he remarked that I looked like an Olympic swimming pool. Just as I was about to respond, probably with a remark about his clip-on tie and short sleeve shirt, we heard gunshots close to the station. We looked out the window and saw people running from the transit center in terror. This is when cops earn their money. Sure, we had just been laughing and joking while waiting for the day to end. But we don't get paid for what we do. We get paid for what we might *have* to do. And right now, it was running toward the sound of gunshots while almost everyone else was running away. A young woman was sitting on the ground, cradling her nine-year-old son in her arms. Her other two sons, six and eight, stood nearby crying. The anguish in her voice, a guttural sound of despair and helplessness, was almost unbearable, so loud it almost drowned out the sirens of an approaching ambulance.

Selwyn Leflore had been sitting on a bus bench in front of the transit center with his mother and brothers. A car driven by two MOB Piru gang members stopped nearby to pick up James "Boo Leg" Harris. Several Santana Blocc Compton Crips, including Victor "Baby Santana" Adegbenro and Tyrone "Thug" Manley, saw them. The rival gang members flashed gang hand signs at each other. Thug pointed at the car, directing Baby Santana to shoot. A stray bullet hit Selwyn in the chest and killed him. A few hours later, patrol officers saw Baby Santana and Thug driving in the SBCC neighborhood. The gangsters threw the murder weapon, a .357 Magnum, out of the window during a high-speed pursuit and were later arrested. Baby Santana should have never been able to kill Selwyn. Just two years earlier, he murdered a rival gang member with an AK-47 during a shootout. Two days later, Officers John Clark and Anthony Easter arrested him, still in possession of the rifle. The DA's office declined to file the case, citing self-defense.

Easter and Clark, known as "Flash" and "Kid Flash," respectively, were regular partners on the PM shift. Everyone on the department loved them; they were like our mischievous little brothers who were always getting into shit. Every night they chased armed gang members or stolen cars. They were a dispatcher's nightmare. Perfect as partners, they could not have been more different. Easter was Black, from the Rolling 60's Crip neighborhood in South (Central) LA, a huge Dallas Cowboy fan, and a former high school track star. Clark was White and from Orange County. He was a former ambulance driver who loved the Minnesota Vikings. And he may not have been a former track star, but he and Jimmy Mac were once the fastest White cops on the department.

I had been seeing Carolyn for well over two years by this point, yet I still had not given her a verbal commitment. Our relationship came up over dinner one night. It wasn't the first time. She would bring it up occasionally, but this time it was different. She demanded a commitment. I told her I couldn't do that. She cried and didn't say a word the rest of the night. During the weekend of my birthday in 1997, she took me on a cruise to Ensenada. She smiled at all the appropriate times, but it seemed superficial. She was finally done with my bullshit, and I couldn't blame her. She deserved better. Despite my reservations, I knew that I couldn't let her go. She had become my lifeline, a bridge that reconnected me to my family, which, unbeknownst to her, had been extremely hard for me to do. She had no way of knowing that before I met her, I cheered for Jenny when she threw stones at her childhood home and clapped when Forrest had it bulldozed. At least for me, she had proven Thomas Wolfe wrong. I *could* go home again.

After the cruise, we sat in front of her house for a few minutes, not speaking. I grabbed her arm when she opened the door to get out. I was overtaken by the sudden knowledge that the greatest love stories ever told start off as happenstance and that God most certainly laughs whenever we plan. I whispered, "Go pack a bag, and let's drive to Las Vegas and get married right now."

She recoiled like she had when I tried to sell her that box of World's Finest and said, "Fool, I ain't getting married without my family being there!"

Two weeks later, we were married at the Flamingo Hilton.

I couldn't afford to buy the type of ring I thought she deserved, so I had the diamonds removed from the one I won at Bo-Pete's house and mounted them into a wedding ring. We were almost late to our own wedding because she was watching me shoot craps. For the first time in my life, I lost at a crap table and walked away from it a winner. During pillow talk a few weeks later, Carolyn told me that she had taken me on the "farewell cruise." She was going to dump me because I wouldn't commit to her. My instincts had been spot on. Had I not trusted them, I would have missed out on my great love story.

A new wedding ring wasn't the only thing I couldn't afford. I couldn't afford a bigger place either, so I continued living at Frailich and Shirleen's condo. Everything had happened so quickly, but I now had an opportunity to reflect. I was married and now had six kids. I had been a bachelor living a dream life by the beach for so long that everything felt surreal, like I was just floating and not really in control of anything anymore. After a few weeks, Carolyn started pressuring me to move in with her and her mother. I kept coming up with excuse after excuse until she finally threatened to take me on another cruise.

I started moving my clothing to my new mother-in-law's house, still not really feeling like I was actually married. It was like I wanted to let go of my carefree life, but not really. I procrastinated, slowly moving my furniture into storage until my aquarium coffee table was the only thing left. I sat on the floor, watching the fish swim around and wishing that my life could be as uneventful as theirs. And then the reason why I had been procrastinating slowly dawned on me. I knew why I had left the table for last. It was because, in my mind, everything that I was before I met Carolyn was connected to it. Once the table was gone, my sense of freedom would be replaced by an obligation to connect to family. But it was *time* to. I gave the coffee table to a neighbor who had always admired it and walked away to my new life.

CHAPTER NINE

WITH MY mind now free and unencumbered, I rededicated myself to police work. Despite my struggles with that elusive gray area, I had forgotten why I decided to become a cop; I had lost all memory of the joy I brought to the victim of that baggage thief all those years before. I had also let Kevin and Jimmy's tragedy turn me down the road opposite the one I should have been on all along. With this recommitment to work as a driving factor, I immersed myself in my job with the belief that they would want me to be the best cop that I could be. It was good news for my family and me but horrible news for the bad guys and theirs. I was damn good at this police shit.

On December 13, 1997, Cat and I were called out to the dead-end of 400 East Gladys Street. Patrol officers had found Andres Ruelas sitting on the curb next to an Acura Legend, bleeding from a gunshot wound to the head. Manuel Labrada was in the front passenger seat of the car. He was still wearing his seatbelt and harness and had a gunshot wound to the back of his head. A large amount of blood was on the car's front seat and middle console, but only a few spots were on the left rear passenger seat. A rolled-up calendar with spots of blood on it was lying on the right rear passenger side floorboard. *No one was sitting there,* I thought. *The calendar would be smashed and there wouldn't be any blood on it.*

Ruelas told the patrol officers that a Black man tried to rob them and shot into the car, but I knew he was lying. The evidence told me that the shooter was sitting in the car behind the driver's seat. Eddie Aguirre, who I called out to assist with translation, found a pager at the other end of the street. Believing that the killer or a witness dropped it when fleeing, we called the last number displayed. An individual who I'll just call Jose answered. He admitted to knowing Ruelas and said a guy named Ramon Garcia, who arrived from Mexico the day before, left Jose's house earlier in the day with Ruelas and another man in Ruelas's Acura.

Jose refused to give us his address. We got it anyway through the reverse telephone directory system, and me, Cat, Aguirre, Code-9 Calvin, and Officers Lanier Freeman and Elizabeth Molina took a drive deep into LA. I sent Freeman and Code-9 to the rear of the house just in case someone decided to take a midnight sprint down the alley. Jose was surprised as fuck when he opened the door and saw us standing there. We found Garcia in a bedroom, packing a small travel bag. He denied knowing Labrada or Ruelas and said he had been at the house all day. We arrested him for suspicion of murder when Cat saw several spots of blood on his pants.

Ruelas sang a different tune when he found out Garcia was in jail. He told us that Garcia had asked him for a ride to Compton. Garcia told him to turn onto Gladys Street. When Ruelas realized it was a dead-end, he was about to turn around when he heard a gunshot, and everything went black. He refused to say that Garcia shot him, but Garcia was the only person in the back seat. I called the LASD crime lab to process the car, and they found Garcia's fingerprints on the interior of the left rear passenger door. Labrada's blood was on the right knee of Garcia's pants, which meant that it landed there when Garcia's knee was between the front bucket seats as he shot Labrada and Ruelas. Had Garcia killed them both and not dropped his pager, he would have gotten away with it. The prints would have meant nothing. Garcia was a Mexican national with no identification and no record of ever being in the United States. The only way we knew his name was because of Jose, who may have even been lied to by Garcia. For all we knew, he was going to kill Jose as well before returning to the anonymity of Mexico.

Ruelas and Labrada were mid-level drug dealers. Labrada got arrested with twenty kilos of cocaine by Long Beach PD several years before his murder. He didn't go to prison, which meant he was probably an informant. Ruelas, on the other hand, had absolutely cooperated with law enforcement on a past case. Garcia had a tattoo of a small pitchfork on his left hand between the thumb and forefinger. It was no great feat of sleuthing to figure out he was a hitman brought up from Mexico to kill Labrada and Ruelas.

Stoney Jackson would have been proud of me for the way I handled this case, relying on the physical evidence. He had always fancied himself an old-school detective, the kind that wore Sherlock Holmes hats and looked at evidence through magnifying glasses while smoking a pipe. Stoney was retired by now, but he had been so much of an influence on my career that I personally gave him an unofficial retirement party. Kid Flash let us use his house for the festivities. Once again, I arranged for stripper friends to provide entertainment. It was quite a party, and because most of the cops in attendance were married at the time, I'm pleading the Fifth regarding their identities. However, Kid Flash was single. The next morning, he woke up with two voracious Black women in bed with him.

Stoney was the type of cop that is disappearing like snow leopards, the kind you hoped would show up at your house when you needed help against the boogieman. I was sad he retired but glad that he could do the job for as long as he had and still get out healthy. The comparison between him and my childhood friend Roney was uncanny. The similarities were more than just their names. Both were tall men with stuttering problems who were extremely proficient fighters. They were a juxtaposition of influence in my life, one an outlaw and one a lawman. Although I felt nothing when Roney died, I felt a tremendous sense of loss when Stoney retired, and I am grateful to them both for providing the duality and balance I would need in my life.

On Sunday, January 25, 1998, I was at a Super Bowl party watching the Denver Broncos play the Green Bay Packers. After the game, four strippers I didn't know made their appearances. I went out on the balcony for some air and saw the host, who just happened to be the cop Darlene had used to exact revenge on me, smoking a joint with one of them while another one was giving him a blow job. The party was way out of control by now, so I quickly made my way home. While in bed watching the news later, I saw that a quadruple murder the news reporter dubbed "The Super Bowl Massacre" had occurred in Compton earlier in the day. I drifted off to sleep, wondering why I wasn't called in.

I was off the next day, but Swanson and all the homicide detectives were still working on the case when I got to the office on Tuesday. They had made a shit-load of overtime. I was agitated Swanson didn't call me. I needed the overtime because Carolyn and I were trying to buy a house. I went into his office to ask him about it, and, without looking up from the overtime slip that he was filling out for himself, he said, "We had enough."

I smiled and replied, "Okay. Let me know if you guys need a hand."

Now he was signing a stack of other overtime slips and didn't bother to stop as he said, "We should be alright. I think this is an easy one. Close the door on your way out."

I went to my desk and started thumbing through the mountain of reports near my phone.

A couple of minutes later, I asked one of the detectives about the case and learned that at 11:00 a.m., Charles "Spanky" Hurd, Michael Hoard, Shawn Potter, and Jessie Dunn were at the Wheels-N-Stuff carwash at 1400 South Sportsman Drive preparing for a Super Bowl party. An employee arriving for work saw two men sitting in a black Honda Accord parked in front. The men followed him inside and ordered him and everyone else to lay on the floor while demanding money and jewelry at gunpoint. One of the men tried to coax the victims into surrendering their valuables, telling them, "C'mon. We all Black."

When the victims still refused, he got upset and said to his accomplice, "Let's smoke these muthafuckas." They then shot Hurd, Hoard, Potter, and Dunn multiple times in their heads and upper torsos. The employee, who had laid near a rolling door that separated one section of the business from the other, managed to get up and run away when one of the gunmen inadvertently kicked it. The gunmen took money and jewelry from the victims and a white Chevrolet El Camino, outfitted with chrome IROC rims. One of them left in the El Camino, the other one in the Honda. A sheriff's patrol unit found the El Camino, destroyed by fire, later that day in Lakewood. The rims were missing.

Despite Swanson's bluster, I could tell that they didn't have a clue as I watched them run around the office like chickens without heads. The detectives were now just sucking up the overtime. A few days after the Broncos came back from Disneyland, Swanson called me into his office. He was still signing overtime slips that didn't have my name on them. He said, "Fred, Scomb is caught up in the middle of several other cases that he is close on, plus he's got a trial coming up. I'm giving you the Super Bowl case. Let me know if you need anything." *The leads must have dried up,* I thought, *so he must think there will be no more overtime.*

I heard Cat laughing in her office as she gossiped on her phone. I said, "Okay. I want Cat to help me."

Swanson chuckled as he looked at me over the top of his readers and said, "Cat, huh?"

Cat and I had solved almost all the cases we caught together and always made overtime on them. Maybe her reputation as being lazy was warranted, or perhaps it was born out of frustration by cops who had unsuccessfully tried to get in her pants. I didn't care one way or the other. She and I were strictly about business and had a great working relationship.

Swanson chuckled again and said, "Okay, Fred. You and Cat." He gestured toward the door with his pen and told me to close it on my way out. I heard him mutter something under his breath as I intentionally left it open this time. Cat had a minimal grasp of the case; some of the overtime slips Swanson was signing were hers. She wasn't upset at all when I told her she was my partner. She smiled and, mimicking the pulling of an old-school slot machine handle, said, "Cha-ching!"

The bloodstains were still on the floor at the car wash. I had the crime scene photos with me so I could get oriented with the location. It would be easy to overlook someone if the roll-a-way door rolled in front of them. We went to talk to the fortunate witness. He was terrified but said he could identify the shooters, so we moved him to an undisclosed location.

Within a day or two, I had found an informant who told me that one of the gunmen was a Long Beach gang member known as Nut or Papa. I reached for the phone to call my new best friend, Mac McGuire. It rang before I could take the receiver off the hook. "Homicide, Reynolds speaking. Can I help you?"

It was Mac. He said, "Hey, you got anything on your quadruple?"

I told him no because I wanted to hear what he had to say first.

He said, "Well, me and my partner Vic Thrash are getting information the shooters are from Long Beach, and one of them is called Popa Nut." I smiled as he went on to tell me that one of his peers, Richard Conant, was working a home invasion robbery that happened near 55th and Atlantic a few days before the Super Bowl massacre. There were two gunmen involved, and they shot and crippled a woman. Mac told me that Conant didn't have a clue who the suspects were, but the Long Beach Mac Mafia Crips claim the area.

A member by the name of Aswad "Nutt" Pops was in the Long Beach PD database. He had been arrested several times for other crimes. I pulled the most recent photograph of him from the booking system and saw that he matched the description of one of the shooters in my case. I checked recent contacts for Pops and discovered that within a few days of the murders, he had been a passenger in a yellow Camaro driven by Byron "Bird" Wilson, also a Mac Mafia member. The car had chrome IROC rims on it.

An informant had also told Mac and Thrash that two other guys with street names of "Smurf" and "Aziz" burned the El Camino. Smurf was a juvenile. He was in custody at Camp Kilpatrick for an unrelated case. Cat and I drove up and interviewed him. He confessed to burning the El Camino with Aziz at Pops's direction but denied knowing about the murders. Smurf also told us that Aziz was Pops's brother. After witnesses identified Wilson and Pops as the shooters in the Super Bowl massacre and the attempted murder in Long Beach, Cat and I got arrest warrants for Pops, Wilson, and Aziz and wrote search warrants for their residences. We found a 9mm round in a seat cushion of a couch in Wilson's apartment. A ballistic check showed it had been cycled through one of the murder weapons. Bird or Pops had probably been unloading the gun at some point, and the bullet ejected and fell in the seat cushion. They either didn't see it or, most likely, forgot about it. The Camaro, still outfitted with the IROC rims, was parked in the driveway at Pops's house. We impounded it as evidence.

The brother of the victim who owned the El Camino was familiar with the rims and could identify them. When he looked at the car the next day, he immediately said, "Those ain't my brother's rims, Reynolds."

Cat and I looked at each other in disbelief before I replied, "What? What do you mean those aren't your brother's rims?"

He squatted and pointed out several imperfections in them and said, "These are knockoffs. My brother's shit was real."

I stormed off in search of the owner of the tow company. I found him sitting in his office, eating BBQ ribs. He licked his fingers, smiled, and said, "Hey, Reynolds! How the hell are you?"

I replied, "Where the hell are the rims that were on that Camaro?"

I wasn't in my usual jovial mood with him, and it caught him off guard. He nearly choked on a baby back. Initially, he tried to say those were the original rims, but he got his mind right after I told him the gravity of the situation. He said, "An LAPD officer saw them and offered to buy them. I didn't think it would hurt, so I switched the rims and sold him the original ones. I didn't think anyone would notice."

I was relieved, but I couldn't let him know that. I said, "Tell you what. You have two hours to get those fucking rims back, or you might be sharing a cell with the owner of that Camaro."

As soon as the victim's brother saw the real rims, he said, "Yeah. That's my brother's shit." The tow company owner and the cop who bought the rims had to appear in court and explain their actions. Perversely, the identification of the rims by the victim's brother became even more reliable. He could very well have identified the knockoffs. No one would have ever known. Cat and I filed the case with DDA John Monaghan, a brilliant courtroom tactician who prosecuted multiple murder cases without a co-chair, often going alone against four to six defense attorneys. Smurf got released from custody just before the beginning of the trial and went into hiding. When Cat and I found him near east LA, he ran from us. I chased him as he scaled fences, finally tackling him at the expense of a nice pair of slacks. It was worth it, though. The next overtime slip Swanson signed from me had an extra eight hours on it for pain and suffering.

I have always been a stickler for details because that is where the devil hides. Not long after we arrested Pops, Wilson, and Aziz, Cat and I were on an elevator with Pops and a custody deputy in the downtown LA Criminal Courts Building. Pops was in surprisingly good spirits for a man facing a potential death sentence. He started flirting with Cat, who batted those feline-like eyes at him but otherwise said nothing.

When neither of us would engage him in conversation, he smiled and said, "C'mon. We all Black." In my eyes, this single statement was more of an indictment than the rims, the witness identification, and the round we found in Bird's couch. It was his motto.

Smurf and Aziz got convicted of arson and receiving stolen property. Pops and Wilson got convicted of the four murders and twenty other felonies and were sentenced to death. On August 29, 2019, Pops committed suicide in his single-man cell at San Quentin prison. Wilson remains on death row. I received my second COPS officer of the year award for this case and my second Employee of the year award. Cat, Rich Conant, and Monaghan also received the COPS award. Even though Conant provided gang testimony during the trial, I felt that Mac and Thrash deserved the award more than he did. This case wouldn't have been solved as quickly without their help. I would never have known about the Long Beach home invasion. Without the bond I had formed with Mac on the Operation Nutty Buster case, no one from LBPD would have ever called me.

The recognition Conant got helped him in his career, too. Immediately afterward, he got assigned to the FBI Violent Crimes Task Force. One year later, he was promoted to homicide, becoming the first Black in the department's history to receive that honor. In 2005, Conant was promoted to sergeant and eventually made it to deputy chief of detectives, becoming the highest-ranking Black on the department until he retired just months before Pops committed suicide. Mac got promoted to homicide shortly after Conant did. After Conant was promoted to sergeant, Mac was the only Black detective in the unit for the next ten years.

In May of 1998, my Grandma Helen died after a horrible and lengthy bout with dementia. My Grandpa Walter and Mom Mary were already gone by now, Grandpa Walter dying of a heart attack while sitting in his beloved rocking chair, my Mom Mary leaving in the relative peacefulness that comes with closing your eyes in bed and never waking up. Grandma Helen was buried in the family cemetery beneath a beautiful dual headstone; my Grandpa Rufus's name and birthdate inscribed in it with the date of death to be determined. The disparity in the information etched on numerous other grave markers revealed a prideful progression of prosperity from slaves who worked in the tobacco fields to owners of them.

I took Carolyn to Rocky Mount for the funeral. After the burial services, family members and friends descended on the house to ravage the best country cuisine imaginable. Unaware of the South's unwritten gender-grouping rule, Carolyn clung to me like the static of freshly dried clothes. As David, Derrick, and I reunited at the house that none of us had any fondness for, Carolyn walked the land surrounding it with us speechless at the beauty of it all. We were joined at one point by my cousin Craig and his mother Sondra, who, rebellious like Carolyn, couldn't care less about silly old rules, written or not. Sondra was among my favorite aunts and was a beautiful woman with long black hair and an infectious personality. She was married to my Uncle Ted, who was my father's assigned best man a lifetime ago.

It was a clear, beautiful night, the sky filled with stars. It was the kind of night that you can never fully appreciate if you're used to seeing the smog-filled skies of LA. It was not hard to imagine that a little over 150 years ago, slaves, some of whom were buried just yards away, walked the same path that we did and looked at the same stars, albeit with different dreams and goals than the ones we currently had. One star was extremely bright. Carolyn pointed at it and asked, "What is that?" We all looked upward, awed by its brilliance. Aunt Sondra, clearly perplexed, asked the same question but with more emphasis and bewilderment.

Derrick was so dark in the night the star nearly paled in comparison to the brightness of his eyes and teeth. He looked upward again dramatically and then back at Aunt Sondra, bucking his eyes widely in his best attempt to transport us back in time as he replied, "That's freedom, Ms. Sondra!"

We laughed so hard it hurt. I realized that what Derrick said had most likely been said before by someone who looked just like him to people who looked like us while looking at the very same star. We were their descendants, still looking at that star to guide us to freedom of a different kind, a world free of the unseen mental constraints still used to control us. This was the first time Carolyn had ever met any of my family. Everyone liked her right away, even my mother. No one knew we were married. My father didn't believe me when I introduced Carolyn as my wife, and he asked her if it was true. She laughed and replied, "I sure hope so because I changed the last name on my ID."

When I was alone with my father later, I told him that Carolyn had three children. He didn't skip a beat as he said, "Shit. What does that matter? They don't have to be yours for you to love them. The only thing that matters is that you love her kids as much as you love your own. *Make* them yours, too." My father's heart of gold had been gilded all those years, so tarnished by the alcohol that I hardly saw the gleam. Now, in his post-drinking years, I realized that he had finally made peace with what had come between him and my mother those many years ago.

CHAPTER TEN

THE FALLOUT from the Tupac and Notorious BIG murders had died down by 1998. It appeared that Baby Lane had gotten away with Tupac's murder, and LAPD was still trying to solve BIG's murder. Persons of interest ranged from rogue LAPD cops to SSCCs to Suge Knight and MOB Pirus.

Meanwhile, Baby Lane was riding the wave of ghetto superstardom in Compton. Buffered by his new status, on May 29, 1998, he and his close friend Michael "Owl" Dorrough got into a shootout with two Corner Poccet Crips over an unpaid drug debt at a car wash behind Compton High School. The shooting left Baby Lane mortally wounded and the two rival Crips dead. Owl took the wheel of Baby Lane's black Chevy Blazer and crashed into a fence near the back of the school as he drove away. According to informants, Owl gave Baby Lane's gun to a Mexican guy walking in the area and told him to get rid of it. Owl then continued driving until he saw Reggie Wright Sr., who had been on the back lot with Aguirre, Richardson, Brennan, and Ladd. Owl flagged Reggie down on Willowbrook. Not knowing what was going on at that point, Reggie handcuffed Owl and told Aguirre and Richardson to stay with him and Baby Lane until the ambulance got there. Reggie then left and went to the location of the shooting where Brennan and Ladd were.

Trying to get a dying declaration, Richardson leaned over Baby Lane and said, "You're gonna die, Lane. Did you kill Tupac?"

Keeping it gangsta to the bitter end, Baby Lane replied, "Why you fucking with me, Cameo?" before losing consciousness. By the time I got to the scene, Baby Lane was in the back of an ambulance speeding down Willowbrook to hip-hop infamy.

Owl was convicted of all three murders and sentenced to forty years in prison. He had no problem being found guilty of killing the Corner Poccet Crips. But when he learned that one of the convictions was for Baby Lane's murder, he screamed at Brennan, "Blondie! Blondie! I didn't kill my homeboy!" while two bailiffs dragged him from the courtroom as his mother Carrie cursed Brennan out.

Owl did not have a gun during the confrontation with the Stones. He could have raised reasonable doubt in a juror's mind had he simply told investigators that after Baby Lane got shot, he grabbed Baby Lane's gun and fired in self-defense. The fact that he flagged a cop down while fleeing the scene is mitigating evidence. But Owl's loyalty was so great that he refused to snitch on Baby Lane even though Baby Lane was dead. Deandre "Freaky Dre" Smith, one of the parties involved in Tupac's murder, according to Keefee D, was morbidly obese and unhealthy. He died of natural causes, supposedly, not long after Baby Lane was killed. Terrence "T-Bone" Brown, the other party involved in Tupac's murder, again according to Keefee D, was killed on September 23, 2015, during a robbery at a Compton marijuana dispensary. Everyone involved in the murder of Tupac is dead now, except for Keefee D, but because of his proffer agreement, unless cops find independent witnesses or physical evidence linking him to the murder, he can never be prosecuted.

I got promoted to sergeant and sent back to patrol in August. Hardly a week had gone by before I was requested to respond to a murder scene at 1509 East Ezmirilian Street. Campanella Park Piru Rodney "Spud" Davis was slumped over in the driver's seat of his car with a bullet in his head. A CV70 gang member named Maximino "Casper" Navarro had driven up alongside him and, armed with a 9mm with red laser sights, ensured that Spud remained forever young.

Richardson and Aguirre investigated the case and had Casper in custody within two months. Casper was later found guilty of murder, and after the judge sentenced him to life in prison, he attacked the prosecutor, DDA Rick Ocampo, with a jailhouse shank. Deputies Louis Suazo and Jeremy Berkshire saved Ocampo's life by heroically wrestling Casper to the floor and disarming him. Years after the courtroom incident, Ocampo became a judge. While in his chambers getting a search warrant signed, I noticed that he has the shank framed and on the wall behind his desk. I asked him why he kept it. He smiled and winked and said, "To remind me that justice is a shield, not a sword."

CHAPTER ELEVEN

ON MARCH 29, 1999, the Lynwood Unified School District placed Superintendent Audrey Clark on paid administrative leave for unspecified reasons. Fred Kennedy was named interim superintendent, and he appointed Omar Bradley, a district teacher, as the assistant superintendent. As scandals continued to rock the Lynwood Unified School District, the Compton Unified School District was still battling state officials. The tension was thick at school board meetings. During one session, Omar and Hourie Taylor had a heated argument. Satra Zurita had to call Danny Sneed to prevent them from coming to blows.

Omar was already fed up with Hourie, and this incident only served to fan the flames. Omar demanded that Howard Caldwell fire Hourie, but Caldwell refused. Caldwell "retired" shortly afterward, and Larry Moore took his position. Moore also refused to fire Hourie, but on June 25, Moore was found dead at the Ramada Hotel due to complications from undiagnosed diabetes. John Johnson, a former classmate of Omar's wife at Compton High and one of Omar's sycophants, was hired as the new city manager. Less than a month later, Johnson called Hourie to his office, where he and Omar offered Hourie an incentive-laden retirement package worth $750,000 which Hourie refused.

During the first week of August, city officials declared a state of emergency after a series of suspicious school fires. One destroyed a wing at a visual and performing arts school, which had been unused since 1992. Another one destroyed a vacated administration building at Compton High. When Omar directed city firefighters and police officers to supplement the efforts of the state-run investigation, the state's representative for the school district insinuated it was just political posturing by the city. Hourie assigned me to assist the arson task force, which already consisted of two LA County arson investigators, an investigator from the state fire marshal's office, two ATF agents, two Compton arson investigators, and a battalion chief.

Less than a week later, I walked into the locker room to get ready for work. Ron Thrash, a likeable young cop who had worked detectives with me, was dressing at a locker near mine. He stepped close to me and whispered, "Hey, Fred, you hear about what happened to Hourie and Percy?" Thinking that they got arrested for drunk driving after leaving the VFW, I shook my head as I put the keepers on my Jim Brown. Thrash went on. "Yeah, man. It's bad. They got suspended in the middle of the night. They had to give up their badges and guns."

Now he had my full attention. "What?! Why? For what?" I asked.

Thrash moved closer and replied, "No one knows. They were just told it was on the orders of the city manager. R. E. is the acting chief now. And believe it or not, Gary Anderson is back. He's the assistant chief."

I put my gun in its holster and snapped the safety strap as I answered, "Bullshit. The city manager ain't got the balls. He's a coward. This is all Omar. And how did R. E. and Scary Gary end up in charge?" Thrash was a helluva nice guy who always smiled and never said a cross word about anyone. He also never wanted any kind of confrontation or drama in his life. Instead of commenting, he shrugged, held his palms in front of him, and moonwalked to his locker, where he finished getting dressed in silence. Knowing the kind of person he was, I didn't push it. Still, I couldn't help but wonder: *What the hell did Percy and Hourie do?*

Gary Anderson, a former lieutenant who retired around the same time as Stoney Jackson, was a middle-aged White man with dishwasher gray hair and pockmarks on his face like Dennis Auner. Anderson frequently bit his fingernails and suffered from lower lip ptosis. He often tried his best to show how in tune he was to the Black culture with his misappropriation of the lingo, and he also had an affinity for coco-skinned women with ample derrieres. While I was working detectives, I had a case where a woman matching the description of his desire was committing fraud at the CUSD. He tried to get me to drop the case, going so far as to tell me what she had done was a victimless crime. It didn't work; I put together an airtight case, and she went to prison.

Anderson was my watch commander for most of the time I worked the yard. He spent a large amount of every shift stealing glances at female dispatchers while playing pinochle with Tom Barclay, one of his field sergeants. John Garrett was the other one. Anderson was known as "Scary Gary" because most of the cops who worked for him thought he was afraid of his own shadow. His hatred for Hourie went back well over a decade to when James Carrington was the chief. Hourie, Red Mason, Pepper Preston, and a sergeant named Willie Mosely had gone to Sizzler's in Long Beach for lunch. They saw Anderson hugged up in a booth with Chief James Carrington's daughter. Red Mason hated Anderson and couldn't wait to let Carrington know. Carrington crawled up Anderson's ass later, and Anderson always believed that Hourie had told on him.

Hourie had also been promoted to lieutenant over Anderson even though Anderson always felt he was the more qualified candidate. R. E. and Percy Perrodin didn't get along either. There was no rhyme or reason for this rivalry other than personality conflicts. Percy despised R. E. because, whereas Percy had been raised in the hard-knock school of Compton, he believed that R. E. was "soft" because of his upbringing in an educated family on the west side of LA.

On the other hand, R. E. thought of himself as more refined and intelligent than the uncouth rube he believed Percy Perrodin to be. I had witnessed them nearly come to blows on at least two occasions. R. E. and Anderson had always been friends, so it was easy for them to form an alliance against common enemies.

Speculation was rampant regarding the sudden change in leadership. To me, it didn't matter who was in charge. There are regime changes in every organization. An organization always outweighs an individual. But loyalty is a reality. The department began to fracture. Not everyone wanted to take a stance against Hourie and Percy getting suspended. It created an unofficial division referred to as the A team and the B team. The officers who supported Hourie and Percy were the self-titled A team. They derisively designated the officers on R. E. and Anderson's side as the B team. The rest were in the gray area like me.

I was now reporting to R. E. regarding the arson investigation. I had to brief him and Anderson about the daily task force meetings, and they, in turn, informed Omar. Omar needed to involve a Compton cop in the investigation so he could monitor the case. Fire department personnel hadn't supported him for years, so he certainly wouldn't get any information from them. The lack of support likely started when Omar's son bounced a personal check from Omar for tuition at the fire academy, and he wasn't allowed to participate in training. Omar was enraged and kicked in the door shirtless, screaming that he was "the fucking mayor" while threatening to get rid of the entire fire department if they didn't reinstate his son. And that was Omar Bradley in a nutshell. His vindictiveness knew no bounds.

Frailich and Bookman helped me with the arson investigation. Mostly we just chased down bullshit leads that went nowhere, but one of them did appear promising. We found a witness who told us that a fifteen-year-old kid named Elijah Cheatham had been bragging about setting Compton High on fire. We never got a chance to interview him, though, because, on September 29, Swanson told me that R. E. wanted me to finish my report and be in the chief's office the following morning.

Officer Jerry Patterson was waiting outside the door when I got there. Jerry was a dark-skinned, mild-mannered, and soft-spoken cop. He had just finished a stint with the Los Angeles Interagency Metropolitan Police Apprehension Crime Task Force (LA IMPACT) and was now in the narcotics unit. Smooth and articulate, he grew up on the west side of Los Angeles like R. E. and Terry Smith and called men "cats". The Black officers on the department who grew up in less-than-ideal conditions teasingly called them all bourgeois. Jerry was meticulous in his attire and was once married to the most sought-after woman on the department, a gorgeous mulatto with sparkling light-green eyes and an out-of-this-world body. She was Sunshine from the movie *Harlem Nights* to at least two cops who almost left their wives for her. Although mild-mannered, Jerry was no punk; he once dotted the eye of the guy most responsible for the demise of his marriage during a "meeting" on the backlot.

Anderson opened the door and invited us inside. R. E. was sitting in a leather chair behind a huge mahogany desk. Framed pictures were spaced neatly apart on the desk. He had both hands pressed together in a pyramid position, resting his chin on the capstone. Anderson stood slightly behind him like a caricature of a Mafia consigliere. The only sound in the office was the bubbling of a forty-gallon aquarium with colorful fish in a back corner amidst several plants. Nice upgrade, but not surprising. R. E. had had plenty of time to put his personal touch to the office. Hourie and Percy had now been on administrative leave for well over a month.

R. E. said, "Sit down, gentlemen." He then broke the pyramid and waggled his left forefinger at Anderson and said nothing else.

Anderson said, "Fred, Jerry, there have been some irregularities in the narcotics vault. We need to find out what's going on down there."

Jerry and I looked at each other before turning our attention back to Anderson. I said, "Irregularities? What the hell does that mean? Is someone stealing, or what?"

Anderson quickly looked at R. E., who nodded almost imperceptibly. "Yes," Anderson answered. "We believe Hourie was in the process of stealing two kilos of cocaine."

I laughed and said, "You're kidding, right?" R. E. never moved or said anything.

Anderson told us that last month, R. E. assigned him to monitor Hourie as Hourie cleaned out his personal effects from the chief's office. Afterward, they went to the vault to confirm the buy fund money amount. Hourie's brother, his attorney, Officer James Green, John Swanson, and Ron Malachi were present in the vault as witnesses. The money count was accurate, and Hourie gave Anderson the key to the locker. Hourie then pointed to several other lockers with locks on them and said he may have items in one of them, but he didn't have the key with him. They agreed to meet in the vault the following day to open the locker. Anderson said he asked Property Officer Ray Hernandez and Sergeant John Wilkinson to be there as well. The next day, Hourie still didn't have the key, so Anderson told Hernandez to cut the lock off. Wilkinson found two kilos of cocaine inside the locker, and Hourie left abruptly. Anderson then told Wilkinson to put the cocaine back and told Hernandez to put a new lock on the locker.

I thought about what Anderson said. Two kilos of cocaine were in a police department's narcotics vault. Big deal. It's only a crime if it's missing. Not when it's still there. You couldn't even argue that Hourie knew the cocaine was in the locker, much less that he had ever had possession of it. He did not have the key to the lock on it, and according to Anderson, Hourie didn't say conclusively that he had anything in the locker. What Anderson had told us was not a crime. None of it made any sense. Neither did why there was a need for so many people to be present for the buy fund verification.

After Anderson finished talking, R. E. finally spoke again, and he said a mouthful. "I am assigning this investigation to the two of you. Reynolds, I believe you are one of the more skilled investigators on the department. I want Patterson to help because he is the most recent addition to the narcotics unit and has worked at LA IMPACT, so he has experience investigating narcotics-related offenses. This is a conundrum and possibly a black hole that could suck the light out of the agency. That being said, and having been provided with a modicum of information regarding this investigation, coupled with the politics and deviltry taking place in the organization at this time, can you conduct an impartial investigation?"

R. E. always thought he was the smartest person in the room, so I answered in a way that wouldn't interfere with his opinion. I said, "Well, I don't know what the hell 'modicum' means, but yeah, even with just knowing a scrap of info, I can do a fair investigation." I was being flippant, but I was serious. Although I did not support every decision Hourie had made as chief, I did believe that he was an honest man. I also had no problem with Jerry, who I thought to be honest as well. Most importantly, he wasn't a part of that A team-B team bullshit.

R. E. said, "Good. You start today. Gary, show them where they will be working." Anderson nodded at R. E. and took Jerry and me to the conference room. He gave us both a key and told us to make ourselves comfortable.

R. E. came in a few minutes later. He was carrying his beloved IBM Think Pad. He said, "Here. Use these." He sat the computer and a floppy disk on the table before turning and gliding out the door in his Bally shoes.

Computers were a rarity on the department. Most of the officers and detectives still wrote their reports by hand. There were only two desktop computers in the detective bureau, one on the floor and one in homicide, and there was one in the report writing room for the patrol officers and one each in the W/C and the watch sergeant's offices. I was eager to use R. E.'s computer, but I was also cautious. He was one of the most tech-savvy people on the department. I had no idea if he was just trying to be helpful or if he was up to *deviltry*. I knew that by saving what I typed onto his floppy disk, he could change and edit the final version to his liking. I decided to buy another floppy disk and save information on both.

Anderson called the conference room phone and asked us to meet him at the narcotics vault. I told Jerry to bring a camcorder. When we got to the vault, Anderson opened the solid steel door which looked like a bank vault door from the 1930s. The camcorder battery was dead, so Jerry went to the narcotics office to get an extension cord. Arnold Villarruel, who was assigned to the narcotics unit, was in the office. Everyone called him Arnie. He was responsible for filing drug-related cases and for the upkeep of the vault.

Arnie was a tall Mexican cop, close to six-three. He had a full beard in typical undercover cop fashion and wore his long, dark hair slicked back in a ponytail. Although he spoke English fluently, he preferred to talk in the dialect of the local cholos. He was persuasive as an undercover cop and blended well with criminals. He had been a lackluster patrol officer, at best, preferring to ride on the coattails of his partners. I had no problem riding with him in patrol because he was a nice guy, appeared to be honest, and didn't do dangerous or stupid shit that could get us killed or in any kind of trouble.

The vault was in the basement to the right of the north staircase. The narcotics office was to the left. Ruby Kenney, custodian of the department's G.R.E.A.T system for years, and Tim Brennan's wife, Joanna, the gang unit's secretary, shared an office next to the narcotics office. The north entrance to the men's locker room was between the stairs and the narcotics office. The rest of the north side of the basement consisted of an indoor shooting range, a boiler room, the property and evidence room, and the weight room. An elbow-shaped ramp at the end of the hallway next to the weight room led to the back lot. Employees who worked on the north side of the basement used this ramp to enter and exit the station. The gang unit's office, complete with walls adorned with gang graffiti, confiscated red and blue rags, baseball caps, and t-shirts and sweatshirts made at the swap meet, was on the south side of the basement.

The vault was a mess. An inventory would have to be tops on our list of things to do. I noticed a sign-in sheet on the vault wall. Whoever enters is supposed to sign it with his name and the date and time. According to Jerry, it was an *honor* system. There was a bank of six green-colored metal lockers just north of the sign-in sheet. Anderson went to one of them and unlocked the master lock on it with a key. He then stood back and gestured toward the locker. I opened it and saw two kilos of cocaine in evidence envelopes on the top shelf. The cocaine was seized by Arnie on December 2, 1992, during a search warrant at 1001 North Muriel Street. A property report attached to one of the kilos showed that a total of four kilos were seized. *Odd,* I thought. *Where are the other two kilos?* As I pondered this, I noticed Arnie walk by the vault door. Although noticeably interested, he never stopped to ask what we were doing.

I put on a pair of latex gloves and grabbed the two kilos. Jerry and I needed to take them to the sheriff's crime lab in Downey to confirm that they were cocaine. On the way, we talked about the investigation thus far. I had never worked narcotics and knew nothing about how the drugs were stored and tracked. I asked Jerry, "Is that normal procedure in the narco unit? I mean, to have just two kilos out of a four-kilo seizure locked inside of a locker in the vault that no one had a key to?"

Jerry answered, "No. Even if there was a special reason that I don't know about, all four kilos should have been together. It's not a crime to store narcotics in lockers in the vault, but it's a violation of unit directives. The dope is supposed to be stored in readily visible blue plastic containers."

"Did Arnie say anything while you were in the office?"

"Yeah, he just asked what was going on in the vault. I told him that they had apparently found something. He was really nervous and asked if I could tell him what they found. I just shrugged my shoulders and walked out. He probably just thinks he's gonna be in trouble because of how unkempt the vault is."

I replied, "Probably" as I squinted my eyes, pursed my lips, and rubbed my chin.

We contacted Senior Criminalist Warren Best at the lab. He broke the evidence seals, took the kilos from their envelopes, and weighed and tested them. One weighed 1021.19 grams, and the other one weighed 1000.62 grams; they were both pure powder cocaine. Best repackaged the cocaine in cellophane bags, and Jerry and I took the original packaging to the crime lab in Los Angeles for fingerprint analysis. We took the cocaine back to the station and put it in the locker. Anderson gave me the key, which I later booked into the property room as evidence.

I looked around the vault. The narcotics were in blue plastic containers with the year, case number, and what should be in the containers written or typed on paper taped to the container. There were also several Xerox boxes in the vault, some of which had information written on paper in the same manner. One box had a pink diaper bag and a Manila evidence envelope filled out by Arnie inside of it. "G055659, 1001 North Muriel Avenue, 12-02-92, Carrillo, J., 11351.5 H&S" was written on the box. The two kilos in question were supposed to be in this box instead of in the locker. *But where were the other two?* As Jerry and I were about to leave the vault, I noticed two sheets of paper with the following information taped to the locker on the east side of the wall near the vault door:

8=1988 (prepared for destruction 7-93)
9=1989 (prepared 1-9-95)
E=1990 (prepared 1-9-95)
F=1991 (destroyed 96)
G=1992 (destroyed 1998-4-1-98)
H=1993 (destroy 6-99)
I=1994 (destroy 6-2000)
J=1995 (destroy 6-2001)
96=1996 (destroy 6-2002)
97=1997 (destroy 6-2003)

I asked Jerry what the information meant, and he said, "That's the narco burn information. The first entry shows that all narcotic evidence from 1988 was prepared for destruction in July of 1993. By law, we must hold onto evidence for at least five years before we can destroy it and only after getting a court order signed by a judge. In 1989 and 1990, the narcotic evidence was prepared for destruction on January 9, 1995. As you well know, before 1989, the first character of our file numbers was the last number of the year. After 1989, we went to letters as the first character in our file numbers, starting with 'E' in 1990, 'F' in 1991, etc. We went back to all numbers in 1996."

Several of the entries had a line drawn through them. I asked, "What do those lines mean, then?"

Jerry looked at the two sheets of paper for a few seconds before rubbing his chin and saying, "Hmmm."

I asked, "What the fuck does 'hmmm' mean?"

Jerry continued rubbing his chin and answered, "The years 1988 through 1992 have lines through them, meaning the narcotics for those years have been destroyed. The only narcotics on that list that should still be in the vault are from 1994 through the current date. We could just be a little behind for 1993, which is why there is no line through that entry, but . . . hmmm." Now I knew what "hmmm" meant. It meant something was fucked up. I walked over to the two sheets of paper and dragged my finger along the line through 1992.

I stopped at the letter G, as in G-055659, looked back at Jerry, and asked, "Then why the fuck are those two kilos from the Carrillo case still in the goddamned vault?"

CHAPTER TWELVE

THE NEXT day Jerry and I spent most of the day discussing strategies, while talking about what we had learned so far. Neither R. E. nor Anderson mentioned Percy's name when they briefed us. *And why did it take an entire month to start the investigation after Wilkinson found the cocaine?* Toward the end of the day, we called Anderson's office and asked him to come to the conference room. When he walked in, I asked him what happened to the old lock on the locker containing the two kilos of cocaine. He seemed surprised by my question and paused for several seconds before answering. He said, "I can't remember, Fred. I know I must still have it, but I just can't remember what happened to it right this instant."

Jerry smelled bullshit just like I did and asked, "Lieutenant, err, I mean Assistant Chief, if this happened over a month ago, why did it take so long to begin the investigation?"

Anderson replied, "The chief wanted this investigation to be in-house, and he wanted individuals who were not only capable investigators but also those who were loyal to the organization and not to certain people. The chief feels that he has found those people in you and Fred. Now, is that it, gentlemen? If so, I got a department to help run."

I nodded my head and turned to Jerry. He shook his head as Anderson walked to the door. I waited until his hand was on the doorknob and said, "Gary, just one more thing."

Anderson sighed heavily. "For God's sake, what else, Fred?"

I leaned back in my chair and replicated R. E.'s hand pyramid and asked, "What role does Percy have in all this? Why is he on administrative leave?"

When Anderson was frustrated or disappointed, his ptosis was more prominent than usual, exposing the vestiges of tar and nicotine on his bottom teeth. I saw that he had been smoking far more than usual. He barked, "That's none of your concern. Now get back to work!" He turned sharply on the heels of his little zip-up black leather half-boots and left, leaving the door open behind him.

I turned to Jerry, who just sat there quietly with a bewildered look on his face. I said, "Let's go home and get some sleep, man. We got a big day tomorrow."

After I got in bed that night, I thought about the paradox of how Ebert and Hourie had essentially both got in hot water because of verifying money in the narcotics buy fund account. Hourie had a young daughter and an ex-wife. There had always been rumors that he struggled with spousal support and school tuition, just as there were rumors that Ebert had a gambling problem. *Is this why Anderson wanted so many witnesses when it was time to verify the buy fund money? Did Anderson and R. E. believe that Hourie was borrowing from the fund occasionally to make ends meet? Did they think they were going to find discrepancies and use that to justify getting rid of Hourie, just like it was used to justify getting rid of Ebert?* I had a strong feeling that when they stumbled across the two kilos of cocaine after the buy fund count was right, they switched reels from potential theft of funds to theft of cocaine, splendidly surprised at the serendipity of it all. Hourie had benefited significantly from Ebert's misfortunes in the vault. It now appeared that it was his turn to be captured in that kaleidoscope of karma, this time in a hue of navy blue and gold.

At about 2:00 a.m., the ringing of the telephone woke me up. I hung up after saying hello two or three times and just hearing heavy breathing. When Carolyn asked who was on the phone, I whispered that it was a bad connection and told her to go back to sleep. I hated lying to her, but I didn't need her to worry about shit. She had enough on her mind, what with working full-time, taking care of the kids, and helping her mother take care of her father. A few seconds later, I heard her lightly snoring as I stared at the ceiling and contemplated the fucked-up timing of the call and the fledgling narcotics investigation.

Anderson opened the vault again the next day, and Jerry and I began the inventory. Plastic baggies containing pieces of crack in sizes ranging from kibbles and bits to baseballs were everywhere. None of them had any identifying numbers or names. Containers of PCP were on the floor along the walls; most of them were also unmarked. The smell was overwhelming. There was no ventilation system in place, which was the single most alarming issue. The following day, R. E. had the vault combination changed. Anderson, Arnie, and Gil Cross, now a sergeant and in charge of narcotics, were the only people who had it now. Jerry and I were against anyone having it other than us, but R. E. disregarded our advice, telling us it would disrupt unit operations if the unit members didn't have it. This indicated to me that the investigation was destined to be out of our control. For us to do a complete and thorough investigation, we had to have full control and autonomy. Otherwise, there would be too many hands in the cookie jar.

Older reports were kept in a room in the back of the jail until they got purged. I told Jerry to get the Carrillo file so we could find out exactly what happened. He came back to the conference room twenty minutes later with a huge binder and said, "I couldn't find the report even though there are a lot of other reports from the same period there. I even checked the search warrant file in the narcotics office, but the Carrillo warrant or the incident reports aren't there either."

I pointed at the binder and asked, "What's that, then?"

"Oh, this is the bible of the narcotics unit."

He handed it to me, and I flipped through a few pages before asking, "What am I looking at here?" Jerry told me that every dope arrest and everything relevant to the case was supposed to be documented in the book. The book was currently Arnie's responsibility. There was also a space for investigator remarks for each entry. Jerry pointed to an entry dated December 2, 1992. It showed that Juan E. Carrillo was arrested for possession of cocaine for sales. Four kilos and 495.7 grams of marijuana got booked as evidence. The Compton PD case number was G055659, filed under court case number TA021802. There was nothing in the remarks section.

There was also an entry regarding a sixty-kilo seizure and the arrest of someone in 1993 by the name of Alvin Haynes. There was nothing written in the book to indicate that the arrest had ever been presented to the DA's office. I specifically remembered the case. A motorhome used to transport the drugs was seized as an asset forfeiture by the department, which became the official

Compton PD command post for years. We also used it for officers to relax in while working the annual fireworks stand when it was at the corner of Compton Blvd and Willowbrook.

Jerry and I continued to thumb through the book until I came across something that caught my eye. On April 23, 1997, someone named Reyes Cano was arrested for sixty kilos of cocaine. The case was a DA reject, but there was no case number. 'Released to the FBI' was the only thing written in the remarks section. I didn't recognize the handwriting. I said, "Wow, Jerry. That's a lot of cocaine to release to another agency. Does this sound right to you?"

He said, "Hmmm." I told him to stop rubbing his chin and answer the fucking question, and he replied, "Well, this isn't the way we release dope to other agencies. If we did, then the chief should know about it, and there should be a substantial paper trail. Especially considering the amount. This was a major seizure."

I reached into my bag for my bottle of Excedrin. Jerry was quiet as he sat across the table from me. Something was fucked up in the narcotics unit, and neither of us had any idea how far down the rabbit hole we had to go before finding out exactly what. I said, "Let's keep this between us for now. And can you see if you can find the index card for the Cano case?"

Jerry nodded and replied, "Sure, Fred, I'll try to, but it's funny. Nothing is where it is supposed to be anymore. Even the court orders for the destruction of narcotics are missing."

About an hour later, Cross came to the conference room and asked, "Hey, you guys got a minute?" Cross had been a detective for nearly twenty years, many of which were while R. E. was over the narcotics unit. I had mad love for Cross, even though he was one of the department's worst detectives and made no apologies about it. Sometimes, he even relished it. Still, he was one cool motherfucker who had a hearty appetite for the finer things in life.

I said, "Hell yeah, I got a minute for you. What's up, Gil?"

He closed the door behind him and said, "I'm worried about Arnie."

I felt Jerry looking at me as I asked Cross why.

The smile that was usually a fixture on Cross's face faded. He said, "Yesterday, he was freaking out. He asked me if he could leave just three hours into his shift.

275

I asked him if everything was okay, and he told me everything was fine, but he just needed to go home immediately." Cross said he had never seen Arnie act that way before.

After Cross left, Jerry and I went to talk to Anderson in his new office, which was Percy's old one. It was still the same, except now Anderson's family pictures were displayed instead of Percy's. There was also a business card holder on the desk filled with gold embossed cards with "Gary O. Anderson, Assistant Chief of Police" on them. Anderson smiled broadly, putting on his best shuck-and-jive routine for us. He asked, "Wuz happn', fellas? Everythang coo?" I dismissed his usual bullshit departure from his own culture and his brief foray into ours.

I said, "Gary, I think that we should change the vault combination again as soon as possible. This time, Jerry and I strongly suggest that only you and Cross have it. Also, and this is per Cross, Arnie is acting strange."

Anderson's smile faded, and he said, "I'll have Barclay call the locksmith to come out tomorrow and change it again if that's what you want, but what does Arnie have to do with Hourie?"

I glanced over at Jerry. I wouldn't get any help from him. He was too busy staring at the toes of his slip-on hush puppies. I said, "Well, I guess he started acting strangely yesterday when we were in the vault." I scanned Anderson's face for signs of guilt, but I didn't see any. He looked more pissed than worried. It was clear that Hourie was the only thing on his mind.

He said, "Don't worry about that, Fred. Arnie's probably just nervous because the vault is a mess, and he's responsible for it. We need to find out why that cocaine was in Hourie's locker. Now, if you gentlemen will excuse me, I have other matters to attend to. Close the door on your way out." I left it open, wondering if one of those matters was a recently paroled big-booty felon who had been convicted of fraud.

Over the lunch hour, I went to Fort Compton and got a copy of the Carrillo case file. Narco destruction orders are not filed with the court; they remain with the requesting agency after the judge signs them. The Carrillo court file didn't contain the police report or any search warrants, but it did hold a minute order which showed that on December 17, 1992, Juan Carrillo pled guilty to possession of cocaine and was sentenced to three years in prison.

I sent Jerry to the narcotics office to continue looking for the Carrillo case index cards. He found them in the rear of the file cabinet. There were four index cards, two filled out by Detective Bryan Gilbreath, who retired several years earlier, and two filled out by Arnie. None of the cards indicated the dope was ever signed out. Jerry also found a memo to the police chief about a narcotic burn reflecting that all narcotics evidence from the year 1992 was destroyed in Long Beach on April 1, 1998. The total weight of narcotics was 368 pounds, including sixty-nine pounds of cocaine, or 31.298 kilos.

Before interviewing Hourie, Jerry and I decided to interview personnel involved in the Carrillo case and the officers present when Wilkinson found the two kilos in the locker. Ideally, the first person we interviewed should have been Jeff Nussman because he was the unit supervisor during the investigation. This wasn't possible, however. He had been arrested the previous year by LAPD after using the internet to arrange a meeting to have sex with a minor. Bobby Baker, a petite, soft-spoken White cop with blonde hair who looked like a teenager, replaced Nussman in the narcotics unit in 1996.

Baker was one of the smartest cops on the department. I called him the "professor." He never raised his voice or used profanity and he used ten-dollar words as part of his everyday vernacular, not just to impress people. Instead of asking over the radio if a gunshot victim could walk, he was the kind of guy who would ask if they were ambulatory instead. He was always thinking. I once saw him contact a gangster who had thrown a bottle of PCP to the ground to destroy the evidence. After handcuffing him, Baker calmly asked another officer for a cigarette, rolled it in the rapidly drying liquid, and put the now saturated cigarette into a sandwich baggie. He then put the broken pieces of the bottle into a bag and booked the gangster for possession of PCP and destruction of evidence. But Baker's biggest claim to fame was that he was part of the major narcotic distribution investigations that targeted Patrick and Fred Johnson and Michael "Harry-O" Harris, three of the biggest drug dealers in California at one time.

Baker was off work because of a neck injury at the time of this investigation. Since retired and personnel off due to injury cannot be compelled to participate in administrative investigations, we interviewed Sergeant Henry Robinson first. Currently one of our helicopter pilots, he was one of the most computer savvy cops on the department and just as smart as Baker. He replaced Baker as the supervisor of narcotics when Baker got promoted to lieutenant. Fat Jack, Gilbreath, Arnie, and Andrew Pilcher, a dark-skinned, muscular, former Marine who was married to Angelia Myles, worked for Robinson. I told Robinson that at least two kilos from 1992 were still in the vault before showing him the chief's memo. After reading it, he said, "I remember this burn. I was there. Jack McConnell got the dope ready for destruction by comparing the dope to be destroyed to the information on the index cards. I helped him. We pulled all the cases listed for the period in question. There is no way in the world any dope from that burn should still be in the vault. Especially not in those green lockers. We don't keep dope in them."

Robinson explained that the dope slated for destruction is put into large plastic bags, weighed, and put against the back wall of the vault. The dope is never removed from the bags again after the weigh-in. The officer will weigh the bags one final time when they arrive at the burn site. After the burn, the destruction order is kept in the narcotics office, along with a memo to the chief.

I thought about what Robinson said after he left the conference room. Basically, after the dope was weighed and placed in the back of the vault, anyone with access to the vault could take it out of the bags later and replace it with items of equal weight. They could then either leave with the dope or hide it in the vault for future use. After all, it no longer existed at that point. There was now a court order and a chief's memo proving it. It was the only explanation of why dope that should have been destroyed was still in the vault. Someone had made it a personal stash house.

Even so, a cop can't move large amounts of drugs without help. Whoever was behind this shit had to have connections with dealers. It was terribly short-sighted not to have foreseen something like this being possible. A surveillance camera pointed at the vault door with a monitor set up in the W/C's office would have ensured adherence to any "honor" system. Failing to do this wasn't entirely on the city, however. The department got thousands of dollars of asset forfeiture money every year to help fight in the war on drugs. It would have certainly been feasible to purchase surveillance equipment to ensure the security of the narcotics vault. This is something that the chief of police should have instituted as soon as that type of technology became available. And because of the failings of the city and several police chiefs, some nefarious shit was taking place in a narcotics vault filled with drugs worth millions of dollars.

I told Jerry to call Arnie and have him bring the Carrillo file to the conference room. Jerry hung up the phone afterward with a quizzical look on his face. He said, "That was strange. It was almost like he knew what I was going to ask for. He didn't even have to think about it, and that case happened almost seven years ago. Hmmm." I knew what Jerry was thinking. No one other than Wilk and Jerry and I knew the name and date associated with the two kilos found in the locker. *Unless Wilk told Arnie the kilos were part of the Carrillo case, how could Arnie be so prepared for Jerry's request?*

About fifteen minutes later, Arnie knocked on the door. He gave Jerry the Carrillo file and told him that he had found it in Joe Velasco's desk. Jerry looked at me and then back at Arnie. Jerry asked, "Why would this old file be in Velasco's desk?"

Arnie shrugged his shoulders and smiled uneasily as he sat down at the table. First assigned to the narcotics unit in 1991, he had stayed in the unit until 1993 when he was removed for, according to him, "unknown reasons." He came back to the unit about a year or two later after repeated requests to Hourie.

I asked him to tell us about the Carrillo case.

He cleared his throat and said, "It was a snitch buy. I wrote the search warrant. We found four kilos of coke, about sixty ounces of crack, and about $20,000 in cash."

I asked him about the marijuana they found.

He said, "Oh yeah. It was in a parked car in front of the house. The car belonged to a brother of one of our dispatchers. She got fired not long ago."

I leaned back in my chair and asked, "It wouldn't be the one who was giving confidential information to a drug dealer, would it?"

Arnie nodded, and Jerry and I glanced at each other.

I asked Arnie if he had ever participated in a narcotic burn, and he said yes before explaining the procedures. He told us that a memo is prepared and sent to the chief to inform him of an impending burn, and then a court order is obtained from a judge. Whoever is responsible for the narcotics destruction prepares it by comparing the weight on index cards with the narcotics log. The weight is added up, and then each type of narcotic is packaged separately.

I looked at Jerry and asked, "You got any questions for him?"

Jerry said, "Yes. Arnie, were the four kilos from your Carrillo warrant stored in the green lockers in the vault?"

Arnie replied, "No, I don't think so, but I don't know. The only reason for that would be if they needed to be photographed or taken to court."

Jerry asked him if all four kilos should have been kept in the locker in that case, and Arnie said yes. Jerry then asked Arnie if he had keys to the green lockers in the vault, and he said only the property officer and the chief did. One of the lockers was for the narcotics buy fund and helicopter money, and the other ones were for valuable property.

I asked Arnie how the burn cases were logged. He said he and Fat Jack kept a record of the burns taped on the wall of the vault. They would mark the sheet after each burn to keep track of what year's dope had been destroyed. Arnie said that any case number on the sheet crossed out had been burned "without a doubt."

When I asked him about the Alvin Haynes case, he said, "I recovered the kilos from a motorhome. They should be in the vault in blue plastic containers." He said the cocaine from the Reyes Cano case was handled by Mark Anderson and an FBI agent. Arnie signed the log authorizing the release of it to the FBI. He and Fat Jack got everything ready for the April 1998 burn. He said Fat Jack prepared it and weighed it, and he (Arnie) took it from the truck and burned it. I asked Arnie about the four kilos from the Carrillo case, and he said they should have been destroyed, too, but if they weren't, they should still be in the vault. He said they could have been kept aside in case they were needed for a reverse sting. If any of the drugs were kept apart, there should be paperwork indicating they were.

I thanked him for talking with us and he nodded and left the room.

An hour or two later, Jerry and I were in the narcotics office looking for other paperwork associated with the Carrillo case when Arnie suddenly yelled, "Jerry! Come to the vault!" Jerry left, and seconds later, he called me to the vault.

Jerry pointed to an unmarked blue bin that Arnie was looking into and said, "Look at this, Fred. Arnie says he found them. He wants to know if this is the cocaine we're looking for." Two kilos of cocaine packaged in evidence envelopes, were in the bin. They were seized on November 24, 1993, from a house in Lynwood. The arresting officer was Nussman. There were also eighteen other kilos in the bin. They only had small blue sticker dots with 'TS197' written on them. It was Terry Smith's initials and badge number.

I remembered that Smith had been involved in a case in the Southside Crip neighborhood where he found a lot of cocaine a few years before. I squatted and picked up one of the kilos and waved it toward Jerry while glancing over at Arnie. I said, "Thanks. We got it from here." Arnie slowly walked out, looking over his shoulder before disappearing around the corner. Jerry told me that when he got to the vault, Arnie had immediately pointed to the two kilos in the evidence envelopes and asked if they were the missing kilos. We never told Arnie how many kilos from the Carrillo seizure were missing during our interview with him.

Jerry said, "Fred, how could he possibly know how many we were looking for unless he knew that only two kilos were in the locker?"

I replied, "Well, I guess Wilk could've told him. The real question is, how did Arnie get in the vault? Didn't we tell Anderson to change the combination and not give it to anyone?"

When Smith got to the vault, we showed him the kilos and asked him if he remembered the case.

He said, "Yeah. I got them from an arrest on Pearl Street in like 94 or 95. One of the cats I arrested was Keenan Handy. I also recovered like $80,000. Word on the street is that the dope belonged to some big-shot Southside Crip they call 'Fink'. About two weeks after I arrested Handy, patrol officers arrested some Mexican cat leaving Handy's house after a vehicle pursuit. He had $100,000 in his car."

I knew Handy. He was a drug dealer who dealt with Mexican drug cartels at various times over the years. His family owned a car wash at the corner of Long Beach and Alondra in the late 80s and early 90s until the sheriffs raided it, got multiple kilos of cocaine, and sent one of his brothers to prison. Not long after Smith arrested Handy, someone shot Handy and Southside Crip Travion "T-Rat" Williams. Handy survived. T-Rat didn't.

Cat and I handled the call-out. Handy placed the blame on an amorphous drive-by shooter. We knew that story was bullshit. There were several shell casings near T-Rat's body as if the shooter was standing next to him and Handy. They got shot just down the street from Handy's house in the SSCC hood. When a shooting occurs in a gang hood, you can always tell if a rival gang was responsible or if it was "in-house." Rival gang equals streets filled with crying females and fellow gang members cursing and swearing revenge. In-house equals streets quiet as field mice. And the night T-Rat got killed, you could hear one pissing on cotton.

CHAPTER THIRTEEN

JERRY AND I interviewed Mark Anderson on October 5th. He had been assigned to the FBI Task Force for almost ten years. His duties included undercover operations involving large quantities of narcotics. According to him, he was never directly involved in the narcotics unit itself other than when large amounts were seized. He remembered the two sixty-kilo seizures and said that the feds were involved in them, and everything happened just like it was supposed to, so he had nothing else to say about it.

He made sure to tell us that under the current burn procedures, there would be no way to know if dope got taken or not. However, he was adamantly in support of the officers assigned to the narcotics unit, saying he didn't believe any dope was stolen out of the narcotics vault to "save his life." He told us, "Yeah, there was nobody stole that dope. It probably just got burned. I don't believe anybody in that unit took that dope out of that locker. Goddammit, they better show me something more than a video because everybody in that unit has always been trustworthy, from Jerry to fucking Velasco to Arnie, even Jeff Nussman, with his fucking problems. There ain't no way anybody stole any dope out of that vault. Now it may have been fucking burned, but no way anybody stole any dope out of there."

Jerry and I were quiet as we listened to Anderson, stealing glances at each other as he ranted his unwavering support for everyone connected to the narcotics unit. There was nothing else that needed to be said. It was clear how he felt. Clarence Darrow couldn't have given a more stirring defense. I stood up and extended my hand dismissively, much like the LAPD oral appraiser had done to me years ago, and said, "Thanks for coming in, Mark."

We interviewed Sergeant John Wilkinson next. He confirmed that there were two kilos of cocaine inside the locker. Wilk could not recall the name associated with the case but thought it was odd that cocaine from 1992 was still around because it should have been destroyed. Wilk also said that Hourie was in the vault when he pulled one of the kilos out. Wilk was as straight a shooter as there ever was, and one of the most ethical, honest cops that I ever met. He would stand behind you and defend you to his dying breath if you were doing your job the right way. But if you crossed the line, Wilk wanted nothing to do with you. If Wilk said there were two kilos in that locker and Hourie was there when he found them, I had no doubt that he was telling the truth. I asked him if he told Arnie what was in the locker. He answered, "I'm sure I did, Fred, but I don't think I told him anything other than some kilos were in there."

Later that day, Jerry told me that when he asked Joe Velasco why the Carrillo file was in his desk, Velasco exploded in a profanity-laden denial. I asked him if he believed Velasco, and he sighed deeply and said, "Yes. He's positive the file wasn't in his desk because he cleaned it out his first day in the unit. Besides, why would a case that happened seven years ago be in his desk? And why that one? The exact case that sparked this investigation? It makes no sense."

I nodded in agreement and said, "R. E. and Anderson gave us this investigation because they think Hourie put those two kilos in that locker. But we haven't found anything supporting that. And remind me what Percy did again?"

Jerry said, "You know what? I've been thinking more and more about Arnie's behavior lately. Not too long before this investigation started, he was bragging about buying a house in Parker, Arizona, and that he was also building a house in Corona. His wife doesn't even work. And they renewed their vows at a wedding reception earlier this year. All this after he filed for bankruptcy and almost lost his house about two years ago."

"I heard about that reception. Bruce Frailich and his wife Shirleen went. I didn't get invited. Did you?" Jerry shook his head, and I continued, "Well, Frailich told me it was in Cerritos on Center Court Drive. There were at least 150 to 200 people there. I'm gonna call the place and see how much a reception like that would cost."

After I got off the phone, I looked at Jerry and shook my head. I said, "Son of a bitch. Wedding receptions at that place with that many people can cost between $9,000 and $12,000. And the balance is due on the night of the function."

Jerry looked at the floor and began shaking his head. I could tell that he was mentally exhausted. Every day was turning up more and more bullshit. I was just as tired as Jerry. The case was beginning to feel just a bit overwhelming. What we thought was going to initially be just an administrative investigation was starting to feel a whole lot like a criminal one. I told Jerry that was enough for the day, and we went home.

The next morning, Jerry was unusually quiet. I knew he wanted to tell me something. Impatiently, I said, "What, muthafucka? Spit it out." He replied, "Well, remember how we were talking about how difficult it would be for a cop to move dope without criminal street connections?"

"Yes. You find something out?"

"I think so. Before you got here, I was talking to Ron Thrash on the back lot about that very same thing. He seems to think that if anyone could do it, it would be the twins who were informants for Nussman. They're two tall guys, from Peru, I think. They used to work at the Swap Meet as security guards until one of them got arrested for impersonating a cop and robbing dope houses. They may have learned how to operate like cops from Nussman's narcotics unit because they used to go on raids with them. But the unit never served warrants in Compton based on the twin's information. The rumor was they were eliminating their competition because they didn't actually live in Compton."

I put my head in my hands and sighed as I told Jerry to get their informant files before they disappeared, too. He returned a short while later with their files and another file for a guy who I knew was a member of the SSCC gang. It was a shock to me. I never would have dreamed that he was an informant.

I called the narcotics office about an hour later. I wanted to talk to Arnie about the twins. Cross answered the phone. He told me that Arnie had called in sick.

Jerry and I talked to Sergeant Willie Mosley next. He had replaced R. E. in the narcotics unit and was in charge until Nussman took over in 1992. He supervised several burns and would enter the destroyed evidence into the computer.

After the computer was updated, the dope was loaded on a truck, transported to Terminal Island in Long Beach, and destroyed. In 1992, the Long Beach City council had voted to approve a request by the California DOJ to allow police agencies to burn about 50,000 pounds of seized drugs a year at the trash-to-energy plant located there. According to Mosley, the information regarding the Compton PD burn was lost when the computer crashed two years before this interview. The data weren't backed up but should have been on index cards.

I asked him why anyone would have reason to be in the vault and if it would be possible to steal dope during the burn preparation. He said, "Other than the chief for buy fund business, an officer should only be in the vault either to store evidence, remove it for court, or on special occasions like the preparation of dope for destruction. There is currently no fail-safe way to prevent theft during a burn preparation. The preparation of evidence for destruction takes place over sometimes one to two weeks. So, yes, based on our current procedures, someone can steal narcotics from bags slated for destruction."

I said, "Well, Willie, that's just fucked up. That should do it, though, unless you have anything else to add?"

He didn't answer. He just glared at me before getting up and leaving the room.

I turned to Jerry and said, "Let's talk to Ray Hernandez next. Call him."

The interview was short. Hernandez was in the vault because Anderson had requested that he be there with bolt cutters. Hernandez had keys to three of the locks, which he opened. He did not have a key to the locker in question, so he cut it off. Hourie and his attorney were present at the time. Hourie said, "There's nothing of mine inside" and he and his attorney left. After Hernandez cut the lock off the locker, Wilkinson found two kilos of cocaine inside. Anderson told Hernandez to throw the lock away and put on a new one. Hernandez then gave the key to the new lock to Anderson.

Hernandez showed me the key he used to open the three locks. The number '3163' was etched into it. He explained that when you buy locks packaged together, the same key unlocks them all even though each lock has its own key.

When Hernandez left the room after the interview was over, I asked Jerry, "Why the fuck would that idiot tell Ray to throw the lock away?"

Jerry just shook his head back and forth as he stared at the floor. I said, "Let's talk to Velasco. I want to ask him about that Carrillo file."

Detective Joe Velasco was one of my former trainees. Smooth and handsome, he was a pint-sized Ricky Ricardo and had been in the narcotics unit for about a year. I told him to have a seat and he stuck his head into the hallway and looked both ways before closing the door behind him.

"Joe, tell us about the narco unit," I said.

He told us that before this investigation, all the members of the unit had the combination to the vault except for Mark Anderson and William Jackson. They were assigned to task forces with the FBI and HIDTA, an acronym for "High-Intensity Drug Trafficking Areas", created by Congress in 1988 as part of the war on drugs. Velasco said that dope over five years old gets destroyed every year. It is not weighed; instead, the weight is added up using what is recorded on index cards. After a judge signs a destruction order, the dope is then set aside until it is taken to get destroyed.

I asked, "So, the containers themselves are never actually weighed?"

Joe replied, "No. It's based on whatever is written on the index cards. It's an honor system."

"Who is responsible for preparing the evidence for burns?" I asked.

Joe said, "Usually, it is the investigator or court officer assigned to the unit. Right now, Arnie has the list of case numbers and quantities of the dope next up for destruction. There is no set date for burns. The prep work is discretionary and not based on the directions of a supervisor."

I showed Joe the Carrillo file. "Arnie said he found this in your desk."

Joe yelled, "That's a fucking lie, Fred! That file was not in my desk! When he said he found it there, I told him he was out of his fucking mind! I know everything in my desk, and I have never seen that file before. It was Arnie's fucking warrant! Why wasn't it in the fucking file cabinet or inside *his* fucking desk?"

I had never seen Joe so upset. He leaned forward in his seat and continued. "Just a few days ago, fucking Arnie and Mark Anderson told me to be careful and watch my back. I asked them why, and Arnie told me he found twenty kilos in the vault when there were only supposed to be two, shit was missing from the vault, and the chief had cocaine in his locker from a warrant he did. Then they tell me that I should get out of the unit. I have known Arnie for over eight years, and for the last year, we have worked together in narcotics. He loves working narcotics. It's all he talks about. Just a few weeks ago, he said he wanted to be a dope cop until he retired. Now, he suddenly wants out of the unit, saying that he's had enough. What the fuck is that about?"

I asked, "Before you go, do you have any idea why Arnie would lie about where he found that file?"

Joe sat back in his chair and curled one side of his mouth while cocking his head to the side as if the answer was so obvious that he didn't need to say anything. Jerry turned to me after Joe closed the door behind him and said, "God, he's an angry cat."

"Not usually," I replied. "But I would be just as upset if I thought someone lied on me like that, too."

The following day R.E. had the vault combination changed again. A few hours later, Jerry and I met with two FBI Special Agents at the Federal Building on Wilshire. We wanted to follow up on the information regarding the sixty kilos. Anderson insisted on going with us. Perhaps he wanted face time with the feds, or maybe he wanted to hear exactly what Jerry and I were going to tell them. We shouldn't have told him and R. E. that we were going to talk to the feds, but a cop going behind his or her boss's back to talk to the feds was ill-advised. It could lead to suspension, ostracism, or even termination.

Jerry and I did most of the talking—after Anderson introduced himself as the assistant chief of police and provided the agents with two of his fancy business cards. We asked them if the FBI took custody of the sixty kilos. They were very standoffish, ultimately telling us that they could not provide us with that information at the time. They ended the meeting by saying they would check their records and "get back with us at a later date." I was vexed. Our request seemed simple enough. Either they took custody of the cocaine, or they didn't. I came away from that meeting believing that the FBI had absolutely no trust in Compton PD.

CHAPTER FOURTEEN

THE NEXT DAY was a Saturday. Jerry and I found a blue milk crate containing fifteen kilos of cocaine hidden next to the north wall behind several blue plastic bins. I looked over at Jerry and saw that he was rubbing his chin. Neither of us saw the milk crate the last time we were in the vault.

"Don't you fucking dare say 'hmmm', Jerry. What's on your mind?"

"Well, we know this is not the way to store evidence because there's no chain of custody. And why is this dope in an unmarked milk crate? It looks like someone was going to take it out of the vault or had recently returned it."

A large, wheeled trash can, containing a broom, a dustpan, a large pair of orange latex gloves, and a cookie can was nearby. A property report dated May 11, 1993, with "Stacey Kelley, 835 ½ West Magnolia Street, Compton" written on it was attached to the cookie can. I said, "I remember this case. Kelley got shot during a dope rip-off, and I helped Branscomb with the investigation. We found that can in the apartment. Arnie responded because there were about thirty-eight bags of weed inside of it. That blue milk crate was at the scene, and he asked us if he could use it to transport the narcotics evidence back to the station. It looks like somebody decided to get rid of everything connected to the Kelley case so they could use the milk crate for those kilos of cocaine."

I considered the pros and cons of getting shit processed for fingerprints that, at some point, had been legitimately handled by personnel assigned to the narcotics unit. *Fuck it.* I told Jerry to call the sheriff's lab on Monday and have them come to the station and print it. We grabbed the narco log-in books and took them to the conference room.

They were a joke. There was no way to confirm who went into the vault other than a signature. Hourie's signatures were all over the books. Most of the time, he entered the vault when he was in charge of the narcotics and gang units. He also had signed in a few times with Chief Ebert. After Hourie became chief, he rarely entered the vault and never alone, according to the log, that is. When officers needed dope for court cases, they gave their subpoenas to the narcotics supervisor, or the detective charged with filing cases. They then signed the log-in sheet and retrieved the evidence for the officer.

Starting on July 21, 1992, Arnie only signed the log-in sheet thirteen times over seven years. The log showed that he was always with someone else. Officers went to court on drug cases several times a day, so his name should have been on the log-in sheet a lot more than that. *And how did he prepare dope for destruction without signing the log-in sheet confirming that he had entered the vault?* For him, signing in appeared to be merely a suggestion.

Jerry and I had worked until night fall. I told him that I would see him Monday morning and left. When I got to my car, some asshole had thrown an egg on it. I was so tired that I just got in, turned on the wipers, and negotiated my way home through the yellow-streaked windshield. I saw a couple of guys across the street when I pulled into my driveway. I put my gun on my lap as I watched them through the rearview mirror. I saw that one of them was just a neighbor when he lit a cigarette. I let out a sigh of relief, realizing for the first time that the case had me paranoid. I went into the house and asked Carolyn if her mother had a pair of bolt cutters while I undressed and told her about my day. She sat up in bed and said, "Babe, you gotta be careful. This is about a lot more than just Hourie and Percy and some stupid code of silence."

I put my gun under my pillow, slid under the covers, and kissed her on the forehead. I said, "I know. I promise to be careful."

She reciprocated the kiss and replied, "You better be. The bolt cutters are in the garage. And don't get used to sleeping with that thing in bed with us."

I got to work later than usual that Monday. I had thought about the case the whole weekend. There were corrupt cops on my department. That was obvious. It was also obvious that Jerry and I couldn't manage a case of this magnitude on our own. It was too wide open and too close to home. We didn't know who to trust, and oftentimes information that we learned was common knowledge before we even had a chance to document it in our reports. The biggest obstacle was the fact that Jerry and I didn't have the teeth to force cops that we had known and worked with for years to fully cooperate.

I parked by the Heritage House because there weren't any parking spaces close to the station. My mind was so preoccupied that I almost got hit by a trash truck driving off the back lot. I went to the locker room to get an extra box of ammo out of my locker. There was white-out on it, and the lock was wired like I figured it would be. I ignored the white-out and just silently cut off the volleyball-sized roll of wire. I got my ammo and walked out as the few officers in there intentionally ignored me.

Jerry was already set up in the conference room when I got there. I was in a foul mood, but I didn't mention the state of my locker. I asked, "Jerry, have you called the lab yet?" He replied, "As soon as I got in."

Just then Gary Anderson came into the room. He told me that Cross and Sergeant Preston Harris, also a former member of R. E.'s Porsche and Harley-Davidson narcotics crew, were in the narcotics office the night before. Cross noticed a lock on one of the wall lockers that he didn't have a key to, so he cut it off and found a large plastic bag containing numerous golf-ball and base-ball-sized pieces of crack inside the locker. Jerry and I went to the narcotics office to talk to Cross. He had put all the crack he found into a box. There were no identifying markings or numbers associated with any of it, so none of it could be used in court as evidence now. Cross gave me the box and the lock he cut off. The three of us then went to the vault to secure the box. I noticed that the trash can was missing and asked Cross about it. He said, "That shit didn't belong in here, Fred. I know Arnie left it with his lazy ass. I wheeled it out last night and threw the trash inside of it away."

Jerry and I both rolled our eyes. We couldn't even be upset with Cross, though. He had no way of knowing it was potential evidence because we never told him. Printing the envelopes was a shot in the dark anyway. Prints are rarely lifted from paper surfaces, as was proven by the lack of any recovered from the packaging containing the two kilos that started this investigation. But the gloves? Prints from those may have helped. Then again, maybe not. They could've easily been explained away if they belonged to someone working in the unit. Still, Jerry and I had made a mistake by leaving the trash can in the vault overnight. Jerry said, "I'll cancel the lab response."

I turned to Cross and asked, "Is Arnie here today?"

Cross had a way of chuckling while talking at times, mainly when he knew he was speaking about someone who had fucked up. I couldn't tell if this chuckle was directed at Arnie or me when he replied. "No, he took today and the next two days off."

"What are his work hours, Gil?", I asked.

Cross replied, "Since he's the filing detective, he works from 0700 to 1630 hours. When I got the unit, I changed everyone else's hours to 1200 to 2130 hours.

In more of a statement than a question, I asked, "So, Arnie works alone from 0700 to 1200 hours, every day, huh?"

"Yes," Cross answered. "He needs to be here to get dope for officers going to court and to take cases for filing. That's why I gave him the combination to the vault again. He needs it to do his job."

After Cross left, I told Jerry, "We're never gonna' have control of that fucking vault. It's time to have a serious talk with R.E. and Gary Anderson. We need help. We got no other choice." Jerry agreed. The FBI had stonewalled us, and the sheriff's department didn't trust us. We would get no help from them or the DOJ without the backing of our administration. And maybe not even then.

We walked to the corner pocket, and R.E. invited us in. The intoxicating sounds of John Coltrane's "My Favorite Things" played in the background as rainbow sharks and clownfish swam seemingly in rhythm to the music. As Anderson sat silently in one of the chairs in front of the huge mahogany desk, R. E. said, "How can I help you gentlemen?"

I answered, "We need help, chief. The case is a lot bigger than we thought it was. To start with, we're gonna need another person."

"Sure, Reynolds. Do you know who you want?"

Of course, I did. I knew a couple of days ago and had even approached him with the offer beforehand. "Kenny Roller," I replied.

Sergeant Kenneth Roller was a young White cop, bone-thin with a bushy mustache. He was the kind of guy who probably dressed up as the town marshal every Halloween when he was a kid and as Woody from Toy Story as an adult. He spoke police jargon and used radio and penal codes to describe people, places, and things, even during general conversation. He wasn't well liked because everyone thought he was *too* much of a cop. He didn't know anything about dope, but he was honest, kept to himself, and wasn't part of any cliques. He was perfect.

R. E. chuckled and asked, "Roller, huh? You got him. Anything else?"

I said, "Well, now that you mention it, it doesn't look like Hourie has done anything wrong. At least not criminally. But we have reason to believe that there is corruption in the unit—"

R. E. held up the palm of his right hand as Anderson groaned and rolled his eyes. R. E. put his hand down and said, "What do you mean, 'Hourie hasn't done anything wrong'? He is the target. Make no mistake about it."

I smirked and said, "Condemnation before investigation is the highest form of ignorance."

R. E. leaned forward and replied, "I beg your pardon?"

"It's a quote by Albert Einstein—"

R. E. snapped, "I know who fucking said it! What did you mean by it?"

I said, "Maybe Hourie was the target initially, but the investigation is pointing toward someone else now. R. E., you were a detective for years. You, of all people, know that the focus of an investigation often changes. Multiple people on the department may be involved. I think we need to get outside help from the DOJ or the sheriff's department. Maybe even the FBI or DEA. It's too big for us."

Anderson rolled his eyes again, specifically when I mentioned the sheriff's department. R. E. was directing the entire conversation at this point as Anderson sat silently. R. E. said, "Reynolds. First of all. We clean *our* own laundry. Is that clear? You are not to contact another agency. Is that clear? I am giving you both a direct order. Now. Is there anything else you need?"

I paused before answering, wondering if Jerry was as shocked as I was that neither R. E. nor Anderson had asked who we thought was dirty in the narcotics unit. I guess if the name Hourie Taylor wasn't attached, they didn't care. It now made perfect sense why Anderson insisted on coming with us to meet the FBI.

I said, "Well, *chief,* now that you mention it. We need to talk to Arnie Villarruel. He took almost the entire week off. We think he's dodging us. You think you can order him in?"

R.E. brusquely replied, "Absolutely. Now get the fuck out."

CHAPTER FIFTEEN

ROLLER CONCENTRATED on completing the vault inventory. R. E. had also agreed to give us two patrol officers on overtime to help, so I asked Roller who he trusted. He asked for Jeffrey Houle and Danielle Slater. I understood the choices. They had recently completed probation and, as such, were not loyal to one side or the other. Jerry and I kept interviewing employees and looking for documents and evidence. We found a confidential informant identification report for one of the twins in the narcotics office. He had been a prolific informant for Nussman, responsible for numerous multi-kilo seizures. The locations he gave up were all in cities that bordered Compton, possibly corroborating information that he and his brother were getting rid of rival dealers. One operation involved an undercover sting using Officer Richard Sanchez in 1994.

On October 13, Arnie came to the station for his interview. Roller sat in as an observer, and at Arnie's request, Terrence Idlebird sat in as his CPOA representative. Idlebird, known as "Bird," was older than most of his peers and a former Marine who was extremely well liked. He was also loyal and believed in giving his fellow officers the benefit of the doubt. We spoke briefly before Arnie got to the conference room. He said, "You don't think anyone is really stealing dope, do you, Fred? Come on, man. I cannot believe anyone would do that."

I answered, "Who said someone was stealing dope, Bird?"

He shook his head and said, "That's the rumor. Most people think it's just bullshit and that you guys are trying to frame Hourie and Percy."

"I can't speak on what I believe or discuss the case with you, Bird. Let's just see how the interview goes." Despite Idlebird's disbelief, by now, I believed that someone was indeed stealing dope. Arnie. I also thought that if this were true, he was not the only one involved.

Arnie only appeared for the interview because R. E. and Gary Anderson ordered him to. As soon as he walked into the room, he began pacing back and forth and clenching and unclenching his hands. He said, "Man, I don't feel right. I need to see a doctor. I want to leave."

I told him to relax and have a seat, but he kept walking around in a circle and pacing back and forth from the door to the chair. As nicely as I could under the circumstances, I said, "Arnie, we just want to ask some questions about the narcotics vault."

He roared, "Fuck that, Fred. I want to see my lawyer, and I want to go see the psych *right* now." I looked at everyone else in the room. The shock on their faces was glaring. *Fuck that,* I thought. He wasn't getting shit right now. If I got disciplined behind my decision, so be it.

I said, "Sure, Arnie. We can make all that happen real soon. But right now, I'm giving you a direct fucking order to sit your ass down so that I can take your statement." He knew he had to. If he refused, it was insubordination. There is no defense against that charge in police work unless the order is unethical, immoral, or illegal. He sat down, his shirt betraying just how fast his heart was beating. I glanced over at Roller, sitting next to me. He was pointing his Beretta .40 caliber pistol at Arnie underneath the table. He reminded me of a gambler in an old Western movie playing poker in a saloon. I was glad. Arnie had the same type of gun holstered on his hip, but he would lose if he tried a quick draw.

In an interview that was more like pulling teeth, Arnie went on to deny anything linking him to the theft of any narcotics. He denied ever having a key to the locks on the green lockers in the vault or any knowledge of the two kilos in the locker. He only remembered the Carrillo case because he wrote the warrant and they got four kilos of cocaine. Arnie said he never saw them again after they were booked as evidence. I asked him about the sixty kilos recovered from the motorhome. According to him, the information was given to him by a Southside Crip informant. The dope was on the way to Little Rock, Arkansas when they pulled over the motorhome. The case was a DA reject, and the cocaine should still be in the vault.

He told us that the informant was now dead, killed in an accident while riding his motorcycle several years earlier in Los Angeles. The driver of the car that hit him was a Mexican national who had his wife and kids with him. By all accounts, it was nothing more than an accident. Still, the informant had given information that led to the seizure of sixty kilos of Mexican cartel-related cocaine. While his death was highly unfortunate for him, it was certainly fortuitous for others.

I showed Arnie the entry in the narcotics bible about the Reyes Cano case. He said that the signature for releasing the sixty kilos of cocaine to the FBI was his. Mark Anderson and an FBI agent handled the case. He believed that Hourie authorized the release. Arnie was adamant that he knew only one of the twins, and only worked with him one time. He swore he had never met the other twin. He also swore that he never socialized or hung out off duty with either of them. He confirmed that he had declared bankruptcy as recently as two years previously, but now owned a house in Parker, Arizona and was in the process of buying another one in Corona.

When I asked him about the large trash can in the vault, he said it had been there for years, and he used it to throw empty envelopes away. He didn't know anything about files in Velasco's desk. I could tell from the way the conversation was going that we weren't going to get anything of substance from him. Several times he even appeared to be on the verge of hyperventilating.

I said, "Thanks, Arnie. Jerry, you have any more questions?"

Jerry thumbed through his notes briefly and said, "No."

After Arnie left, Idlebird looked at us like he had seen a ghost. He walked uneasily to the door, turned around and said, "Damn. Just damn. I'll talk to you guys later."

Roller, Jerry, and I just sat there after Bird left, alone in our thoughts until Jerry broke the silence. He said, "That fucking cat is dirty." Jerry didn't curse much, so I knew that he was upset.

Kenny, however, had a potty mouth. He bellowed, "Fuck that dirtbag! Arnie's a fucking thief, but he ain't no fucking criminal mastermind. He can't be doing this shit alone, Fred! You know he 459'ed that dope, and he would have needed a code-9 to do it. I guarantee you he's 10-7."

I tuned them both out, lost in thought as they continued talking. The department had made it too easy to steal dope from the vault. We had different opinions from current and former members of the narcotics unit, but it all came down to this. All you had to do was mark whatever the dope's weight was based on the index cards, put it on the court order, and then put something else of equal weight in bags, seal them, and burn them. After that, the dope no longer exists even though it *does*. Hell, you could even sell it back to who you took it from or to their competition. Yeah, Arnie was done. And so was this fucked-up investigation.

Gary Anderson stopped me as I was about to go home for the day. He told me that he had received a call from one of the FBI agents we spoke to, and he confirmed that the Reyes Cano cocaine was in fact in the possession of the FBI. Anderson also ordered me not to make any more contact with Arnie because he had just turned in his badge and gun and gone off on stress. Like Roller thought, Arnie never intended on coming back to work. We later found out that he had entered the vault and uncharacteristically signed the log-in book before our interview with him. *What the fuck was he doing in there?* He had also apparently cleaned out his locker, which was the strongest indication to me that he had no plans on ever returning to work.

The next morning, Jerry and I were in the narcotics office looking for index cards, reports, destruction memos, and court orders in case we had overlooked some of them. Jerry looked in Arnie's desk and found a set of keys on a "Wild Bill's" keychain and five other "Master" lock keys. Each of the Master keys had the numbers "0536" on them.

While checking the file cabinets, we found two master locks. I tried the keys on these locks, and on the one Cross had cut off the locker containing the unmarked cocaine. The keys opened all three locks. The keys also opened another lock that was on one of the lockers on the west wall of the office. We had five keys that opened four locks. One lock was missing, and it was most likely the lock Gary Anderson had Ray Hernandez throw away. We had a collective "aha" moment. This meant that Arnie had possession of keys to both lockers containing large quantities of cocaine, some that should have been destroyed, the rest unmarked. Motherfucking Anderson, he of the gold-embossed business cards, had literally directed Ray Hernandez to throw away the smoking gun.

I felt sick to my stomach. I went to the conference room and packed my stuff without saying another word to Jerry.

Since I had worked on Haley's birthday and hadn't seen her or Dominic for a couple of weeks, Carolyn and I decided to take all the kids to Medieval Times in Buena Park that night to celebrate. Medieval Times is a show about knights jousting and competing for the hand of a princess. It reminded me of King Arthur and his knights of the round table. As I watched the tournament winner give Haley a red rose, I wished that life was as black and white as it was for the gray-armored knights of the round table. The good guys and bad guys were clearly delineated. More importantly, the good guys always won.

CHAPTER SIXTEEN

ON OCTOBER 15, I was home asleep when the phone rang. I looked at the clock. It was 2:00 a.m. I answered the phone, my annoyance apparent, and heard the familiar heavy breathing on the other line. I hung up. About two minutes later, the phone rang again. I said, "Hello," and this time, the person on the other end replied, "You're dead," before breathing heavily again.

In a whispering roar of fury, I asked, "Who the fuck is this? Tell me who you are, dickhead!"

The caller replied, "You're dead, motherfucker! You and that dispatcher bitch!" He hung up before I could tell him to kiss my ass. The sound of me slamming the receiver down woke Carolyn up. "Babe, who was that?" she asked.

I replied, "Just a bill collector. Go back to sleep."

She sat up in bed, clearly perturbed. "No, Frederick! That's bullshit! Who the hell was that calling?"

Carolyn rarely, if ever got upset or raised her voice (that was my job in the relationship). She was scared. I had to make her feel safe, but I couldn't lie to her. I sighed, held her hands, and looked directly into her eyes. I said, "I don't know, but it has to do with this investigation. Someone threatened me." There was no way I was going to tell her everything said by the cowardly caller. She got my .38 from the top shelf in our closet and put it under her pillow. Then she kissed me before putting her head on the pillow and closing her eyes. After all this time, I had no idea just how much of a rider she was. I reciprocated the kiss and said, "Just don't get used to sleeping with that thing in bed with us."

I called Jerry and Roller after she fell asleep and let them know about the threat. No one had called them—only me. I notified the W/C next. He told me he would have a unit come by my house periodically throughout the night.

I got my pistol and an extra clip out of my bag and sat near the front door for added security. Not once did a Compton PD unit drive by my house. The next day over the lunch hour, I walked to Bookman's house. He lived on the corner of Myrrh and Acacia, directly across the street from Compton High. It was less than a block from the station, so he walked to work and usually went home for lunch. Despite living so close, he was late every morning, walking in just as Swanson was giving his usual opening statement of, "Death came calling last night . . ." before briefing us about the previous night's events. D-dub always embarrassed Bookman by telling Swanson that he was late because of a Sigalert at the corner of Willowbrook and Myrrh. No matter how many times he said this, it was always fucking funny.

Bookman was licking his fingers and holding a fried chicken breast when he answered the door. He said, "What's up, money? C'mon in." Bookman had started calling me this after seeing my bankroll the day after a good night at Bo-Pete's. I sat down in the living room and explained what was going on. He said, "Man, fuck them crooked motherfuckers. What you need from me?"

I answered, "Some firepower. Something small and compact, but powerful."

Bookman continued licking his fingers as he put the breast on the kitchen counter. He said, "Come with me." I followed him into his bedroom, where he moved clothes hanging on hooks aside in his closet, exposing a large wall safe. After he opened it, I saw multiple semi-automatic rifles and pistols inside. "Try this," he said. He handed me a Mac-10 with a suppressor and two 32-round clips.

He said, "It's a little heavier than a Mac-11, but it shoots fo-fives instead of nines. Put it in here." He handed me a briefcase he got from under the bed. It had slots for the weapon, suppressor, and extra clips.

After putting everything in their specific spaces and closing the briefcase, I noticed a button covered by a small hinge near the handle. "What's this for?" I asked.

Bookman grabbed the briefcase, smiled, and said, "Peace of mind, money." He then flipped the hinge and pushed the button, which exposed the weapon, fully ready to fire. I left his house and walked to the station past Fort Compton, looking like just another attorney, except while their briefcases carried the means for a legal death, mine had the means for an actual one.

I went to the corner pocket. Gary Anderson was sitting in one of the chairs talking to R. E. He stood up just as R. E. offered me the other one. I said, "No, thanks. I'll stand. Someone called my house last night and threatened to kill my wife and me. I think we should take it seriously. I need a unit to watch my house until this investigation is over, or at the very least, for the next few days."

R. E. and Anderson glanced at each other before R. E. spoke. He said, "We heard about that when we got to work this morning, but we don't have the resources or the money for that. The city is in dire straits. We're already paying overtime on the vault inventory." Frustrated, I turned to leave, and R. E. asked, "By the way. What's in the briefcase?"

I glared over my shoulder just before walking out the door and replied, "Peace of mind, sir. Peace of mind."

I met Jerry and Roller in the conference room and showed them my new toy. Jerry nodded silently. Roller was more vocal in his approval, yelling, "Fuck yeah! 417 like a motherfucker! That's what the fuck I'm talking about!"

I filed a report with the Carson sheriff's station about the threatening phone calls when I got home that evening. They were extremely responsive and had the district unit drive by my house as much as possible. Patrol units even sat near my house when they had paper to scratch. Despite my newfound peace of mind, I was becoming more and more paranoid. Whenever I left work, I was suspicious of all cars that followed me past three blocks. I began to consider my mortality daily and realized that I wanted to leave a part of me with Carolyn in case something happened to me. I tried my best to conceal my concern, but she knew the case was getting to me.

While having dinner one night, she said, "I'll be glad when this case is over. It's driving you crazy. But that's not what's bothering you tonight, is it?"

I answered, "No. Lately, I've been thinking about something else." She asked what, and I replied, "Well, I know that we agreed that we didn't need any more kids when we got married. I've changed my mind. I want a baby with *you*."

She smiled and began shaking her head back and forth. I grabbed her chin and lifted her face to mine, I said it again, just to let her know I was serious. This time, she said, "Yes. Okay, babe."

A month later, she was pregnant.

CHAPTER SEVENTEEN

R. E. AND ANDERSON were getting impatient for me to interview Hourie and Percy. I knew why they wanted the interviews done as quickly as possible. It was because the city couldn't fire Hourie and Percy before then. Once R. E. found out how fucked-up the vault was and the ineptness of the narco unit, he figured that it was curtains for Hourie. Percy would simply be collateral damage. A leader of any organization is responsible for everything that happens under his or her watch. Daryl Gates wasn't directly accountable for Rodney King's ass-whipping, but it occurred on his watch, so he retired instead of potentially getting fired. Now, R. E. believed he finally had what he needed for the city to just make Hourie and Percy go away. It didn't matter what they said. Nothing could justify the condition of the narcotics vault, and if they refused to talk, it was insubordination.

I interviewed them both on October 19. Percy was first. Gary Anderson and Kenny Roller sat in as witnesses. Percy's attorney was by his side. Percy refused to talk until he was ordered to do so by Anderson via the city manager.

Percy was promoted to captain by Hourie in 1993. He was currently the commanding officer of the Investigative Services Bureau, and part of his responsibility was the management of the narcotics unit. He did not know about any of the significant narcotic seizures but opined that if the department were to release a large quantity of narcotics to another agency, then there should be a "significant paper trail" and it should not occur without his and/or the chief's knowledge. He knew nothing about the two kilos in the locker. He had never ordered an audit of the narcotics vault and was unsure when the last one had occurred. Basically, I came away from the interview thinking that Percy may just have been the rube R.E. perceived him to be. He seemed utterly clueless as to what was going on in his unit. Other than that, the interview was as pleasant as it could be under the circumstances. I didn't have too many questions for Percy. How could I? He still hadn't been accused of anything.

I interviewed Hourie next. He was represented by the same attorney as Percy. Hourie also refused to cooperate until ordered to. Putting his bear paws on the table as he leaned forward, he fixed his eyes on me in an attempt at intimidation and said, "*Mister* Reynolds, you better be sure you know what you are doing." After that, he condescendingly referred to me as "*sergeant*" as if to drive home the fact that he was my superior. He was adamant that there were no kilos of cocaine in the locker in the vault. He said Wilk and Anderson also looked in the locker, and they both know that there was nothing there. Hourie called Anderson a liar multiple times during the interview, causing Anderson to give credibility to his nickname. He never looked Hourie in the face, preferring to keep his eyes glued on the paperwork on the table in front of him as he nervously shuffled it around.

Like Percy, Hourie said he never participated in an inventory of the vault nor ordered one. He said that narcotics were destroyed consistent with departmental orders. Also, like Percy, Hourie didn't seem to know too much about what was going on in the most sensitive unit in his department. Although he admitted to knowledge of the Alvin Haynes arrest, he said that it was only because the department got a motorhome out of the deal and the suspect was supposedly going to Little Rock, Arkansas, which is where he just happened to be lecturing on gangs at the time.

When I showed him the Reyes Cano log entry regarding the release of sixty kilos of cocaine, he said that he was "absolutely not" familiar with the case. He also said that he didn't involve himself in the day-to-day operations of narcotics, so he wouldn't necessarily know the disposition of drugs. Interviewing Hourie was even more frustrating than interviewing Arnie. I had been put in a most unenviable position, that small area between a rock and a hard place. If Hourie got his job back, I was fucked. If I messed up the investigation and R. E. somehow remained the chief, I was fucked even harder. I did the next best thing. I decided just to be objective and let the chips fall wherever they wanted to.

After the interview, Hourie left the room first, followed by Anderson at a safe distance. The attorney looked at me and said, "You should be careful. You better think about what you're doing."

I asked him if he was threatening me and he said, "No, now you are trying to twist my words around." Just like a damned lawyer. No one, except for politicians, twists up words better than they do. I glared at him as I zipped up my bag and replied, "Whatever, man. Fuck you." I was amazed at how composed I managed to stay as I walked away from him.

The following day, Jerry and I helped Roller and the two patrol officers with the inventory. We found a blue narcotics bin against the back wall that contained twenty-seven kilos of cocaine with "ORO" stickers affixed to them. Each kilo had coffee grounds in the cellophane packaging. A brown paper bag containing four kilos of cocaine dated 03-02-93 was hidden away in the corner of the vault. There was a Xerox box next to the paper bag with file number 9727325 written on one side and Arnie's initials and "6,931 grams" written on the other side. Six kilos of cocaine were in the box. Another bin had a total of fifteen unmarked kilos of cocaine in it. None of them had any identifying information. We also found a second blue narcotics bin containing a box of marijuana and thirteen kilos of cocaine. Several of the kilos were dated 10-05-94, but the rest were unmarked.

While Kenny and Houle and Slater continued the inventory, Jerry and I interviewed Internal Affairs Sergeant Rick Petty. Before his current assignment, he was the chief's adjutant from February 1992 through May of 1998. He served under Chief Ebert for about four months and then under Hourie when Ebert got fired. After R. E. took over, R. E. replaced him with Officer James Green. Petty's primary duty as adjutant was to assign projects from the chief's office to other supervisors. A kindly, affable man with a million-dollar smile and a cocoa-brown complexion, everyone liked Petty, probably no one more than me. I asked him if Hourie ever had the narcotics vault combination or if Hourie ever went in there alone. He replied, "I don't know if he ever had the combination or not, Fred. I suppose it's possible, but whenever he told me he was going to the vault, it was always to meet someone."

I asked Petty if he remembered any information about a sixty-kilo cocaine seizure coming through the chief's office in April of 1997. He said, "I don't recall seeing anything regarding that much cocaine. And I looked at all the paperwork coming into the office every day before giving it to R. E.'s wife, Wanda, who was the chief's secretary for a long time. I would absolutely remember something as significant as a sixty-kilo seizure. Every supervisor submits a daily log sheet to the chief's office, and Hourie read them all. I guess it's possible for the chief not to know about a seizure that large, but only if the paperwork never came through the office. I just couldn't see the supervisor of the narcotics unit not putting something like a sixty-kilo cocaine seizure in his daily log, though."

Petty told us he remembered a motorhome transporting cocaine being seized because he saw the paperwork justifying the seizure. Hourie signed off on the seizure so he would have to know the circumstances of the case.

"Have you ever seen Hourie meeting with Nussman, Rick?"

"Oh, hell yeah, Fred! They met all the time. It was always just the two of them in closed-door meetings. They met two, sometimes three times a week, and the meetings would last between ten and twenty minutes. I never heard what they talked about. I just assumed it was about the activities of the narcotics unit. Hourie would call me into his office for certain things if he met with other supervisors, but never if a narcotics supervisor was in there. Mark Anderson met with Hourie a lot, too." Petty said he never saw anything about narco burns come through the chief's office while he was the adjutant.

Jerry and I interviewed Officer Richard Sanchez next. Sanchez, or "Richie," as everyone called him, was a baby-faced Puerto Rican originally from the Bronx, NYC, who loved to hear himself talk. He was about five-foot-five and 130 pounds. Richie worked undercover on loan to Nussman's narcotics unit in 1994. We asked him about the undercover sting case that he worked. He told us that he and one of the twins posed as dealers and sold three kilos of cocaine to a buyer in the city of Southgate. The twin ran the entire operation briefing beforehand, telling everyone where to be and how to approach the buyer.

Arnie was also involved in the operation. The twin and Nussman told Richie that he couldn't carry a gun even though the twin had one. After the sale, somehow, the buyer got away even though he was surrounded by cops. Apparently, he never even got a chance to get the cocaine. Nussman and the twin, along with Arnie, brought the money and the cocaine back to the station. Richie overheard Nussman telling them that the buyer had shorted them. Richie was also familiar with the other twin because they both used to hang out in the narcotics office and socialize with everyone. He had seen them in the station on more than twenty occasions, and they walked around unaccompanied as if they were police officers.

I couldn't believe what I was hearing. Nussman violated a cardinal rule by not allowing his undercover to be armed, not to mention breaking the law by allowing an informant to carry a concealed firearm. *And that part about being shorted? What the fuck was that?* Richie also said he knew nothing about the burn procedures. What he did confirm, however, was that the twins pretty much had the run of the station and the narcotics unit and were apparently overly friendly with Nussman and Arnie.

On October 21, Jerry and I interviewed Lieutenant Reggie Wright. Sergeant Roller and Marvin Branscomb sat in on the interview. Reggie had requested that Branscomb sit in as his CPOA representative. Reggie refused to give a voluntary statement and told me that someone was going to have to order him to talk. I let Gary Anderson know, and he then gave Reggie an order to cooperate. Reggie was agitated during the interview, and I don't know if he was more upset that it was me asking the questions or whether he was insulted by even being interviewed.

Reggie was currently assigned to patrol as a W/C after R.E. had reconfigured the gang unit, replacing arguably the best gang detectives in LA County with B-team members. Before that, Reggie had been the supervisor of the gang unit since 1994 and was given the extra responsibility of supervising the vice and narcotics units in 1997. He knew the twins, because one of them had worked at the swap meet before. They were both informants for Sergeant Nussman. He saw them going in and out of the narcotics office all the time. He knew about the sixty kilos from the Reyes Cano case and the sixty kilos from the motorhome case because they were both joint efforts between Compton PD and the FBI, and Mark Anderson spearheaded the operations.

When I asked Reggie if he gave the authorization to release the Reyes Cano kilos of cocaine to the FBI, he replied, "Hell no, Fred! I never got involved in shit like that during my command. Even if something like that came through me, then the chief or Percy, more than likely the chief, would have to make that authorization." Reggie said he never had the combination to the vault because he never had a reason to go inside. If he had adhered to the honor system over the years, this would appear to be true. In reviewing years of signatures on the log-in books, Reggie's did not appear. Reggie also said he never participated in any narcotics burns because sergeants are in charge of the burns.

Jerry asked Reggie if he knew that Arnie had at one time experienced financial difficulties, and Reggie replied, "Unofficially. I just heard rumors about it, that's all. Arnie seemed happy working narcotics and was good at his job. I thought he was solid." Jerry then asked Reggie if he knew that Arnie and Pilcher had concerns about him always wanting to know search warrant locations before they were served.

Reggie exploded, screaming, "I never wanted to know where a search warrant was, so whoever told you that told you a damn lie! I never wanted to know until it came to my attention that Arnie and Pilcher brought up going to Fat Melvin Hoard's spot! And the only reason I was concerned is that they were looking for the same guy that my gang unit was looking at for a shooting, and he had guns, and I wanted his ass! That is the only reason I got involved. If it wasn't for that, I would have been somewhere on the other side of town. I never asked Pilcher and Arnie where they were going. They would come to me and try and tell me, and I would tell them that I didn't want to even know!"

I thanked him for his cooperation, and he and Branscomb walked out the door without saying another word.

The next day, Jerry and I interviewed Fat Jack. He was now in charge of subpoena control, responsible for keeping cops from milking the city for overtime by appearing in court and just sitting around all day. Many of them resented Fat Jack because he was very proficient at his job. Fat Jack worked narcotics as the filing detective from 1993 until 1998. He said that when he took over the responsibility of the vault, dope was everywhere, kilos of cocaine were on the floor, on the shelves, "just all over."

Fat Jack said that whenever he was off or on vacation, Arnie was responsible for the vault. Fat Jack said dope slated for destruction was put inside a plastic trash can and then weighed. The gross weight was recorded onto a manifest list and submitted to a judge, who, in turn, issued a destruction order, which was kept filed away in the narcotics office. The narcotics were then loaded onto a truck and driven to an incinerator company in Long Beach by an armed escort. Fat Jack admitted that someone could remove the drugs and replace them with equal weight without anyone knowing.

I asked, "Who was the lead investigator on the motorhome case, Jack?"

"Arnie", he answered. "As a matter of fact, I asked Nussman about it just before I left narcotics because that was a lot of dope in the vault. None of it had any case numbers attached which had screwed up the chain of custody. He told me the case was over, so I prepared it for destruction. Why do you ask?"

I just looked at him.

When I didn't answer, he sat back in his chair and blew out a big gust of air. He said, "That dope didn't get burned, did it? Those sons of bitches!" He was outraged. I hadn't seen him this upset since Doyle's buffoonery with Slim and Nitro. I asked him what checks and balances were in place to prevent theft, other than the officer's integrity and honesty. He answered, "None, son. That's it. But if we as cops don't have those qualities, then what in the fuck good are we?!"

Several hours later, Jerry and I interviewed Detective Mikey Paiz. Paiz was a middle-aged, balding Mexican cop with a beer gut who chewed gum nonstop and laughed a lot. He was a far cry from the former semi-pro baseball player with a head full of hair that he had when he was a rookie. There was a time when Paiz could run like the wind and had an arm like a cannon. He always carried a baseball with him that he called his "freeze ball." Instead of chasing criminals and yelling freeze, Paiz would just throw the ball with pinpoint accuracy and hit them with enough force that it knocked them to the ground. Paiz was legendary then. Nowadays, he used his cannon to hoist cans of beer to his mouth instead.

He worked narcotics for Nussman for a short time before getting thrown out of the unit after accusing Arnie of breaking into his desk and stealing $1,800. After that, Paiz was known as a snitch, and no one in narcotics wanted to work with him. He said he never participated in any narcotic burns while he was assigned there. I asked him if he ever saw some twins around the narcotics office. He laughed loudly, smacking the wad of pink bubble gum in his mouth even louder than usual. He said, "Fred, you're shitting me, right? They were Nussman's informants, and they practically worked there! One of them was there almost every day! He pretty much had the run of the narcotics office and was very friendly with Nussman and Arnie. They even hung out together, off duty, and drank at bars. They asked me to go with them once, but I refused. It's not proper for a narcotics officer to socialize off-duty with informants." Paiz got deadly serious at the end of the interview and said, "Watch yourself. Those twins are dangerous."

We finished the vault inventory the following day. We found twenty-six additional kilos of cocaine that were confiscated from a house in Lynwood on October 3, 1994. One of the twins had been the informant on this case. We also found a multi-colored carry-on bag with ten kilos of cocaine inside, each one with gold ORO stickers affixed to them and containing coffee grounds in the cellophane wrappings. This indicates that they were part of the other twenty-seven kilos with ORO stickers, for a total of thirty-seven kilos. We couldn't find any corresponding information to explain where they came from. If these kilos were part of the motorhome seizure, then where were the other twenty-three? Major dealers usually *brand* their product with a specific identifier, hence the stickers.

And there was still the question of the fifteen kilos that we found in the blue milk crate. Although there was no indication that they were part of the cocaine recovered from the motorhome since they didn't have any stickers on them, there were no other seizures of just fifteen kilos. Even if the sticker kilos and the fifteen kilos in the milk crate were part of the seizure from the motorhome, then that would still only be a total of fifty-two kilos, or eight too few. Absent any other identifying information or reports, this would make the most sense. *But if the 15 kilos were part of the Alvin Haynes case and the ORO kilos weren't, then where were the other forty-five kilos? If they were burned, then why weren't these burned as well?*

The FBI had advised Gary Anderson that they had in fact taken custody of the sixty-kilos from the Reyes Cano case, so the sticker kilos were part of something else.

Over the course of the investigation, we had interviewed dozens of cops who had either worked narcotics before or who had been present when Wilkinson found the two kilos of cocaine in the locker. None of them could even remember the last time someone inventoried the vault to find out what was supposed to be in there and what wasn't.

Combined with the two kilos of cocaine that started this investigation, we now had found 138 kilos of cocaine in the vault, most of which couldn't be attached to cases, almost all with questionable chains of custody. A best guestimate would be that there were three kilos of cocaine missing and unaccounted for, at least thirty others that should have been destroyed but were still in the vault, and possibly eight of the sixty-kilos seized in the Alvin Haynes case missing and unaccounted for as well.

Kenny Roller prepared the following document at the conclusion of his portion of the inventory:

A review of the destruction manifest from the 1998 destruction (which would have been narcotics seized or recovered from 1992 with case numbers beginning with the letter "G") indicated the Department destroyed the following narcotics by weight:

Cocaine:	*69 pounds (approx. 31 kilograms)*
Marijuana:	*225 pounds*
PCP:	*24 pounds*
Heroin:	*2 pounds*

A review of the narcotics property index cards (for the year 1992 with case numbers beginning with the letter "G") that are completed and maintained by the narcotics investigator, indicated the following narcotics were booked, by weight:

Cocaine:	*1,604.1 grams (approx. 2.5 pounds)*
Marijuana:	*9,654.47 grams (approx. 20 pounds)*

PCP:	*761.113 grams (less than one pound)*
Heroin:	*76.25 grams (less than one pound)*

These weights are based on the weight of the narcotics, as indicated by the laboratory receipts.

Obviously, there are discrepancies between the destruction manifest and the narcotics evidence index cards. A portion of the weight discrepancies may be explained by the fact that some narcotic evidence (ie: PCP) is commonly booked with or in the container it was seized or recovered in. Additionally, what are commonly referred to as "buy narcotics" and "non-lab narcotics" are not sent to the crime laboratory for analysis or weighing.

The containers, if any, and the buy and non-lab narcotics notwithstanding, there still remain discrepancies. For example:

Cocaine reported as having been destroyed: 69 pounds	
Cocaine indicated on the index cards:	*2.5 pounds (approx.)*
Difference:	*66.5 pounds*

This would, if accurate, indicate that there was either 66.5 pounds of containers and evidence envelopes, and/or there were 66.5 pounds of buy and non-lab narcotics destroyed in the 1998 destruction operation."

The vault inventory had revealed some highly troubling information. In addition to the unmarked kilos, there were 1,765.92 grams of cocaine, 585.858 ounces of PCP, 94.05 grams of heroin, twenty-seven sticks of Sherm, and over twenty pounds of marijuana---all from cases dated in 1992. None of this dope was supposed to exist anymore; all dope from that year was destroyed according to the Chief's memo and officers assigned to the unit. Yet it was all still in the vault. But the most troubling result of the inventory was the fact that three kilos of cocaine were missing for certain: the other two kilos from the Juan Carrillo case, and one kilo connected to an arrest made on June 12, 1998. Jerry was very familiar with this case. He and Officer Sue Nelson had been assigned to conduct a stop of a pick-up truck at the behest of the FBI and Mark Anderson. Jerry and Officer Nelson stopped the vehicle in Carson. K-9 Officer Luis Mrad and his dog "Benny" assisted, and Benny alerted to the bed of the truck. Jerry searched and found two kilos of cocaine. Arnie took custody of the cocaine and booked it as evidence. Now, just over a year later, only one of them was still in the vault.

I have never believed in coincidences. Just as the attacks on 9/11 occurred on a date synonymous with an emergency call for help, the so-called drug destruction by Compton PD occurred on April 1, a date for exploiting fools.

CHAPTER EIGHTEEN

A FEW DAYS after we finished the vault inventory, I was walking across the back lot when Detective Phillip Bailey stopped me. He lived near Riverside County, so he got to work early most mornings to beat traffic. Bailey, just old enough to have started dying his hair, was well off financially. Besides having the Swap Meet's lucrative security contract, Bailey owned a late-model Mercedes Benz, a beautiful 3,800-square-foot home, and a string of shitty apartments on Magnolia and Acacia where gang members sold their dope in front of. The only thing he loved more than himself was his huge Rottweiler and his 1957 Chevy. Bailey was also a braggart, telling anyone close enough to hear that he couldn't care less about police shit; he was all about the money and only cared about how his bank account looked. But today, something about his demeanor was different. He was calm, almost somber, as he asked, "How's the investigation going, Fred? I heard Arnie went off on stress?"

I was taken aback by his behavior change and didn't know whether he was fishing or just making small talk. But no. He never made small talk with me. He didn't even fucking like me. I said, "It's problematic, Phil. What's up?"

He said, "I don't know if this has anything to do with it, but when y'all first started this investigation, I saw Arnie walking across the back lot toward the station at around three or 4:00 a.m. I ain't never seen him here that early before. He was carrying a blue milk crate with both hands. There was some type of sheet or blanket covering it. I walked over to speak to him, but he had this shocked look on his face when he saw me. He spoke to me but turned his body like he was hiding the milk crate and walked away real quick-like, down the ramp to the basement. It was strange because he usually bullshits with me. I figured maybe he wasn't feeling well, so I just let it go."

I replied, "Probably" as I squinted my eyes, pursed my lips, and rubbed my chin before walking away, wondering if Bailey had any idea that the milk crate had fifteen kilos of cocaine in it and that Arnie may have been bringing it from home.

I met with Jerry and Roller and told them about the conversation. Based on what Bailey had seen, I believed that we had probable cause to write a search warrant targeting Arnie, but I knew I was reaching. If we had the lock that Anderson ordered Hernandez to throw away and could show that Arnie had possession of the key, the probable cause would have been a lot stronger. I decided to go with what we had. I volunteered to write the warrant because I had the most experience. I took it to JSID, where two DDAs reviewed it while I sat in the lobby. Thirty minutes later, they told me that I didn't have enough probable cause and would need an informant or an eyewitness. I was undeterred. "Then what about a wiretap?"

They both looked at me like I had lost my mind. One of them said, "Sergeant, if you don't have enough for a search warrant, what makes you think you are anywhere close to having enough for a wiretap affidavit?" I took my warrant and left, like a little boy with a ball who no one else wanted to play with. When I got home, I grabbed a bottle of booze and no glass. I probably shouldn't have called Roller and Jerry with the bad news. They certainly didn't deserve my drunken, misdirected wrath.

The next morning, I went to the chief's office and met with R. E. and Gary Anderson and told them what I had done and about the subsequent denial by JSID.

R. E. was shaking his head as he sat there with his hand pyramid in front of his face. He could barely contain his rage as he hissed, "Of course, you didn't have enough probable cause. And what does this have to do with Hourie?"

I answered, "I won't know until I find additional evidence. No doubt it will lead to additional search warrants—"

R. E. held up a long, bony forefinger and snapped, "Stop right there. No assistance from outside agencies. No more warrants. You should have come to me before you even wrote it. This investigation was over after you interviewed Hourie and Percy. Give me whatever you guys have written up to this point and the inventory results from the vault. I'm sending you back to detectives next week."

The following day, I was finishing up the report when dispatch called about a kidnapping. A woman had taken eleven-month-old Rafael Torres from his home. The child's uncle had met her in a bar and brought her to the house because she told him she had nowhere to live. When the man and the baby's mother went to sleep, the woman took the baby. Stranger abductions are always frightening. In most cases, the person kidnapped is killed or never seen again. R. E. assigned me to head the investigation. He told me to do whatever it took to get the baby back, and he didn't care how much it cost the city.

With R. E.'s permission, I called the FBI for assistance. We didn't believe this was a kidnap for ransom case, so they set up a command post at the house. More than likely, the abductor had been unable to have a child of her own, had lost a child due to homelessness or domestic issues, or in a worst-case scenario, had taken him to sell on the black market. Bloodhounds tracked the baby's scent to a bus stop on Long Beach Boulevard and Compton. There was no way to tell if the woman got on the bus. She could have very well been picked up by a car, or she could have been at a homeless shelter. The possibilities were like needles in a haystack. We notified LAPD and the sheriffs as we painstakingly began checking homeless shelters in Compton. We also had "Information Wanted" posters created and distributed throughout LA County. Additionally, we ensured that as many homeless shelters as possible got the information.

Frailich and Reserve Officer Rudy Johnson were with me on the case from the beginning. We worked all night, finally falling asleep at our desks. My phone rang at about 7:00 a.m. A downtown bus driver and several passengers recognized the baby and the kidnapper as they got on the bus at Union Station. The kidnapper had caught the Long Beach bus to downtown LA and taken the baby to a homeless shelter for the night. LAPD officers detained them at 14th Street and Grand Avenue. I woke up Rudy and Frailich. I said, "Hey. Go get that bitch and the baby. They're downtown with LAPD."

One of the highlights of my career was seeing the mother reunited with her baby. Besides catching a killer, saving a baby is one of the most fulfilling acts a cop can perform. It was indeed a feather in R. E. and Anderson's respective caps.

FREDERICK DOUGLASS REYNOLDS

Everyone was watching on this one, and no one more than Omar. Although the department was mired in muck, the quick and safe resolution of such an enormous crime shone a bright light on R. E.'s crown.

Jerry and I gave everything related to the narcotic investigation to R. E. and Anderson the following day. Anticlimactically, it was over. No one cared about Arnie stealing dope. Unless Hourie Taylor was involved, it just didn't matter. There was a lot more work that Jerry and I could have done with this investigation. It was a major case and should have been assigned to a task force using personnel from other law enforcement agencies and carried out in secret.

The powers that be didn't want a sprawling investigation, though. They wanted a nice, neat little package to justify unjustly firing Hourie and Percy. I'm not saying that Hourie was the greatest chief ever, and Percy was certainly no Sir Robert Peel, but the city officials and R.E. and Anderson fucked them over, but good. They were placed on administrative leave simply because Hourie, who had run afoul of Omar Bradley, refused to retire, and Percy, simply because he was Hourie's friend.

It was a witch hunt, certainly, but by God, did we miss an opportunity to clean up Compton PD and start fresh. At one time, Arnie was so broke that he almost lost his house, had his car repossessed, and was a frequent borrower of money from coworkers. In short order and without any valid new income source, he had spent at least $9,000 on a frivolous wedding reception in Cerritos, bought a house in Parker, Arizona, just fifty-nine miles from a house owned by one of the twins, and was trying to buy another one in Corona. And after going off on stress and ensuring that the city of Compton would be paying him for the rest of his life, Arnie later opened a restaurant, doing it all with a wife who didn't have a job. If he wasn't a crook, then his financial acumen is epic. In their zeal to run the department, R. E. and Anderson had unknowingly launched an investigation that uncovered mass theft of cocaine from the narcotics vault that was brilliant in its simplicity. Arnie would have undoubtedly been in narcotics for years if not for Jerry and me stumbling across his bullshit while investigating Hourie, so I guess we could be thankful for that. At least he was no longer a cop.

After I left the station, I stopped by Bookman's house, where I relinquished my peace of mind, both figuratively and literally. What I had learned about my department, the city of Compton, and the lengths some people will go to achieve power would bother me for the rest of my career. I also learned that contrary to what my Grandpa Walter told me those many years ago, snakes don't always hide in tall grass. Sometimes they hide in plain sight.

I went to the VFW to have a drink before going home. Percy, Hourie, Eric Perrodin, and a couple of senior firefighters were at a table drinking when I walked in. The VFW was now their war room, used for planning strategies to fight against Omar. They stopped talking when they saw me. I had often sat with them in the past. However, that day, other than me overhearing "R. E.'s boy" and snide remarks about my character and loyalty, they ignored me. I sat at the bar alone. Even the pretty, normally chatty Filipina bartender rescued from the P.I. years ago by one of the VFW members ignored me, quietly pouring my drinks, and walking away.

When I got home, staggering, and feeling sorry for myself, Carolyn was crying. I said, "What happened? What's wrong?"

She hugged me tightly as she sobbed into my chest. She looked up at me and said, "I had a miscarriage. I'm so sorry, babe." I was devastated and didn't even know how to react. I was just . . . numb. When she had needed me the most, I was somewhere having a pity party for one. I felt like a complete jackass.

If I thought I was going to get a break from being assigned high-profile cases after the narco and kidnapping investigations, I was wrong. On November 21, 1999, an article written by Staff Writer John L. Mitchell appeared in the *LA Times*. The article described Mayor Omar Bradley as being "livid" after a weekly newspaper compared him to the late Haitian dictator Papa Doc Duvalier. Known for not only his charm but also his temper, Omar's critics dubbed him the "King of Compton" and that under his leadership, the city purged anyone who disagreed with him. In addition to the suspensions of Hourie and Percy, City Clerk Charles Davis put in a one-million-dollar claim accusing the city of creating a hostile working environment. The city controller went out on stress, the fire chief went out with a bad back, and City Treasurer Wesley Sanders filed a police report claiming he was held hostage in his office by Omar, John Johnson, and Laurence Adams.

About a month before the article was written, Sanders was in a local bank discussing city finances with the bank manager. Omar's wife was in the bank and overheard the conversation. Afterward, Sanders was summoned to city hall by Omar, where Johnson and Adams were also present. Sanders later reported that he was verbally and physically assaulted by the three men, who demanded to know what he told the bank manager. R. E. assigned the case to me. Omar, Adams, and Johnson all denied the allegations. Ultimately, the case came down to one person accusing three others with no evidence or corroboration. Witnesses at the bank confirmed that Omar's wife and Sanders had been there, but other than that, there was nothing to support Sanders's accusations. The bank manager refused to tell me what he and Sanders discussed. The DA's office rejected the case, but do I believe Sanders was telling the truth? You goddamn right, I do.

CHAPTER NINETEEN

R. E. AND GARY Anderson were now firmly in charge. No one believed that Arnie was a crooked cop or that other cops on the department were possibly corrupt, too. Over half the department believed I had been part of the conspiracy to get rid of Hourie and Percy. Jerry and Roller felt the tides of ostracism as well, but I had become the face of the investigation and bore the brunt of the crashing waves. R.E.'s reconfigured gang unit was now comprised of six uniformed officers under the leadership of Sergeant Preston Harris. They focused more on selective enforcement than gathering gang intelligence. R. E. also reconfigured the detective bureau, combining robbery with homicide and burglary with forgery. Brennan and Ladd were assigned to the newly created robbery/homicide team, which increased the team to six detectives. Swanson remained the supervisor of the unit. I was now the floor supervisor, and Eddie Aguirre was working on my side. Mark Anderson and William Jackson had been reassigned as well, with Jackson being sent back to patrol and Anderson being sent to the gang unit to provide just a *modicum* of legitimacy. James Lewis replaced Arnie in narcotics, and Sue Nelson and Mark Metcalf replaced Anderson and Jackson. These reassignments were crucial mistakes and poured fuel on the fire in the wake of the suspensions of Hourie and Percy.

Two months after the narco investigation, R. E. assigned me to homicide as the supervisor and moved Swanson to the floor. This was another mistake. It drove a deeper wedge in the department. Swanson was a popular sergeant, particularly among the homicide detectives, who were the most senior and influential members on the department. They were now in open rebellion and not answering their phones after hours, forcing me to respond to almost every murder, sometimes twice a night.

Aguirre, Ladd, Brennan, Mark Anderson, and Branscomb led a movement to recall Omar and have Hourie and Percy reinstated. Brennan, Ladd, and Ray Richardson ran for CPOA board seats to gain the political clout needed to put teeth in the recall. Aguirre won the presidency, and Brennan, the vice presidency. Richardson won a board seat. There was now non-stop picketing in front of city hall by off-duty Compton cops. The signs had not so subtle things written on them along the lines of, "No more Omar!", and "Omar is a crook!" "Recall Omar!" and "Arrest Omar!" were two of the most popular signs. Omar retaliated immediately, launching a smear campaign on the entire department now, not just on Hourie and Percy. We had averaged about the same number of murders and shootings his entire time in office. But *now*, after his police department had turned against him, crime was out of control and the city needed the sheriff's department. It was almost as if he had said to himself, "Get rid of me? I'll show them who is in charge!" Members of the fire department had long ago seen his rage and vindictiveness first-hand and up close.

A few days before the CPOA elections, R. E. called me to his office and said, "Reynolds, I want you to investigate the shooting of a Long Beach cop. The gun was supposed to have been in our property room at one time. You know anything about the case?"

Of course, I knew about that case. Willow Street gang member Aaron "White Boy" Hefflin, who had only been out of prison for about fifteen days after doing time on one of my carjacking cases, shot Officer Brian Watt when Watt pulled him over on a traffic stop. The car had been taken in a carjacking. Watt's helmet partially deflected one of the bullets and saved his life. Still, his injuries were severe enough that he had to retire. The gun Hefflin used had a serial number showing it was registered to Compton PD.

LBPD eventually found out that Hefflin was hiding out at an apartment complex on Myrrh Street just a block from the police station. They never notified us that Hefflin was hiding so close to our station, which put our officers in danger. They had been willing to potentially sacrifice the life of a Compton cop to apprehend him. Had they contacted me as soon as they identified him, I could have told them exactly where to find him. But they didn't trust Compton PD beforehand, and the shooting only exacerbated the distrust.

321

I said, "I'm vaguely familiar with it, chief. I thought the department already investigated that shit. Why are we investigating it again?" R. E. smiled smugly before answering. "Damn, man. You need to watch the news more. Haven't you heard Omar condemning the department for selling guns to gang members? Or are you one of those cats who only looks at sports?"

I wanted to tell him no, that the news was fake and that I read Keats and Poe and actually knew what a fucking event horizon was and what modicum and perineum meant. But I didn't. Instead, I kept it simple as I walked out of the office and said, "You know how I love my Tigers, chief."

Almost two years after Hefflin got arrested for trying to kill Officer Watt, the trial had put the case back in the news at the most inopportune time for Compton PD, and Omar seized on the negative publicity. He not only had the crime rate to beat us up on, but he now had allegations of corruption as well. When the shooting happened initially, Omar said nothing about it. Now, coupled with the ineptitude of the narcotics unit and theft allegations, it all made Hourie look incredibly incompetent and the department fantastically corrupt. Omar now began beating on the incident like war drums. Hefflin was convicted and sentenced to fifty-one years in state prison by "Jolting" Judge Joan Comparet-Cassani, a no-nonsense, by-the-book judge who looked like a combination of Jane Robbins and Lucille Ball. She had earned her colorful sobriquet after ordering deputies to put a 50,000-volt stun belt on a disruptive defendant in her courtroom just three years earlier. The next time he had an outburst, she had the bailiff activate it.

The missing gun case file was nowhere to be found, so I had to start from scratch. The computer system showed that the gun was registered to the department in the mid-1980s. Watt didn't get shot until ten years later. There had been four police chiefs during this period. *How could Hourie be blamed if it couldn't be confirmed when the gun went missing?* Annual inventories would have turned up missing evidence, firearms, or dope. But no one knew when the last audit had even been done, which was actually another strike against Hourie. The gun had been entered into the system as a semi-automatic. The weapon Watt got shot with was a revolver, the same type of gun the female security officer misplaced years before.

A secretarial mistake could have accounted for this, however. Something like this could also have explained why a weapon reported as stolen got issued to Aguirre. Record-keeping at Compton PD had obviously been less than stellar over the years. *Omar posited that Compton cops were stealing guns from the evidence room and selling them, but how does one old-ass .38 caliber revolver finding its way onto the streets prove this?* There was never one shred of evidence proving or suggesting this. There were hundreds of high-quality, high-capacity firearms in the Compton PD property room. Most of them went for as much as $3,000 to $5,000 on the streets. *Why would a crooked cop choose a low-grade revolver over one of them to sell?*

I requested that the ATF do a trace of the serial number. The results showed that the gun was owned by a now-defunct security company in Compton before Compton PD got it. The weapon that I used as a Compton security officer was the same gun I used in the academy. It seemed plausible that, assuming that the gun had been in the possession of Compton PD at one time, someone could have stolen it from the armory and later sold it on the streets. It didn't necessarily have to be a cop, either. Anyone working at the station could have easily accessed the armory as often as the door was left open.

I was juggling this case while also responding to murders and supervising investigations on the other cases. About a month after R. E. had assigned me the missing gun case, Anderson told me not to worry about it because the city was going to settle with the officer. I guess Omar had gotten all the political traction out of the case that he needed. Stolen narcotics, gang members in possession of guns registered to Compton PD; it all provided justification for the PD's dismantling and perhaps, rightfully so. It appeared as if we couldn't take care of our own shit. In the words of the streets, we were a hot mess.

As far as Arnie's case was concerned, it was clear as day that he hadn't acted alone. Who knows who he would have implicated had we been able to develop enough probable cause to arrest him? He would've folded like a tent in a Category Five and brought down the whole house of cards. Sadly, I never got the opportunity to see white-out all over *his* fucking locker.

CHAPTER TWENTY

THE NEW millennium started off in Compton with a bang. Only thirty minutes before the New Year, someone fired a .45 caliber pistol multiple times into 601 West School Street and hit seven-year-old Marianna *Yanez* multiple times. She was pronounced dead just after midnight. Two days later, twenty-four-year-old Mark Hopper was at 1207 East Tucker Street looking to purchase marijuana. A Santana Blocc Crip had demanded Hopper's money and gold necklace at gunpoint. Hopper ran toward Long Beach Boulevard, and the gunman fired at him multiple times, killing him and Francisco Arellano, who was pulling into his driveway after returning home from Blockbuster with movies for his children. Six hours after that, a bandit taxicab driver pulled next to the curb at Central Avenue and Brazil, and the passenger threw a suitcase out. A passerby saw blood coming from it and called the police. Terry Smith, Bobby Ladd, and I responded. Forty-four-year-old Carmen Villegas was naked and folded up like a pretzel inside the suitcase. The autopsy later showed that she had been sexually assaulted and stabbed over one hundred times.

We got lucky and found a witness who had seen the cab and was able to get the name of the cab company. I asked Eddie Aguirre to help out in case a Spanish-speaker was needed. We tracked the fare down to an upstairs apartment above a corner liquor store near downtown Los Angeles. There were streaks of blood in the hallway leading to the door. We broke in just in case there were other victims and found a bloody knife, more blood, and signs of a struggle. The two occupants, Rodolfo Garcia and Luis Hernandez, were gone. We obtained warrants for them after we learned they had fled to Mexico. They apparently chose Compton to dump their luggage, thinking one more body just wouldn't matter.

Meanwhile, Omar kept his foot on the political gas pedal, alleging that Compton cops in patrol cars had shouted profanities at him and tried to run him off the road. R. E. and Gary Anderson did whatever Omar told them to. Omar could have easily had them suspend the officers had this been true, but he never named them. Instead, he made a blanket accusation against the entire department. A few days later, someone began writing a weekly propaganda rag called *The Truth* and circulated it anonymously throughout city hall and the police department. The writer(s) attacked and smeared city politicians and any officers deemed B team members. Omar was most often the primary target, although R. E., Gary Anderson, and I were in the writer's crosshairs on multiple occasions.

Omar didn't take the written abuse as tolerantly as I did. He was furious and had Lawrence Adams, back with the city as the assistant city manager, promote Reggie Wright Sr. to captain, thinking Reggie would be able to get the officers opposed to Omar under control. Adams also promoted Danny Sneed to captain, who was well liked in the city although not as popular with the officers. R. E. supported Sneed's promotion, but he didn't think it was a good idea to promote Reggie. He was concerned that Reggie's loyalty to Hourie and Percy could motivate him to try and use his new position to their advantage. It was a costly mistake to promote Reggie. The rebellious officers turned on him, calling him a sell-out and a traitor, and stepped up their recall efforts against Omar.

Swanson must have thought it possible for him to make lieutenant when Sneed and Reggie got promoted, as he toed the line for R. E. briefly. Only Swanson didn't have the cache with city hall as Reggie and Sneed did, so there was no benefit in promoting him. It didn't take him long to realize this, and he switched from the B team to the A team and went back to patrol as a field sergeant. Ron Malachi replaced him on the floor.

This did not sit well with the veteran homicide detectives, and it didn't take long for me to find out how they truly felt.

On January 16, 2000, at about 10:50 p.m., two of my detectives were called out to investigate a suspicious death at 219 North Santa Fe Avenue. Three-year-old Devinn Howard had been found dead in a half-filled bathtub. The detectives interviewed the mother's boyfriend, twenty-four-year-old Myron

Bables, when they got there. The mother had left him there to watch Devinn and her other two toddlers while she went out to a nightclub. Bables told the detectives that he put Devinn in the tub to bathe him before going into another room to check on the other kids. When he came back, Devinn was submerged in the water and appeared to have drowned.

When I got to the office the next morning, I called the detectives into my office to ask about the case. I noticed that the overtime slips that they left on my desk reflected they had spent almost eight hours on the investigation. They walked in, told me that it was just an accident, and proceeded to leave without offering any further information. They were sarcastic and discourteous, which infuriated me. I said, "Where the fuck are you guys going? Close the door and have a seat."

Once again, they told me that it was an accidental death, so they didn't take any scene photographs or collect any potential evidence. They showed me a couple of Polaroid photographs of the child. He had what appeared to be burn marks on his upper legs and buttocks. They explained it away by saying the water was too hot when Devinn got in the tub because Bables didn't run enough cold water.

I couldn't believe what I was hearing. Eight hours of overtime? For that? The department was on the verge of collapsing, morale was low, and most detectives had little respect for me as a supervisor now. Still, a three-year-old child drowning in a bathtub while in the care of a twenty-four-year-old? Regardless of the bullshit that was going on, we were still a goddamn police department, and that child deserved more consideration than he had received.

As the two detectives got up to leave, probably because they had to get started on their anti-Omar campaign for the week, I signed their overtime slips, threw them across my desk, and said, "Here, don't forget these." I then grabbed my camera and the evidence kit that I purchased with my own money. Shortly after I was assigned as the homicide supervisor, someone sabotaged the unit by stealing the roll-a-tape, measuring instruments, evidence markers, and camera. I drove to Thrifty's drug store to get some film before going to the apartment where Devinn died. Bables wasn't there, but Devinn's mother was adamantly in favor of him, stating there was no way that he would hurt her child. She allowed me inside to look around. I began the tedious process of looking for evidence and taking photographs.

Devinn's mother still hadn't cleaned up. I guess trauma affects us all differently, but this was fucked up. Or not. More than likely, it was indicative of regular everyday life for her. I saw a pizza box on the bed, which only contained maybe one or two slices. There was a large amount of vomit on the floor. *Curious,* I thought. *Vomiting could be caused by many things, such as overeating, illness, and drowning. But it could also be caused by head trauma.* The bathtub still contained the water. I measured the width and depth of the tub. There was no way a conscious three-year-old could have drowned in the bathtub. Devinn's arms were undoubtedly long enough to grab the side of the tub and pull himself up if he had slid underwater. After processing the scene, I told Devinn's mother that I needed to talk to Bables. Before leaving, I took a quick look in the closet to see if there was evidence of solace-seeking. Nothing. Just the usual for impoverished people in the inner city; dozens of expensive tennis shoes and designer jackets.

Bables came to the station later that day, walking past the two flabbergasted detectives. He sat in my office, spinning lies for the next twenty minutes. He said that Devinn had soiled himself after throwing up. He spanked the child, but only once on the buttocks. Bables then sat Devinn in the bathtub after the tub was about a third of the way full, but the water was too hot. He ran cold water and left the bathroom for a few minutes. When he came back, Devinn was dead. Bables was nervous as he talked to me, but that doesn't always indicate guilt. But he wouldn't look at me. Instead, he looked down at his hands the entire time. I imagined he was thinking about how they could have committed such a horrible act. I grew tired of listening to him, so I smiled and thanked him for coming in. As we shook hands, I snatched him close to me and whispered, "You're full of shit."

He finally looked at me. "It's the truth! I didn't kill that kid!" he screeched. Aha. Victim disassociation, a classic sign of a guilty conscience. I convinced him to take a polygraph examination. Even though the test results are inadmissible in court, cops frequently use them to stimulate conversation and coax confessions.

The test revealed that Bables was deceptive in two areas: the cause of Devinn's death and his role in what happened. The results rattled him enough that he admitted to killing Devinn, but only by accident. The autopsy showed that Devinn had died due to drowning. I believe that Bables, tasked with babysitting small children, lost his temper when Devinn soiled himself and he struck Devinn on the head, rendering the child unconscious. He then carried Devinn to the tub to cleanse him. He ran hot water and put Devinn in the tub, which burned him. Realizing that the water was too hot, he then turned on the cold water. Bables had to leave the bathroom, most likely to tend to the other children for whatever reason, so he turned the water off. Devinn was unable to regain consciousness due to the injury to his head and subsequently slid underwater and drowned.

The DA's office didn't want to try the case due to the incompetent initial investigation, so Bables was allowed to plead guilty to involuntary manslaughter in exchange for only a five-year prison sentence. I didn't like it, but I understood the rationale. A jury may very well have found him not guilty. A few days after the DDA filed the charges, I saw one of the original detectives on the case. To his credit, he apologized and thanked me. The other detective didn't care one way or the other.

On February 1, 2000, an article appeared in the *LA Times* titled, "Police Vote Criticizes Mayor, City Manager." Newly appointed CPOA President Eddie Aguirre told reporters the union had voted no-confidence in Omar and the city manager. It was an unprecedented move in the history of Compton politics. In the 1930s, the police chief and mayor had come to blows during a council meeting. Even then, a vote of no-confidence in the mayor didn't happen.

The CPOA never took such a vocal stance against political corruption before either, even though city officials had gone to prison occasionally.

The very next day, another article appeared in the *Times* titled, "Compton Chief Accused of Negligence, Evidence Loss." City officials had formally accused Hourie of negligence in handling two kilos of missing cocaine and improperly storing two other kilos in a locker under his control, even though it was never proven. The personnel complaint also accused Hourie of maintaining lax oversight of the department's property room, which possibly resulted in a gun being used to shoot LBPD Officer Brian Watt. Since I never finished the investigation, I don't know who made this deduction. The thirteen-count complaint, accusing Hourie of a wide range of misconduct and seeking his termination, was reported to be the first official indication of why he was suspended five months earlier. Neither Kenny Roller, Jerry, nor I ever saw the complaint. Had we been called to testify in court or any other hearing, we would have confirmed that the complaint's finding was not our conclusion. First of all, there were three kilos of cocaine missing for sure, not two. There were most likely several others missing as well, but we couldn't prove just what had been destroyed and what hadn't.

Carolyn and I bought our first house in March. The down payment took every penny we had, plus some help from Carolyn's mother. Dominic and Haley visited often, but inevitably jealousy reared its ugly head. Gilda called me within a week of us buying the house and told me that Dominic had to live with me now. I knew she thought I was going to say no so she could tell him and Haley what a horrible father I was. For years, whenever I dated someone with children, Gilda would tell them that I could take care of another woman's kids but couldn't take care of my own. At the time, I couldn't begin to understand the damage she was doing to them. When I told her that I would be right over to get Dominic, the silence on the other end of the line was rare but expected.

The transition was smooth. Dominic moved in as if he had been living there all along. We set about the business of being a blended family, but there was a darkness about him. The more we pulled him to us, the more he pulled away. Dominic became increasingly disrespectful, no matter how much Carolyn and I did for him. He told me that I should treat him better than Carolyn's kids because he was my biological son. I was troubled by this. I had always gone out of my way to treat them all the same. Still, I could not have dreamed that it would be a contributing factor in costing me my relationship with Dominic. He stopped going to school and even began smoking marijuana in the house. He also became an extremely negative influence on Deon, who followed in his footsteps.

When I confronted them about the weed-smoking and how detrimental it was to the entire family because I could get fired because of it, they told me they hated me. I was losing control of my family. And while I was trying to hold it together at home, the Grim Reaper was working overtime in Compton.

CHAPTER TWENTY-ONE

MARCH 11, 2000 was a Saturday. I was at a matinee in Long Beach with Carolyn. The year had started with the double murder on Oaks Street, the discovery of Carmen Villegas in a suitcase three days later, the murder of Devinn Howard, and four others by this date. Morale was for shit, so I was working seven days a week, sometimes sixteen hours a day. I responded to every one of the murders.

Settling into our seats with shared boxes of popcorn and Milk Duds, I put my arm around Carolyn and prepared for a much-needed escape from reality. In the middle of the coming attractions, my pager went off. Carolyn looked at me, rolling her eyes and groaning at the gentle sound of the vibrating. I went to the payphone in the lobby, dropped in a quarter, and called the station. "Watch commander's office, Sergeant Swanson speaking. Can I help you?"

I said, "This is Reynolds. Who's dead, and how many?"

Swanson sounded surprised that I had answered the page. He said, "Oh, hey, Fred. Sorry to bother you. I paged the on-call detectives, but neither one of them called back. Death came calling today. You got a dead teenager on Wilmington."

I pictured Swanson on the other end of the line getting a perverse pleasure at disturbing me on the first day off I had had in a month. I knew that he harbored resentment toward me because of Hourie and Percy. Even so, I still had a tremendous amount of respect for him. But right now, he was getting on my fucking nerves. I asked, "What's the story, John?"

He went on to tell me that seventeen-year-old Latoya Powers had been killed during a drive-by shooting at 2200 North Wilmington. A man walking with her had also been shot. They were both transported to MLK, where she was pronounced dead. Her companion was in critical condition.

FREDERICK DOUGLASS REYNOLDS

I said, "Okay. I got it. How you been?"

--CLICK--

I then called my old stand-by Frailich. He answered in his usual carefree manner. "Kool! How the hell are you, meshugana?"

I smiled as I replied, "I'm good, Brucie. Look, I know it's your day off, but I need some help."

He already knew what I wanted. He said, "Freddy, I'm on my way. Who got smoked?"

I filled him in on the details and then called Cat. Like Swanson, she was also salty because of Hourie and Percy. Although we had formed a bond when we inventoried Kevin and Jimmy's bloody uniforms and worked several exceptional cases together, she got caught up in the station bullshit and believed that she had needed to pick a side. She chose the A team.

"This is Cat."

"Hey, Cat. It's Fred. You busy?"

Despite everything, she seemed glad to hear from me. She said, "Hey, Kool! What's going on? I just got my hair done, and now I'm just sitting here at the nail shop. What's up?"

I was impressed and said, "I thought this was your home number. You got a cell phone? Damn! Must be nice."

She answered in her typical classy way, showing off without rubbing your nose in it. "C'mon now. You know how I do it. What's up, Kool?" She had given me this nickname because of the rapper Kool Moe Dee, who had the hit singles "Wild, Wild West" and "How Ya Like Me Now?" in 1988. No one else called me Kool except Frailich when he was trying to be a smart ass. Cat loved money. After telling her about the case, she put the A and B team shit aside in the interest of economics.

The movie had just started when I got back to my seat. Carolyn wasn't happy, but she understood. I didn't even have to tell her the circumstances of the case. It didn't matter to her. All she knew was that someone had lost their life, most likely in a horrible way, and I had been entrusted with trying to make sense of whatever tragedy awaited me. By now, she had grown accustomed to the late-night callouts and me sleeping for up to sixteen hours after working a difficult case. She knew the importance of my job; she knew that I was trying to provide closure for the survivors of people taken far too soon for reasons that didn't even make sense most of the time. Although she had never gone on a single call-out with me, she was the best partner I ever had.

I got to the scene within an hour, and as usual, Frailich, a notorious stickler for promptness, was already there. Cat got there about an hour later, proudly sporting the finest hair weave money could buy. The only evidence at the scene was a blue-fisted Afro pick on the ground near a payphone, which she asked about and pointed to with a long, red acrylic fingernail. Frailich and I quickly brought her up to speed. A witness saw a white Mitsubishi Galant occupied by gang members pull next to the victims. The front-seat passenger yelled, "Fuck all Crabs!" before he and possibly one other occupant opened fire.

The surviving victim was a Front Hood Crip, and the pick had been visible in his hair when he was shot. The shooter he saw was dark-skinned and armed with a black revolver. Since the shooters called him a Crab, I knew the suspects were Bloods. I narrowed the suspect list down even further because the Front Hood Crips were feuding with the Athens Park Bloods, who were aligned with the Miller Gangster Bloods.

We found a witness who got almost the full license plate of the car. We ran down every combination that would complete the license number, and only two Mitsubishi vehicles returned as potential matches. One was a white Galant rented from Alamo that had been reported stolen. By now, we had worked non-stop through the night and were exhausted. We entered the vehicle into the system as armed and dangerous, and I sent Cat and Frailich home. We would contact the rental company when it opened later that day, but I had a strong feeling that the car had most likely been clucked off by a crackhead. I drove home, praying that no one else got killed because I wasn't confident any other detectives would answer their pagers. I had just started to get undressed when the house phone rang. Carolyn woke up, wiping the sleep out of her eyes as she attempted to focus on me. She asked, "What time is it, babe?"

"It's 3:00 a.m. Go back to sleep."

Slightly perturbed, she yawned and said, "That's got to be the station calling this late. Didn't you just get home?"

"It's okay. I'm sure it's just an update on the case."

I picked up the phone, praying that death hadn't come calling again. Swanson was on the other end. With a heavy sigh, I asked him what was up.

He said, "You're not sleeping, are you? I hope not." His words were sympathetic, but his tone permeated indifference. "The sheriff's stopped your suspect vehicle at El Segundo and Main about fifteen minutes ago. Three people inside. Might be your shooters."

I said, "I'll be right in." I hung up on him mid-sentence and put my shoulder holster and shoes back on. I didn't need to hear shit else he had to say. Leaning down to kiss Carolyn, I relayed Swanson's information, and she was snoring before I turned the lights off.

The driver of the car was a member of the Athens Park Bloods. He told me that he gave a smoker a twenty-piece to use the car. He wanted to use it to get revenge for an APB member who got shot by a Front Hood Crip a few days before. He was also the driver during the shooting on Wilmington, and there were two other APBs in the car with him. They shot because of the blue Afro pick, which suggested the male victim was from Front Hood. The girl just got in the way. Just like I thought. Another senseless fucking murder.

After the interview, I began checking recent arrest reports. I found out that not long after the murder, sheriff's deputies had arrested a Miller Gangster Blood in possession of a .38 caliber revolver. When I interviewed him at the county jail, he admitted that it was the murder weapon. He picked it up after the shooter ditched it. I wrote a multi-location search warrant and arrested the other two occupants of the Mitsubishi. Gary Anderson dubbed the warrant "Operation Rescue." I don't know why he named it that. I wanted to call it "Operation No Naps," but I was too tired to argue.

A week later, I was sitting in my office when four of my homicide detectives walked in, led by Scomb, who hadn't spoken to me socially since I interviewed Reggie Sr. I said, "What's up, gentlemen? Have a seat."

Scomb tersely replied, "This won't take long. We're not working for you anymore. We want to work the floor." I had replaced Cat with Van Wie about a week prior, which more than likely was the straw that broke the camel's back for Scomb and the other three detectives. Cat was well liked in the detective

333

bureau. I liked her, too. But in recent years, her work on sex crime cases had been less than stellar. My decision wasn't personal. It was just business.

I looked at the other three detectives standing behind Scomb and asked, "Does he speak for the rest of you muthafuckas?" They nodded collectively, and I said, "Okay. Move your shit before the end of the day. Leave the door open after you leave so I can watch." I was devastated but fuck them. I walked over to the floor side and pointed at Dave Cameron, George Betor, and Terry Smith, three brand-new detectives who had replaced three recently retired ones. I said, "Move your shit to my side. You're working homicide now."

Other than Mikey Paiz and Bobby Ladd, no one else wanted to work for me, and Eddie Aguirre was too busy with CPOA business. I didn't ask Bookman or Frailich because although they didn't mind helping out on callouts, they didn't want to be responsible for the long-term handling of a homicide investigation. I had lost one homicide investigator in the exodus. Now, I was a brand-new homicide supervisor in charge of five homicide investigators, three of whom didn't know their heads from their asses.

The animosity between Omar and the CPOA had reached a boiling point, and Omar made no secret of his desire to get rid of the police department. The connection between Omar and the upper echelon of the sheriff's department came courtesy of one of his cronies, Melvin Stokes. Stokes was the President of Carmel Enterprises, which sponsored bullfighting tournaments at the former site of the Alameda Auto Plaza. Compton cops, with Captain Sneed supervising the scheduling and assignments, worked overtime at the events.

Lendell Johnson knew Stokes well. While Lendell was working overtime one weekend, Stokes asked him if he knew any high-ranking Blacks at the sheriff's department. Omar was livid that "his" police department was being so disrespectful toward him, and he wanted them gone. Stokes wanted to put Omar in contact with someone to discuss replacing the department. Lendell's first cousin was Chief Curtis Spears, the highest-ranking Black on the sheriff's department at the time. When Lendell put Spears in contact with Omar and Laurence Adams, the demise of Compton PD was underway. Sheriff Leroy Baca desperately wanted the contract with Compton, especially after a recent failed attempt to wrest control of the north end of Long Beach city from Long Beach PD.

Compton's contract would increase Baca's power base tremendously and give the sheriff's department jurisdiction over the vital hub portion of LA County. Additionally, it would increase the sheriff's department's multi-billion-dollar budget, thereby eventually increasing Baca's salary. Baca created a transition team. They took over the Code-7 room, laying computer wires while patrol briefings were being conducted. We were told not to worry; it was just a feasibility study. I knew this was bullshit. Computer wires don't need to be laid for that. This was a hostile takeover. They had come into the station as if it were a foregone conclusion that the city would contract with the sheriff's department.

Omar said that he had nothing personal against the police department. Initially he said it was just business; the department needed to go because it was systemically corrupt, and crime was out of control. But later on, he added that the city could no longer afford the department and could get the sheriff's department's services for much less. Both of these were blatant lies.

Were we supposed to really believe that civil rights advocate Omar Bradley, the so-called champion of diversity and social justice, really wanted to disband one of the only predominately Black police departments in the state for those reasons? And bring in an agency that had a long and storied history of racism and abuse toward minorities? Why didn't he do this right away instead of suspending Hourie and Percy and installing his puppets? The real reason was exactly what Melvin Stokes had told Lendell Johnson. He hadn't counted on the extreme opposition from the rank and file after removing Hourie and Percy from power. Making the entire department go away would also make his headache go away. I had heard Omar call deputy sheriff's racist rednecks on several occasions. His Star Wars metaphor was one of his kinder thoughts when it came to White people. Now, he was willing to turn them loose on the citizens of Compton.

Omar was a walking revolutionary. He was assuredly "woke" at the time and, according to him, had read *The Autobiography of Malcolm X* at age nine, *Soul on Ice* by Eldridge Cleaver at eleven, *Mein Kampf* at eighteen, and later *The Rubáiyát* and the writings of Mao Tse-Tung. I refuse to believe that he overlooked the sheriff's department's history regarding its dealings with minorities. Getting rid of Compton PD had nothing to do with the welfare and safety of

335

the citizens. We were in Omar's way and making shit way too uncomfortable. And that part about cleaning up Compton and making it safe? That was just a political platitude. Every area similar in racial makeup and economic status that the sheriff's department patrolled was just as violent despite the presence of the Century Regulators, now the flagship of the department since the closure of Firestone and Lynwood, the East LA Cavemen, and Lennox Grim Reaper cliques at those stations.

While I was having problems with detectives answering their pagers, it was business as usual for the A team. On April 24, Brennan was invited to a community meeting to discuss the possibility of the sheriff's department taking over Compton. Omar and Lonnie Howard came in uninvited. When Omar tried to speak, several citizens walked out, and the meeting ended. Brennan overheard Omar telling citizens that Brennan had hired gang members to kill him, and Brennan called Omar a liar. Howard yelled, "Someone better tell that White, blond asshole that this is my city, and he better get the fuck out."

When I heard about the accusation, I was unsettled by the mayor's veracity. Just under five hours after Jerry and I started the narco investigation, Compton resident Eugene Cannon got shot and killed on West 156th Street. Omar was kneeling next to him when patrol officers arrived. He later intimidated the young cop protecting the crime scene, entering it on at least two other occasions with Lonnie Howard. Brennan was the investigator on the case and interviewed Omar several times. With every interview, the dialogue between the two men grew more contentious.

An LA County deputy district attorney related to Cannon attended the funeral. Omar and several friends were also in attendance. Cannon's relative overheard Omar bragging that he had paid for the services, and he and his associates talked amongst themselves as if they knew who killed Cannon and why. Three months later, someone shot and killed a guy named Andre Campbell at the Zodiac Club in Century City. Surveillance cameras captured the cars used by the suspects. One of them was registered to someone named Kelvin Scott, who LAPD later arrested on January 20, 2000. They found three handguns at Scott's residence and his car parked at Omar's house. There was no mistaking the fact that although Omar, on the surface, appeared to be a prominent member of the community and pillar of society, he was comfortable in the underbelly of society and walked the fringes of criminality seamlessly. His giving the appearance of being afraid of anyone, let alone cops in the city he was the mayor of, seemed a bit contrived and rang hollow.

The day after Omar accused Brennan of trying to have him killed, Brennan was ordered to report to R. E.'s office. R. E. brought up Omar's accusation and told Brennan that he had not decided whether to suspend him or not. R. E. told Reggie Wright Sr. to take a solicitation-for-murder report naming Brennan as a suspect. When Reggie contacted Omar, he told Reggie that he did not want to file a report, he just wanted to "pass on what he heard." In other words, lay groundwork for future lies. That's all politics is. It is an ongoing contest to get what you want by telling lies, which confuses and pits people and groups against each other. In prison, especially among prison gangs, politicking is cause for a shank in the shower or headfirst fall from an upper tier. And Omar was proving to be a master at dirty politicking.

On April 29, 2000, at about 3:15 p.m., a woman was pushing a stroller carrying ten-month-old Kylah Witrango in front of 117 East Cypress Street. It was the same apartment complex where the infamous "Cover Me" incident occurred almost eight years previously to the day. Several Spook Town Crips were standing in front when a white Ford Mustang with three CV-70 gang members drove up and stopped. They yelled racial epithets and fired multiple shots from an AR-15.

I was in my office and heard the shots. I was one of the first cops on the scene. I almost broke down in tears when I arrived. Struck in the face by an errant bullet, the baby was still in the blood-soaked stroller. Three other women, including the baby's aunt, were also wounded in the shooting. Numerous .223 caliber shell casings were on the ground. Reggie Sr. was devastated. He had a personal connection with Kylah's parents, as he had seen them grow up. We created an in-house task force comprised of both A and B team members to work the case. The department was bitterly divided. Some officers had stopped speaking after knowing each other for twenty, and in some cases, thirty years. Still, we came together one last time in the face of this monumental tragedy. I was never prouder. It was Compton PD at its finest; it was why we wore the badge, not to

337

engage in politics and fight city hall. Omar laced up his war boots anyway and immediately went full attack dog mode, using the murder as another example of why the sheriff's department needed to police Compton.

Less than twenty-four hours later, Long Beach PD Officer Daryle Black and his partner, Rick Delfin, were driving an unmarked police car on North Lime Street in Long Beach. Without warning, eighteen-year-old Ramon "Gumby" Sandoval, a Barrio Pobre gang member, began shooting at them with an AR-15, emptying a banana clip and striking their car twenty-eight times. Daryle, shot twice in the head, was killed instantly. Delfin suffered a graze wound to the head and a devastating wound to the left leg. A forty-five-year-old pregnant woman inside her home got hit several times as errant bullets penetrated the walls. One of the shots that hit her just missed her seven-month-old fetus. Sandoval was later sentenced to death.

Thirty-three-year-old Daryle Black was a well-liked and popular six-year veteran of the department. Mac and Vic Thrash were good friends with him, and they had all worked in the gang unit together. Mac and Vic told me that Daryle was a helluva nice guy who would do anything for you. It was one more thing that Mac and I shared: the indescribable pain of losing a friend and co-worker to violence. I knew Daryle, but only on a professional level. Like me, he was a Black man from Michigan who had joined the Marines, moved to Southern California, and became a cop. He was just one more of the genuinely good guys who seemed to be so prone to losing their lives in this line of work.

While Long Beach PD was mourning one of their officers and conducting a massive investigation, we were still diligently working on Kylah's case. We followed up on multiple leads from the public, but it all came down to a phone call to Reggie. The caller told him where one of the shooters and the car was. During the late hours of May 1, undercover officers staked out the location while Brennan and Ladd wrote the search warrant. We arrested Jesse Sosa, the alleged shooter, near Pacific Avenue and 20th Street in Long Beach. We found the white Mustang in a nearby alleyway. There were several shell casings on the back seat and floorboard, which matched the shell casings found at the murder scene. Several hours later, we arrested the driver, Abel Gonzales Jr., at a house on East 144th Street in Compton. Witnesses couldn't identify Sosa, and he was released. Gonzales was sentenced to life in prison, but the third suspect remains unknown.

Seeing a baby with her face shot off and then learning that Daryle got killed less than twenty-four hours later caused me to break down. The world had gone crazy. No one was spared from the madness—from infants to the elderly, to those sworn to protect them. It was just too much death, over and over again. I had to find some light in all this iniquity. Since I left home those many years ago, I had survived by believing that I didn't need anyone, that I could get through life walking alone in the darkness. I knew I should not have had to feel like that anymore. Carolyn was there for me now, but I still couldn't cry in front of her. I had sworn that I would never cry in front of anyone again after my mother and the grey monster had last witnessed it, so I held it in until Carolyn went to sleep. Then, I went into the bathroom, turned on the shower, and cried like a baby.

CHAPTER TWENTY-TWO

IN MAY, Elisha Cheatham got shot to death at Santa Fe and Cocoa Street, not far from the Compton Unified School District Headquarters. There were no witnesses, leads, or evidence. Cheatham had never been interviewed regarding his possible involvement in the school arsons. He was a gang member. I am sure there could have been at least a dozen reasons for his murder. Still, the report I gave to R. E. contained all the information I gathered during my investigation, including Cheatham's name. Word on the streets was that certain city officials had the fires set to regain control of the school district. R. E. would have made the report available to them. I just pray that the murder had nothing to do with anything contained in it.

Dissemination of *The Truth* and the picketing in front of city hall continued nonstop. While pissing off Omar, it also illuminated the dealings of Compton politicians. Some roaches shy away from luminosity, and the politicians in Compton were no different. Although they needed a light turned on in another part of the house, they got a spotlight in the living room instead.

On June 28, at 4:45 p.m., thirty-eight-year-old Gary Beverly was shot to death on the 91 FWY westbound as he waited to exit at Wilmington. He was on his way home from work. During this time of day, because of the traffic light at Wilmington and Artesia, traffic getting on the off-ramp is at a standstill, although it remained steady in the other westbound lanes. I knew this because it was the same way I took home while I lived with Carolyn's mother. Terry Smith and I were in the office when the call came in, so we responded to the scene. Beverly's vehicle, a wine-colored Chrysler Sebring, had bullet holes in the driver's window. Beverly had already been transported to MLK, where he was pronounced dead.

Frank Wheaton was the city spokesman and a longtime friend of Omar. He arrived on scene shortly after Terry and me and stood nearby talking on a cell phone. When interviewed by news reporters at the scene, Wheaton said, "It could have been road rage, it could have been an intentional hit, or just a random act of violence. We just don't know right now why this happened." He gave this statement without any input from Terry or me.

Reggie Wright Sr. escorted Omar into the scene. I saw this and immediately confronted them. I was livid and told Reggie to take him out of the scene as Omar yelled, "It was Branscomb! He thought it was me in that car!" Reggie and Omar left. Reggie later told me that Omar had requested that Reggie take him to the hospital to view Beverly's body, at which time he told Reggie how much he and Beverly looked alike.

Terry and I knew that Omar's accusation against Branscomb was bullshit. There was no mistaking Omar. He never met a crowd or microphone that he didn't like. Anonymity was something he never, ever embraced. If he was accused of something, he wouldn't hide from it. He would spin it to look favorably toward him. Omar never, ever, let a good tragedy go to waste. Branscomb, even more so than Brennan, Ladd, and Aguirre, had been the biggest thorn in Omar's side during the recall effort and often called him a crook to his face. There was no way Branscomb would have mistaken Beverly for Omar. He hated Omar so much he would have looked him in the eyes before pulling the trigger had he wanted to kill him.

And Branscomb was certainly no shrinking violet. A former professional ballplayer who played in the Cincinnati Reds farm system and once roomed with Davey Concepcion, Branscomb worked out every day. He was in phenomenal shape. His oldest son was a shot-caller in a Crip gang out of the Paramount area. Known as Bobcat for his fighting skills, he learned them from his father. If Branscomb wanted Omar, he would've had no problem getting him or whipping his ass. In accusing Branscomb, Omar immediately threw out a red herring while calculatingly trying to derail Branscomb's career and get rid of his most dangerous adversary.

Gary Beverly was the principal at Lynwood High School for three years. He had recently been promoted to Director of Student Services and Special

Education for the Lynwood Unified School District. Part of his duties was to help students who were pregnant or who were new mothers. According to Laurence Adams, the former personnel director of the Lynwood Unified School District, Beverly was a "fast riser in a hard-knocks school district." It was déjà vu all over again, Adams in the middle of a blatant Lynwood political murder.

After processing the crime scene, Smith and I met with Beverly's wife at her home in Carson. She told us that everyone loved her husband, and he did not have an enemy in the world. She said her husband loved the school district and was passionate about his student's welfare and safety and was always devastated when they got pregnant. Beverly was a simple man, unconcerned with flashy clothing and cars. The most enlightening thing that Mrs. Beverly told us was that her husband took the same route home every day at the same time.

Later that night, Smith and I drove to MLK Hospital to view Beverly's body. Omar, Lonnie Howard, Frank Wheaton, Paul Richards, Laurence Adams, and two women I didn't know were in the parking lot. Smith muttered, "What the fuck are all these motherfuckers doing here?" We both thought it unusual that Omar and the others were at the hospital at that hour. Omar approached us, asking if we had any new information on the case before requesting to see the body. Again, unusual, but we let him come with us.

I wanted to see how it played out and what he was going to say. The morgue attendant unzipped the body bag. Beverly had at least one bullet hole in the left side of his head. Omar said, "Look at that. He looks just like me. Branscomb was trying to get me and got him by mistake."

Branscomb could pick up the spin on a curveball or a fastball coming at him at 95 mph. There was no way he would have mistaken this man for Omar. Smith and I quietly looked at him as he continued to hammer home his belief that the only reason Beverly got killed was because of their "uncanny resemblance." Smith and I couldn't figure out why Omar would take such an interest in a body at the morgue.

The victim's wife hadn't even seen him yet. Omar had visited crime scenes and thrust himself into investigations to try and get details on other occasions. But this was the first time he visited a morgue to view a body once, let alone twice. We had had numerous children murdered during Omar's reign in office, but he had never requested to view any of them. *Why Beverly?*

From the beginning of the investigation, Terry and I believed that Beverly had been targeted, not the victim of road rage or gang violence. We knew that Beverly wasn't killed by Branscomb or any other Compton cop due to mistaken identity. We *all* knew what Omar looked like. Furthermore, he drove a black Lincoln Town Car at the time. Magnanimous beyond belief, he sometimes held court at the Roscoe's Chicken-N-Waffles restaurant on Central Avenue, where the Omar Bradley Special occupied a space on the menu between dishes named for MLK and Dr. Charles Drew.

Omar and Gary Beverly, much like Hourie and R. E., couldn't have been more different. Omar would not have been caught dead in a Chrysler Sebring, nor would he wear the type of clothing that Beverly was wearing, which was cheap and off the rack. Omar was a bespoke man, partial to alligator and crocodile shoes and boots and tailor-made suits. This was no mistaken-identity murder. It was a planned assassination by someone who made sure they were killing the right person before pulling the trigger. *But why Beverly? He was a well-loved school administrator who loved his students. Who the fuck would want to kill a guy like this?*

Less than twenty-four hours after the strange contact with Omar and friends at the morgue, Smith and I got called out to a triple murder at Compton Boulevard and Central. Willie Calhoun, Anthony Colbert, and Lisa Butler were riddled with bullets fired by Campanella Park Piru gang members armed with an AR-15. Seven more people would be murdered over the next five weeks.

The sheriff's department was full steam ahead in their quest to take over Compton PD. Negotiations between the city, sheriff's department, and the CPOA were set to start the following week. I had once been one of the most respected and popular officers on the department, previously holding positions of CPOA board member, vice-president, and president on various occasions. Now, I was a pariah because of the narcotics investigation, and hardly anyone talked to me.

Despite the way most of the cops felt, Eddie Aguirre still respected me and asked me to be a part of the CPOA negotiation team. Eddie was always the type of person who could read a room. He had fought hard to save the department, but he was a realist. He knew that the clock was winding down on a police department that had been in existence since 1888. Nothing could halt the Omar freight train. Not *The Truth*, the vote of no-confidence, the officers picketing in front of city hall, or the strategy meetings at the VFW orchestrated by Eric Perrodin.

I loved Compton PD. It had saved my life and given my kids medical and dental insurance. But enough was enough. Why *were* we trying to save a department that couldn't adequately protect its citizens at that point? A department where most of the cops had just simply stopped caring? I decided to put myself in a position to help my fellow cops get the best deal possible once we put on tan and green. First, though, I wanted to get Fat Jack's opinion on what was going on.

I went to his office, where he was still grinding away as the subpoena control officer. He looked up, smiled, and said, "Come on in, son. Have a seat . . . hold on." He held up a finger as he answered the phone. "Subpoena control, Sergeant McConnell speaking." After a few seconds, he said, "NO! You don't need them all in court, and I don't care what they are saying! I know this case. You only need the arresting officer! Tell the rest of those numb nuts to go home!" The slamming of the phone onto its base briefly reverberated through the small office. Fat Jack looked at me and said, "What can I do for you?"

I replied, "Do you think this is it, Jack? Do you really think the sheriffs are going to take over?"

He sat back in his seat and blew out perhaps the last raspberry I would ever hear from him. He said, "Hell yeah, I do! Maxcy Filer ain't walking through those goddamn council chamber doors. But I'll be goddamned if they stick my old fat ass in a courtroom or jail and I'm too old to work the streets. I'm fucking retiring!"

On Tuesday, July 11, just four months after proposing to disband the department, the Compton City Council voted 3-2 to contract with the sheriff's department, citing a wave of recent killings as the reason to make the change. Omar, Amen Rahh, and Delores Zurita voted in favor, saying that the police department was powerless to stop the out-of-control violence. Zurita stated, "People are prisoners in their own homes. Change is the only hope of making

Compton safer. Honest to God, I want to feel safe in this community. Maybe we can sit on the porch again."

Sheriff Baca attended the council meeting and pledged to offer employment to any eligible Compton officer. "The best officers should be able to stay in the city," he said.

Captain Chuck Jackson, head of the sheriff's transition team, said precisely what Omar wanted to hear. "When the sheriff's department takes over, we're going to get away from politics and down to business."

Councilwomen Marcine Shaw and Yvonne Arceneaux cast the dissenting votes, citing opposition from residents who believed the decision violated the city charter and was more about politics than public safety. Shaw also pointed to unresolved issues with the union that represented the county's 6,000 deputy sheriffs. Omar responded by saying, "The value of human life is greater than the city charter or any union." This is something that Omar and I wholeheartedly agreed on. Yet, regarding the murder of Gary Beverly, the silence of his political war drums was now deafening.

On August 29, 2000, LA Superior Court Judge David P. Yaffe dismissed a legal challenge to the city's decision to disband its police force. The judge did not stop the decision because although the 1924 charter indicated that a citizen's vote was required to get rid of the police department, a more recent version of the city charter, approved in 1983, did not. Several hours after Judge Yaffe dismissed the motion filed by the CPOA, thirty-two-year-old Ronald Kennedy was shot to death on West Cypress Street. This brought the murder total to thirty-six in just nine months and put the city on pace for fifty-four for the year. Terry Smith was the investigator. He arrested someone, but the DA's office rejected the case for insufficient evidence. The last murder case in the history of Compton PD remains officially unsolved.

The negotiations with the sheriff's department began a week after I spoke with Fat Jack. The CPOA was represented by Eddie Aguirre, William Jackson, Attorney Jerry Lennon, and me. Lawrence Adams and Captain Jackson represented the city and the sheriff's department. The negotiations went quickly; it was clear that Adams wanted the deal done as soon as possible. We got almost everything we wanted. The chief would be allowed to be a captain because sheriff's captains are de facto police chiefs of the stations they are assigned to. Compton PD captains would go over as lieutenants, and lieutenants and sergeants would retain their ranks.

Detectives and FTOs would not keep their positions, and this was an issue the sheriff's department refused to negotiate on. The Memorandum of Understanding forged between the CPOA, the city, and the county was the absolute best deal we could have gotten. We would retain our seniority, and patrol officers with more than six years seniority would not have to go to the courts or work the jails. Best of all, the city agreed to cash out our sick and compensatory time, which totaled five million dollars.

After one of the negotiation sessions, I walked close to Lawrence Adams and whispered, "I know who killed Gary Beverly." His eyes wide in disbelief, or perhaps even fear, he grabbed my arm tightly. He then pulled me further away from the other people present and whispered back, "Who?"

I looked around like I was CIA, and he was KGB and said, "I think it has to do with a Las Vegas-based sports agent who was illegally trying to recruit a Lynwood High School athlete."

Adams breathed deeply, released my arm, and replied, "Good work. Make sure you keep Omar and me updated."

During an interview with a Lynwood school employee, Smith and I found out that Omar and Beverly almost came to blows during an argument just hours before Beverly was murdered. Interviewing Omar was a no-brainer, yet R. E. ordered us not to contact him. This was very peculiar. R. E. had no problem with me interviewing Omar about the city treasurer's allegations or with Brennan interviewing him about the murder of Eugene Cannon, but R. E. refused to let us interview him about Beverly.

R. E. and Anderson wanted daily briefings regarding the status of the investigation. They may have instructed us not to talk to Omar, but they couldn't tell me what to write. I knew they were giving case specifics to city officials, so I decided to take a page out of Omar's book. Smith and I lied and diverted, telling R. E. and Anderson the same thing that I had told Adams. To support this theory, I semi-plagiarized a *Sports Illustrated* article about the agent and let them read it every time I updated the report. At the same time, Smith wrote a separate report detailing the actual investigation. Too bad R. E. wasn't one of those who watched or followed sports all the time. He would've recognized the piracy.

According to Omar, city hall was no longer a safe place to meet officials on the weekends because of death threats from Compton cops. Sheriff Baca then provided him with around the clock protection by deputies from the Major Crimes Bureau. One of those deputies would eventually ascend to the rank of commander. Omar's bodyguards also interfered in the Gary Beverly murder investigation, following witnesses, and reinterviewing them after Smith and I had already done so. At least two witnesses expressed apprehension about the deputies and felt that their conduct was improper.

Baca assigning bodyguards to Omar wasn't to protect Omar from us. It was to protect Omar from suspicion. Why else were the bodyguards going behind our backs during the Beverly investigation? We had obviously underestimated Omar's resolve to get rid of us. And Leroy Baca, who made no secret of his desire to take over Compton, was the perfect ally, even to the point of possibly turning a blind eye to a murder investigation. Baca conducting business with Omar would've been bad optics if his department considered Omar a person of interest in a murder, and the Compton contract had to be secured at all costs.

As head of the homicide bureau, I was the liaison between the department's murder cases and the Sheriff's Homicide Bureau. I discussed several open cases with their representative, specifically the high-profile murder of Gary Beverly. I told him that Smith and I considered Omar a person of interest in the case who absolutely needed to be interviewed. We were told that the sheriffs couldn't investigate Compton murders until after the final contract was done. I knew this wasn't true, however. The sheriff's department is obligated to investigate murders in municipalities upon request. I wasn't requesting at that point. I was almost begging. Smith was so frustrated by the lack of interest in the case he lost himself in the battle, eventually getting fired from the sheriff's department several years later for an alcohol-related incident and losing his wife in the process.

I have visited him in his small, one-bedroom apartment. It looks like a war room dedicated to the case. He obsesses over it, and the only thing missing is a tinfoil hat at this point. Still, Smith has made headway and unearthed some fascinating information. His frustration lies in the fact that he has sent letters to the LA DA's office, the DOJ, and Kamala Harris's Attorney General's office, and none have chosen to investigate the case. After languishing for years, the murder investigation of Gary Beverly, one of the most notorious and brazen murders in the history of Compton, remains unsolved.

Interest in the Gary Beverly case slowly diminished. Omar didn't use this case as a platform to bring in the sheriff's department. If there was ever a case to support lawlessness in Compton and the police department's inability to stop it, this was it. And yet, in shocking contrast, he hardly spoke about it. Gary Beverly was beloved in the community and by his students. He has a memorial at Lynwood High School, and a nearby street is named after him now. He was a decent man who possibly had a secret, a secret so devastating that it would be ruinous for the person who had him killed. Usually, the motive in a murder doesn't necessarily reveal the killer. Someone who kills a shopkeeper during a robbery could be anyone, as the motive is financial gain. However, I believe that in the Gary Beverly case, the secret itself is the motive which if revealed will unmask the killer.

All the murder cases were overwhelming my depleted homicide team. Once the CPOA had hammered out the MOU with the sheriff's department, I went to R. E. and requested that the sheriff's department start investigating *ALL* murders in Compton. He refused, telling me that so long as there was a spark of life in Compton PD, we would continue investigating our own murders. A few days later, he and Gary Anderson simply stopped coming into the office. No one was running the department. Most of the detectives had also stopped coming in. The second floor was so vacant on some days it looked like an abandoned building.

Laurence Adams and Omar appointed Danny Sneed to the chief's position. A week later, R. E. came back to work. He and Sneed got into a heated argument, which ultimately ended with Omar and Adams deciding to let R. E. remain the chief until the end. At that point, it should not have even mattered who the chief was. It was like someone challenging Edward John Smith for the captaincy of the *Titanic* after it hit that fucking iceberg. But it did matter. It mattered to R. E.'s ego, which in his mind allowed him to be the last chief of

Compton PD so he could write his own Wikipedia epitaph. It also mattered to the smart and calculating Sneed, but for a much different reason. He knew that only the current chief could transfer to the sheriff's department as a captain. In the end, they were both wrong. Hourie and Percy had never been fired. They were still on administrative leave and drawing their full salaries when the sheriff's department took over Compton. In the annals of history, Hourie Taylor will always be the last official chief of the Compton police department.

On September 7, 2000, just nine days before the sheriff's department officially took over, R. E. issued a memo indicating that the sheriffs were to be called out on all homicides, suicides, officer-involved shootings, and suspicious deaths. Later that day, every Compton officer who had been accepted by the sheriff's department gathered in the city council chambers, where we were sworn in by Sheriff Baca. Followed by a grinning Omar Bradley, Baca walked along the first row and shook hands with his newly appointed deputy sheriffs.

Several cops, most notably Scomb, refused to shake Omar's hand. Omar took it in stride and pointed at Scomb's badge and mouthed, "I turned that into a star." Scomb simply mouthed, "Fuck you" in reply. Omar just chuckled and walked away.

The following week, we had to turn in our city equipment. Omar had vindictively ordered that our duty weapons be destroyed. A few officers disregarded Omar's directions and kept theirs. In yet another glaring example of the shoddy record-keeping and tracking of firearms by the department and the city, no one was the wiser. Not only did the city keep our weapons, but they also kept our badges.

On September 12, 2000, the LA County Board of Supervisors approved a four-year contract for the sheriff's department to patrol Compton. Five days later, Compton PD was officially disbanded. Compton was now the forty-first, and most lucrative contract city the sheriff's department had. The last shift to patrol Compton was fittingly the PM shift. Omar Bradley, Lonnie Howard, Frank Wheaton, John Johnson, and Laurence Adams were on the back lot, glad-handing and back-slapping with Leroy Baca and other high-ranking sheriff's department officials. Omar, shining like new money, was wearing a black leather walking suit, crocodile boots, and a gold-and-diamond-encrusted Rolex

Presidential. I finally realized why the parking lot had always been called the back lot. You see, the term "back lot" refers to an area near a movie studio and is used in filmmaking or TV shows. And what I was witnessing was dramedy at its finest.

Preston Harris was the watch commander that night. After he gave the last Compton PD briefing, I had the officers meet me in the report writing room. As some of them openly wept, I told them how proud I was of them and that although Compton PD was now history, their own narratives were just beginning. I told them the best way to honor the department's legacy would be not to do anything to tarnish it. Lastly, I told them they were well prepared. We had been Hub City cops, and no one else would ever be able to say that, not even the incoming sheriff's deputies.

Preston later led the Compton units through the city with their overhead lights flashing to show their gratitude to the citizens. While the Compton cars were in the streets, a fleet of gleaming LA County Sheriff's cars with "City of Compton" on the doors pulled onto the back lot and replaced them. The marquee above the gas pumps now bore the words, "LA SHERIFF", as did the marquee affixed to the front entrance to the station. Afterward, the Compton cops parked their vehicles by the Heritage House and went to the locker room. Fifteen minutes later, they emerged wearing tan and green uniforms with stars on their chests instead of shields. Omar had given us a sound ass-whipping, and he knew it as he placed his cigar in his mouth and watched the sheriff's cars drive off the back lot to begin patrolling the city. The first unit to clear the back lot was Captain Jackson, the first commanding officer of the sheriff's department's 28th Station. And with a simple, "280-Charles, show me 10-8," spoken into his vehicle's radio mic, the Compton Police Department was history.

In the months before the sheriff's department took over, Blue, Andrew Pilcher, and a cop by the name of Luther Fore transferred to Rialto PD. Joe Velasco transferred to Redondo Beach PD, joining the five others who transferred there years before. Just about all the detectives retired. After the sheriffs took over, Swanson, arguably one of the best homicide detectives who ever worked Compton PD, was transferred to Carson Station, where he worked as a patrol sergeant. He desperately wanted to work sheriff's homicide, but he wasn't even considered. Thoroughly humiliated by the dismissive attitude of the homicide captain when he interviewed for the position, he never considered applying again and finished out his career in patrol. It was an insult that Swanson never got over, and he remains bitter about it to this day.

It was mismanagement at the highest level to not keep Compton homicide detectives if for no other reason than to provide insight into the 1,400 murders the sheriff's department had assumed responsibility for. Despite the blatant disrespect shown toward us, I tried to help as much as I could by authoring a 640-page memorandum documenting numerous murders, gang rivalries, and the most active shooters in the city at the time the sheriff's department took over Compton. It is now known as the "Gang Book."

Mark Anderson went from a celebrated undercover narcotics officer assigned to federal task forces to giving tickets to fare evaders on the Metro Rail trains and buses. Most of the patrol officers were moved to the courts as bailiffs, the jails as custody deputies, or the Transit Services Bureau. Brennan, Richie Sanchez, and Ray Richardson stayed at Compton Station for a brief period, working with the OSS team. But Brennan quickly wore out his welcome and rubbed many deputies the wrong way by continually talking about what he did as a Compton PD gang detective. Predictably, the deputies could give less than a fuck. Brennan must have genuinely felt maligned. Formerly a whale in a goldfish bowl, he was now a minnow in the Nile. After being a homicide detective for most of his career, Branscomb went to court services at Fort Compton. Ladd also worked there as a bailiff briefly before quitting and applying to Garden Grove PD. He eventually retired as the supervisor of their gang unit.

Aguirre transferred to West Hollywood station patrol for several years before being selected to work gangs at East Los Angeles station. Richardson went to work patrol at Temple station. While Brennan was assigned to Compton OSS, he and Omar came across one another. Brennan smiled and drove away while giving Omar a one-finger salute. Within a week, Brennan was transferred to Lakewood station and working as a traffic unit. Sanchez managed to hang on with the gang unit by changing his status from a mediocre Compton cop to a knowledgeable gang investigator simply by using his Bronx gift of gab. Percy

Perrodin and Hourie Taylor eventually retired, and Hourie was hired as the Chief of the Compton Unified School District PD.

The narcotics investigation was ultimately a good thing. Even if no one was ever brought to justice, the theft was stopped. Who knows how long the thieves would have continued if not for the investigation? It was clear that the administration had no clue. *Or did they?* I was never allowed to see how deep the rabbit hole went. I will just take solace in the fact that I was able to disrupt corruption and make my peace with that.

During the weekend of October 14, 2000, Carolyn and I went to my cousin Craig's wedding in Augusta, Georgia. The reception was at a facility on the Master's golf course. Craig's father was my mother's brother Ted, a high school principal in Dayton, Ohio. Ted and his wife Sondra were both holders of master's degrees in education. Craig majored in political science in college and later worked on President Bill Clinton's staff. Craig's family had always stressed education. He attended Albion, one of the most expensive colleges in Michigan, and his friends and classmates were rich White kids who lived in Gross Pointe, Michigan's equivalent to Beverly Hills.

On the night before the wedding, my sister Linda's fourteen-year-old son got arrested for stealing a car. No one volunteered to help pay his bond. Linda didn't have the money, but I did. I wasn't going to leave her son in jail if I had the means to get him out. I went to the sheriff's station with my father, David, Derrick, and my cousin Wendell, a modern-day version of Uncle Bus and skilled at making moonshine of every flavor imaginable. After I bonded Linda's son out, we all tried talking sense into him, telling him that the path he was on was no good. I could tell it was going in one ear and out the other one. I knew he was a real nice kid who was probably dealing with the same type of shit as I once had, as his parents had recently gone through a turbulent marriage that devolved into a tumultuous divorce.

Later that night, Carolyn and I were lying in bed in our room. I told her I was concerned for my nephew's future and that he might not catch the breaks that I had caught. She stroked my head and whispered, "It's okay, babe. You did the right thing. That's all you can do."

A month later, Carolyn was one month pregnant.

Omar Bradley killed the Compton PD, but Judge Yaffe buried it on October 24, 2000, denying a motion for a restraining order filed by Hourie and Percy. I stayed at Compton Station as a field sergeant for a few months until Captain Jackson asked me if I wanted to go to another patrol station. I asked him which station was the slowest, and he answered, "Probably Cerritos, Walnut, or Lomita." Lomita wasn't far from where I lived at the time. I started there two weeks later. I went from chasing gang members, seeing dead people, and being bombarded with political shenanigans to brown-bagging my lunch and eating it on the beach while feeding screaming seagulls. Life was good again.

CHAPTER TWENTY-THREE

ON DECEMBER 19, 2000, the city council conducted a public hearing regarding a proposed franchise with HUB, a trash company created by Michael Aloyan. After realizing the amount of severance pay the city had to pay the former Compton PD officers, Aloyan approached Laurence Adams and offered the city five million dollars to take over the in-house waste disposal operation on a franchise basis. Adams recommended to the city council that due to the urgent need to address the fiscal commitment, they should negotiate only with Aloyan rather than solicit bids for a franchise.

Aloyan's criminal history and the city's failure to solicit bids from competing waste haulers were topics of discussion at the hearing. Despite concern from almost every citizen who addressed the council, Omar would not allow any discussion of Aloyan's background or relationship with councilmembers. Even Patricia Moore appeared to voice her opinion after spending twenty-eight months in federal prison. Her opinion of the no-bid trash contract as corrupt fell on deaf ears. The city council awarded Aloyan the contract, worth about $25,000 a month, and an annual salary of $300,000, making him the highest-paid city official. The agreement also allowed him to share in the profits from the city's collection activities and gave him a right of first refusal on any potential future waste franchise.

HUB hired or gave monetary gifts of approximately $1,000 each to Omar's relatives, including his nephew Jaumal Bradley. Bradley, an Elm Lane Piru gang member who was fiercely loyal to Omar, had a prior conviction for a gang-related murder in 1989. Aloyan hired Omar's brother Henry even though he had no waste management experience because Aloyan said he was "the biggest bookie in Compton." HUB contributed $43,000 to Omar's campaign committee over the next year.

In January of 2001, Compton agreed to sell some of its best city-owned land to Paul Richards for millions of dollars less than it was worth. A 1997 appraisal had placed the property's value at $3.6 million. Richards, who had no experience as a developer, would not be required to put up any of his own money. Instead, the city loaned him over $2 million, covering the land's purchase price and planning costs. He only had to repay the loans—without interest—whenever he sold the 231 houses he planned to build. When the loan was approved, the city did not publicly disclose the appraisal value. The agreement Richards had with the city ensured that he would receive $6 million in management and "preferred profit return" fees before splitting any remaining profits with the city. Several months after the deal, Richards, who was still the Mayor of Lynwood, voted to pay his sister up to one million dollars for negotiating a billboard deal in Lynwood that he already had in the works. When Richards lost an ally on the council during the November election, the new majority voted to cancel his sister's no-bid contract.

Eric Perrodin got vengeance for his brother Percy and Compton PD on June 5, 2001, when he was elected mayor after a bitterly contested mayoral race against Omar. The King of Compton was dead; long live the king. Eric immediately created the Compton Public Safety Office and hired his brother Percy to run it. Within three months of the election, the LA DA's Public Integrity Division served eleven search warrants targeting Omar Bradley, Delores Zurita, Amen Rahh, Yvonne Arcenaux, and John Johnson for theft of public funds. Their offices and homes were searched, in addition to the offices of the city manager, controller, treasurer, and clerk. The warrants also asked for the confiscation of safes, purses, and wallets belonging to Laurence Adams. The DA's office also served a search warrant at Compton Community College, where Omar and Rahh's connections ran deep. Both of Fat Jack's predictions had finally come to pass. The sheriff's department had taken over Compton PD, and a metaphorical bus had pulled up to city hall and carted the occupants off to jail. A little more than eight months later, Michael Aloyan pleaded guilty in federal court for taking part in a million-dollar bribe of several elected officials in Carson. He had offered them a bribe in exchange for their votes on granting Carson's solid waste disposal contract to HUB.

Now firmly entrenched in office, Mayor Perrodin questioned the merits of the deal the city had given to Paul Richards. The land was now worth $8 million. Richards, a longtime Lynwood councilman and mayor, had served for years as an assistant city manager and labor negotiator for Compton and as a paid advisor to the Compton community college board. Without question, he was awarded the sweetheart deal because he was a political ally of Omar Bradley and Laurence Adams.

My oldest daughter Haley graduated from high school two weeks after Eric Perrodin was elected mayor. She joined the Navy, and my baby daughter Lauren was born the first of July. Lauren wasn't breathing when she came into the world, and her skin was blue. The doctor calmly turned her over on her stomach in his hands and rubbed her back. The blood rushing throughout her body created an olive skin tone as she screamed and made her entrance to the world. The doctor gave her to me after I cut the umbilical cord. I cradled her gently like she was a vase from the Ming Dynasty and looked at her. She didn't open her eyes until I cut the cord. Then, just for a second, she looked at me with the most beautiful green eyes I had ever seen before closing them. She looked just like Carolyn's mother. Her skin tone and green peepers caused me to call her "my sheriff baby." She was an omen that I took to mean I had nothing to fear at the sheriff's department.

My parents were there for both events. My mother was mellower, and she hardly yelled at my father now. My father looked healthy and robust. He had been retired from Ford for more than ten years and hadn't had a drink in almost as many. Now, in the twilight years of his life, he basked in grandfather-hood. I would often catch him just sitting back and smiling as he looked at all his grandkids.

After Lauren arrived, Dominic grew even more defiant, and Deon followed right along behind him. Neither one of them was going to school now, preferring to spend their time smoking marijuana. But I wasn't going to put up with that shit. As soon as they got old enough, they had two choices: go live somewhere else or join the military. They chose the latter. Jeremy followed suit, and I now had four kids in the Navy. I thought it was going to do Dominic and Deon some good. I wasn't worried about Jeremy or Haley. Jeremy was strong-willed, smart, and not prone to follow stupidity, and Haley was now married to a great guy named Habib, who was also a sailor. They had two daughters, Madison and Kennedy.

When Dominic got out of the Navy, he was even more disrespectful, not only to me but also to Carolyn. Nothing I did or said helped. From the moment I married Carolyn, he had grown colder and colder. It got so bad I could no longer let him live with us. He moved out of state and left no forwarding address. I was heartbroken. It is challenging to deal with a child who is angry and bitter to the point he or she continually disrupts a home's sanctity, but being a parent is tantamount to being a leader, as well as a teacher. A parent cannot let one wayward child poison the rest of them.

Carolyn has always told me it wasn't my fault for how Dominic turned out, but I was tone-deaf to her reasoning. To me, I had failed him as a father, no matter how you looked at it. It turns out that life is a continuing saga of cross-bearing. Once you unburden yourself of one, there is always another one to take its place. Sometimes we carry multiple crosses at a time, shedding them like skin as we transition through life.

Paul Richards got recalled in 2003 after he and two other councilmembers had voted to allow a seven-year trash contract to Kosti Shirvanian, owner of Western Waste, the same company that Patricia Moore confessed to receiving bribes from. In February of 2004, Omar, Amen Rahh, and John Johnson got convicted of misappropriating public funds. The charges against Zurita and Arceneaux were dropped. Two years later, Richards got sentenced to sixteen years in prison for federal bribery and kickback charges for steering city contracts to a front corporation he secretly owned.

Mayor Perrodin, now with a council that supported him, voted to terminate the trash contract with Aloyan. Aloyan then filed a suit for breach of contract. In October of 2006, a jury returned a unanimous verdict in favor of Compton, finding that Aloyan obtained his franchise in violation of Government Code Section 1090, which prohibits public officials from having a personal interest in contracts awarded on behalf of their cities. Compton was awarded $22.5

million in damages. It was a symbolic victory, as Aloyan had recently declared bankruptcy.

After working at Lomita Station for a year, I was accepted to OSS, one of the better assignments on the department. I supervised gang teams at Century Station, Carson Station, and Compton Station. While at Carson, my team received four consecutive awards from the city for lowering the rate of gang crime to all-time lows. Our success was dampened by the tragedy of the death of yet another cop I knew personally. On June 24, 2006, thirty-five-year-old Jerry Ortiz, extremely well liked and one of the most popular deputies in the gang unit, was killed in the Hawaiian Gardens by a twenty-nine-year-old gang member named Jose "Sepe" Orozco. Jerry had been looking for him because he was shooting people just because they were Black. While Jerry was following a lead and standing in the doorway of a house, Orozco stuck a two-inch revolver between the doorjamb and shot him in the head.

My team and I were at work when it happened. We heard over the radio that Jerry was being airlifted to Harbor General Hospital in Torrance, about three miles from Carson Station. I directed my team to meet me there. The helicopter landed just as we parked. Hospital personnel were waiting on the tarmac. The helicopter personnel lifted the stretcher bearing Jerry out of the helicopter and rolled him to the trauma room where a team of surgeons were waiting. My team and I stood guard at the door as the surgeons feverishly worked on him.

After a few minutes, one of the helicopter personnel came out of the room with tears in his eyes. He said, "God, I'm sorry, guys. We did everything we could." He then walked slump-shouldered back to the helicopter and flew away. One of the guys on my team, Mark Wedel, a good-natured White deputy who was one of the best people I ever worked with, started crying. I hugged him like he was my brother, his tears staining the iconic green windbreaker of the gang unit. I looked over his shoulder into the operating room where Jerry lay lifeless on the table with the sheet covering his face. It took everything I had not to cry, too.

Murders in Compton had steadily been on the rise since the sheriff's department took over. By 2005, they had gone up to seventy-five in one year. I was happy at Carson. Carolyn's mom still lived there, and my house was only three miles away. I didn't want to go back to Compton, but when Chief Cecil Rhambo asked me to go back when the gang-related murders continued to spin out of control, I said yes. I had come to respect him tremendously after he replaced Captain Chuck Jackson at Compton Station in 2001. Compton was Rhambo's first command after being promoted to captain. After reading the gang book I had written, he drove to Lomita Station at 3:00 a.m., where I was a patrol sergeant to talk to me about Compton gangs. By 2008, Rhambo, a brilliant man and conscientious cop who truly cared about the community, would be the highest-ranking Black on the department.

After a year at Compton Station, my team received a Distinguished Service Award for lowering the number of gang-related murders in Compton to the lowest in over twenty-five years. It wasn't just luck that my teams were able to accomplish these things. I was good at investigating gang-related crimes but even better at picking good, smart cops who knew how to treat the citizens we worked for. We wore velvet gloves over our fists. In over nine years, no one on my gang teams shot anyone or crashed any cars. We had fewer than five citizen complaints and only two reported uses of force, yet we routinely led the entire Bureau in arrests, search warrants served, guns recovered, and filed cases.

Joe Gooden was the second-in-command at Compton Station. When he was promoted to captain, he was assigned the Internal Affairs Bureau command and personally requested that I come with him. I was now responsible for investigating deputies accused of misconduct. The worm had undoubtedly turned.

In 2012, Rhambo, now an Assistant Sheriff, and Captains Gooden, James Thornton, and Ralph Ornelas, my supervisors for many of the years I spent in the gang unit, all vouched for me to go to homicide. Rhambo and Gooden are Black. Thornton and Ornelas are White. But they all had the same opinion of my work. None of them cared about my skin color. Even with their blessings, I was reluctant to apply for homicide again after being turned down three other times. One of the captains who turned me down had even been rumored to have said, "No motherfucker from Compton PD will ever work homicide if I have anything to do with it." I didn't let this phase me. I just continued to do my job until my peers and supervisors had to recognize me. Should it have taken this long? Of course not. Obviously, there were racists at the sheriff's department. But I wasn't going to fight fire with fire. Instead of discrimination lawsuits, I brought buckets of water. I didn't want anything given to me because I was Black, but I wasn't going to be deprived of anything because I was.

During the merger process between Compton PD and the sheriff's department, rumors were rampant. According to some, every Compton cop would get fired within five years; the department was filled with racists, and we would find nooses on our lockers and be called niggers. None of this happened. Whenever I did feel like someone had a problem with me, I just asked them about it. I wasn't there to make friends. I was there to do police work. The biggest problem I had was with other Black deputies. Some of them didn't want to associate with me because of the perceived stigma of all Compton cops being corrupt. It was almost like they thought something was going to rub off on them, that they were having a bad enough time fitting in already. They badmouthed me to the White deputies. I wasn't dealing with racism as much as I was dealing with multiple crises of character on the part of my own people worried that "Massa" was favoring me more so than them.

Dominic moved back to California later that year. He had a new girlfriend who had three kids, and she was pregnant with his child. Carolyn and I soon found out that the Department of Children's Services had taken her other children due to physical abuse. As a cop, I had assisted DCS as they took children out of homes on many occasions. I knew this was something DCS did not take lightly, and they only did it when presented with children who had significant signs of abuse. I was a kindred spirit with abused children, and for this reason, Dominic's girlfriend wasn't welcome in my house. A parent physically abusing a child was unacceptable to me and non-negotiable. Still, when she had Dominic's child, Carolyn was at the hospital. Carolyn called me at work to tell me, screaming, "It's a boy! He's beautiful!" I left and drove to the hospital. When I held him, he looked into my eyes, and I rubbed one of his hands with a forefinger. He grabbed it in a death-grip and wouldn't let go. It was a sign of things to come.

When they were released from the hospital, Dominic asked me to drop them off at a seedy motel nearby where they had been staying. The next day, a social worker came to my house looking for them. When I told her that they didn't live with me, the social worker panicked. She said, "Oh my God! Do you know where they are?" She told us that the only reason they were allowed to leave the hospital with the baby was that the mother told them they lived with Carolyn and me. Otherwise, the baby would have been placed in protective custody like his siblings. I told the social worker the baby could stay with us, but his parents weren't welcome because the mother was abusive, on drugs, and I didn't trust her in my home. Dominic, for his part, wouldn't go anywhere without her.

Carolyn and I took the social worker to the motel, and she gave the baby to us. Dominic and his girlfriend were strangely ambivalent during the entire incident. It was almost like they had been playing house. It was so surreal; I felt like I was out of my body watching a bad *Lifetime* movie. Everything had happened so fast. Less than four days after the baby was born, Carolyn and I were taking him home with us alone. We stopped at the local supermarket and bought Pampers, baby food, and Enfamil. The next day we took the baby to a scheduled appointment at the DCS building. Dominic, his girlfriend, and my friend Henry's ex-wife Valerie were there. We sat in a large office with the social worker, her supervisor, and several other social workers.

Unless someone volunteered to take the baby, he would be placed in a foster home because Dominic and his girlfriend were under investigation and weren't allowed around their children. Valerie, in an endearing act of selflessness, especially since she was already raising two autistic kids, volunteered initially. But then Carolyn leaned over and whispered to me, "Babe, we should do it." After some additional conversation with the social workers, we walked out with a seven-day-old infant. The agreement was for us to take care of the baby while his parents went through six months of parental schooling and court appearances. A judge could then give them the baby and her other three kids. Six months turned into two years.

The baby was a ward of the court, so we had to get fingerprinted, have background checks, and have our home inspected to ensure that it was "up to standards" for a child to live in. Courtney and Lauren, the last kids living at home, had to submit to the fingerprinting and background checks as well. Carolyn and I were working full-time. She worked from 6:00 p.m. to 6:00 a.m., and I worked from 8:00 a.m. to 4:30 p.m. This meant that when she was at work, I took care of the baby, and when I was at work, she did. Plus, either Carolyn or I had to make the forty-minute drive to children's court for hearings. Our hours made it impossible to get adequate sleep. We couldn't use babysitters because of the fingerprint and background requirements, and we refused to put the responsibility of taking care of a newborn on the girls.

I was working internal affairs when we first got the baby. One of my academy classmates, Steve Vaughn, was my supervisor. My situation was embarrassing. I didn't want my personal business aired, but I had to tell him. Some of the court appearances were interfering with my attendance and productivity. My concerns were completely unnecessary. He told me to take whatever time I needed, even if I had to leave work for a few hours every day. Steve just happens to be a White guy, and in yet another instance of character taking precedence over skin color, he treated me as well as any man I have ever known. I had worked for Black supervisors in the past who would write me up if I was two minutes late, but Steve was as understanding and compassionate toward my situation as if I was his blood brother.

In 2014, my father was diagnosed with stage-three multiple myeloma. I met my brothers in Detroit so we could spend time with him. When we were children, he had always talked about taking us to the NFL Hall of Fame one day, but something always seemed to get in the way. Now, we decided to take him and made the two-hundred-mile drive to Canton, Ohio. Once we got there, we walked around for a little while before I noticed how easily fatigued my father was getting. After less than twenty minutes, he said that he was tired and ready to go. He stopped as we were leaving and looked up pensively at a giant bronze statue of Jim Thorpe. I watched him, wondering if he knew that the great athlete, a Native American member of the Sac and Fox Nation, had also suffered from alcoholism during his life. My father smiled slightly before turning and walking out the door.

We were mostly quiet during the drive home, restricting our conversations to the Tigers' dominance at the time and the brilliance of pitcher Justin Verlander. We made a promise to go to the Negro League Baseball Hall of Fame next time. When I got on the plane to California the next day, I was melancholy. I knew that my father's days were numbered. I had doubts that we would make good on that promise.

Carolyn and I quickly fell in love with the baby. His parents had named him Dezmend. After going to court off and on for four years, Carolyn and I decided to adopt him when their parental rights were terminated. It was either that, or he would have been placed in a foster home, and none of us would have ever seen him again.

Our good friends Nicole and Bryan Bavis were in court when the adoption was finalized. We asked them to be the godparents. I am forever grateful to them, as they were with us every step of the way during the horrible ordeal of dealing with the court system. Once on the verge of having no parents, the baby now had four. Carolyn and I named him "Charles *Desmond* Reynolds," after my father. I let Dominic visit him shortly after the adoption, and he tried to take Desmond from the house. When I stopped him, he attacked me as Desmond cowered in a corner crying. That was the last straw. Dominic was no longer welcome in my home. I refused to subject Desmond to the kind of emotional dysfunction that I had to deal with as a child, and I was going to make damn sure that he didn't have to witness it again in the future.

Desmond was going to a daycare not far from the house, and I would drop him off in the morning. He was alert, strong for his age, and had started walking before he was one. But he was three now, and he still wasn't talking. Something didn't feel right to me, so I parked across the street after dropping him off one day. I watched as the children came out to play and noticed that he didn't interact with the other kids. He would just go off to a corner by himself and kick a ball over and over. Although Carolyn and I had been diligent about taking him to the doctor for check-ups, I started feeling a sense of dread. Desmond wasn't acting like the other kids.

I had transitioned quite well to the sheriff's department. When all was said and done, I would receive sixteen evaluation ratings of "outstanding" and one rating of "very good" in the seventeen years that I worked there. I got the rating of "very good" my second year at homicide after solving even more cases than I did my first year. It was written by a lieutenant who referenced that I was a former Compton PD officer even though I had been on the sheriff's department for thirteen years by then. The only other time it was mentioned was in my first evaluation, for obvious contextual reasons. It is obvious that the lieutenant had rated me on something other than my work product.

Eddie Aguirre was promoted to sheriff's homicide during my third year there. I immediately thought about how great it would be to work as his partner before retiring. He and I were on different teams at the time, but there was a particularly rude detective on his team who wasn't well liked and rubbed everyone the wrong way. No one wanted to work with her. I told their team lieutenant that I would gladly work with her, knowing that eventually, she would do something to justify me not wanting to continue working with her. It took four months. She insulted me at a crime scene in front of several other people, some of whom she had insulted in the past as well. Eddie didn't have a partner at that point, so they put us together. It wasn't luck. I totally planned that shit. Two former Compton PD cops, who were not even supposed to be good enough to work sheriff's homicide, were now partners.

My career had come full circle. Eddie was one of the best detectives I had ever worked with. Although I once taught him, now he was often teaching me. We solved almost every case we caught, often working sixteen hours every day. We both had something to prove—that we were every bit as good, and in most cases better, than the best homegrown sheriff's homicide detectives at the bureau. Carolyn had retired from work by then due to a back injury, so I was free to work a lot of overtime, stacking up the money for my retirement.

On the sheriff's department alone, I had received twenty-five commendations, a Legendary Law-Man Award, two Distinguished Service Awards, one Meritorious Service Award, four consecutive Meritorious Service Awards from the city of Carson, and dozens of awards from senators, congressmen, assembly members, mayors, city councilmembers and even a future vice-president of the United States. I had also represented the department as an expert on Black street gangs, traveling throughout the country and teaching law enforcement officers at the city, county, state, and federal levels. Still, something was missing. My career, although satisfying and productive, was incomplete.

CHAPTER TWENTY-FOUR

DURING THE first week of August 2015, my mother called and told me my father wasn't doing well. I flew to Detroit the next day. I was devastated when I saw him this time. Shriveled and being pushed in a wheelchair by a nurse at the oncology clinic, he forced a smile when he saw me, a death head's mask struggling to find joy. The doctor and nurse took us into an office, and as the nurse sobbed gently, the doctor said, "I'm sorry. There is nothing else we can do. The best place for him now is in hospice." I got angry and stormed into the hallway. I put my head on the wall, begging God to make my father better.

I knew what hospice was. It was where you went to die in comfort with a morphine drip. Instead of going to one, however, my mother had the ambulance take my father to a nursing facility. My Uncle Ted drove up from Dayton the next day. Impromptu best man to my father at the beginning more than fifty-years before, he was now here at the end, as well. We gathered around my father's bed, not really knowing what to do as he lay there, unable to speak, his eyes darting back and forth as we prattled on about everything and nothing. On the third day, he started coughing badly. An ambulance took him to the hospital. Once again, a doctor told my mother nothing could be done for him. Rather than send him back to the nursing home, the doctor admitted him.

The next day, David and I went driving around the city. For him, it fed the hunger of nostalgia. For me, it was tantamount to a farewell tour. There were just too many bad memories there for me. Tiger Stadium was just a vacant field now, the old cable tracks on Michigan Avenue still visible through the asphalt at various places. The Olympia Stadium, also known as the Old Red Barn, was gone as well, now the site of the Michigan National Guard's Olympia Armory. Detroit had been devastated by crack. Strawberries still walked the streets, offering sexual favors for little or nothing. Very few stores on Grand River were still open. Liquor stores with denizens of dope loitering in front broke up the blocks and blocks of boarded-up businesses riddled with graffiti. Most of the apartments we lived in had been demolished; others were like props from horror movies. Numerous streets, formerly the sites of beautiful, well-kept homes, now had multiple vacant lots overrun with grass as tall as children. Some blocks only had five or six houses on them. Some had more, but half were empty, with some missing porches and roofs and others gutted by fire.

Instead of seeing children playing in the yards, crackheads shuffled down the streets, some stopping and getting on their hands and knees as they picked objects off the ground, no doubt thinking someone had accidentally dropped a piece of crack. We drove to my mother's aunt and uncle's house, a place that I hadn't seen in thirty years. Dreadful memories stirred within me as I looked at it—how my father never seemed comfortable there, how I always believed that it was a house that held dark secrets never revealed but that I knew existed, nonetheless. As we drove away, I saw two men smoking crack in the driveway on the side of the house while a woman was on her knees giving one of them a blow job.

David and I went to the hospital that night. It started raining as we drove into the parking lot. We hurriedly walked into the hospital and took the elevator to my father's floor. We went into his dark, somber room, eerily quiet except for the monotonous beeping of an EKG machine. He was lying in bed with numerous tubes connected to him. He appeared even frailer than he was just the day before, a shadow of the man who used to hoist me onto his shoulders to see Santa at the parade. He didn't even seem to know we were there. When David began fighting back the tears, I left so he could have some time alone with him. David came out a few minutes later and hugged me. I hugged him back briefly before walking into the room. The gentle beeping of the medical machinery seemed strangely at odds with the thunderous beating of my heart. It was raining much harder now, the pitter-patter against the window creating an emotional symphony with the beeping and my father's rhythmic, pronounced breathing through the tube in his mouth.

I put my face close to his and whispered that I loved him, realizing that I had never told him this before. The realization brought forth a flood of tears as my body convulsed like the mother of a murdered child when receiving the death notification. I cried unabashedly, apologizing for everything that I had put the family through, the shame of dropping out of school, the embarrassment of going to jail over and over, telling him that none of what I did as a child was his fault. I told him that any success I had in life was because of him. My words became indecipherable, butchered by my sobbing, further masked by a sudden loud crack of thunder followed by a flash of lightning. Just then, for the first time in days, my father made a sound. It was only a loud grunt, but I knew what it meant. It meant that he was proud of me. It meant that there was no need for me to cry and that he loved me too, even if he had never told me either. Most importantly, it meant that he forgave me. As it dawned on me that the most meaningful conversation that I had ever had with my father consisted of a single, pain-filled grunt, I realized that he was the greatest man I never knew.

The following morning, David and I rented a car to drive back to Minnesota. We stopped by the hospital before leaving. It was overcast outside, the sun peeking in and out of the clouds periodically before retreating. My father was lying in his bed at the far reaches of his room now, the only noise the leitmotif of machinery that keeps a person alive. The fickleness of the overcast sky caused the shards of sunlight cutting through the window blinds onto his face to slowly disappear. Inexplicably, I thought of Dylan Thomas's anguish, commiserating with him as I prayed for my father to *"rage against the dying of the light and not go gentle into that good night."* David and I decided not to disturb him and left. We spent a few days together in Minnesota, reminiscing about our childhood and familial questions that would never be answered.

I flew back to Long Beach on August 17. In a curious bit of irony, my father died the next day at 12:24 p.m., a number synonymous with his wedding day. Carolyn held me as I got the news, crying and offering support. I hugged her back stoically, believing that I had left all my tears on the floor next to my father's bed. My mother had him cremated within days of his death. The day after he died, Desmond was diagnosed with autism. When Carolyn and I got home from the doctor's office, I was sitting in our bedroom, alone, in front of the closet mirror, trying to collect my thoughts. I thought about how my father's death and Desmond's diagnosis came so close together. I looked at myself and saw tears streaming down my face. I put my face in my hands just as Carolyn walked into the room. She had never seen me cry before, and it startled her. "What's wrong? Did you hurt yourself?" she asked.

I looked up at her, no longer concerned with trying to hide my tears. I said, "I can't help Desmond, Carolyn. I'm lost right now. I have spent my whole life helping others, but now I feel so helpless. What did he do to fucking deserve this?"

Carolyn put my head against her stomach and said, "Babe, we *got* this. No matter what happens, Desmond is going to be alright. We got this."

I knew she was right. In the middle of these two tragic events, I found the lucidness of purpose. Desmond wasn't put in our lives to make ours harder; we were put in his to make it easier. If not for us, who knows if he would have ever gotten diagnosed? The earlier an autistic child is diagnosed, the better it is in the long run. There are numerous school programs and special services designed for autistic children, but they have to have been diagnosed to avail of these opportunities. Now that Desmond was with Carolyn and me, he would never be shuffled from foster home to foster home. We were going to ensure that he was nurtured and well taken care of. We knew that his road was going to be rough. Suddenly, the image of my father turning away from Jim Thorpe smiling came to my mind. Of all the memories I had of my father, why this one, and why now? Then it hit me like a linebacker. Jim Thorpe's Native American name was Wa-Tho-Huk, which translates as "Bright Path."

CHAPTER TWENTY-FIVE

ALMOST EVERY cop killed in the line of duty in California has a freeway memorial dedicated to him or her, but Kevin and Jimmy didn't. Neither did Dess Phipps. Over the years, I had periodically inquired of city politicians and police administrators about it, but nothing was ever done. I finally decided to look into it myself. I found out that all I needed was money for the signs and for the state assemblyman for the 54th District to present a resolution in Sacramento. Simple. That was it. It was a tragedy that something so easy hadn't been done years before for so noble a cause. Mike Gipson, a friend of Lendell Johnson's, was the assemblyman. Lendell put me in contact with him, and he agreed to sponsor the resolution. Gipson told me that I would be working with his field deputy, Michelle Chambers, to complete the project.

Eddie Aguirre and I went to a Compton city council meeting to ask for the money. Janna Zurita, daughter of Delores Zurita and now a councilwoman herself, secured the funding within two days. I authored the resolution and drove to Sacramento, where I met with Assemblyman Gipson. We presented the resolution to the assembly, and they voted unanimously in favor of it. Satra Zurita arranged for a venue to host the dedication ceremony. I then put together a committee consisting of Reggie Wright Sr., Eric Strong, Paul Mason, Tim Brennan, Carl Smith, and Gary Davis to plan the ceremony. Chambers, seeking to turn a solemn event into a political grandstand, designed the program and put Mike Gipson's face prominently on the cover with small photographs of the fallen officers in the upper corner. It read, "Mike Gipson presents a freeway memorial service," in big, bold letters. We told her this was unacceptable, and she threatened to withhold the mock freeway signs to be displayed at the ceremony unless we capitulated to her demands. We contacted Gipson, told him about our concerns, and Chambers had the programs redone.

The ceremony was held on November 19, 2016. The families of all three officers were present. Sheriff Jim McDonnell was the keynote speaker. Just over one month previously, he had been tasked with speaking at the funeral service of Lancaster Station Sergeant Steve Owen. Owen had responded to a burglary in progress when he was shot to death by a parolee with a lengthy criminal record. Like so many other fallen officers, Owen was highly likable and a beloved cop in the community.

The Mayor of Compton, Aja Brown, didn't attend the ceremony for Kevin, Jimmy, and Dess Phipps, citing a previous engagement. She and Janna Zurita were bitter rivals at the time, however, and this most likely was at the root of her non-appearance. Chambers never told any committee members or the fallen officer's families when the actual dedication of the signs on the freeway would occur. Gary Davis just happened to find out because a friend of his worked for Cal Trans and helped make the signs. Gary's friend called him and told him they were putting them on the freeway in two days. When I called Chambers to tell her that the families wanted to be present, she said, "That's not possible. It's too dangerous for you guys to be on the freeway." It wasn't too dangerous for her, however. A week after the freeway signs went up, she posted a picture on Facebook of her posing alone next to them as cars whizzed past. After all that I had done to ensure that the three Compton officers were remembered, Chambers didn't even give me one of the mock signs. Instead, she kept one for herself.

Chambers later rented an apartment in Compton just to run against Janna Zurita for her council seat. She used the freeway memorials as a platform, even taking credit for drafting the resolution. She also told voters that if it weren't for her, I would never have been able to get it passed because no one else wanted to help. This was bullshit. It took so long to get the memorials up because apparently none of the Compton politicians or police administrators gave a shit or thought it was necessary. Along with Aja Brown, Chambers is now part of Compton's current kakistocracy, where—much like Jack Burden had found in Robert Penn Warren's *All the Kings Men*—the roots of the corrupted flowers from the crannied walls of city hall have always sprawled throughout the city and beyond. When I think about the lack of integrity Chambers displayed and how little consideration Brown gave to fallen Compton police officers, it makes me realize that the more things change in Compton, the more they stay the same.

After the freeway dedication, I visited the site where Kevin and Jimmy were murdered, and I could still see them. The imagery was vivid for me, but to pass-ersby, the only evidence of that night's horror is the brass plaque embedded in the cement marking the site. It is weather-beaten and dirty and has succumbed to a greenish-blue layer protecting it from further corrosion. It has multiple dents, and pieces of the concrete surrounding it are missing and broken as if someone tried to remove it. I drove to a nearby hardware store and bought a bottle of Brasso, the same solution cops use to polish their badges and belt buckles and keeper snaps for their Sam, Jim, and Sally Browns. And while Michelle Chambers was congratulating herself and feathering her political nest with the blood of fallen heroes, I was on my knees polishing a monument to two of them, unconcerned with the people laughing as they walked past me. When I stood up, I looked down approvingly as the sun shone brightly on it. I got in my car and drove off, glancing in my rearview mirror, my mind now at peace. I had finally rid myself of the cross I had borne the longest.

CHAPTER TWENTY-SIX

I RETIRED on November 5, 2017, which was the best birthday gift I could give myself. The freeway memorials had brought me full circle. After all the death and misery that I had dealt with for thirty-two years, it was time for me to enjoy my family.

During my career, I had witnessed the best and the worst of humanity. As I watched some of the most violent people alive become best friends with the revolving doors of the judicial system, I often felt like Sisyphus, pushing an immense boulder up a hill, only to watch it roll back time and time again.

I had fallen short of being the father Dominic and Haley needed, and I hadn't even been there for Abree. I was wrong for that. They certainly deserved better, and those lost years are gone forever. I was never able to reconcile with Dominic, even as my heart hurts every day. It tells me to forgive, but my head tells me to protect the greater good and the welfare of the family. Surprisingly, Abree contacted me from Northern California several months after I retired. Although I had never been in his life or been there for him, he was cordial on the phone and expressed a desire to meet me and spend time with me. I was floored. He told me he had a two-year-old son, Abree Jr., and he wanted me to meet him as well. I told him they were more than welcome in my home and gave him the address. When I hung up, I told Carolyn. She had known about Abree since the beginning of our relationship. She was ecstatic and couldn't wait to meet him.

The day they were supposed to arrive, I was anxious and nervous. I didn't know how it was going to go. He could very well curse me out for being a shit father and for not being there when he needed me, and I would understand. If this was what he wanted to say, I would stand there and listen, deserving whatever vile names he chose to call me. I answered the door when the doorbell rang and saw a tall, handsome man. He smiled broadly and said, "What's up, Pops?" I smiled back, and we hugged each other tightly, and started crying. I looked over his shoulder and saw his girlfriend, also crying and holding my grandson. Abree and I hugged each other for what seemed like forever; neither of us wanted to let the other go.

When we finally broke our embrace, I looked at him and blubbered, "I'm sorry I wasn't there for you, son." He would've had every right to vent his anger at me right then and there, but he simply hugged me again.

We sat in the backyard and smoked cigars, and I broke out the best cognac I had. Abree Jr. ran around the house, and Carolyn and Abree's girlfriend got acquainted in the living room. We talked and tried as well as we could to catch up on the last twenty years. His mother had done right by him. He was a smart, respectful young man. I expected him to hate me, but he told me that his mother had never said anything bad about me. She had always told him that I was a good man who had been put in a position I wasn't ready for. She was too kind in that regard, but unlike Gilda had been with Dominic and Haley, she didn't want him to grow up hating me, so she never poisoned him toward me. I am grateful to her for that. As I said earlier, there are no do-overs in life, but there are *make-it-rights*. I could never get back the years we lost, but I could be there for him if he needed me now.

As we continued talking, I noticed that Abree Jr. never stopped moving or running around, much like Desmond when he was that age. When I asked about it, Abree said, "Oh, he's autistic." I was floored, but I knew that also, like Desmond, Abree Jr. was in good hands. During the short time I had spent with his father, I found out that he was an amazing man. It is said that the fathers of autistic children take it much harder than the mothers, who are natural nurturers. My *make-it-right* with Desmond would have to be things other than the normal father-son activities. A lot of fathers faced with this scenario find it difficult. Having met Abree, I knew he was the right type of father for his son. He would never need a do-over. He would make it right from the beginning.

After they left, I went back to the backyard and poured another drink. I thought about the unpredictability of life and the ever-present synchronicity of seemingly random events. I had expected Abree to hate me and never would have dreamed that his son would be autistic. I thought about the job, which had almost destroyed me and taken a considerable part of me, but I was still standing. Carolyn had finally gone to college at my urging and graduated with honors from Cal State Dominguez University. She continually pushes me to go back to school, but I am content with my GED and a never-ending thirst for seeking knowledge on my own accord. Courtney, Haley, and Deon have all graduated from college, and Lauren is currently attending. I am proud of the blended family that Carolyn and I have raised. We should be enjoying the fruits of our labor, but we now have another responsibility to tend to. This one will be more difficult than the others.

The symbol for autism is a multicolored puzzle, and there could not be a more appropriate one. Just when we think we have Desmond figured out, he throws us a curveball. Some days are better than others. He is quirky, for sure. He eats popcorn with a spoon and has a Ninja Turtles blanket that he takes everywhere, folding it and holding it close to his nose. He will only smell the yellow shell of Donatello. Even in the dark, he knows where that part of the blanket is. He also has difficulty learning, and enunciating words at times, and he has asthma that requires daily medicine, but he is exceptionally talented, rendering works of art so beautiful I have had several of them professionally framed and hung on the walls in our house.

I have learned to embrace the term "meltdown", as I bear witness to them several times a week. He demands everything in a certain way—a toasted Nutella sandwich not cut diagonally causes a meltdown of an epic proportion; likewise, so does a hamburger with pickles. It's not sufficient to just take them off. He has to have an entirely new burger, even if I had just waited in line at In-n-Out for thirty minutes. I have also learned to ignore the honking horns of cars waiting behind me as I go through the order ensuring it was made just right. Carolyn and I know that Desmond will most likely need to be cared for his entire life, but like all the challenges we have faced in our lives together, we will meet this one, too. Thankfully, Carolyn has taught me not to see certain things as misfortune but rather as opportunity.

Haley has four kids now, Jeremy has one, and Deon has three. Six of the kids are half-White, one is half-Filipina, and one is half-Mexican. My family is a melting pot of the spirit of what America is supposed to represent. Carolyn and I saved our money well over the years and purchased our forever home. I wanted it more so for her than for myself. She brought me back from the dark side and reunited me with my family. Most importantly, without hesitation, she had agreed to adopt *my* grandson. Most people would tell you it was only right, and anyone else would have done the same thing. Wrong. It takes a special person. And I had married one who deserved a beautiful home.

It is big enough for all our children and grandchildren to be comfortable, and it has a large backyard with a swimming pool, which Desmond gets in almost every day. He swims like a fish and has never had a single lesson.

There is a park just down the street from our house where I sometimes take him to play. It is hard watching him play with the other kids, the so-called "typical" ones. Sometimes they laugh and tease him. Children can be so unapologetically cruel to each other. The hardest part is that Desmond isn't even aware of it. I find myself fighting back tears occasionally. However, at times, the wonders of life will surprise me when I least expect it. One time while we were at the park, I was sitting on a bench watching him play with a little White girl with Down syndrome. After a while, Desmond grabbed her hand, and they walked over to me. He said, "Papa, this is my new friend." He then hugged her just as her mother walked up smiling and said, "Come on, Emma. It's time to go home."

As Emma and her mother walked away, I marveled at the wonder and synchronicity of life once again, thinking about how we are all connected in one way or another and that racism is learned, not inherent. The memory takes me back to a much simpler time, a time when I held onto my Mom Mary's apron while she went about the business of making my biscuits and gravy at the directions of a different Emma.

Carolyn and I have come a long way, carefully avoiding the pitfalls and sand traps of life. Through hard work and commitment, we have achieved the American dream despite our skin color. We didn't need welfare or any other type of government assistance. We didn't complain or gripe. Instead, we took advantage of everything available to us and worked hard to realize that dream. Of our military kids, only Jeremy is still in service. When he was promoted to chief, Carolyn flew to Italy to help his wife Nikki pin his anchor on him.

375

Carolyn cried when they pinned it on, the emotions just too much as she realized that she and Jeremy had proved all the naysayers wrong who predicted they would end up on welfare.

Navy boot camp photos, along with college diplomas and my academy graduation photo, adorn a wall in our family room, strategically placed around the shadow-box-encased flag from the coffin of Carolyn's father. It is the room that we are proudest of. That flag represents the true spirit of this nation. It tells us that although we still have far to go, it is also a reminder of how far we have come. We are all brethren in this country. We are definitely a dysfunctional family, but we are family, nevertheless. Many have died for that flag, and many will die for it in the future. It is so much more than just a "rag" or piece of cloth. It represents the living embodiment of dreams yet to be fulfilled but dreams still worth fighting for.

Six months into retirement, I'm sitting in my backyard watching Carolyn and our opportunity frolic in the pool. The pool lights are the latest LEDs, and I have the setting on random, causing a beautiful undulating rainbow effect, not unlike the fish in the coffee table aquarium that was so hard for me to let go of. I light a Padron series 1926 cigar and sip Avion Extra Anejo tequila from a lead crystal glass. I then look up at the night sky. It is uncommonly clear for Southern California, and I see a star brighter than any other near it. It is close to the moon, which just happens to be super full and casting light downward on the rippling water and intermingling with the pool lights. I wonder if the star could be the same one that brought such joy and laughter to my Aunt Sondra, Carolyn, Craig, my brothers, and me as we tread the ground our forefathers had tread before us. I imagine that they dared not dream that their descendants would one day live the life that I have been blessed with.

I take a long sip from my glass and say a prayer for Kevin, Jimmy, Dess, and all the other cops who have lost their lives in the line of duty. But I can't just stop at them. I also say a prayer for Gary Beverly, Smokey, Kylah, and all the other children who are among the 1,154 people murdered in Compton during the time I worked there. At times, the melancholy is suffocating, but I cry much easier now, finally understanding that the suppression of tears and emotion has absolutely nothing to do with masculinity. Sometimes, I even cry when I see the hummingbirds suckling from the birds of paradise plants near my swimming pool.

I think about my father, and the last time I saw him doesn't even come to mind. Instead, I think about Thanksgiving parades, Tiger games, and Dot and Etta's shrimp hut. I have forgotten the suffocating smallness of the closet and the thud of boots that didn't belong to him as I clutched the quilt made by my grandma's hands. And although his battle with alcoholism is a bitter taste in my mouth, the memory of our family trips to Canada remains as sweet as ever.

I have forgiven my mother for the stinging lashes in front of the grey monster. I now realize that I have always loved her dearly and somehow understand that her loss of innocence and Paradise Lost may have been at the core of the beatings. And as I continue watching Desmond laughing in the pool and splashing water on Carolyn, I smile and think about days gone by and things that might have been.

EPILOGUE

ON JANUARY 10, 2011, Maxcy Filer died quietly in his sleep at the age of eighty. Like Tucker Jr., Filer was laid in state at city hall. Tucker had officers from the department he tried so desperately to get rid of standing guard near his body. In contrast, Filer had deputies from the department he tried so desperately to keep out of Compton standing near his. They are all dead now—Walter Tucker Jr., Bob Adams, Floyd James, Jane Robbins, and Laverta Montgomery—people I looked at as Compton royalty as I obsequiously opened doors for them, not yet realizing that save for Maxcy Filer and Jane Robbins, they were all emperors who never wore any clothing.

Percy Joseph Perrodin Jr. died of prostate cancer on January 4, 2017. He was a good cop who died under a cloud of suspicion, and he deserved a better ending than he got. Reggie Wright Sr. and Reggie Wright Jr. were indicted by the feds a few months later for their roles in an illegal drug operation that spanned three states and involved members of the Grape Street Crips. Carolyn and I were devastated when we heard the news. I wasn't shocked when I heard Reggie Jr. was involved, scorpions hitching rides on the backs of frogs across rivers often suffer similar fates. But no one expected Reggie Sr. to be accused of involvement in something like this, or maybe it was just me. Rumors had persisted for years that the glittering of Reggie Sr. wasn't all gold. Regardless of his legal problems, I still respect him for what he did for the city of Compton. I also respect him for what he did for me and understand that, more oftentimes than not, love for family is unconditional to the point of detriment.

In April of 2017, Compton city officials found two hundred firearms in a vault at the old city hall located at 600 North Alameda. Among the guns found were sniper rifles, stun bag shotguns, and .40 caliber pistols. There is no doubt that these were weapons formerly used by the Compton police department. In yet another example of the shoddy oversight of city-owned guns, there was no paperwork to confirm this. Apparently, the guns were just shoved away in the vault after the city got rid of us. If the firearms had hit the streets, no one would have ever known of their existence until they were used in a crime, or someone was arrested with one. The sheriff's department took possession of the guns and inventoried them. When deputies returned to the vault later to move the weapons to a more secure location, twenty-three Beretta .40 caliber and eight Glock .40 caliber pistols were missing. They have never been located.

In March of 2018, an article in the LA Times by Angel Jennings reported that "Compton officials overpaid themselves, charged questionable trips on city-issued credit cards, and failed to safeguard taxpayer money, resulting in a staffer stealing millions of dollars over years, according to a state audit." Under Mayor Perrodin's leadership, by 2008, the city had turned around a deficit decades in the making into a general fund surplus of $22.4 million. By 2014, under Perrodin's successor, the city was once again in debt, this time to the tune of $49.1 million. The California State Controller reported that the city had received failing marks in 71 out of 79 measures assessing internal accounting and administrative controls, ranking Compton's accountability as "nonexistent" and that, "The City Council's brazen overspending had contributed to the city's financial hardship." From July 1, 2013, through June 30, 2016, Compton had a budget 300% higher than the average budget of cities of similar size and population.

In November of 2018, a White off-duty deputy sheriff dressed in uniform and driving a department vehicle robbed a medical dispensary warehouse of six hundred pounds of marijuana and $100,000 in cash. He was accompanied by three other men. During the robbery, an on-duty LAPD unit drove up and the deputy told them they were serving a search warrant. The deputy and his accomplices were later arrested and sentenced to prison. It was bittersweet for me. Anytime a cop does something like this it stains the reputation of us all. But after all the years of Compton PD being labeled crooked Black cops, there was a perverse vindication that a corrupt White deputy had done something far worse than any Black Compton cop had ever done. Corruption is not department, gender, or race specific. It has everything to do with character. Period. Sometimes cops slip through cracks in crannied walls, too. Some say the roots are just as deep as the roots of corruption spawned by politics. I couldn't disagree more.

IN MEMORIAM

IN ADDITION TO Officers Kevin Burrell, James MacDonald, and Dess K. Phipps, there were two other officers killed while giving their lives to protect the citizens of Compton.

On April 4, 1967 fifty-year old Officer Ralph Kay Reeves had responded to Compton High School to investigate reports of a student under the influence of drugs or alcohol. When he got there, the intoxicated student started fighting with Officer Reeves and a group of other students surrounded them and tried to take the student from Officer Reeves. During the struggle, Officer Reeves collapsed due to a heart attack. His condition never improved, and he subsequently died on March 26, 1968. His son, Kay Reeves, was also a Compton police officer. Officer Reeves also had a brother, Richard Reeves, who was a patrolman for the Kansas City police. He was also killed in the line of duty on October 2, 1957.

On February 12, 1967, Reserve Sergeant James Turner was working off-duty as a clerk at Jim's Oasis Liquor store at 910 S. Central Avenue when Raymond Lloyd Johnson entered the store armed with a handgun and announced a hold-up. Sergeant Turner pulled his gun and a shoot-out occurred. The store's owner, Mayer Zeidenweber was shot and killed. Turner, who lived less than six blocks from the store, was mortally wounded. Johnson was also wounded during the shootout. He took Turner's gun as he lay on the floor bleeding and fled the location. Johnson was apprehended by Glen Smith, an employee at a business next to the liquor store, who held Johnson at gunpoint until other police officers arrived.

I didn't learn about the deaths of Officer Reeves and Sergeant Turner until well after I obtained the approval for the freeway memorial signs for Burrell,

MacDonald, and Phipps. I found out about their deaths while I was assigned to sheriff's Homicide and took it upon myself to review and synopsize all the murders that occurred under Compton PD. The fact that five Compton officers had lost their lives in the line of duty and there were no dedications or memorials to any of their memories until the freeway memorials for Burrell, MacDonald, and Phipps were injustices. Perhaps someone will right the injustices to Officer Reeves and Reserve Sergeant Turner in the future.

Since the Los Angeles County Sheriff's Department assumed policing responsibility for Compton in 2000, only one law enforcement officer has lost their life in the line of duty. On October 24, 2016, forty-seven-year-old Sergeant Alfonso Lopez was responding to assist other deputies involved in a high-speed pursuit when he suffered a fatal heart attack and crashed.

May these law-enforcement officers all rest in peace.

THE FOLLOWING are the names of the courageous men and women who worked for the Compton police department during the time that I did:

Chief James Carrington
Chief Ivory Webb
Chief Terry Ebert
Chief Hourie Taylor
A/Chief Ramon E. Allen
Assistant Chief Gil Sandoval
Commander Thomas Armstrong
Commander Dallas Elvis
Commander Anthony Ruiz
Captain Percy Perrodin
Captain Steve Roller
Captain Danny Sneed
Captain Reginald Wright Sr.
Lieutenant Gary Anderson
Lieutenant Robert J. Baker, Jr.
Lieutenant Mardrue Bunton
Lieutenant James Fette
Lieutenant Joe Flores
Lieutenant Evelyn Malachi
Lieutenant Douglas Slaughter
Lieutenant Alfred Smith
Lieutenant William Wallace
Lieutenant Jerry Wortman
Sergeant Cornelius Atkins
Sergeant Rick Baker
Sergeant Thomas Barclay
Sergeant Gilbert Cross
Sergeant Robert Davis
Sergeant John Faber

Sergeant John Garrett
Sergeant Preston Harris
Sergeant Barry Lobel
Sergeant Ronald Malachi
Sergeant Edward "Red" Mason
Sergeant Jack McConnell
Sergeant Willie Mosley
Sergeant Brent Nielsen
Sergeant Walter Nelson
Sergeant Michael Nunez
Sergeant Jeffrey Nussman
Sergeant Eric Perrodin
Sergeant Richard Petty
Sergeant Willie Mosley
Sergeant Angela Myles-Pilcher
Sergeant Alfred Preston
Sergeant Henry Robinson, III
Sergeant Kenneth Roller
Sergeant John Swanson
Sergeant Ronald Thrash
Sergeant John Wilkinson
Sergeant Willard Williams
Sergeant Giles Wright

Detective Eduardo Aguirre
Detective Dennis Auner
Detective Phillip Bailey
Detective Ken Baratta
Detective George Betor

Detective Duane Bookman
Detective Marvin Branscomb
Detective Timothy Brennan
Detective David Cameron
Detective Catherine "Cat" Chavers
Detective Dwight Dobbin
Detective Bruce Frailich
Detective Bryan Gilbreath
Detective Alfred Green
Detective Stoney Jackson
Detective Lendell Johnson
Detective Robert Ladd
Detective Betty Marlow
Detective Michael Markey
Detective Marion Ming
Detective Norman Nelson
Detective Michael C. Paiz
Detective Ray Richardson
Detective Rich Rivera
Detective David "D-dub" Smith
Detective Terry Smith
Detective John Soisson
Detective Oscar Van Wie
Detective Dolph Wagner
Detective Robert Weems

JUVENILE SPECIALIST:
Chester Hammond

Officer Michael Abbott
Officer Stephen Aguilar
Officer Calvin Allen
Officer Guiseppe Amato

Officer Mark Anderson
Officer Albert Archuleta, III
Officer Victor Ayala
Officer Samuel Bailey
Officer Richard Balogun
Officer Ray Banuelos
Officer Harout Bazukian
Officer Juli Boyd
Officer Keith Bowen
Officer Bobbington Brandt
Officer Bernard "BB" Brown
Officer Bill "Junkyard" Brown
Officer Raymond V. Brown
Officer Ted "T-Bone" Brown
Officer Jason Buckley
Officer Kevin Burrell
Officer Willie Bundage
Officer Belinda Byrd
Officer Herman Camacho
Officer Gonzalo Cetina
Officer Robert "Chilly" Childs
Officer Anthony Christian
Officer John Clark
Officer Howard Coolidge
Officer Danny Correa
Officer Raymond Cruz
Officer Daniel Dail
Officer Gary Davis
Officer Myron Davis, Sr.
Officer Jose De La Cruz
Officer Timothy Dobbin
Officer Michael Doyle
Officer Charmaine Drew

Officer Jose Duran
Officer Anthony Easter
Officer Gary "Jaws" Eaves
Officer Thomas Eskridge
Officer Sean Essex
Officer William Farrar
Officer Wesley Fenderson III
Officer Rene Fontenot
Officer Luther Fore
Officer Terry Foss
Officer Lanier Freeman
Officer Brett Garland
Officer Henry Gaxiola
Officer Fernando Gonzalez
Officer James Green
Officer Peter Grimm
Officer Jose Guarderas, Jr.
Officer Carlos Guerra
Officer David Halsey
Officer Linda Hollins
Officer Clarence Holzendorf
Officer Jeffery Houle
Officer Randy Hudson
Officer Terrence Idlebird
Officer Carlos Jackson
Officer Jasper "JJ" Jackson
Officer William Jackson
Officer Edward Jackson
Officer Henry "Bud" Johnson
Officer Telly Johnson
Officer Bettye Jones
Officer Julio Jove
Officer Michael Jules

Officer John Khounthavong
Officer Kordell Knox
Officer Robert Labarge
Officer Michell Lambdin
Officer Sergio Lepe
Officer David Leverick
Officer James Lewis
Officer Mark Lobel
Officer Victor Locklin
Officer Sean Logan
Officer Anthony Lucia
Officer Mike Mageo
Officer Julio Mata
Officer Paul E. Mason
Officer Steve McMorris
Officer Steve McKesey
Officer Louis Mendez
Officer Mark Metcalf
Officer James "Donnie" Miller
Officer Julio Miranda
Officer Serette Mitchell
Officer Elizabeth Molina
Officer Pamela Moore
Officer Cain Mora
Officer David Motts
Officer Luis Mrad
Officer Cipriano Nainggolan
Officer Samuel Naylor
Officer Ricardo Negrette
Officer Susan Nelson
Officer Oscar Nunez
Officer Samuel Orosco
Officer Robert Page

Officer Marcos Palafox
Officer Christopher Paredes
Officer Jerry Patterson
Officer John Pena
Officer Henry Perez
Officer Karen Pewitt
Officer Ed'ourd Peters
Officer Roderick Pettus
Officer Andrew Pilcher
Officer Marvin Pollard
Officer Randy Poulos
Officer Adam Ramirez
Officer James Real
Officer Hector Renteria
Officer Joseph "Joey" Reynolds
Officer Rodrick Roach
Officer Cornelious "Pete" Robertson
Officer Helen Ross
Officer Jimmy Russell
Officer Wilbert Rugama
Officer Jaime Ruiz
Officer Henry Saenz
Officer George Sagen
Officer Richard Sanchez
Officer Latayna Scott
Officer Dante Serrechia
Officer Garrett Shah
Officer Alfred Skiles
Officer Danielle Slater
Officer Jeffrey Slutske
Officer Julius Smiley
Officer Anthony Spatola
Officer Carl Smith

Officer Gene Smith
Officer Eric Strong
Officer Ivan Swanson
Officer Russell Townsley
Officer Larry Urrutia
Officer Roberto Valentin
Officer Carole Valdez
Officer Michael Vasquez
Officer Joseph Velasco
Officer Michael Verlich
Officer Eduardo Verdugo
Officer Gerardo Verdugo
Officer Arnold Villarruel
Officer Lee Williams
Officer Randall S. Williams
Officer Robert "Blue" Williams
Officer Ronald Williams
Officer Jaeton Wilson
Officer Paul Wing
Officer Gary Winfield
Officer James Whitmore
Officer Glendal Whitney
Officer Lowell "Dean" Wright
Officer Reginald Wright, Jr.
Officer Thomas Zampiello
Officer Christian Zavalza

K-9: ARY; Preston Harris
K-9: BENNY; L. Mrad
K-9: BILL; Ed Jackson
K-9: DANN; K. Roller/J. Duran
K-9: SARONI; T. Zampiello

RESERVE OFFICERS

Calvin Blakely
James Brown
Richard H. Bryant
Sidney Cross
Allen Doby
Alex Fortune
Tom Gibby
Fernando Gomez
Brian Hanhart
Ed Hicks
Ricky Hill
Carl Houston
Eugene Hubbard
Darrell Inouye
Rod Johnson
Rudy Johnson
Lionel LeDuff
Emil Lewis
James MacDonald
Eugene Mitchell
Clarence Parson
Joe Queenie
Brian Reyes
John Rey
Johnny Rolling
Marvin Todd
Robert Thundercloud
Osvaldo "Val" Villareal
Dave Wharton
Bruce White

DISPATCHERS:

Carolyn Baker
Martha Barajas
Signe Barnes
Sofia Bracken
Gina Butler
Yolanda "Yo-Yo" Caballero
Dorothy Carey
Cecilia "CC" Carter
Monica Chambliss
Pamela Edwards
Anita Fox
Lorna Gipson
Andrea Hawkins
Cynthia Hoffman
Tamara Hunt
Debra Fowler
LaGina Jackson
Dorothy Johnson
Odessa Johnson
Patricia Larkin
Melanie Logan
Eva Lopez
Veronica Lopez
Sherri Miller
Kenna Neal
LaDonna Norman
Ada Palafox
Gloria Ponce
Beatrice Riley
Shaun Roberson
Veronica Toro
Sandra Torres
Kyi Whitmore

JAILERS:

John Bryant
Wayne Garner
Albert Hughes
Daniel Valdez
Victoria Rymer
Lawanna Moore
Lee Cody

SECRETARIES:

Wanda Allen
Joanna Brennan
Ruby Kinney
Pam Maddox
Mary Neal

RECORDS CLERKS:

Cynthia Anderson
Jo Ann Anderson
Yvette Amani
Tungelin Beene
Renee Bracy
Claudette Charles
Hazel Citizen
Darlene Daniel
Rosie Daniels
Meriel Dearmon
Vivian Dodson
Janice Fitisemanu
Lavera Hardwick
Rodney Herndon
Blossie Johnson
Renee Johnson-Jacobs

Demetra Klines
Allyson Lavalais
Kimberly Longmire
Betty Limbrick
Jennell Noble
Teresa Nazel
Mozella Paul
Adrianna Pizarro
Elaine Reynolds
Beatrice Riley
Victoria Rolling
Patricia Simpson
Patricia Tate
Leslie Tojin
Mateo Torres
Leza Tucker
Josie Twine
Christine Washington
Lana Wortham

LEGAL ADVISORS:

Ronnie Hawkins
Cal Saunders

SECURITY OFFICERS:

Roderick Carter
Cecil Chavers
Ruther Daniels
Larry Fisher
Darrell Grimes
Keith Hamilton
Hermetta Harper
Vernell McDaniels

Martha Pickett
Donald Sayles
Charles Scott
Charles Webb
Harold Williams

COMMUNITY SERVICE OFFICERS:
Robin Broom
Patrice Carmichael
Sidney Commodore
Cedric Hicks, Sr.
Charlotte MacCaster
Michelle Mercier
Angie Whetstone
Lamahr Wilkins
Irma Espinosa
Guadalupe Gil

PROPERTY OFFICERS:
Archie Childers
Gevena Clay
Maria Gonzales
Ray Hernandez

MECHANICS:
Alan Butler
Thomas Itty
Leslie Williams

PARKING CONTROL OFFICERS:
Tenita Galloway
Frank Garces
Arlene Partlow

DEPARTMENT CHAPLAIN:
Father Daniels

TIMEKEEPER:
Shirley Grisham

IT:
Bobby McDowell

THE FOLLOWING are the members of the Los Angeles County Sheriff's Department who welcomed me to their department with open arms:

Assist Sheriff Cecil Rhambo
Assist Sheriff Todd Rogers
Chief Anthony Rivera
Chief April Tardy
Commander Joseph Gooden
Commander Kevin Goran
Commander Willie Miller
Commander Oceal Victory
Captain Bernice Abrams
Captain Shaun Mathers
Captain Vickie Stuckey
Lieutenant Yolanda Clay
Lieutenant Yvette Christopher
Lieutenant Robert Dillard
Lieutenant Alicia Malone
Lieutenant Kathy Renner
Lieutenant Cee Cee Strong
Lieutenant Steve Vaughn
Sergeant Blanca Arevalo
Sergeant Jeff Fleming
Sergeant Michelle Hall
Sergeant Scott Graham
Sergeant Robert Windrim
Detective Liz Aguilera
Detective Mark Brooks
Detective Barry Fitchew
Detective Dion Ingram
Detective Cliff Jones
Detective Mike Maher

Detective Jerry Ortiz
Detective Luis Suazo
Deputy Roberto Bayes
Deputy "Big" Eric Lee
Deputy Aura Sierra
Deputy Daphne Terrell
LASD "Love" class #229

HOMICIDE:
Captain Duane Harris
Captain Martin L. Rodriguez
Lieutenant Derrick Alfred
Lieutenant Dave Coleman
Lieutenant Michael Rosson
Sergeant Slyvia Brossoit
Sergeant Tim Cain
Sergeant Kenneth Clark
Sergeant Bill Cotter
Sergeant Bobby Gray
Sergeant Shannon Laren
Sergeant Ray Lugo
Sergeant Rob Martindale
Sergeant Dan McElderry
Sergeant Sandy Nava
Sergeant Ken Perry
Detective Ed Aguirre (CPD)
Detective Dean Camarillo
Detective Mike Caouette
Detective Gina Eguia

Detective Adam Kirste
Detective Paul Mondry
Detective Dameron Peyton
Detective Traci Healy
Detective Mike P. Rodriguez
Detective Q. Rodriguez
Detective Rich Tomlin

CRIME ANALYST:
Romy Haas
Danielle Ponce De Leon
Lizzette Rosales

EVIDENCE:
Cheryl Garrett (HOM)
Deborah Jackson (HOM)
Rosa Williams (CSN)

SECURITY OFFICER:
Manny Amaya
Jonvive Anguiano
Benny Carbajal

LET:
Dwayne Rhine

CSI:
David Alonso

CARSON OSS TEAM
Commander Ralph Ornelas
Captain James Thornton
Lieutenant Ishmael Chavez

Lieutenant Luis Trejo
Sergeant Eric Arias
Sergeant Michael Gomez
Sergeant Eric Ehrhorn
Sergeant Amy Hanson
Sergeant Mark Pope
Detective Dennis Chuck
Detective Gail Durham
Detective Nina Gonzales
Detective Mark Wedel
Detective Shawn Young
Secretary Oly Ang

COMPTON OSS TEAM
Captain Doug Fetteroll
Captain Robert Jones, III
Lieutenant Bobby Lawrence
Sergeant Eric Arias
Sergeant Bobby Dean
Sergeant Brian Richardson
Sergeant Jose Salgado
Sergeant Jose Sandoval
Sergeant A. Spatola (CPD)
Sergeant Joe Valencia
Detective Oscar Calderon
Detective Al Carrillo
Detective Gail Durham
Detective Nina Gonzales
Detective Eric Gomez
Detective Mike Hernandez
Detective Raul Magadan
Detective Dennis Salcedo
Detective Rich Sanchez (CPD)

Detective Joe Sumner
Secretary Cecilia Miranda

And special recognition to Lieutenant Dana Ellison and his GET Team, which helped my Compton OSS team drive the gang related murders in Compton to the lowest number in 25 years.

CPSIA information can be obtained
at www.ICGtesting.com
Printed in the USA
LVHW021539070921
697214LV00014B/564